OBSERVATION SKILLS FOR EFFECTIVE TEACHING

OBSERVATION SKILLS FOR EFFECTIVE TEACHING

Third Edition

Gary D. Borich
The University of Texas at Austin

With Contributions by
Debra Bayles Martin
San Diego State University

Merrill,

an imprint of Prentice Hall

Upper Saddle River, New Jersey   Columbus, Ohio

Library of Congress Cataloging-in-Publication Data

Borich, Gary D.
     Observation skills for effective teaching / Gary D. Borich, with
contributions by Debra L. Bayles.—3rd ed.
          p.   cm.
     Includes bibliographic references (p.) and indexes.
     ISBN 0-13-860396-0
     1. Observation (Educational method) 2. Teaching   I. Bayles,
Debra L. II. Title
LB1027.28.B67   1999
371.102—dc21   98-22994
                                                                                  CIP

Editor: Debra A. Stollenwerk
Production Editor: Mary Harlan
Photo Editor: Carol Sykes
Design Coordinator: Karrie M. Converse
Text Design: Custom Editorial Productions, Inc.
Cover Design: Brian Deep
Cover Photo: ©Stock Market
Production Manager: Pamela D. Bennett
Director of Marketing: Kevin Flanagan
Marketing Manager: Suzanne Stanton
Marketing Coordinator: Krista Groshong
Production Supervision: Custom Editorial Productions, Inc.

This book was set in Stone Serif by Custom Editorial Productions, Inc., and was printed
and bound by Banta Company. The cover was printed by Banta Company.

 © 1999 by Prentice-Hall, Inc.
Simon & Schuster/A Viacom Company
Upper Saddle River, New Jersey 07458

Earlier editions © 1994 by Macmillan Publishing Company; 1990 by Merrill Publishing
Company.

Photo Credits: pp. 1, 21, 235, Anne Vega/Merrill; pp. 7, 121, Scott Cunningham/Merrill;
pp. 39, 65, 93, 149, 179, 209, 263, Anthony Magnacca/Merrill

Printed in the United States of America

10 9 8   7 6 5 4 3

ISBN: 0-13-860396-0

Prentice-Hall International (UK) Limited, *London*
Prentice-Hall of Australia Pty. Limited, *Sydney*
Prentice-Hall of Canada, Inc., *Toronto*
Prentice-Hall Hispanoamericana, S. A., *Mexico*
Prentice-Hall of India Private Limited, *New Delhi*
Prentice-Hall of Japan, Inc., *Tokyo*
Simon & Schuster Asia Pte. Ltd., *Singapore*
Editora Prentice-Hall do Brasil, Ltda., *Rio de Janeiro*

PREFACE

People in all walks of life have always wondered how to acquire the skills and competencies of a professional. Individuals strive to advance in their professions and to acquire the salary and status of highly respected members of that profession: The result of this effort is called *intelligent behavior*. All of us want to acquire the intelligent behavior frequently observed among those we call *experts* or *professionals*, but we know that becoming an expert or a professional requires more than simply a desire to be good. This book focuses on one of the prime means by which to become a professional: observing others and incorporating what is seen and heard into one's own behavior.

To be sure, more is required than simply watching others who are competent in their jobs. To become competent at teaching, you must know what to look for, and you must have a framework or structure by which what is observed can be made meaningful for your own behavior. Other skills are needed, too. You must be psychologically ready and physically prepared to observe, have tools for categorizing and recording what is seen, and have a knowledge of content and teaching methodology. But even this is not enough: To become an expert, you must understand the patterns and sequences of effective teaching that make all the parts work as a whole.

Where do effective teachers learn to make the parts work as a whole? How do they bring their natural abilities, knowledge of content and teaching methods, and professional goals together into a harmonious pattern of intelligent behavior? It isn't from books or training sessions alone—these can focus on only a small number of activities. It isn't from teaching experience, either—the hectic pace of the classroom makes it impossible for many teachers to reflect on their own patterns of behavior.

Only through observing more experienced teachers can all these ingredients be brought together into a meaningful pattern to be modeled in your own classroom. These patterns of practice—not individual techniques, strategies, or methods—make teachers effective.

As we will see in this text, the purpose of observation is to improve yourself. Plans for self-improvement are realistic when they are based on your own unique strengths and weaknesses and on the school context in which they are to occur. The importance of this latter point is seldom recognized: A teaching activity that is effective in one school or classroom may not be effective in another. No amount of student teaching experience or formal instruction can prepare you to teach in every classroom context. Although student teaching and instruction can point you in the right direction to maximize student growth, the realities of a specific classroom and the students within it will determine *how* and *how much* you learn and grow as a teacher. This is the unique function of classroom observation: to understand teaching within a specific classroom of learners, and to develop a program of self-improvement based on that understanding. In short, the dimensions of effective teaching ultimately must be defined by the qualities and characteristics of those who must be taught. This is why classroom observation is so important: It reveals the patterns of practice by which teachers refine and match the dimensions of effective teaching to a specific population of learners.

To accomplish this goal, this book presents effective teaching practices that can be observed during three career stages—preteaching, student teaching, and induction- (first-) year teaching. It provides competencies for preparing to observe, learning how to observe, and knowing what to observe.

Organization of This Text

Chapter 1 focuses on the close and necessary relationship between the personal attributes for successful living and professional competence. It explores the characteristics that make an individual successful as a person as well as a professional—characteristics from which you will profit and will learn from classroom observation.

Chapters 2 and 3 focus on what real classrooms are like and the psychological preparation and mental perspective important to observing the complex sequences of events that occur in classrooms. These chapters explain why observation is important (Chapter 2) and how to prepare for transforming the casual process of *looking* into the systematic process of *observing* (Chapter 3).

Chapter 4 is devoted to the technical competence that must precede systematic observation. This chapter provides a knowledge of the tools that observers use to record life in classrooms and to organize their observations in useful ways. You will learn how to develop and use simple tools of observation, and to revise them to fit a particular school context or self-improvement goal.

Chapters 5 through 12 detail the framework or structure through which life in classrooms can be organized and made meaningful. Observation skills are presented according to eight areas found by researchers to be related to positive outcomes in learners. These eight areas, each containing patterns for observing effective teaching, are: learning climate, classroom management, lesson clarity, instructional variety, task orientation, student engagement, student success, and higher thought processes. Each of these chapters combines a study of observation skills with the patterns of effective teaching practice identified in the research literature. The methodological concepts, observation instruments, and dialogues they contain are designed to help the observer see and practice research-based patterns of effective teaching. This is the unique focus of *Observation Skills for Effective Teaching*, Third Edition.

New to This Edition

Readers of the earlier editions of this text will notice this third edition has a new look. To make this book even more practical than earlier editions, we have enlarged the physical dimensions of the text to allow for the full size copying of more than 40 observation instruments and records.

Second, this edition has spotlighted the realistic classroom dialogues of earlier editions by moving them "up front" to the beginning of each chapter, to set the stage and to provide an advance organizer for the "reactions" to them and the discussions that follow.

Readers of previous editions will also notice that we have integrated our discussions of theory with observation practice by placing our observation instruments and records within a discussion of their rationale. These changes make this edition even more user friendly than previous editions and provide the flexibility of a handbook that can be carried into the classroom.

Uses of This Text

This book can be used in several ways. First, it may be used as a companion volume to *Effective Teaching Methods*, Third Edition (Borich, 1996), in which some of these same pedagogical concepts are presented in a methods text format. In *Observation Skills for Effective Teaching*, students learn how to observe and practice many of the behaviors and patterns of practice presented in *Effective Teaching Methods*.

Second, this text can be used for a preteaching or observation course taken prior to, or in conjunction with, a methods course. Thus, it can serve as an advance organizer for more specific and pedagogically oriented courses that follow.

Third, this text may be used as a resource during student teaching and beginning teaching to provide a direction and foundation for a program of self-improvement, training, and mentoring. It provides many practical tools for teacher self-development, renewal, and redirection throughout the early years of teaching. In each of these applications, the major goal of this text is to sensitize the beginning teacher, through observation, to patterns of effective teaching—and to begin the process of self-improvement based upon the results of this observation.

Special Features

Some special features of *Observation Skills for Effective Teaching*, Third Edition, are

❑ Beginning chapters (*Getting Ready, Why Observe, Preparing to Observe*, and *How to Observe*) that prepare the teacher for the psychological, technical, and cognitive demands of observing in classrooms

❑ Integration of major research findings on the dimensions of learning climate, classroom management, lesson clarity, instructional variety, task orientation, student engagement in the learning process, student success, and higher thought processes and performance outcomes, with discussions of why these dimensions are important and how they can be integrated to form patterns of effective teaching practice.

❑ Examples from the research literature of effective and ineffective teaching indicators. Through the use of realistic classroom dialogues, integrative discussions, and summary charts and tables, readers see effective teaching practices alongside less effective practices.

❑ Classroom dialogues at the beginning of each teaching effectiveness chapter (Chapters 5–12) in a variety of subject-matter areas, grades, and levels of schooling. The reader can practice recording key dimensions of effective teaching in the context of naturally occurring classroom dialogues at the elementary, middle school, junior high, and secondary levels.

❑ Author reactions to each of the classroom dialogues. These interpret and place in perspective the most relevant features of each practice dialogue from the observer's point of view.

❑ More than 40 full-page easy-to-copy instruments, scales and data-recording formats, grouped at the end of the chapters, for observing and implementing major patterns of effective teaching.

❑ Discussions at the end of each chapter that sensitize the reader to cultural, ethnic, and gender issues pertaining to the observation of each pattern of teaching behavior.

❑ Activities at the end of each chapter that engage the beginning teacher in the observation process and the development of patterns of effective teaching.

ACKNOWLEDGMENTS

Many individuals have contributed to the preparation of this book, not the least of whom are the many professionals whose studies of classroom life have contributed to the "effective teacher" described here. The work of these professionals has made possible a synthesis of effective teaching practices, representing a variety of data sources and methodological perspectives. Although I accept responsibility for my translations of their research into practice, any strengths the reader may see in this approach must be shared with those who have contributed to the research upon which this book is based.

I would also like to thank those teachers who have shared their insights about the teaching process with me over the years. Among these have been teachers in the Austin, Texas, Independent School District, especially Travis Heights Elementary and William B. Travis High School. They have provided many opportunities for observing the effective teaching methods described in this text. For their helpful reviews of the manuscript, both past and present, I extend my gratitude to Nicholas Anastasiow, formerly of Hunter College; Jeanie Amlund, Pennsylvania State University; Mary Bendixen-Noe, The Ohio State University; Phyllis Blumenfeld, University of Michigan; Paul Cook, Brigham Young University; Bettye Jones, Virginia State University; Ann Neely, Vanderbilt University; Michael Perl, Kansas State University; Marleen Pugach, University of Wisconsin–Milwaukee; Thomas Rakes, Memphis State University; Barak Rosenshine, University of Illinois; Ann Schulte, North Carolina State University; Elizabeth Simons, Kansas State University; and Allen Warner, University of Houston.

I would also like to thank Dr. John Rogan for his revisions of the teacher concerns instrument in Chapter 5; Dr. Gerhard Klinzing of the Center for New Learning Methods at the University of Tuebingen, Germany, for his instructive suggestions and documentation; and Regina Neef for providing me the opportunity to observe important crosscultural differences.

Finally, I would like to thank Jeanie Amlund, Pennsylvania State University at Mckeesport; Mary Noe-Bendixon, Ohio State University at Newark; and Sharon Griffin, whose experience in using this text provided helpful suggestions for this third edition.

G. D. B.

CONTENTS

LIST OF INSTRUMENTS

WHY OBSERVE?

To see a world in a grain of sand
And a heaven in a wildflower:
Hold infinity in the palm of your hand,
And eternity in an hour.

William Blake

What we see is often determined by what we want to see—or are prepared to see. Have you ever noticed that when you look closely at something, you discover details never seen before? When your observation is focused, even the slightest variations take shape. With this chapter we begin our journey of learning to observe—to notice grains of sand in the span of a single lesson, and to see eternity in an hour.

Johnson, Caesar. (1972). *To see a world in a grain of sand.* Norwalk, Connecticut: The C.R. Gibson Company, p. 7.

Playing in the park, 3-year-old Jake looks up to see his mother approaching. He runs down the sidewalk to greet her. In his haste, he trips on an uneven stone and lands, unceremoniously, at his mother's feet.

For a moment, Jake looks stunned—about to cry. His mother wonders if he is hurt as he glances up at her face with a questioning look.

Laughing, Jake's mother scoops him into her arms. "Hi, honey!" she chuckles. "What fun to have you so excited to see me!"

The imminent clouds on Jake's face clear, and the toddler smiles.

How often have you observed a similar event—noting that split second when a child seems to decide how to respond to a given situation? Like Jake, each of us experiences many interactions with the world every day. As we try to make sense of these events, we create a personal framework or set of expectations about the nature of the world and our appropriate responses to events within it. This set of expectations influences what we see in a particular setting, as well as what we choose to ignore.

Many psychologists believe that professionals create frames for understanding within their chosen fields, just as individuals construct a frame for interpreting the events of daily life. *Experts* know what to look for and rapidly learn from what they see, and thereby rise to the top of their profession long before others who do not have a structure for sorting out the least relevant from the most relevant details. Sternberg (1995) believes that intelligent behavior may be marked more by the structure or frame one brings to a problem or task than by what one knows about the problem or task beforehand. Thus, developing a professional frame from which to evaluate and act on events is a critical skill for becoming an expert.

From observing the actions and interactions of professionals, less experienced individuals gain a sense of what is valued in a particular discipline and how professionals working in that field typically respond to events. But, while observation seems as simple and commonplace as dressing, eating, or driving a car, it is important to remember that, like Jake, each of us interprets the world and responds to it according to our personal frame. Without some outside direction, it is possible that our classroom observations may serve to validate much of what we already "expect" to see—allowing us to overemphasize some things and overlook others. As a result, observations need to be focused if they are to be helpful in our professional life.

The focused observation techniques described in this book draw upon more than twenty-five years of research on effective teaching. This research has identified strategies, methods, and practices used by effective teachers to achieve desirable outcomes in learners. This research, included in this text, will help you expand your professional framework to include insights about teaching in eight areas.

1. Learning climate
2. Classroom management
3. Lesson clarity
4. Instructional variety
5. Teacher's task orientation and content presentation
6. Students' engagement in the learning process
7. Student success
8. Students' higher thought processes

This book devotes a chapter to each of these dimensions of effective teaching. Within each chapter you will find teaching methods and research and observation instruments to help you better understand, observe, and eventually implement these key aspects of teaching in the classroom.

Much of this text focuses on ways you can observe other teachers to learn about the teaching profession; this book also addresses ways to apply these observation techniques and insights to your own teaching. Thus, while you are observing others to learn about their approaches to teaching, you will also be learning to observe yourself—and to be observed by others. These observations will provide important insights about your growth as a teacher.

The ability to consciously consider your personal growth is called *reflection*. There are many goals you will want to work toward in order to reflect on your own behavior. But some of the most important for focused observations are to achieve empathy, establish cooperative relationships, become realistic, establish direction, attain confidence, release enthusiasm, become flexible, and become self-reliant. As you observe professionals working to achieve each of these goals, you will want to reflect on your own development—and then set some goals for yourself. Because a cycle of observation, reflection, and goal setting is so important to becoming a productive and successful professional, let's consider these eight goals for focused observation in more detail.

GOAL 1: TO ACHIEVE EMPATHY

Effective teachers exhibit *empathy*—a willingness to see events from different points of view and to appreciate others' interpretations or reasons for acting the way they do. An empathic approach can help you to understand student behavior from the student's point of view—which often provides insights for effective ways of dealing with problems or challenges. Your ability to empathize during classroom observations will serve you well both as an observer and as a teacher. For example, when you observe a teacher implementing an unusual classroom rule, you may be tempted to pass judgment on the teacher's effectiveness or on the rule's appropriateness—from your point of view. While your own experiences are an important source of information in evaluating what you observe, you will also benefit from trying to understand events from the teacher's vantage point. You may ask yourself, "Is what I am seeing working within the context of this classroom? Why or why not?" As you consider these questions, you may discover that a seemingly inappropriate strategy in one context may be appropriate in another. As a result, your observations will extend beyond your personal and textbook knowledge of teaching to include an awareness of the variety of social and emotional contexts that can influence a teacher's decisions. Enhancing your ability to empathize will help you approach your own teaching with more flexibility—and with the instructional alternatives you need to be an effective teacher.

GOAL 2: TO ESTABLISH COOPERATIVE RELATIONSHIPS

Early on, effective teachers identify people who can help them in their teaching. They understand that, in the hectic and stressful environment of the classroom, people need people to offer ideas, support, and collegiality. As you become involved in student teaching, and later in your beginning years of teaching, you will find a need to develop cooperative relationships with your colleagues. Experienced teachers have a wealth of information about students, curriculum, textbooks, and media with which you will be working. As you observe in different classrooms, you can and should take the opportunity to discover how professionals create and maintain cooperative relationships and how you can become an active participant in these relationships. These experienced teachers can answer many questions you will have now—and later (Ayers & Schubert, 1994).

In addition to answering questions about lesson formats, grouping of students, and instructional methods, your colleagues can be an important source of emotional support. During student teaching and your beginning years of teaching, you will often desire to express concerns and problems in a nonevalu-

ative context. If you have established a network of professional colleagues, you will have a safe place to share unanticipated problems and to brainstorm solutions. Teaching can be a lonely profession at times—facing a full day of classes filled with surprises and challenges can occasionally dishearten even the most enthusiastic or experienced teacher. Recognizing the need to turn to others for emotional support and having created a network for collegial sharing can help you to overcome difficulties and to renew your dedication and vigor.

GOAL 3: TO BECOME REALISTIC

Most beginning teachers understandably have an idealistic view of schools and teaching. While idealism motivates us to renew and extend our efforts, it also creates pitfalls when we are unreasonable in our expectations of students or ourselves. For example, beginning teachers who believe that schools *should be* a certain way may spend a great deal of time and effort trying to change a particular setting—failing to see and accept the strengths of the context they are working with. From your classroom observations, you will learn that schools and classrooms vary widely—and that each context offers both advantages and challenges. As you observe and reflect upon different classrooms, you will become more realistic in evaluating both what is desirable and what is less desirable in different classrooms.

In addition to seeing life in different classrooms, it is important to place your own successes and failures in learning to teach in proper perspective. In the classroom, just as in life, it can be tempting to attribute successes to factors outside ourselves (e.g., the students are bright, the lesson topic was inherently interesting) and to attribute failures to personal failings (e.g., the students would have passed the test if I had covered more content, the class wouldn't have misbehaved if I had been more prepared). It's important to realize that events involving misbehaving students, running out of time for a lesson, or other "failures" may not always result from our personal inadequacies or lack of effort. There are times when some events would be beyond the control of *any* teacher. As you observe, you will become increasingly aware of just how frequently these types of events occur in classrooms, regardless of almost any effort on the part of the teacher to prevent or alter their occurrence. Indeed, observation reveals the important role of serendipity in classrooms—that many unplanned outcomes happen in spite of, not because of, the efforts of teachers.

Serendipity is sometimes difficult for a beginning teacher to accept. We tend to derive a feeling of success or failure from those events for which we feel we *should* be responsible. Yet a class of very bright, easy-to-manage learners, preselected for advanced placement, may produce outcomes astonishingly different than those of another class learning the same subject. Knowing which outcomes are under your control, and as a consequence accurately judging the influence of your own actions, is one of the most important goals a teacher can attain. An ineffective teacher may work countless hours to change student behavior that cannot be changed in the course of a lesson or a unit—or a semester. This teacher may never see the desired results and attribute to herself an unrealistic sense of failure. Effective teachers, on the other hand, work to improve behavior that can be attributed to the strategies, materials, and methods they select. They learn where to look for improvement daily, and attribute to themselves a realistic sense of success. By observing which behaviors are changeable in classrooms, you can learn to more accurately attribute success and failure to particular actions of the teachers you observe and, later, to yourself.

GOAL 4: TO ESTABLISH DIRECTION

Another purpose of classroom observation is to establish the professional goals toward which you will want to work during your student teaching and first year of teaching. By observing others, you will identify characteristics and practices you will want to emulate in your own teaching. Recording these characteristics and practices during observation can form the basis of short- and long-term goals of self-improvement. One of the advantages of focused observation is the opportunity to identify particular patterns and sequences of teacher behavior and to evaluate their effectiveness in a variety of settings. Over time, you should be able to identify teaching strategies specific to particular purposes and contexts that you value and to integrate them into your own teaching.

GOAL 5: TO ATTAIN CONFIDENCE

Most of us in the course of learning to become teachers make judgments about what we believe is effective teaching (Clark & Peterson, 1986; Polanyi, 1958). In the course of teaching, we then make decisions that follow from these judgments. Many of these decisions about what and how to teach represent gut feelings, the exact source of which may not

be known to us. Some writers refer to this way of knowing as *tacit knowledge*. Tacit knowledge represents what we know by experience, but rarely, if ever, articulate. Just as in the example with Jake, each of us compiles vast amounts of tacit knowledge through everyday experiences (Alexander, Schallert, & Hare, 1991). This knowledge often guides our actions as effectively as does the knowledge we gain from formal instruction. Our tacit knowledge is put to use by acting, sometimes unconsciously, on thoughts and feelings acquired from day-to-day experiences. Tacitly acquired knowledge often helps us distinguish what is right from wrong, appropriate from inappropriate, and effective from ineffective.

Even though tacit knowledge has guided them in many ways throughout their lives, many beginning teachers reject their tacitly acquired knowledge in favor of less familiar and less appropriate responses. Some seem afraid to trust their instincts, perhaps fearing that these instincts are too subjective to be trusted. Unfortunately, many problems encountered by beginning teachers stem, in part, from a lack of confidence in their ability to act spontaneously in a given situation. This can prove unfortunate, because sometimes spontaneous judgments and instincts may serve the decision-making process better than a less relevant mechanical or academic response. It is important for beginning teachers to learn to trust their initial responses to a classroom problem or decision—especially when those decisions are also informed by academic knowledge. This trust can be developed, in part, by considering *what we feel* as we observe particular classroom events and then by reflecting on whether our intuitions are borne out. Effective teachers learn to contrast academic ideas with their personal intuitions and to compare the results. Through observation, beginning teachers learn to test their judgments and to trust their instincts.

GOAL 6: TO RELEASE ENTHUSIASM

Effective teachers demonstrate an enthusiasm for the subject matter they teach, and for the teaching profession. The ability to release enthusiasm stems from a belief that what we do matters. Having an image of a future self who is growing provides us with the courage to work hard and attain the goals we select.

Interestingly, the ability to release enthusiasm can also be accompanied by fear. Sometimes, even though we desire to learn and to grow, we fear that releasing our imaginative potential and trying to realize our goals may leave us open to failure. Indeed, some people want to improve but are afraid to leave the safe confines of the familiar (Borich, 1993). As a result, we may *want* to be enthusiastic about teaching, and yet fear the ramifications of letting ourselves truly seek that goal.

We can enhance our personal enthusiasm and learn to calm our fears by seeing others attain goals, perform activities, and produce results that we ourselves would like to accomplish. As you observe successful teachers, you will find yourself saying, "I want to be like that." From this, you will set goals such as, "I want to *try* that." As you try various techniques, you then discover that you *can* accomplish particular goals, and your enthusiasm for teaching grows. Focused observation of successful, enthusiastic teachers can help you dare to release the enthusiasm within you.

GOAL 7: TO BECOME FLEXIBLE

A part of setting and achieving any goal is being willing to take risks. Effective teachers most often achieve their goals in the context of trial and error. This means that to develop as a professional, one must try new things and risk occasional failure. We seldom succeed in attaining a goal, performing an activity, or achieving the desired results the first time we try something. The key to our improvement is to persevere long enough for success to occur. This is why enthusiasm and the energy it releases are so important for self-improvement. Enthusiasm provides us with the stamina to prac-tice desired behaviors in the face of failure (or less-than-perfect results) until success arrives. Since some failure is inevitable in becoming an effective teacher, it is important to develop a flexible attitude. For example, you may practice a behavior exactly as you observed it in a particular classroom—and not achieve the desired results. If you continue to repeat the same behavior, little growth or success may occur. At this juncture it is important to consider various aspects of the behavior that could be adapted or altered in some way. A history of focused observations will help. The fact that you have observed teachers in many different settings will likely suggest variations you can try to improve your strategy. In other words, as you see different teachers interpret similar ideas in numerous ways, you, too, can gain the ability to see and act more flexibly in your own teaching.

GOAL 8: TO BECOME SELF-RELIANT

Perhaps the most important goal of focused classroom observation is becoming self-reliant. As you observe across many educational contexts and approaches, you will be building a professional frame from which to interpret events and make decisions. The greater the detail and scope of your frame, the greater your sense of personal confidence, enthusiasm, and flexibility in setting goals for teaching—and in achieving those goals. Focused observation in classrooms will reveal that teaching is a complex profession for which no amount of formal training can provide sufficient preparation. It will also underscore the fact that effective teachers exist in spite of the challenges of teaching—and that, with careful thought and effort—you can join their ranks.

A BEGINNING THOUGHT

This book will address many of the facets of becoming a skilled observer. But mastering the contents of this text is no guarantee that classroom observation alone will improve your teaching. A carpenter, plumber, physician, or lawyer may know the mechanics of a given trade and still not be expert at providing the service required. Something more is needed to achieve expertise—something beyond factual, observational, or academic learning. That something is a desire for, and an openness to, change and development. No one becomes effective or achieves the status of a professional without the desire to continually adapt to the ongoing stream of challenges and problems in his particular work environment. Schools are no different than executive boardrooms, hospital emergency rooms, or tenth-inning baseball games: They all require split-second decisions—new and spontaneous reactions that sometimes defy even the best-laid plans. As you seek to become a professional, you will need a willingness to open yourself to new ways of responding to your world—ways beyond the set of expectations you have developed over the years. Learning to teach is a process of expanding one's personal frame to include new insights, and accepting the fact that frame building is a lifelong process. Effective executives, surgeons, and athletes, as well as teachers, bring to their work the personal attributes (empathy, cooperativeness, realism, goal orientation, confidence, enthusiasm, flexibility, and self-reliance) that make success happen. You can enhance both your personal and professional development in each of these areas through the focused observations described in the chapters ahead.

Chapter 2

LENSES FOR OBSERVING

Could a greater miracle take place than for us to look through each other's eyes for an instant?

Thoreau, Henry David

What we see is often determined by our own view of life. This view is often personal, sometimes unstructured, and occasionally biased. In this chapter we offer a framework for observing, more objective than our own, that represents different lenses for viewing life in classrooms. It is a framework developed from classroom research that is shared by many who teach and observe in classrooms. With this chapter you will begin to see classrooms through the eyes of others, a view that is less personal than your own.

As you prepare to observe in classrooms, it is important to consider what sort of "lens" you will observe through. As noted in Chapter 1, all of us develop our own views of the world or ways of looking at life. Our view is influenced throughout our lives by the experiences we have, the emotions we feel, and the way we choose to interpret them. What are the characteristics of your world view? How might they affect the way you "see" particular teachers or classrooms? Let's try a little experiment to find out. Read the sentence below (from a study by Sanford & Garrod, 1981, p. 114) and create a mental picture from the words.

John was on his way to school.

What picture formed in your mind as you read the sentence? How old is John? What does he look like? What time of day is it? What is the weather like? Remember what you pictured and read on.

He was terribly worried about the math lesson.

Now what is the picture you see? Has it changed? Does being worried about a math lesson "fit" the picture you have already developed in your mind about what John is like? Keep reading.

He thought he might not be able to control the class again today.

Has anything in your mental picture changed? What? Why? Now keep reading.

It was not a normal part of a janitor's duties.

What do you see now in your mental picture? How old is John? What does he look like? Were you surprised at the information in the last sentence? Why?

Just as you formed mental images and expectations while reading about John, you have probably formed a number of mental images and expectations about schools and classrooms. To explore a few of these images, take a minute and make a list with the headings shown in Figure 2.1

Now, take a minute to create a second list with the headings in Figure 2.2.

What do you notice about the two lists you have created? Can you think of any specific experiences that may have influenced each of your lists?

WHAT REAL CLASSROOMS ARE LIKE

As you make formal (and informal) observations on your way to becoming a teacher, it is important to realize that you are about to enter a complex and demanding profession—a profession that requires not only intelligence, physical stamina, and motivation, but also an acute sense of sight and sound. Your ability to perceive what is happening in a classroom will be critical to your success as a teacher. Because the teaching profession is complex, it is important for you to consider how your preconceived ideas about teaching may influence what you see and hear—and how you interpret that information. No doubt you have already formed, from your years as a student, a set of beliefs about good and poor teaching, teachers, and lessons (Palmer, 1993; Richards, Gipe, & Duffy, 1992). While these opinions and beliefs comprise an important part of your view of education, they can also act as "blinders." In order to look beyond personal experience to obtain a more complete view of classrooms, let's consider four characteristics of classrooms that may affect what you see: *rapidity, immediacy, interruption,* and *social dynamics.*

FIGURE 2.1 Positive Images of Schools and Classrooms

The Perfect Classroom	**The Perfect Teacher**	**The Perfect Lesson**
(how it looks, smells, feels, etc.)	(his classroom management, instructional methods, presentation style, etc.)	(subject, duration, type of activities, etc.)

FIGURE 2.2 Negative Images of Schools and Classrooms

A Terrible Classroom (how it looks, smells, feels, etc.)	A Terrible Teacher (his classroom management, instructional methods, presentation style, etc.)	A Terrible Lesson (subject, duration, type of activities, etc.)

Rapidity

One of the first things you will notice from observing in classrooms is that events move rapidly. In fact, some authors (Verloop, 1989; Clark & Peterson, 1986; Jackson, 1968) estimate that there are up to one thousand teacher–student interchanges in most classrooms in a single day. These interchanges include asking questions, soliciting information, clarifying answers, probing for details, reciting facts, and responding to student requests. In other words, events do not move slowly in classrooms; they are constantly changing at a rapid rate from teacher question to student response, and from student question back to teacher response—creating a momentum of classroom activity that puts the teacher on the front lines practically every minute of the day. The teacher's ability to move the class along at a brisk pace, keep transitions between major instructional events short and orderly, and establish milestones toward which all students work contributes momentum and a sense of accomplishment to the classroom.

Being able to see how the rapidly changing events in a classroom can be used to establish momentum is an important observation skill. But even more important will be your ability to discern why a teacher responds in a particular manner to a particular event. For example, you may at first judge a teacher's response to a given student as unnecessarily abrupt. But, to maintain the momentum of the classroom, this teacher may have decided it is more important to move the group forward and to come back to the student at a later time. Your sense of how rapidly events move in classrooms will be an important observation skill.

Immediacy

Closely related to the rapidity of life in classrooms is the immediacy of the interactions that occur within them. Immediacy pertains to the need to respond quickly to rapidly occurring events. For example, teachers often do not have time to think about how they will respond to a student question, but rather must have an answer—some answer—ready for almost any question or situation that may occur. To delay or ponder for very long over what to say may create an awkward void in the flow of classroom events that can, and often does, result in a loss of momentum and problems in classroom management (Emmer, Evertson, Clements, & Worsham, 1997). But even more important, the momentum of the classroom must be maintained with responses and interactions that satisfy student needs and instructional goals. Few reactions or responses of the teacher can be put off until tomorrow, until the end of the period, or even for a minute. Most of the queries, questions, and solicitations made by students need immediate responses if they are to be effective in satisfying student needs. This makes practically every exchange a test of the teacher's responsiveness. It also tests the teacher's skill at keeping the flow going in ways that respond to, rather than put off, student needs for information, clarification, or further discussion.

Interruption

Think back to some of your experiences as a student. How often were classroom routines interrupted by an unexpected announcement from the office or someone at the door? A third characteristic of classroom life that you will notice is the number of times the natural flow of the classroom is interrupted. A source of frustration for most teachers, such events can so alter the momentum within a classroom that both student achievement and classroom discipline can be affected by them. Perhaps in no other profession are individuals interrupted so frequently in the course of delivering or providing a message than in teaching. Even unsolicited salespeople generally are allowed to complete their messages—and who ever heard of a surgeon being interrupted during an operation by a messenger at the door! Messengers, public address bulletins, students straggling in late for class, changing course schedules, getting parent signatures, and making announcements are only some of the many interruptions that invade the instructional routine of daily classroom life. As even your earliest classroom observations will reveal, teachers do a lot more than teach, and are often interrupted more than they teach.

Researchers have noted that the amount of uninterrupted time students spend actively engaged in the learning process (for example, contributing to a discussion, answering a question, or completing an assignment in a workbook) is an important condition for learning. This time is even more valuable when it is spent on learning tasks that afford students the opportunity to achieve moderate to high levels of success. However, interruptions can make it difficult for students to become actively engaged in a learning task. Results of research studies have shown that, even though fifty minutes may have been assigned to a subject, students may be actively engaged in learning only about half that time due to clerical interruptions and distractions (Berliner, 1984). An even smaller portion of that time may be devoted to tasks with which the students are achieving at a moderate to high level of success (Pasch, 1991). Being able to see the many types of interruptions that occur in classrooms and how effective and ineffective teachers manage these interruptions is another important skill for observation—and, later, for your teaching.

Social Dynamics

The fourth characteristic of classrooms is social dynamics. Teaching is a group process. Even in one-on-one encounters, students are aware of other members of the group, and so rarely perceive themselves as individuals in the classroom. As a result, teachers confront many important instructional and management decisions related to group dynamics.

Many teachers implement discussion sessions, student teams, small groups, and the sharing of in-

structional materials to create opportunities for positive social interaction among their students. These various forms of cooperative learning provide alternatives to the traditional lecture format that can heighten motivation and the excitement of learning (Slavin, 1991; Johnson & Johnson, 1987). But learning in groups can also create opportunities for social distraction—which may inhibit the learning process. Friends and enemies are often found in the same class, and excitement and expectations that often start outside class are easily carried into the classroom. There is, in other words, ample opportunity for groups in school to behave as groups do outside of school, with all the same characteristics: jealousies, competition, playfulness, laughter, and argument. Although common outside the classroom, these characteristics can create social distraction and off-task behavior within the classroom. Few professions require their members to work in such a confined space with so many individuals for so long a time during the day as does teaching. Add to this scene the fact that some individuals do not want to be there, and you have the perfect social setting for learners to become distracted by one another. The teacher's ability to plan and carry out activities that promote cooperative interaction and discourage social distraction can make the difference between an effective and an ineffective classroom. Observing the social dynamics of classrooms will help you discover what types of activities minimize social distraction and maximize cooperative interaction among students. It will also help you understand how and why teachers can sometimes be unaware of how their own behavior contributes to or detracts from establishing a cooperative and cohesive learning environment.

BECOMING AWARE OF CLASSROOM BEHAVIOR: LENSES FOR SELF-IMPROVEMENT

Given the rapidity, immediacy, interruption, and complex social dynamics of classrooms, it is easy to see why teachers are busy people. Few occupations could boast of having a thousand or more interactions with clients or customers in a single day, yet teachers customarily do this not just for one day, but for practically every day of the school year. Add to this the fact that the teacher's job is to facilitate the learning of subject matter content and to ascertain that what is taught is learned, and we have a particularly demanding job. The effect of this ambitious undertaking is that most of a teacher's attention is focused on the subject matter and the students rather than on herself. Within the busy schedule of a school day, teachers do not have many opportunities to reflect on the relative merits of the strategies and methods they use. To pause for contemplation during instruction could disrupt the rapidity of classroom events, and almost surely would result in a loss of momentum; to pause after class or at the end of the school day would require the ability to accurately recall events that may have occurred hours earlier. As a result, teachers frequently can be observed performing behaviors that are unintentional and that they are unaware of, such as dominating discussions and allowing too little response time for students to think through an answer (Swift, Gooding, & Swift, 1988), staying with or encouraging answers from high-ability students more than low-ability students (Good & Brophy, 1990; Rist, 1970), calling on members of one sex more than the other (Sadker & Sadker, 1991; Good & Brophy, 1986), and giving preferential treatment to high-achieving students and more frequently criticizing the wrong answers from low-achieving students (Good & Brophy, 1986). These behaviors have been observed even among experienced teachers, suggesting that at least some teachers may be so involved in conveying their subject matter content that they are unconscious of many of their own patterns of interaction.

A second reason teachers may be unaware of their teaching behavior is that they are not always given specific signs that define "good" teaching. Broad indexes of effectiveness, such as the number of students completing homework, high grades on classroom quizzes, accumulated points for work completed, and improvement from year to year on standardized tests, are often used to gauge progress within a classroom. Although these are convenient end products of individual student progress, their disadvantage for determining a teacher's effectiveness is that many factors other than the instruction being provided can contribute to them—student motivation, aptitude, past achievement, learning readiness, and home life, to name only a few. Also, since end products often result from many different instructional activities over an extended period of time, they rarely point explicitly to what should be changed to improve the quality of the outcome, and therefore provide little corrective or remedial value for changing teacher behavior.

Without clear signs of what to look for to evaluate their teaching, and without the time to consider and reflect on classroom events, many teachers fail to adequately consider their teaching effectiveness. The focused observation activities and accompa-nying observation tools provided in this book are designed to help you develop professional "lenses" for observing others, as well as for assessing your own development as a teacher. As you learn to observe through these lenses, you will be working toward four major goals: (1) to become aware of your own behavior (now and later, as a professional); (2) to discover alternative instructional practices and explore solutions to instructional problems; (3) to determine your personal teaching strengths; and (4) to focus your reflections on important areas of teacher effectiveness. Let's look more closely at each of these goals.

To Become Aware of Your Own Behavior

Although teachers make many decisions each day about the instructional process (how to capture student attention, who they will call on, how they will structure the content, how to summarize the lesson, how misbehavior will be handled, what seatwork to assign, etc.), they sometimes make these decisions unconsciously in the course of meeting the demands of the classroom. They may become bound by routine, failing to recognize how easily decisions can be altered. Instead of being pulled along unconsciously by the stream of rapidly paced events in the classroom, teachers can and should be active decision makers who influence the quality and nature of events in the classroom. As you observe in classrooms, you will become aware that the stream of events is not the same in every classroom, and that sometimes teachers make decisions simply as a result of convention and tradition. If your observations lead to questions such as "Should I be doing that?", "Could that work in my classroom?", or "Would I have done that?", your observations are beginning to make you more aware of your own teaching. That awareness can help you discover some of your own unconscious decisions and unchecked assumptions. Even after you complete your university preparation, taking the opportunity to observe others will help remind you of your own behaviors—and how they may appear to others.

Learning to observe carefully and listen astutely will be your vehicle to becoming a reflective teacher. Just as a medical student observes a procedure many times before attempting it alone, you too will observe master teachers as part of your professional development. As you reflect on the actions and intentions of professionals, you will learn more about yourself. Some of this learning will be exciting, as you discover your personal strengths and talents for teaching. Other aspects of this learning will be challenging, as you identify areas in which you want to improve. One of the advantages of focused observation is that you can accomplish much of the reflection necessary for professional growth in the privacy and security of your own mind. As you observe others, take the opportunity to reflect on what you see: What you see will tell you as much about yourself as it will about those you are observing.

To Discover Alternative Instructional Practices and Explore Solutions to Instructional Problems

Another purpose for observing is to seek information and example behavior related to a specific area of interest. While each of us has experienced a number of instructional practices as a student, there are many we did not experience—or that we experienced in a limited context. As you enter the teaching profession, it is natural to wonder about new instructional practices, methods, and strategies, and whether new and different educational ideas will help you become a more effective teacher. As you read textbooks, observe other teachers, and practice teach, you'll develop questions about the "how-to's" of teaching. Whether the basis of your curiosity stems from wondering about your own experiences as a student, from wanting to see some textbook procedure come alive in the classroom, or from having experienced a seemingly intractable problem in your own teaching, observation of other classrooms is often a practical solution for discovering and applying new ideas.

Developing a professional curiosity can help you refine the focus of your observations. For example, as you watch a teacher lead a class discussion, you may wonder how a teacher can successfully blend fact- and concept-type questions in the midst of the same discussion. Or you may encounter a problem with misbehavior in your own classroom and want to learn more about the variety of rules used by other teachers for keeping students from calling out without being acknowledged. Focused observations can be among the most rewarding, because they occur in response to an immediate need that has some sense of urgency for your thinking—and later, for your teaching. When you focus your observations on specific questions, your observations can result in a special sense of satisfaction when you discover new approaches worth trying. They can also be a source of comfort when you encounter a problem that seems to have no easy solution, and discover, through your observations, that others struggle with similar challenges, and that the source of the problem may lie outside yourself.

To Determine Your Personal Teaching Strengths

Aside from helping you find solutions to instructional problems, focused observation helps put your personal teaching strengths in perspective. Teachers do not always see that a decision they have made, either consciously or unconsciously, could solve an instructional problem of another teacher. This may be due to the fact that many teachers rarely observe others and do not have sufficient opportunities to describe to others the positive achievements in their own classrooms. As you observe, you will discover areas where *your* knowledge and experience provide insights that can help other teachers address a particular challenge. Taking the opportunity to share insights about successes and challenges builds a healthy sense of competence and shared professionalism. This benefit alone is why career-ladder and professional development programs are increasingly requiring peer observation.

To Focus Your Reflections on Important Areas of Teacher Effectiveness

Handbooks and reviews of classroom research, such as those by Brophy (1989), Duncan (1987), and Wittrock (1986), summarize the results of more than twenty years of research in classrooms. In these and related texts (for example, Borich & Tombari, 1997; Borich, 1996, 1995, 1993), the processes used by teachers to instruct students (for example, activity structures, questioning strategies, methods of organizing content, use of incentives and consequences, defining classroom rules, and ways of pacing and sequencing instruction) are related to student outcomes (such as performance on classroom and standardized tests, attitude, problem-solving skills, and engagement in the learning process). This research has identified guidelines for effective teaching practice in eight areas: (1) learning climate of a classroom; (2) classroom management; (3) lesson clarity; (4) instructional variety; (5) teacher's task orientation; (6) students' engagement in the learning process; (7) students' success; and (8) students' higher thought processes and performance outcomes. Since so much effort, experience, and time has been devoted to researching these areas, it is important that you become aware of them.

The easiest and most efficient way to learn about effective teaching practices and to understand their application in the classroom is to observe them. Thus, it is important that the beginning observer enter the classroom with a plan of what to look for. Rather than simply waiting for interesting events to occur, the observer begins by looking for evidence of effective teaching practices already identified by researchers, to which, later, related practices can be added. Let's look more closely at the eight areas of effective practice that can help guide your initial classroom observations.

EIGHT AREAS, OR LENSES, TO FOCUS CLASSROOM OBSERVATION

Because classrooms are complex, observers often choose a particular lens, or focus, to gain insight regarding a particular aspect of classroom life. Over time, observations are completed using different lenses, resulting in a more comprehensive and detailed understanding of teaching and learning. While the eight lenses we will use are not the only ones that could guide observation in classrooms, each has been researched and has been found to influence the performance of learners. Other lenses for viewing classroom behavior are also available, and new lenses will undoubtedly emerge from classroom research in the future. For our purposes, the following lenses will serve as an introduction to acquiring classroom observation skills and beginning to teach effectively. We will discuss each in greater detail in later chapters.

Area 1: Consider the Learning Climate

The *learning climate* of a classroom refers to its physical and emotional environment. Some observable features of the learning environment are (a) the warmth, concerns, and expectations conveyed to students by the teacher; (b) the organization of the physical aspects of the classroom, which promotes or precludes cohesion and interaction among students; and (c) the competitiveness, cooperation, or independence encouraged by the structure of activity within the classroom.

As you observe the learning climate of a classroom, you will want to note how students seem to feel about themselves, about one another, and about their classroom, and what activities and materials promote those feelings most conducive to learning.

Area 2: Focus on Classroom Management

Classroom management involves organizing the classroom and anticipating and responding to student behavior to provide an environment for efficient learning. Some observable features of classroom management are organizing the physical aspects of the classroom to match instructional goals; preestablishing and communicating classroom rules; developing and communicating instructional routines; establishing a system of incentives and consequences; and using techniques for low-profile classroom control.

Because many beginning teachers find effective classroom management challenging, you'll want to pay close attention to how effective teachers orchestrate and facilitate learning with their classroom management skills.

Area 3: Look for Lesson Clarity

Lesson clarity refers to a teacher's ability to speak clearly and directly, and to present and facilitate instruction at the students' current level of understanding. Some observable features of lesson clarity are informing learners of expected skills and understanding; providing advance organizers that place the lesson content in the perspective of past and future learning; reviewing and summarizing; and using examples, illustrations, and demonstrations that expand and clarify lesson content.

Area 4: Verify Variety

As you recall from your own experiences as a student, *instructional variety*, using different modes of learning (visual, oral, and tactile) maintains interest and attention. Effective teachers select an appropriate mix of instructional approaches to support particular learning objectives. Some observable features of instructional variety are the use of attention-gaining devices; variation in eye contact, voice, and gestures; use of alternate modes (seeing, listening, and doing) through which learning is to occur; and using appropriate rewards and reinforcers to sustain student interest and engagement.

Area 5: Observe Task Orientation

Task orientation involves maximizing students' opportunity to focus on instructional tasks. It includes managing classroom activities efficiently; handling misbehavior with minimum disruption to the class; reducing instructional time devoted to clerical duties; and maximizing time devoted to content coverage. Some of the most observable features of task orientation are lesson plans that reflect the text and curriculum guide, use of rules and procedures that anticipate and thereby reduce misbehavior, and established milestones (for example, tests, reviews, and assignments) for maintaining instructional momentum.

Area 6: Examine Engagement

Students learn best when they become actively engaged in the learning process. Teachers promote *student engagement* by providing exercises, problem sets, and activities that allow students to think about, act on, and practice what they learn. Some observable features of teachers facilitating student engagement in the learning process are the provision of activities for guided practice; the use of feedback and correctives; the use of individualized and self-directed learning activities; the systematic use of meaningful verbal praise; and checking and monitoring of classroom assignments during seatwork.

Area 7: Measure Student Success

Students' learning is enhanced when they complete work at moderate to high levels of success. Some of the most observable features of teaching focused on student success are unit and lesson organization that reflects prior learning; timeliness of feedback and corrections; gradual transitions to new content; and a classroom pace and momentum that builds toward major milestones (for example, reviews, projects, practice exercises, and tests).

Area 8: Look for Higher Thought Processes and Performance Outcomes

Higher thought processes are those such as critical thinking, reasoning, and problem solving that alone cannot be measured by tests of cognitive achievement. Some observable features of teaching for higher thought processes are using collaborative and group activities; demonstrating mental models and strategies for learning; arranging for student projects and demonstrations; engaging students in oral performance; providing opportunities for independent practice; and using performance assessments.

CHALLENGES TO OBSERVING IN CLASSROOMS

So far we have discussed four purposes for observing in classrooms. These are to

1. Become aware of your own behavior, which will provide feedback for making decisions that help consciously control and alter the stream of events in your classroom.
2. Discover alternative instructional practices and explore solutions to instructional problems.

3. Determine your personal teaching strengths.
4. Focus your reflections on important areas of teacher effectiveness.

Before undertaking an actual observation, let's take one more step in preparing to observe by considering how easily biases and personal experiences, if not controlled, can influence your observations. Let's listen to three imaginary teachers who have been instructed by the school counselor to write down their impressions of Peter after observing him during their first day of class. As each teacher "speaks" about Peter, make some notes of your impressions about Peter and about the teacher.

Teacher A Peter arrived late to my classroom and took a seat in the last row without acknowledging that he was late. Most of the class brought the required supplies—paper, pencil, and ruler—but Peter had none of these. I have had students like this before—lazy and irresponsible—and it's like pulling teeth to teach them anything. I don't know for sure, but I'm willing to bet I am going to have trouble with him this year.

Teacher B Well, you've asked me to comment on Peter, but I don't have much to say so early in the school year. In fact I wouldn't have even noticed Peter if he hadn't walked in late, probably due to all the commotion and noise in the halls this morning. At any rate, Peter seems like a quiet, maybe even shy, boy since he seemed embarrassed to even say he was late and went directly to a seat in the last row. I predict Peter won't have much to say during my class this year.

Teacher C When you asked that I give you my impressions of Peter, I looked up his achievement scores and grades from last year. After meeting him for the first time today, everything made sense. Peter is going to be a very high achiever in my class. He's the type that gets right down to work. For example, when he came into the class, he went to the corner of the classroom to get away from the commotion caused by students arriving late. Peter seems like a sensitive, high-achieving student who probably will have to be given extra work to keep him challenged this year.

What did you notice about the three reports? Could these different perceptions of the same student emerge on the same day? Researchers such as Good and Brophy (1990), Willis (1972), and Rist (1970) have noted such instances among teachers, attributing differences in observation to selective perception. *Selective perception* involves seeing what we want to see, or allowing our perceptions to be unduly influenced by things outside the immediate context of the observation. Notice how each of the three observers saw different aspects of Peter's behavior, and interpreted the meaning of what they saw in terms of the rest of the school year.

Teacher A seems convinced that Peter will be a troublemaker and, therefore, will need close watching if he is to learn. Teacher A assumes that Peter has a poor disciplinary record—often comes late to class, fails to follow school rules, and will, if given the chance, seize any opportunity to become a troublemaker.

Teacher B's description suggests that Peter will need no special attention, that he will blend into the woodwork of the classroom. In fact, Teacher B predicts, based on only a single class period, that Peter will be easy to handle.

Teacher C believes that Peter is a high achiever. Teacher C's observations focus on Peter's academic skills and, after checking the records, she seems convinced that Peter will require supplemental learning materials to keep him challenged.

Each of these observations of Peter could eventually prove to be accurate—or just as easily could prove to be false. The point is that the observers had no choice but to observe and comment on only a small part of Peter's behavior—that which each assumed was the most important, without knowing the reason why Peter's behavior was of concern in the first place. In other words, they unconsciously selected what they saw.

Each of the three teachers not only made some selective observations, but also some interpretations to go along with them. In their written accounts, facts about Peter's behavior were blended with interpretations about what these facts might mean. Teacher A felt pretty sure that what was observed meant Peter would be a troublemaker—and, therefore, she should be on her guard. Teacher B thought that what he saw meant Peter was quiet and shy. And Teacher C believed that what she saw was a sign of a high achiever with academic talent and a responsiveness to school. In each instance, these teachers not only recorded the facts as they saw them, but interpreted them according to their own opinions, formed by, for example, their past experiences with similar students, their own values about the appropriateness or inappropriateness of the behaviors observed, and what they thought the counselor to whom they were reporting wanted them to see. Each of these teachers unknowingly set up different expectations for Peter, which may lead them to treat Peter in special ways for the rest of the school year. These initial impressions may encourage them to selectively perceive Peter's future behavior in ways that reinforce their initial impressions.

We will have more to say about how to recognize and control selective perception. For now, let's identify some of the sources of influence outside the immediate context of an observation that can create selective perception—and which you will want to consider as you complete your classroom observations.

SOURCES OF INFLUENCE ON OBSERVATIONS FROM OUTSIDE OURSELVES

One of the most significant sources of selective perception comes from the school and classroom environment in which you will be observing. Some of the specific school and classroom characteristics that can affect your perceptions are described in the following sections.

Student Ability and Achievement

One of the most persuasive influences on your observations will come from the known or presumed mental abilities of the students in the classrooms you will be observing. Although student abilities are often a legitimate focus of observation and an obvious influence on what goes on in a classroom, they can bias an observation if their influence is not recognized and limited to a specific area of observation. High-IQ or high-achieving classrooms, which may be denoted by tracked classes or advanced subject matter, can establish expectations that force seemingly neutral or irrelevant data to confirm that everything is going well in these classrooms. Conversely, when low-ability or remedial classes are observed, expectations may focus your attention on student inattention, poor quality of work, lack of student participation, or teacher difficulty in controlling the class, to the exclusion of the many positive events that may be happening in the classroom. Although these factors may be part of the legitimate focus of the observation, they should not influence you to selectively perceive or overemphasize these characteristics simply because they are expected. Especially when observing predesignated categories of students (for example, gifted, high-ability, or less able), regardless of whether such categories are established informally by the teacher or formally by the school, it is important to recognize that many such categories represent stereotypes. These categories, in reality, capture a wide range of student and teacher behavior and may include the unexpected.

Classroom Characteristics

A second source of potential influence on your observations will be the immediate physical context in which the instruction takes place. This includes the general attractiveness of the classroom (for example, neat and clean, bulletin boards filled with interesting displays, desks and chairs in order), as well as some less tangible aspects of the classroom, such as its apparent warmth and congenial atmosphere. Although these can be important areas of observation, they can preclude your ability to perceive other important areas of classroom behavior if they are allowed to dominate your attention. In other words, observations preceding instruction, and especially those pertaining to the physical context in which instruction takes place, should not lead you to presuppose anything about the learning process. Physical characteristics of the classroom will naturally yield both positive and negative expectations, but these impressions should not be allowed to color your observations. If physical characteristics of the classroom are to be the explicit focus of an observation, they must be studied apart from stereotypic expectations.

Participatory and Cooperative Student Behavior

A third influence on what an observer sees is the responsiveness of the students to the instruction and the teacher. These behaviors often represent a cooperativeness or willingness on the part of the students to become active participants in the classroom. They are particularly influential because they are often the most obvious to observers. For example, the willingness of students to comply with a teacher's instructional demands and obedience to classroom rules can quickly establish a tone of effective or ineffective instruction long before any other event takes place. But student cooperative or participatory behavior can result from many factors outside the control of the teacher, and effective or ineffective instruction can, and often does, go on in spite of such behaviors. Every teacher is fearful of students acting up just when an administrator or observer is present, especially when such an observation is scheduled for a particularly unruly class. A trained observer, however, while noting the responsiveness, participation, and obedience of the class, should not necessarily presume that such behavior is the result of effective or ineffective classroom management or poorly chosen instructional practices. Observations specifically targeted in these and related areas must reveal the extent to which the teaching practices observed are the result of, or the cause of, these student behaviors. The cooperative and participatory behavior of the students should not influence the observation of other important classroom events that may be occurring simultaneously.

Experience and Education of the Teacher

Most observers generally know the number of years a teacher has been teaching, if only by the teacher's age. Some observers also know whether or not a particular teacher has received an advanced degree, has attended special seminars or workshops, or has special honors related to teaching. These, too, can influence what an observer sees or fails to see in a classroom if their influence is not recognized at the outset of an observation. As a result of what is called a *halo effect,* these characteristics of the teacher can easily intimidate an observer and influence what data are perceived as relevant to the observation. They may also influence the degree of emphasis that is placed on events. For example, better classroom management skills are usually expected from an experienced teacher. The truth is that years of experience, advanced degrees, and special recognitions do not always result in effective teaching. These may represent important avenues for becoming an effective teacher—but they do not guarantee effectiveness. This is not to lessen the value of experience and advanced training, but rather to suggest that they are not the only way of becoming an effective teacher. For some, they may not even be the best or quickest way of becoming an effective teacher. The point is that, unknown to many observers, perceptions of events within the classroom are often influenced by the presumed stature a teacher has attained outside of it. Such presumptions can lead you to notice events that fit your expectations.

School, Grade, and Subject Matter

Another influence leading to selective perception comes from a knowledge of the school, grade, or subject matter to be observed. Poor and rich neighborhoods are a fact of life; they have spawned their own expectations. Similarly, certain expectations surround various instructional levels or grades, as well as certain subject matter areas. Observers in schools in poor or high-crime neighborhoods, for example, often approach their task fearing the worst. Observers who visit schools with better reputations often come with an optimistic attitude. One often hears reference to students in the elementary grades as "sweet," in junior high as ``difficult,'' and in the twelfth grade as "mature." Vocational and technical courses, remedial or basic track classes, and college preparatory or advanced placement courses have stereotypes as well. The point is that stereotypes can restrict what you see, according to what the stereotype implies. If stereotypes could predict life in classrooms, they would have long ago become accepted facts rather than the inaccurate caricatures of classroom life that they often are. Effective teaching does not occur any more often, on the average, in advanced college-bound classes with high-IQ students taught by experienced teachers with master's degrees than in any other setting, contrary to many expectations and stereotypes. This is one of the best reasons for not allowing school, grade, and subject to unduly influence what is, or can be, observed.

Individual and Cultural Diversity

Another outside influence on observation is the individual and cultural diversity found in every classroom. Although the physical school setting has remained largely unchanged over the past seventy-five years, the major participants—the students—have changed. The typical classroom of today contains a more diverse group of learners than at any time in our history. This diversity reflects not only the motivational and cognitive abilities that children bring to school, but also the culture that accompanies them. It is no longer accurate to say that we are a nation and an educational system *with* minorities; rather, we are a nation and an education system *of* minorities. By the year 2000, nonwhite students will make up more than 40 percent of all students in America. Nonwhites currently make up the majority of learners in our twenty-seven largest school districts.

Added to the medley of cultures in our schools is an assortment of family patterns. It is estimated that by the year 2000, the majority of children entering school will have, by their eighteenth birthday, lived with just one parent; there will be at least four million latchkey children of school age at home alone (Hodgkinson, 1988). The steadily shrinking number of two-parent families will more than likely have both parents working full time. The homes of these families are just as likely to be organized as disorganized, democratic as authoritarian, structured around rules and routines as absent of any predictable living arrangements.

The result of this cultural, familial, and socioeconomic diversity is an ever-increasing range of individual differences in the classroom. This diversity will be equaled by the diversity in how teachers deal with it. For example, the research of Tharp and Gallimore (1989), Dillon (1989), and Bowers and Flinders (1991) presents convincing arguments that different cultures react differently to the nonverbal and verbal behavioral management techniques of proximity control, eye contact, warnings, and classroom arrangement. Furthermore, these authors cite numerous examples of how teachers from one cul-

ture interpret disruptive behaviors of children differently than teachers from another culture.

As we observe in classrooms, we need to explore our potential biases related to diversity. For example, gender-, racial-, and ethnic-specific clothing, dialect, and mannerisms can lead us to expect and look for one type of behavior more than another, or to place stereotypic interpretations on classroom behavior to which gender, race, and ethnicity actually have no relationship. For now, it is important to know that some of the patterns of effective teaching techniques you will observe are culturally sensitive. The astute observer must consider instructional and management techniques not only in relation to classroom context, but also in relation to the cultural history of the learner or learners with whom they are being used. We will deal with the issue of individual and cultural diversity as it applies to the observation and recording of specific teaching and student behavior throughout this text. Remember that the mistaken relevance of gender-, racial-, and ethnic-specific behavior to learning can influence your observations.

SOURCES OF INFLUENCE ON OBSERVATIONS FROM WITHIN OURSELVES

In addition to the ways observations can be influenced by external factors, several factors within yourself can determine what you choose to perceive.

Your Own Experiences in School

We often compare present experiences with past ones, and our experience with school is no exception. As noted in Chapter 1, much of what we see and hear in classrooms can be related to what we saw and heard in school when we were growing up (Lortie, 1975). This creates a strong tendency on our part to make comparisons between what is being observed and what classrooms were like when we were in school. There is a tendency to hold up the past as a standard against which present classrooms should be measured. Therefore, aspects of a classroom that are unlike those in our own school experience may be placed in a negative light, or instructional activities that worked well in our own past experiences can inadvertently become the standard for today's classrooms. For example, a tightly managed lecture format from our own school days may lead us to see a classroom with a high degree of student talk as a poorly managed classroom (Cazden, 1988). Whenever we allow our previous school experiences to form the basis of what we see, our observations are being influenced by selective perception. While we cannot, and should not, ignore our past experiences, it is important to continually examine how they may influence our current perceptions.

Recent Influences and Training

Aside from our past experiences in school, our perceptions and judgments are often influenced by our most recent experiences and training. Workshops on new teaching techniques, books on innovative instructional methods, problems related to education covered in the mass media, and university coursework can all influence what we see. These experiences and events can provide a useful additional focus to our observations—or they can serve as a distracting influence. We tend to be enthusiastic about our most recent experiences, perhaps because they are more memorable. A halo effect is formed by our excitement about something new and different, which can exaggerate its true effects. At first we use or see the new approach at every turn, and expect others to do so as well. At this stage, even inconsequential events can sometimes be mistaken for evidence that the approach is or is not being used. In time, however, the newness of the idea subsides, and it is placed in the context of other ideas. Our perspective broadens, changing our initial absolute acceptance of a new or innovative approach to an acceptance that is more conditional. In other words, influential events, ideas, or experiences occurring in the life of the observer at the approximate time of an observation can unconsciously direct an observer to overemphasize the importance of what has been learned in another context. This is another instance when the focus of an observation can be clouded by selective perception.

Who May Be Watching; Who May Find Out

It is no secret that we often change our interpretations because of who may be listening or who may use the data from the observations we make. This is one of the reasons observations of teachers by school administrators as part of yearly appraisals and career-ladder enhancements are often discredited by teachers and sometimes, privately, by administrators.

Teachers may change their typical behavior—even rehearse desirable behaviors—for the sake of an observation, and then revert to the original behavior immediately afterward, as almost any of us might in a similar evaluative situation. Observers change their behavior as well. Teachers believed to be less competent by an administrator-observer may be given somewhat inflated ratings to minimize a potentially argumentative confrontation with the teacher; conversely, teachers perceived to be more competent by an administrator-observer may be given somewhat deflated ratings to keep the teacher working toward higher levels of performance, and to minimize the disappointment of others who may think their performance is equally effective. For these reasons, peer observation may be far more conducive to the professional development of teachers than administrator observation, because many of the political factors apparent in administrator observation are minimized when teachers observe other teachers. It is important, therefore, that the purpose of a peer observation, self-improvement and professional development, always be clear to both parties.

CHOOSING A USEFUL LENS: THE NEED TO STRUCTURE OBSERVATIONS

Wise observers separate the informal process of looking from the systematic process of observing. The difference between just looking at an event and carefully observing it lies in the structure an observer brings to the observation. This structure provides a framework to separate relevant events from irrelevant events, and to sort the myriad events of the classroom into manageable and comprehensible categories that have professional relevance for the practice of teaching. Without this structure, an observer is left to cast about for relevant events, and runs the risk of not knowing when minor details are of major importance or vice versa. In short, without an appropriate lens for observing, we would be in the same position as Teachers A, B, and C, who attempted to record their observations of Peter without knowing what aspects of Peter's behavior were of concern to the counselor. A lack of focus leaves our observations open to selective perception, contradictory explanations, and false expectations. All of these can confuse or distort our observations, rendering them of limited value.

Structuring an observation simply involves directing our attention to a certain area of classroom life. Many possible structures, or lenses, exist and have been used in the study of classrooms. An effective lens for the purposes of classroom observation, however, is one that captures important classroom events within a well-defined context. As we have noted, classrooms are busy places of rapid interchanges between students and teachers, in which action sequences do not always have definable beginnings and ends. This makes placing structure on what we see even more important. Without some guide, we may see everything that can be seen, but nothing in specific demands our attention. Choosing a particular lens for viewing, a specific question for study, helps us manage the huge amount of information available during a classroom observation. It also helps us consider which external and internal factors may influence what we see and how we interpret our experiences.

The eight patterns of effective teaching practice described in this chapter will become the lenses through which we will learn to observe life in classrooms. In Chapter 3, we will see how these patterns of practice occur simultaneously and in rapid succession in a quickly paced classroom. In Chapter 4, we will present some of the recording methods that can be used to observe each of our lenses. And in Chapters 5–12, we will focus on the individual and interactive effects of each of these areas of classroom life, providing recognizable patterns of effective teaching practice. We turn now to these important steps for observing in classrooms.

Chapter 3

MAKING CLASSROOM VISITS

David says
that since he
made his bed
this morning,
there's a
train track
in his blankets.

Before,
when I looked,
I only saw
that it was
wrinkled.

Eleanor Schick

Like the poem's author, each of us sees what we expect to see most of the time. Interestingly, when someone points out another view, or when we look at a situation with a different perspective, we often gain new insights. This is true of classroom observation—and it is an important notion. In this chapter we'll consider various perspectives we may want to take in observing classrooms, and why those perspectives may be useful to us.

City Green. New York: Macmillan Publishing Company, Inc., 1974.

Although you'll often want to observe classrooms with very specific questions or goals, your first few observations may be more general so that you can get a feel for particular grade levels or schools. The eight lenses discussed in Chapter 2 can be used to help you consider the overall picture of a classroom. To see how all eight lenses can work together to inform your observation and suggest specific questions for further study, let's visit a fictional classroom taught by Ms. Koker. Complete the *General Observation Form* (Instrument 3.1) at the end of the chapter and make notes next to each topic area as you read about the events in Ms. Koker's class.

A CLASSROOM DIALOGUE

The scene is a seventh-grade social studies classroom. Ms. Koker is beginning a unit on forms of government. It is early in the school year, so the class is still new to her. The first several weeks of school were a bit rough for Ms. Koker because she was somewhat unprepared for the aggressive talking-out behavior of some of the students, and because of the new textbook, which devotes less time to some of her favorite topics. Things have calmed down somewhat now that Ms. Koker has established some classroom rules and has decided to organize her class more tightly with drill and practice exercises. Ms. Koker's goals for this lesson are to introduce three types of government, and then begin to develop the concept of democracy. Aside from a tendency to be loud and talkative, this class is composed of students of mostly average abilities, with a few who are bright and a few who regularly challenge her authority.

Ms. Koker Today we begin a unit on various forms of government. In the next few days, we will study the concepts of monarchy, oligarchy, and democracy, and how governments are formed using each of these three concepts. In fact, we will cover these three forms of government so thoroughly that at the end of the week, each of you will know how to create a government of your own using each—but, please, don't start any revolutions with what you learn! [Class laughs.] Let's start by defining what a monarchy is. Does anybody know? [At this point, some class members turn to their neighbors to ask if they know the answer.]

Ms. Koker Please, no talking. Bobby, do you know what a monarchy is?

Bobby No.

Ms. Koker Christina, do you have any idea?

Christina No, I'm afraid I don't, Ms. Koker.

Ms. Koker Tim, you're not in your seat, so I'll have to ask you. Do you know what a monarchy is?

Tim Yep, it's a butterfly. [Class bursts out in laughter.]

Ms. Koker That's an extra assignment for you tonight. Okay, I'll tell you. A monarchy is a government that is ruled or governed by a single person. It's a form of government in which a single person, a king or queen for example, is the supreme head of a state for his or her entire lifetime. Now, what other names besides "King" or "Queen" do we have for individuals who serve as head of a country for a lifetime? Let's go from left to right across the first row.

Mary I'm not sure what you mean, Ms. Koker.

Ms. Koker Next. Felipe?

Felipe You mean, what do we call someone who is just like a king, but called something else?

Ms. Koker You're on the right track. Next. Anna?

Anna Well, I would call a king an emperor.

Tim [Talking out] Yeah, like in "The Emperor's New Clothes!" [Class laughs.]

Ms. Koker Okay, that's the second time you've spoken out of turn, Tim. You will answer two extra homework questions tonight if you don't want me to write up a detention slip. Now, go up and write your name on the board, so I won't forget to give you the assignment. [By now, talking has grown louder and a few students have left their seats waiting for Tim to return from the board.] Let's see now, where were we?

Student [From somewhere in back of room] We were talking about emperors.

Ms. Koker Yes, emperors, like kings, usually indicate a monarchy—or rule by a single person over a long time. Other names for heads of state that indicate a monarchy are czar, which was a title once used in Russia; kaiser, which was a term used in the early German empire; and sultan, which is a word still used today in the Middle East. These individuals, like kings and emperors throughout history, have often had absolute power over the people and lands they ruled. Traditionally, these rulers gained their power from the family they were born into, and not from any accomplishments of their own. In some cases today, a type of monarchy exists alongside some other form of government. Can anyone think of a country like our own that has a king or a queen? Let's go across the second row this time. Rashaun?

Rashaun England. They have a queen and royal weddings and that kind of stuff that we don't have in this country.

Ms. Koker Good, Rashaun. Some present-day monarchs, like the Queen of England, still exist. However, in England the queen possesses only minor authority and exists for mostly symbolic purposes, or as a way of showing the country's historical roots. Although kings and queens did at one time have absolute authority over England, today they serve mostly ceremonial functions. That was a good response, Rashaun. Now, before we move to another form of government, called an *oligarchy*, does everyone understand what a monarchy is? [No one responds.]

Ms. Koker Okay, I guess we can go on. Let's see, where did we leave off in the second row? [Tricia meekly raises her hand.] Can you tell us what an oligarchy is, Tricia?

Tricia I don't know.

Ms. Koker Next. Raul?

Raul Don't know.

Ms. Koker Well, I guess I'll have to tell you—but it's in the chapter, which you should have read. An oligarchy is a form of government in which absolute power or authority is given to a few persons, instead of a single ruler as in a monarchy. These individuals usually come to power not through heredity or being born into the right families, but through some political struggle or compromise. Oligarchies, which were common in ancient times, are hard to find today, but some governments almost like an oligarchy still exist. Can anyone think of one? Jeff, Kathy, you're the last two in the second row. Any ideas?

Jeff I'm not sure, but is it like a mother and father in a family?

Ms. Koker What do you mean?

Jeff Well, my parents have a kind of agreement—not written or anything like that—in which my mother is responsible for taking care of the house and my brothers and sisters, and my father is responsible for his job and doing repairs. That's a kind of sharing of responsibility, isn't it?

Ms. Koker Yes, maybe. But it's not what we're talking about here. Kathy?

Kathy I can't think of any examples.

Ms. Koker Well, you probably never heard of the Peloponnesian Wars, but shortly after one of these, in about B.C. 400, ancient Greece was ruled for a brief time by a group of persons called the Thirty Tyrants. This may have been the very first oligarchy. Also, we've been hearing a lot lately about a country called Yugoslavia. In that country power and authority used to be divided among individuals representing each of the states or regions. Now, let's compare the two forms of government we've been discussing—monarchy and oligarchy—with our own form of government. First, let's remind ourselves of what our form of government is called. Let's pick up with the first person in the third row. Quann?

Quann I'm not ready.

Ms. Koker Everyone should be ready when I call on them.

Quann Well, I didn't get to read this yet. [Class begins to snicker at Quann getting in trouble.]

Ms. Koker Okay, I'm going to make the rule that everyone must read the assignment before we begin a topic. That means that the reading for the entire week must be done by class on Monday. [Loud moans are heard.]

Tim [Speaking without acknowledgment] But that means we'd have homework over the weekend, and no other teacher makes us do that.

Ms. Koker [Ignoring Tim's comment] We still have one more form of government to discuss. Joan is next. [Class becomes noisy and restless at the thought of weekend homework.]

Joan We live in a democracy.

Ms. Koker What else can you tell us about a democracy?

Joan Well . . . [Just as she is about to begin, the public address system clicks on.]

Principal [On P.A.] I'm sorry to interrupt, but two lunchtime jobs are still available for any students who want to be paid for working in the cafeteria during the second half of their lunch. We need some workers for today, so, teachers, if anyone is interested, please write them a hall permit and send them to the office immediately. Thank you. [Roberto and Tim raise their hands, indicating their interest in the job. The teacher ignores Tim and writes a pass to the office for Roberto.]

Ms. Koker Okay, we were discussing democracy. Time is short, so take out paper and pen and write down everything I say. Another rule we will start tomorrow, since you're not doing the reading, is to take notes on everything I say. The word *democracy* comes from the Greek word *demus*, which means "the people," and the Greek word *kratein*, spelled K-R-A-T-E-I-N, which means "to rule."

Brittany [Calling out] How is that first word spelled?

Ms. Koker [Responds by spelling the word.] D-E-M-U-S. So, who's next to be called on? [Rhonda raises her hand.] Okay, Rhonda, putting these two words together, what does the word *democracy* mean?

Rhonda It means that the people rule.

Ms. Koker Good. And who are the people in a democracy? Sam?

Sam I guess it's all of us—everyone that lives in a certain place.

Ms. Koker Okay, a democracy differs from a monarchy and an oligarchy by who is given the authority to rule. As we have seen, in a monarchy, a single person, usually chosen through heredity, is given absolute authority, and in the case of an oligarchy, a small number of persons, representing only a fraction of all the people in the land, are given the authority to rule. In a democracy, however, authority to rule rests in the hands of all the people. But how could such a system work when everyone has authority over everyone else? Next person. Diana?

Diana We—or I should say all the people—elect persons to represent us. I guess that's what our senators and representatives do.

Ms. Koker So when we say that all the people have the authority to rule in a democracy, we really mean . . . Next. That's you, Phil.

Phil We elect persons—like Diana said—representatives and senators, and we give them the authority to rule.

Ms. Koker Yes. So in a democracy like ours, the people have authority, but indirectly, through the election of individuals that represent their interests. In our form of democracy, called *representative democracy*, a legislature composed of senators and representatives is elected by the people. Does anyone know of any other kind of democracy? Mark, you're next.

Mark Nope.

Ms. Koker Did you take notes on the chapter?

Mark I was going to do that tonight.

Ms. Koker I will begin checking notes at the end of every class. Since some of you haven't read the assignment, we'll use the remaining time to read Chapter 7.

REACTIONS FROM OBSERVING MS. KOKER'S CLASSROOM

Although this dialogue represents only a small slice of classroom life, classroom exchanges such as this occur frequently at almost all levels of schooling (Cazden, 1988). They are, to be sure, uneven, rough, and sometimes even crude attempts to convey information in the midst of all sorts of competing forces—misbehaving and unprepared students, interruptions, quickly sketched lesson plans, and insufficient instructional time, to name only a few. The flow of events in a classroom, as shown in the dialogue, is not always a neatly packaged, smooth unit of instruction. Instead, teachers and students often struggle, sometimes with themselves and sometimes with each other, to complete the day's lesson. Although Ms. Koker's classroom may have had some problems, these problems are not uncommon for any teacher at one time or another.

Think back for a moment on the dialogue you have just read. In your opinion, was it an example of effective teaching or ineffective teaching, or did it contain some examples of each? What are your impressions of Ms. Koker as a person and as a teacher? What about her knowledge and use of instructional methods? Did she do all the right things most of the time, even though not all the students conveniently cooperated, or did some of her decisions make it less likely that the goals of the lesson would be achieved? Do you believe the goals for this lesson, as stated before the dialogue, were met? If not, whose fault was it—Ms. Koker's, for not motivating the students; the students, for not reading the assignment; Tim, for misbehaving; or the principal, for creating a distraction at a crucial time?

Of course, all of these factors (and others) were instrumental in the way life in this classroom unfolded. But if we were to attempt to fully understand life in this classroom, each of the questions we asked ourselves would point us in equally narrow, and perhaps even biased, directions. A broader set of lenses than individual questions or idiosyncratic concerns that happen to gain our attention would be necessary to view classroom life.

As you consider the interactions in Ms. Koker's classroom, look over the *General Observation Form* (Instrument 3.1) you completed. In what areas did you notice positive interactions? In what areas do you feel concern? Did completing the form help you observe Ms. Koker and her students more effectively?

The eight areas of effective teaching can help us achieve the breadth of vision we need to understand the events in Ms. Koker's classroom. Let's use each of these areas as a lens to achieve a more focused observation of life in Ms. Koker's classroom as it unfolded during this lesson. After viewing the events through each of these lenses, we will bring all our data together to form some general impressions of the strengths and weaknesses of Ms. Koker's presentation. As you read the following discussion, add some notes to your *General Observation Form* to help you remember key points about viewing any classroom through each of the eight lenses.

OBSERVING THE LEARNING CLIMATE

Recall that the learning climate of a classroom involves the social and emotional environment in which learning takes place. In Chapter 2, we noted that some of the most noticeable features of a learning climate are the warmth, concerns, and expectations conveyed to students by the teacher; the organization of the physical aspects of the classroom that promote or preclude cohesion and interaction among students; and the competitiveness, cooperation, or independence encouraged by the teacher's instructional routine. Using these aspects of the learning environment as our lens, let's look back at the dialogue to see how the learning climate may have influenced the achievement of Ms. Koker's goals for the lesson.

In many ways, the learning climate in Ms. Koker's classroom appears tense. On one hand, Ms. Koker seems genuinely committed to having students contribute their ideas to the development of the concepts of monarchy, oligarchy, and democracy. On the other hand, few students seem to feel free or relaxed enough to share anything but the most obvious answers. As a result, very little genuine discussion takes place.

The manner in which Ms. Koker responds to students increases the tension in the classroom. Rarely is an answer followed by another question to the same student. In the case of an inaccurate answer or no answer, the teacher quickly moves to the next student instead of staying with the student to correct a partially wrong answer, or drawing out a partially correct response that another student might build on. Even when opportunities present themselves to stay with a student and develop his response further, such as when Jeff equates the sharing of responsibilities among members of an oligarchy with the sharing of responsibilities between his mother and father, the teacher responds with a curt "But it's not what we're talking about here." These moves on the part of Ms. Koker enhance the competitive nature of this classroom by treating each individual student response as either all right or all wrong, thereby missing the opportunity to connect the discussion to the students' own experiences.

Another aspect of the tense learning climate apparently results from Ms. Koker's desire to keep firm control of the events occurring in her classroom. Ms. Koker decided on a carefully controlled row-by-row recitation of answers instead of an open discussion. Perhaps in an effort to enhance classroom management, she restricts any interaction that is not a direct response to her questions. Consequently, she restricts the very type of response that her discussion-oriented agenda seems to call for. Without realizing it, Ms. Koker sets up a learning climate of opposing forces. The students resist being drawn into the discussion to avoid saying anything unacceptable; the teacher asks for student participation but responds with mostly unrewarding answers. Had the atmosphere of the classroom been less rigid, this class might have been more conducive to the cooperative interchanges being sought by the teacher. We will return to the concept of the learning climate and how to observe it in Chapter 5. For now, however, let's get a feel for some of the other lenses through which life in Ms. Koker's classroom can be observed.

OBSERVING CLASSROOM MANAGEMENT

What did you notice about Ms. Koker's classroom management style? Did it appear to be more of a reaction to student behavior than a well-organized system of rules and procedures thought out in advance? At several points in the lesson, Ms. Koker seems to make up rules on the spot. Although sometimes necessary, this practice is risky. It can convey to students a sense of arbitrariness about the rule itself, making it seem less credible, and therefore less likely to be obeyed. Apparently, Ms. Koker failed to convey some basic rules earlier in the school year

(for example, when to complete assigned reading and take notes). Without a well-organized system of rules and class procedures, Ms. Koker may continue to react defensively, at first tolerating a wide range of behavior, and later using valuable class time to respond to behaviors she didn't foresee.

Ms. Koker's classroom also exhibits problems with conduct. Talking out, for which presumably a rule was communicated earlier, seems to be a persistent problem. This comes as no surprise, because Ms. Koker's response to talking out, even in this short episode, was inconsistent. Notice that Ms. Koker is adamant at first about not speaking out. After reminding the class at the beginning of the lesson, "Please, no talking out," and reprimanding Tim for talking out, she accepts without reprimand a call out, "We were talking about emperors," from an anonymous student after she asks the indirect question "Let's see now, where were we?" This question, the result of losing her concentration after dealing with Tim's misbehavior, results in the very behavior she wishes to avoid. The conflict occurs when she switches unexpectedly to a nondirective style ("Let's see now, where were we?") more suited to an informal discussion session than the row-by-row recitation format she had pursued from the beginning of the lesson.

Did you also note the amount of class time and resulting problems created by Ms. Koker's response to Tim's misbehavior? Although Tim's misbehavior might have been unpredictable, Ms. Koker's response to it may have created an even bigger problem. First, she responds by assigning extra homework, thereby equating homework with punishment. Second, during the time it took for Tim to leave his seat, go to the board to write his name, and return, the rest of the class waited without direction. The momentum, or pace, which previously kept the class moving forward and focused on the lesson, was lost. These momentary lapses, whether due to interruptions from misbehaving students, public address announcements, or visitors at the door, require special classroom management procedures to keep students engaged in the learning process. Ms. Koker's costly use of instructional time for discipline might have been avoided had she established and consistently reinforced an organized system of classroom rules and procedures from the start of the school year.

OBSERVING LESSON CLARITY

Lesson clarity involves communicating clearly and directly, and presenting content at the students' current level of understanding. Clarity involves not only the visual and oral clarity of a teacher's delivery, but also the proper organization and structuring of the material to be taught. For example, to organize and structure the material to be taught, the teacher must know how much knowledge the students already have about the day's lesson. Notice that Ms. Koker begins the lesson by saying, "Let's start by defining what a monarchy is. Does anybody know?" The responses she receives, however, are not too encouraging. The first two students called on say no, after which Ms. Koker says, "I guess I'll have to tell you then." This beginning involves two aspects of clarity: checking for relevant prior knowledge, and summarizing or reviewing when it is discovered that the students do not have the knowledge necessary to understand the day's lesson. Had Ms. Koker not discovered early in the lesson that students had little or no knowledge of the day's topic, she might have gone on to more advanced concepts, never realizing her students did not have a basis for understanding the material she was presenting. As it was, most of the lesson seemed to cover the basics of what the students should have already learned from reading the text. Phrases such as "Okay, I'll tell you" and "It's in the chapter" are clues that this class may never have encountered the text before, leading Ms. Koker to make explicit a rule that, in the future, all assigned reading be completed before a topic is discussed in class.

Some other aspects of clarity involve informing the students of the skills or understanding expected at the end of the lesson, and organizing the content for future lessons. Recall that, to some extent, Ms. Koker's opening remark reflects both these aspects of clarity. The students are informed of the three forms of government to be covered, and are told that they are expected to know how to form the three types of government at the end of the unit. Both of these ingredients of the day's lesson worked to make Ms. Koker's lesson more understandable.

OBSERVING INSTRUCTIONAL VARIETY

Another lens through which to observe Ms. Koker's classroom is instructional variety. Instructional variety includes the varied use of rewards, reinforcements, and types of questions asked (for example, recall vs. application) as well as the flexibility of the teacher to change strategies or shift directions when needed. Variety can be enhanced by a teacher's animation (through variation in eye contact, voice, and gestures), as well as through the use of different instructional strategies and methods within the same lesson. We did not see Ms. Koker teaching, but from what we read, there seems to have been little variety

in her classroom. She persists with her questioning technique, even though she seems to have little success with it, until finally, out of necessity, she assumes a more direct lecture approach at the end of the lesson. Also, her questions call only for basic facts and definitions: "What is a monarchy?" and "Can you tell us what an oligarchy is?" instead of "What are its advantages and disadvantages?", "How is it formed?", or "What value should we place on the three forms of government for governing ourselves?" Focusing only on factual recall may fail to engage some students in the learning process.

Instructional variety is also achieved by choosing specific activity structures to convey lesson content. The term *activity structures* refers both to how the students are organized for learning and how the lesson is organized. Both categories of structure appear in Ms. Koker's classroom. For example, we note that Ms. Koker chooses to organize her instruction around student recitation in a drill-and-practice format. We noted previously the possible mismatch between such a format and what appears to be the discussion-oriented goal of her lesson. At that time, we suspected that this structure was selected more as a way to manage classroom talk than as an effective vehicle for achieving the goals of the lesson. The choice of a recitation format led Ms. Koker to call on students one by one in a predesignated order, as might be done if students were giving their answers orally to questions from a workbook. The results were factual responses that avoided any risk on the part of the students, rather than the type of responses that could result in more complex or integrated learning.

Perhaps due to her concern about classroom management, Ms. Koker relies on questions and lecture to transmit the content of the lesson, and devotes little time to applying the concepts learned, checking for the accuracy of understanding, or summarizing and reviewing. All of these activities may not have been equally appropriate for this lesson, and need not all must always be present for effective instruction. However, the conflict between Ms. Koker's activity structure and the goals of the lesson suggests the need for more instructional variety than was offered. Ms. Koker might have also used group discussion and questions having several right answers to elicit critical thinking, reasoning, and problem solving.

OBSERVING THE TEACHER'S TASK ORIENTATION

Task orientation, the percentage of time allocated to a lesson in which the teacher is actually teaching material related to the topic, provides another lens for observing Ms. Koker's classroom. In the dialogue, attention to the misbehavior of individual students, time spent introducing new rules about conduct and academic work, and interruption from the school administrator all took their toll on the time that could have been devoted to instruction. As a result of these interruptions, the time Ms. Koker actually spent teaching the content was limited. When teachers inefficiently handle misbehavior or spend large amounts of class time doing clerical chores (for example, passing out papers, collecting money for school projects, or stapling and collating), instructional time may be only a small percentage of the total amount of time allocated to the lesson. Although we have no way of knowing the exact amount of time Ms. Koker's instruction was interrupted by noninstructional demands, a simple count of the total number of lines of dialogue minus the number of lines containing dialogue unrelated to the goals of the lesson reveals that about 34 percent of Ms. Koker's teaching was off-task. If this continued throughout the school day, more than 18 minutes of every hour would be devoted to noninstructional events.

Noninstructional events that compete for instructional time include formulating classroom rules, giving directives, administering reprimands, dealing with interruptions, creating orderly transitions between subjects or activities, and engaging in activities that structure the learning environment. The amount of time actually devoted to instruction often depends on how efficiently noninstructional activities are managed. Poor classroom management can detract from time spent on instructional tasks, decreasing students' engagement in the learning process and, predictably, interfering with success in completing assignments correctly. Although we saw only a brief view of Ms. Koker's classroom, she made some important decisions about classroom rules, the use of reinforcement, and the handling of misbehavior that affected the amount of time devoted to instruction during this lesson.

OBSERVING STUDENTS' ENGAGEMENT IN THE LEARNING PROCESS

A sixth lens through which to observe a lesson is student engagement in the learning process. Like the task orientation of a teacher, this behavior is often measured as a percentage of time. Student engagement in the learning process pertains to the percentage of time the teacher presents instructionally relevant content (is task oriented) and the students are acting on, thinking about, or otherwise using the content being taught. In contrast to a teacher's task orientation, a student's engagement in the learning process may be much more difficult to determine. A student may look attentive or appear to be working through the workbook, but her thoughts may be miles away. In the example, part of the time Ms. Koker was teaching, at least some of her students were not engaged in the learning process.

By relying on individual recitation, Ms. Koker does little to involve students in the lesson. Aside from her questions and a few attempts to reward a correct answer with praise, Ms. Koker seems to encourage only a passive or mechanical involvement in the lesson. Absent from Ms. Koker's lesson is a broad range of questions that might excite the imagination of students and encourage them to keep trying after a wrong answer or no answer. Perhaps most relevant to the apparent disengagement of some of the students was Ms. Koker's drill-and-practice style, which requires students to respond in order across rows. This ordered-turns approach is often recommended for content in which many discrete pieces of knowledge with clearly defined right and wrong answers is being recalled. But Ms. Koker's content seems concept-oriented. After a time, students in the back half of the room could pretty much guarantee that they would not get called on during the class, providing even more opportunity for these students to disengage from the learning process. This, together with Ms. Koker's sometimes critical responses to a wrong answer or no answer, may have provided a reason for those who had already responded to turn their attention elsewhere. If more complicated and time-consuming responses were being sought, it may have been better for Ms. Koker to call on students who volunteered and who, therefore, may have provided answers around which she could have built lesson content. Ms. Koker could also have implemented any of a number of small-group-response activities to encourage greater student participation.

And, did you also note the unevenness of the praise given to students during this dialogue? Ms. Koker did not do much to encourage participation in the learning process or to reinforce effective performance, and so failed to offer much motivation or a reason for students to work harder. The word *good* to acknowledge a correct answer was used only twice during the entire lesson and, when used, was not accompanied by any specifics to make the praise meaningful to the learner. A *meaningful* system of praise and feedback is essential to encourage students to engage in the learning process.

Observing Student Success

What signs of student success did you see in Ms. Koker's classroom? Student success pertains to the percentage of correct responses given to classroom questions, class exercises, and workbook assignments. When an expository or didactic approach (which seems to fit Ms. Koker's recitation format) to learning is used, the percentage of student success after the first time through the material should be 60 to 80 percent. This encourages further response and engagement in the learning process. When the success rate is, on the average, less than 60 percent, it may indicate that the lesson content is too difficult or that the exercises are inappropriate for the material being taught. Ultimately, homework and further assignments should create an average success rate of 90 percent or higher.

Ms. Koker's students seemed reluctant to participate, avoiding, rather than engaging in, the lesson. Students found it safer to say "I don't know" than to risk a wrong or partially wrong response and be criticized for it. Ms. Koker seemed to accept only a narrow definition of correct responses. As a result, the success of her students in answering questions was not very high. Most students avoided answering altogether, and others failed to provide the correct answer. These two student behaviors tell us a lot about Ms. Koker's classroom. Failure to actively involve students in the lesson and present instruction that most students can respond to correctly are indications that the level of the lesson may not have been properly matched to the students' current level of understanding.

As was the case with student engagement, there are certain teacher activities that encourage a moderate to high success rate. These include providing correctives immediately following a wrong or partially right answer, dividing lesson content into small segments at the learner's current level of understanding, planning transitions to new content in small, easy-to-grasp steps, and continually relating the parts of the lesson to larger objectives and goals.

It also seems that Ms. Koker's questions function more as a test, to see how much the students already know, than as a way to build on their existing knowledge. Instead of using her questions to fine tune and lift student responses to higher levels, Ms. Koker uses her questions to cover broad, undigested areas of content. Some retrenchment— or returning to simpler concepts or divisions of content—might be called for in Ms. Koker's classroom. Seatwork assigned prior to the day's lesson is one way to check student success rate. If a low success rate is confirmed, Ms. Koker could provide more practice opportunities to actively engage students in the learning process before embarking on the next lesson, or she could utilize cooperative learning activities to better engage students during the lesson.

Observing Higher Thought Processes and Performance Outcomes

The final lens through which to observe Ms. Koker's classroom takes the previous lens, student success, to a higher level. For this lens our focus turns from the recitation of correct responses to higher thought processes, which arise out of teaching and learning activities that promote critical thinking, reasoning, and problem solving. These processes cannot be measured by tests of cognitive achievement alone. The higher thought processes required for analyzing, synthesizing, and decision making in adult contexts are stimulated by interacting with peers and adults and by increasing awareness of one's own learning.

By requiring oral responses, Ms. Koker encourages students to exhibit higher thought processes. But, Ms. Koker fails to follow up on her students' responses and lift them to a higher level. Recall that most of her responses were short and noncorrective, often moving to another student if the response was right, or failing to probe more deeply with another question if the response was incorrect. Ms. Koker saw each answer as either correct or incorrect—not as an opportunity to make a wrong answer right or a good answer better. This left her students responding at the lowest level of behavioral complexity, even though her lesson seemed, at times, aimed at acquiring concepts, patterns of thinking, and judgments.

In other words, Ms. Koker's presentation lacks a plan for helping her students learn the content. For example, alerting her students at the start of the lesson to look for some of the features that could be used to distinguish a monarchy from an oligarchy from a democracy might encourage her students to analyze the differences between various forms of government, their purposes in history, and advantages or disadvantages in today's world. Although not every lesson will achieve these types of higher thought processes, teachers can and should capitalize on potential opportunities whenever possible.

Also, while student collaboration was not a lesson objective, students collaborating with one another or building on the responses of others could have created classroom interaction that engaged more students and improved student understanding of the concepts being presented. Ms. Koker could have shaped responses in small steps or allowed the thoughts and judgments of individual students to inform the group, so that larger concepts, patterns of thinking, and judgments could have accumulated gradually. By using student responses and collaborative learning activities to encourage problem-solving and judgment skills, routine recitation at the beginning of the class might have turned into higher thought processes by the end of the class. In later chapters, you will learn about many alternative strategies and decisions that can be used to achieve higher thought processes in your classroom.

PREPARING TO OBSERVE IN REAL CLASSROOMS

If you thought our description of Ms. Koker's classroom seemed a bit unfair, you're probably right. A lot happened to Ms. Koker in less time than it generally takes to teach a single lesson. Although our picture of Ms. Koker was compressed for illustrative purposes, teachers at all levels of experience and training are confronted with, and must manage, similar events. Real teachers in real classrooms are never immune from these and similar problems, despite the extent of their training or years of experience.

As we conclude our discussion of Ms. Koker's class, it is important to note the interrelationship among all eight lenses through which we viewed these classroom events. Seldom is the behavior observed under one lens independent of that being observed under others. This reflects the interactive nature of life in classrooms. In other words, if we were to observe Ms. Koker's classroom with only one or even a few of our lenses, an incomplete and possibly distorted observation would result. This is especially obvious when we consider how the learning climate established by Ms. Koker, her classroom management techniques, and the presentation of content all work to influence student behavior. Remember, too, that Ms. Koker's behavior, classroom management style, and presentation were influenced by her students' behavior during the lesson. Thus, it would be futile to separate these interactive aspects of a classroom in real life. Although in future chapters we will cover each of the lenses individually to reveal their unique features, our final goal as experienced observers is to understand overall patterns and rhythms of classrooms.

Reflecting on the ways teachers (both fictional and real) handle various challenges will help you develop important professional insights—especially as you observe classrooms through the eight lenses of effective teaching practice. Additionally, your obser-

vation visits to real classrooms will be even more productive if you plan (1) what to do before your classroom visit; (2) what to do during your visit; and (3) what to do after your visit.

ACTIVITIES BEFORE THE OBSERVATION

Except for an occasional observation by a school administrator, most teachers are not accustomed to being observed. As a result, the teachers you observe may feel some anxiety, and may even wonder if their professional competence will be questioned or judged. During an observation, these concerns can interfere with a teacher's performance and make it less representative of her typical behavior. This is why establishing a congenial relationship with those you will be observing is an important first step to observing in classrooms. In the first part of this section, we look at some of the ways you can create and maintain a positive relationship with the teachers you will be observing. In the second part, we introduce some of the tools needed to make this relationship enduring and productive.

One of the first tasks you will face in observing is selecting whom to observe. If you are observing prior to practice teaching, the targets of your observation will most likely be chosen for you, and their cooperation will be ensured through prior agreement. During your practice teaching, however, some observation outside your cooperating teacher's classroom may be expected of you, which you will need to arrange on your own. It is here that you will need to make some important decisions concerning whom to observe and how to introduce yourself and the observation task.

Whom to Observe

As you become increasingly familiar with your school, many subjects of observation will appear as a result of your day-to-day interactions with teachers and students. Your initial observations should be of those who are teaching in your major area, and preferably those teaching the subjects you will be assigned to teach. Your first subject of observation, therefore, naturally should be your cooperating teacher. This will create a convenient opportunity to rehearse the observation skills you will need later in less familiar settings.

Your next priority for observation should be a teacher who teaches grades or subjects similar to those of your cooperating teacher. This will provide the opportunity for your cooperating teacher to introduce you to others teaching at the same grade level or content area. Over time, your observations can include other teachers in the school who are teaching grades or subjects that you are not likely to teach in the immediate future, but which you might like to teach at some subsequent time.

Finally, observations should be made in classrooms where your experience within the school, communication with other teachers, and attention to student comments indicate something of special importance is happening. These observations may afford you the opportunity to observe particularly dynamic personalities, the use of innovative teaching methods, or instruction devoted exclusively to a particular type of student (for example, gifted English Language Learners or lower achievers). Since these targets of observation may come to your attention informally, they may be far removed from the grade level and/or subject matter you will be teaching. These excursions into unfamiliar subjects and grades are well worth the effort because of the new ideas, creativity, and excitement they'll return to you, the observer.

Introducing Yourself

During your first days in a school, introduce yourself to as many teachers as possible. Few teachers will simply say no to a request to observe, but some may provide excuses why it would not be advisable to observe in their class that day or that week, until they know something about you. As odd as it may seem, even some of the best and most experienced teachers are sometimes defensive and shy about being observed. This may mean that, without extra effort on your part, some of the teachers from whom you may benefit the most may not comply with your request to observe them. This is all the more reason that a pleasant introduction should precede a request to observe. Blurting out "I'd like to observe you during fourth period today" before a teacher has even had the opportunity to get to know you is likely to create some defensiveness on his part. The purpose of a prior introduction is to reduce the defensiveness and dispel the fear of the unknown. Identifying yourself by name, the institution at which you are studying, and the cooperating teacher with whom you are working may be a sufficient introduction. But, if time permits, mentioning your career goals ("I would like to teach _____ in such and such type of school.") and how the course or grade you are requesting to observe relates to those goals ("You are teaching the type of students I am likely to face on my first job.") will enhance your chances of obtaining permission to observe. Your request to observe, therefore, should follow a friendly exchange in which the teacher from whom you are requesting permission learns your name, institution, supervising teacher, immediate career goals, and how your career goals relate to the responsibilities of the teacher whom you will be observing. Once permission is obtained, the important information described in the following sections should be exchanged with the teacher prior to your observation.

Identifying Your Goals for the Observation

It is important to convey to the teacher your goals for the observation. This need be only a sentence or two that communicates your reason for being there (other than that the observation is being required of you). Your reason can be general ("I would like to see a class of _____ graders," "learn about classroom management techniques") or specific ("I would like to get familiar with the texts and instructional material being used at this grade level"). Relaying the goals of your observation tends to reduce the anxiety a teacher might otherwise experience due to a belief that your observation may include a personal value judgment of her professional competence.

Finding Out the Day's Lesson

Next, you will need to determine the teacher's goal for the lesson, and how this goal fits into some broader sequence of instruction. Without knowing the purpose of the day's lesson, what you see can easily be taken out of context. Goals can be misunderstood, procedures misread, and reasons behind activities confused unless you find out where a given lesson is coming from. Knowing long- and short-term lesson goals will help you avoid wasting precious observation time trying to figure out the purpose of the day's lesson.

Finding Out About the Students

Before your observation, you will want to learn about the ability level of the students. This may seem obvious in some cases (for example, when the course you will be observing is a tracked or pre-grouped class devoted entirely to the needs of less able, average, or more able learners). Yet every group has unique characteristics and a wide range of abilities—no matter how it is labeled. Ask if any students in the class are being mainstreamed, are English Language Learners (ELL), or have learning disabilities that may influence what you see. Although your observation may confirm or challenge these labels, your knowledge of how the teacher views this class may be as important for making sense out of what you observe as the observation data itself. Knowing how a teacher perceives the class may provide valuable insights as to why she engaged in one activity over another, or why he used some materials rather than others.

How to Be Introduced

You will also need to consider how you wish to be introduced. Often, the teacher you are observing will have a preference for introducing you. At other times, however, you will be asked how you wish to be introduced. Typically, such introductions are short, involving a phrase such as "Ms./Mr. ____ will be visiting with us today and she/he is from ____." It will be to your advantage if the introduction is limited to only a few brief facts about you, so as not to draw attention to you during your observation. If the class experiences frequent visitors like yourself, the teacher may choose not to introduce you. However, if the class is unaccustomed to having visitors, an introduction is desirable, because the students' attention during much of the class may be devoted to figuring out who you are and why you have come to their class.

Where to Sit

Prior to your observation, you'll also need to determine where to sit. While the existing arrangement of desks and chairs in the classroom may limit some options, it is preferable for your chair to be outside the center of action. Front row seats or seats in which the majority of students are facing you usually deter effective observation by making your every move noticeable. Consequently, your placement in the classroom, preferably toward the back and out of the center of attention, can be an important aid to your observation. When, out of kindness or respect, a teacher places you in the center of attention, you should politely request a change if an alternative seating arrangement is available.

In summary, prior to an observation you should

1. Decide whom to observe.
2. Introduce yourself.
3. Identify your goals for the observation.
4. Determine placement of the lesson in the curriculum.
5. Find out about the students to be taught.
6. Arrange for your introduction to the class.
7. Arrange a place to sit.

Steps 1–5 are best completed during a conference period prior to the lesson you will be observing. Because these steps may require more than a few moments on your part or the teacher's, they should not be completed in the few hectic minutes before class, when the teacher may be trying to prepare for the next class or make the transition to the next subject. Steps 6 and 7 may be, and often are, completed immediately before the observation begins.

ACTIVITIES DURING THE OBSERVATION

The next set of activities begins at the start of the lesson. These activities are designed to help you feel comfortable in the role of an observer, and to avoid some of the problems that typically confront an observer attempting to record events in a fast-paced classroom.

Unless you feel comfortable physically, you will not feel comfortable psychologically. This means that your body comfort often takes precedence over, and can even control, your thoughts and actions. Your comfort and ability to feel natural in the classroom therefore may be of paramount importance to being able to accurately perceive the events around you. As we will see in subsequent chapters, some types of observations require that many classroom events be coded and recorded rapidly and systematically. To do this you must be seated in a way that allows you to see all the events occurring in a classroom. You'll need a practical writing surface that can be supported effortlessly, such as a desk top or clipboard. Sit at a desk, or in a chair with a back, so that your notes and records will not have to be taken from an awkward or artificial position. These choices will help you avoid fatigue, writing cramps, and frustration at not being able to record your observations quickly and legibly. Although your choice of seat will be determined by the type of furniture in the classroom, avoid the use of stools, chairs of awkward height, and tables covered with equipment or materials, and don't try to write against a wall or on the top of a file cabinet or bookcase. While some of these suggestions may seem unimportant before you observe, you'll discover that the task of observing and recording classroom events is demanding enough that, even when you are seated comfortably, you may tire before the end of a single class period.

Once you're seated comfortably, wait until things calm down to begin your observation. You'll probably be the center of attention for the first few moments, regardless of your out-of-the-way placement in the classroom and low-key introduction. Depending on the number of other recent visitors to this classroom, an initial period of turbulence set off by your presence may last from a few seconds to several minutes. Before useful observation can begin, you will want to wait out any disturbance your presence may have caused in the natural flow of events. To help reestablish a normal routine, try waiting calmly, with a pleasant expression and with your eyes focused on the teacher.

As classroom activities unfold, a source of distraction to your observations may come from the students seated around you. These students may ask questions about you, your purpose for being there, or even about their schoolwork. Usually, a polite but firm refusal to be drawn in will help students turn their focus away from you. You may find it helpful to avoid direct eye contact, especially with those students seated closest to you. Scan the room broadly, focusing most of the time on the teacher and, when necessary, on individual students seated at more distant points.

ACTIVITIES AFTER THE OBSERVATION

At the conclusion of your observation, give a brief word of thanks to the teacher you have observed. Teachers rarely have more than a few moments of free time between classes or periods, and even less when changing from one subject to another at the elementary level, so a quick comment such as "Thanks, I enjoyed the class" is always welcome. Just as your introduction before class served to break the ice and turn possible anxiety about your presence into a more constructive feeling, so can your goodbye dispel any remaining anxiety or apprehension. The intent of both these communications—before and after—is to dispel any belief that value judgments are being made about the professional competence of the teacher.

Because this moment is very important in setting the stage for future observations, try to relate to the teacher an upbeat or memorable event that occurred during the observation. For example, you could mention just how the observation session was helpful to you: "Seeing how you used the overhead projector was helpful to me because I'm required to use visuals in my next presentation," or "The approach you used to handle Jason's off-task behavior seemed really effective." Although it is important not to exaggerate or to make up the importance of seeing a particular event, nearly all observers see interesting, if not effective, techniques during a single period of instruction. Make a mental note to look for such an event before your observation begins, write it down when it occurs, and relate it to the teacher at the time you communicate your thanks for being allowed to observe.

Finally, immediately following your observation you will need to find a quiet place to review and enhance the notes and records you made. As we will see in subsequent chapters, these notes and records can take many forms; however, they seldom will be in final, usable form immediately following an observation, due to omissions, vague references, incompleteness, and illegibility. Classroom events occur far too rapidly for notes to perfectly represent the events that took place. Therefore, some filling in is usually necessary while the events of the classroom are still fresh in your mind. Even an hour's delay can make an important difference in filling in the subject of a vague reference, remembering an antecedent event that makes a later event more logical, or correcting illegible handwriting, which may be the key to deciphering important words later. Since the observation will still be fresh in your mind, this period of reflection can also be a time of insight and understanding. You will want to make more notes—or notes about your notes—reminding you of and highlighting those events that you may want to bring up later in discussions with the teacher you observed, your cooperating teacher, your college or university supervisor, or in a methods class in which you may be enrolled.

Now that we have covered some of the basics of what to do before, during, and after an observation, you're ready to work through the activities below to apply your knowledge. In the next chapter we will look at some ways of recording your observations, and, in the chapters ahead, we will consider each of the eight lenses in greater detail.

ACTIVITIES

1. Using the format in Figure 3.1, identify subjects and grade levels you would like to observe. Assign numbers to the boxes to indicate the order in which you would like to observe these classrooms. For each of these entries, identify one purpose that you would have for observation in that area. Express your purpose in a form suitable for communicating to the teacher being observed, such as "I would like to see your class of _____ graders in _____ to observe _____."
2. Pictures of the seating arrangements in two different classrooms appear in Figures 3.2 and 3.3. Place an *X* on two seats in each classroom to indicate suitable observation positions. Now refer to the classroom diagram in Figure 3.4. Assume you can move a seat to a point from which to observe. Indicate where you would place it with an *X*.
3. Reread the dialogue from Ms. Koker's classroom and look for other observable signs of effective teaching. Make a list of the signs you notice. Include both positive and negative instances. Compare your list with that of a classmate, and revise yours to include any additions or omissions suggested by your classmate. Using the signs you and your classmate listed, in what ways could Ms. Koker improve her teaching?
4. With a classmate, arrange to observe a classroom for approximately one class period. During this time, use the second copy of the *General Observa-*

FIGURE 3.1 Subjects and Grade
Levels to Observe

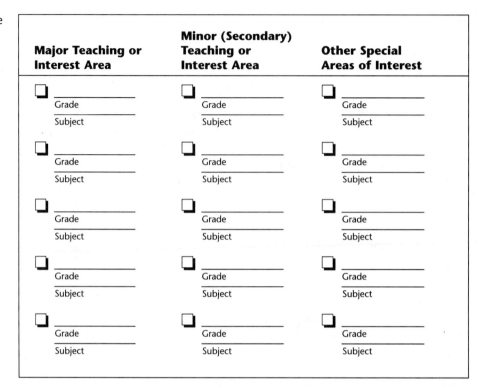

Major Teaching or Interest Area	Minor (Secondary) Teaching or Interest Area	Other Special Areas of Interest
❏ _____ Grade _____ Subject	❏ _____ Grade _____ Subject	❏ _____ Grade _____ Subject
❏ _____ Grade _____ Subject	❏ _____ Grade _____ Subject	❏ _____ Grade _____ Subject
❏ _____ Grade _____ Subject	❏ _____ Grade _____ Subject	❏ _____ Grade _____ Subject
❏ _____ Grade _____ Subject	❏ _____ Grade _____ Subject	❏ _____ Grade _____ Subject
❏ _____ Grade _____ Subject	❏ _____ Grade _____ Subject	❏ _____ Grade _____ Subject

FIGURE 3.2 Classroom 1
Seating Arrangement

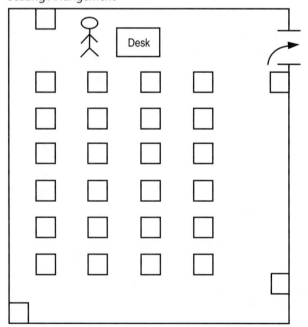

FIGURE 3.3 Classroom 2
Seating Arrangement

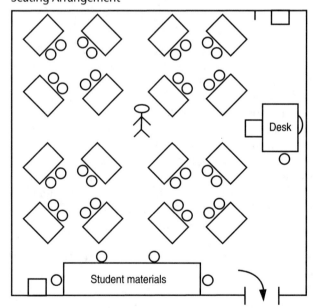

tion Form (Instrument 3.1b) to focus on the eight patterns of effective teaching. Immediately following the observation, compare your ratings and create a common rating on which you both can agree. What are your overall conclusions pertaining to each of the eight lenses?

5. To gain a sense of the pace of and common interruptions in a classroom, arrange to observe in a classroom where there is likely to be some teacher–student interaction (questions and answers, discussion, or oral checking and feedback). Divide the time devoted to your observation into three equal

Figure 3.4 Classroom to Be Observed

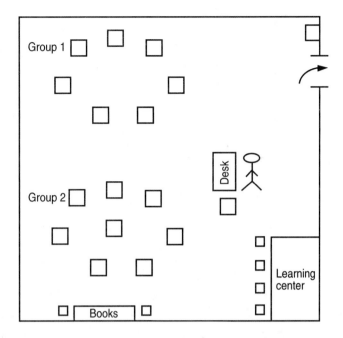

parts (for example, three 15-minute segments). This activity may be completed in pairs.

a. During the first 15 minutes, count the number of teacher-to-student and student-to-teacher interchanges that occur, and record the occurrence of each with a tally in the appropriate box in Figure 3.5. For example, a teacher question addressed to a student would count as one tally, and a student response back to the teacher would count as another.

b. During the next 15-minute segment of your observation, continue observing teacher–student interaction, but this time record the number of student-to-teacher and teacher-to-student exchanges that pertain to (a) lesson content, (b) procedural matters (directions and clerical tasks), and (c) discipline or classroom management (restating rules, giving warnings, or assigning punishment). Use the boxes in Figure 3.6 to tally the number of teacher–student exchanges in each of these areas during this part of your observation.

c. During the last 15 minutes of your observation, continue observing teacher–student interactions. This time, record your tallies according to whether the exchange is brief (lasting approximately five seconds or less) or extended (lasting more than five seconds), using the boxes in Figure 3.7. Include the complete exchange as a single tally—record the teacher-to-student statement and the student response to the teacher (if applicable) as a single unit.

d. After the observation, state three general conclusions, supported by the data you have collected in each of the three boxes, about the pace of the classroom.

6. Reflecting on the classroom you have just observed, write down on the back of the *General Observation Form* (Instrument 3.1b) any interruptions

Figure 3.5 Classroom Interactions Between Teacher and Students

Teacher Exchange Directed to Student	Student Exchange Directed to Teacher

FIGURE 3.6 Classroom
Interactions in Three Areas

Exchanges Involving Lesson Content	Exchanges Involving Procedural Matters	Exchanges Involving Discipline or Classroom Management

FIGURE 3.7 Duration of
Classroom Interactions

Brief Exchange (5 seconds or less)	Extended Exchange (more than 5 seconds)

you can recall that may have occurred either for administrative/clerical reasons or as a result of student misbehavior. How typical do you feel these interruptions are of this and other classrooms throughout the school year?

7. In the classroom you have just observed, identify one significant event, behavior, or episode that you noticed but the teacher did not. Suggest some reasons why, in this instance, the teacher may have been unaware. If the teacher had noticed this event, behavior, or episode, would it, in your opinion, have changed in any way the manner in which this lesson was presented?

8. Think about whether your impression of this classroom was generally positive or negative. Now consider the following sources of selective perception both from outside ourselves and from within ourselves:

❑ Student IQ and achievements
❑ Classroom characteristics (physical context)
❑ Participation and cooperativeness of the students
❑ Experience and education of the teacher
❑ School, grade, and subject matter
❑ Individual and cultural diversity
❑ Your own level of experience with similar classrooms
❑ Recent educational influences and training
❑ Who may be watching (for example, your supervisor, the students)
❑ Who may find out (for example, the teacher)

Place a checkmark beside any of the statements that you believe might have influenced your ratings on the *General Observation Form* you completed for Activity 4.

Iɴsᴛʀᴜᴍᴇɴᴛ **3.1a**

General Observation Form

Instructions: For each lens, place a check mark on the blank closest to the word that best describes the classroom you are observing.

	Learning Climate Teacher Centered __ __ __ __ __ __ __ Student Centered
	Classroom Management Orderly __ __ __ __ __ __ __ Disorderly
	Lesson Clarity Clear __ __ __ __ __ __ __ Unclear
	Instructional Variety Varied __ __ __ __ __ __ __ Static
	Teacher's Task Orientation Focused __ __ __ __ __ __ __ Unfocused
	Students' Engagement in the Learning Process Students Involved __ __ __ __ __ __ __ Students Uninvolved
	Students' Success in Basic Academic Skills High __ __ __ __ __ __ __ Low
	Higher Thought Processes and Performance Outcomes Many __ __ __ __ __ __ __ Few

INSTRUMENT 3.1b

General Observation Form
Instructions: For each lens, place a check mark on the blank closest to the word that best describes the classroom you are observing.

Learning Climate

Teacher Centered __   __   __   __   __   __   __ Student Centered

Classroom Management

Orderly __   __   __   __   __   __   __ Disorderly

Lesson Clarity

Clear __   __   __   __   __   __   __ Unclear

Instructional Variety

Varied __   __   __   __   __   __   __ Static

Teacher's Task Orientation

Focused __   __   __   __   __   __   __ Unfocused

Students' Engagement in the Learning Process

Students Involved __   __   __   __   __   __   __ Students Uninvolved

Students' Success in Basic Academic Skills

High __   __   __   __   __   __   __ Low

Higher Thought Processes and Performance Outcomes

Many __   __   __   __   __   __   __ Few

Chapter 4

"SEEING" BEYOND PERSONAL EXPERIENCES AND EXPECTATIONS
LEARNING TO OBSERVE SYSTEMATICALLY

There is no such thing in anyone's life as an unimportant day.

Alexander Woollcott

One assumption of an experienced observer is that nothing observed is unimportant. What the experienced observer is saying is that "everything is related to everything else" and that there are few, if any, coincidences in life—or in classrooms. In this chapter we will provide tools and techniques that can help you make sense out of the myriad relationships that occur in classrooms—relationships between students and teacher, among students, between students and text, between teacher and media, as well as the more subtle relationships and patterns that occur over days, weeks, and months in a classroom. When you use the tools and techniques of this chapter to observe systematically, you will soon realize that nothing is as important to life in classrooms as that which, at first glance, appears unimportant.

FIGURE 4.1

Larson. G. (1984). The Far Side Gallery. Kansas City, MO: FarWorks, Inc., p. 26

In Chapter 3, we learned that structure—or focus—is a key element that distinguishes *observing* from *looking*. We also discussed the fact that our personal observations are colored by our experiences and expectations. Learning to observe in a focused or systematic way can help us balance what we expect to see with what actually occurs in a classroom, resulting in a more complete understanding of teaching. In this chapter we present several methods for observing systematically and recording what is observed.

WHY OBSERVE SYSTEMATICALLY?

Like the humans in the cartoon (Figure 4.1), we often go through life seeing what we expect to see, often failing to question our assumptions and our conclusions—even though they may be erroneous. If we approach learning to teach in the same manner, we will likely miss many learning opportunities. But how does a person learn to *observe* rather than merely *watch* or *look* at classroom events? Systematic observation, defining a specific purpose for observing and choosing a method for recording the observations, is one way to enhance observation skills. In Chapter 3, eight structures—or lenses—for observation were introduced. Some specific purposes for observing in these areas were also described, such as the extent to which

1. A teacher's classroom conveys a balance between warmth and control (learning climate).
2. A system of rules and procedures operates to minimize interruptions and time spent on non-instructional tasks (classroom management).
3. The instruction presented is at, or slightly above, the students' current level of understanding (lesson clarity).
4. The teacher conveys enthusiasm and animation through variation in eye contact, voice, and body movement, and selects appropriate experiences to engage students in a wide variety of learning activities (instructional variety).
5. The teacher exhibits a systematic cycle of review, testing, and feedback (task orientation).
6. The teacher monitors work in progress and checks for student understanding (student engagement in the learning process).
7. Feedback is given immediately following student responses to firm up, extend, or correct responses (student success).
8. Models or strategies for learning are provided that promote critical thinking, reasoning, and problem solving (higher thought processes and performance outcomes).

Although a classroom observer could gain much insight into classroom processes and events by asking teachers and students about their thoughts and feelings, opportunities for such interviews will probably be rare, given the busy nature of most classrooms. Furthermore, interviews do not always accurately reflect a person's interpretation of the world, because interviews can be influenced by many other factors, including the participant's view of why she is being interviewed. For example, a student or teacher may answer your interview questions the way she thinks you want them answered, rather than the way she actually feels. As a result, we must find other ways to gain insights about teaching. One alternative involves the use of classroom visits. While classroom visits usually involve limited verbal interaction between the observer and the teacher and students, much useful information can be gained by noting observable behaviors and the contexts in which they occur. Figure 4.2 identifies some observable signs that might be used to record behavior in each of the eight focus areas. These signs can be recorded independently of the

subjective perceptions of the classroom participants. This allows you, as the observer, to determine what to observe as well as what importance to assign to particular events.

Although making such choices allows you to be more objective in your observations, it also places a responsibility on you. The questions that guide your observations will influence the behaviors you notice—and how you record them. Single events or unusual occurrences will often command your attention, but it is important not to overestimate their importance. A single sign under any of the eight question areas is unlikely to provide a complete picture of classroom behavior.

Generally, you will want to watch for multiple signs that indicate a consistent pattern of behavior. Herein lies one of the main differences between systematic observation and informal observation. Systematic observation uses data-collection instruments to record multiple signs that reveal consistent patterns of behavior. This helps focus your attention on a specific area of interest, and yet avoid overvaluing a single behavior or event. Making a record of what you observe *while you observe it* will also help you remember events you might otherwise forget after the visit is over—*and* notice patterns you didn't recognize while in the classroom.

METHODS FOR OBSERVING AND RECORDING

Because systematic observation involves observing and then recording behavioral signs in a form that can be retrieved and studied at a later time, it usually involves a form, or instrument. The instruments used for recording classroom behavior can range from relatively unstructured (taking notes), to highly structured (involving explicit procedures for when and how long to observe specific behaviors). In this chapter, we discuss three general methods that are useful for recording behavior in classrooms. These methods are arranged in order from least structured to most structured, and include examples for actual use in classroom observation.

Method 1: Narrative Reports

Narrative reports represent the least structured of our three general categories. Narrative reports do not specify the exact behavioral signs to be observed, but instead simply describe events, in written form, as they occur. Little guidance is given to the observer about what to include or exclude from the observation. Thus, narrative reports are

FIGURE 4.2 Observable Signs Pertaining to the Eight Question Areas

Question Areas

Learning Climate	Classroom Management	Lesson Clarity	Instructional Variety	Task Orientation	Student Engagement in the Learning Process	Student Success	Performance Outcomes and Higher Thought Processes
Degree to which students can express their feelings and opinions Frequency with which student responses are used and extended Amount of interaction and sharing among learners	Use of preestablished classroom rules Use of instructional routines System of incentives and consequences	Frequency of examples, illustrations, and demonstrations Percentage of students who can follow directions given Use of review and summary	Use of attention-gaining devices Changes in voice inflection, body movement, and eye contact Use of a mix of learning modalities (visual, oral)	Orderliness of transitions Teacher's preorganization of administrative tasks Cycles of review, testing, and feedback	Use of exercises and activities to elicit student responses Monitoring and checking during seatwork Use of remedial or programmed materials for slower learners	Number of correct or partially correct answers Number of right answers acknowledged or reinforced Number of delayed corrections vs. immediate corrections	Use of teaming, pairing, or other cooperative activities that encourage student problem solving Display of student products and projects Opportunities for independent practice and application

sometimes referred to as *open-ended*, meaning that considerable flexibility about what events to record is given to the observer. You may find it helpful to think of narrative reports as note-taking activities. While there are many ways to take notes, four methods will be particularly helpful for you as you observe in classrooms: anecdotal reports, ethnographic records, thematic notes, and visual maps.

Anecdotal Reports

An anecdotal report describes a critical or unusual incident that occurs in the classroom, which may be related to an event of larger consequence. It takes the form of a written paragraph that describes what, how, when, and to whom the critical incident happened. Because of the special significance of separating fact from interpretation, anecdotal reports are divided into two distinct parts: (a) facts and (b) an interpretation of the facts. Example 4.1 illustrates the form of an anecdotal report.

Notice how Seana divided fact from interpretation in her report. In the first part, she writes a matter-of-fact description of what happened; in the second, she speculates about John's self-concept, and even offers a judgment about the effect of this teacher's behavior

on potential volunteers. Example 4.2 shows how the first part of this anecdotal report might have been written had both parts been blended together by a less skilled reporter.

Notice how Katy blends fact and speculation in her description. How did she know, for example, that John raised his hand *shyly*, came to the front of the room *nervously*, began to read *reluctantly*, *broke down from nervousness*, or returned to his seat *crushed*? All this may have been true, but no description in the narrative pointed to the factual character of these expressions. As you can see, separating fact from interpretation can help you challenge your personal lenses—and remind you that additional observations in other contexts will be needed before your interpretations can become facts, or can be discarded as isolated incidents that do not reflect John's (or his teacher's) typical behavior.

Anecdotal reports are most useful when they occur over time. For example, after an observer makes an initial interpretation, she returns to the classroom at a later date (perhaps several times) to clarify that interpretation. The focus of later observations is to expand on the interpretation's usefulness and validity. Later anecdotal reports should help clarify ambiguities,

EXAMPLE **4.1**

> **Teacher:** Robins
>
> **Class:** Fifth grade
>
> **Subject:** English
>
> **Date:** January 17
>
> **Place:** Oakleaf Elementary
>
> **Purpose:** To observe student participation and engagement
>
> **Observer:** Seana Hawkins
>
> **Incident:** As class started, the teacher asked if anyone would like to read the story they had written for last night's assignment. John raised his hand. The teacher gave him permission, and he came to the front of the room. John began to read the story in a very low voice; when he had been reading for about 30 seconds, the teacher asked him to read louder, saying "Speak up, or you'll never be any good at public speaking." At this point, John stopped reading, returned to his seat, and remained silent for the rest of the class.
>
> **Interpretation:** John appears to enjoy writing and sharing his creations with others. It seems, however, that he is very sensitive and gets upset easily when he receives the slightest criticism, indicating he may not have confidence in himself or in his abilities as a public speaker. The teacher's comment to John in front of the class may have reduced his confidence even further, and may discourage him and others from volunteering in the future.

EXAMPLE **4.2**

> **Teacher:** Robins
>
> **Class:** Fifth grade
>
> **Subject:** English
>
> **Date:** January 17
>
> **Place:** Oakleaf Elementary
>
> **Purpose:** To observe student participation and engagement
>
> **Observer:** Katy Williams
>
> **Incident:** As class started, the teacher asked if anyone would like to read the story they had written for last night's assignment. John shyly raised his hand. The teacher gave him permission, and he nervously came to the front of the room. John reluctantly began to read the story in a very low voice, probably because he was having second thoughts about volunteering. After what surely seemed a long time for John, the teacher asked him to speak up, scaring him with the possibility that he will never be a good public speaker. At this point, John broke down from nervousness and returned to his seat, crushed by the insensitive remark of the teacher.

identify misinterpretations in past reports, and update and enhance factual descriptions with more recent data. Most importantly, when anecdotal reports focus on the same target behaviors over time (for example, John's subsequent performances in front of the class), they can reveal patterns and regularities that may reveal the true cause of the original critical incident. For example, maybe it was the personal nature of the topic and not the teacher's behavior that was the primary cause of John's behavior in the first observation. Patterns and regularities observed over time can then be used to form a single, coherent interpretation that identifies what should be changed in the classroom or environment for improvement to occur.

Anecdotal reports offer several advantages, which include:

1. Behavior is observed as it occurs in the natural setting of the classroom.
2. Data can be gathered unobtrusively, without involving those who are being observed.
3. The observer is not restricted in what to look for, and is therefore free to record seemingly minor or unexpected behaviors that may be of significance later.
4. The observer needs little or no special training.

However, anecdotal reports also have their limitations, which include:

1. The time required in maintaining and interpreting anecdotal reports can be extensive when many reports are accumulated over time.
2. The objectivity of the "facts" in a record may be overly influenced by the past behavior of the persons being observed and/or the beliefs of the observer about the appropriateness of what is observed.
3. Incidents recorded may be taken out of context or interpreted incorrectly due to an inadequate sampling of behavior, especially when records are not cumulative.
4. Narrative descriptions can be difficult to analyze and interpret when the behavior being observed is complex or has many different causes (school, home life, peers).

Ethnographic Records

A second method of observing and recording that takes a narrative form is an ethnographic record. Ethnographic records report events sequentially, as they occur, without selecting a specific focus or incident. Ethnographic records differ from anecdotal reports in that the observer records a continuous stream of events, usually for the duration of an entire class period and occasionally longer, and records all the behavior occurring, not just selected incidents. As with anecdotal reports, it is important that the observer record only what is observed, and avoid judgments or interpretations unless they are clearly divided from the factual portion of the record, as illustrated in Example 4.3.

Notice how this ethnographic record captures the flow and sequence of events, which the anecdotal report could not. Also note how it captures almost everything, whether or not it appears to be relevant to the instructional goals of the classroom. During

the class, or immediately afterward, the observer can write, in the margins, comments that bring particularly noteworthy events into focus (for example, effective use of rewards, student restlessness and inattention, or revealing expressions on student faces). The numbers running down the left margin can help reference each comment for later discussion and analysis.

Unless a lesson is taped and then transcribed, it is almost impossible for an observer to record every word or action that occurs. Therefore, the realistic objective in creating an ethnographic record is to capture the essence of what occurs and not every detail—with the aid of a laptop computer, when possible. In this example, the observer did an effective job of recording the flow of activity in a factual, nonjudgmental manner. Later, he could highlight certain aspects of the record with a transparent marker, or add interpretative comments in the margins. These could be points for discussion with a supervisor, topics to be discussed in a college or university methods class, or ideas for other lenses for subsequent observations.

An ethnographic record has several advantages for capturing life in classrooms.

1. It provides a comprehensive picture of the continuous flow of events from the beginning to the end of a period of observation.
2. It places events in perspective by indicating possible cause-and-effect sequences that occur in a classroom.
3. Like the anecdotal report, it requires little training or special skill.

However, there are also several disadvantages to using an ethnographic record.

1. It can be fatiguing to record for long periods.
2. Some events can be easily missed due to the intense concentration required to write down everything that occurs.
3. It can be inefficient and incomplete when different but equally important activities are occurring simultaneously: three or four small groups working at the same time; low-, average-, and high-ability groups pursuing their own activities; or Mike, Sue, and Betty all acting out at the same time.

Further, compiling an account of events during even a single class period can produce voluminous handwritten notes that are time-consuming to read and comment on. If others are expected to read your running record, you may have to retype it, or recopy it in neater, more legible handwriting, requiring still more time before the record becomes useful. These

EXAMPLE **4.3**

Teacher: Mrs. Tyler and a teacher aide

Date: November 12

Subject: Second-grade class, open classroom with teacher and aide. I will be simultaneously observing 18 children in two reading groups, 9 children, in each group.

Observer: Keiffer Sunden

8:30

1. The children have just been let into the
2. classroom, taking their coats off and
3. wandering around the room. Several boys
4. are in the corner, and some girls
5. are sitting on the floor playing with a puzzle.
6. The teacher is walking back and forth in the
7. back of the classroom, attending to some of
8. the children. Then, teacher and teacher aide
9. go to desk to talk to one another.

8:35

10. Mrs. Tyler leaves room. Teacher
11. aide stays seated behind her desk.

8:40

12. Mrs. Tyler comes back into
13. room. She walks to the desk at
14. far left-hand side of the classroom,
15. where there is a round table, and sits on
16. the edge. She says, "Blue Group, get your
17. folders and go up to the front. Green Group,
18. come here." Noise level drops and
19. children begin to follow orders. She
20. says, "Anybody lose a quarter?" No one
21. responds, and she repeats the question.
22. She says, "I know someone found—
23. someone lost a quarter because it was
24. found in the coat room. Look in your
25. pockets and see." No one says anything.
26. She now stands up and pulls a pile of
27. workbooks from across the table over to her.
28. They are the reading workbooks.
29. She opens the one on the top.
30. "Ah, Daniel!" she says loudly. "Your

31. work yesterday was not too bad but you
32. need some help. Evidently there are still
33. some words you don't understand." She
34. thumbs through the rest of his lesson. Danny
35. is standing at the outside of the circle around her,
36. not listening to what she is saying. Mrs. Tyler
37. now stands and gives instructions to the Green
38. Group. She tells them to go through pages
39. 8–13, reading the two stories between those
40. pages and to go over the work in the workbooks
41. that she is about to give back. She tells them
42. that they may sit anyplace but not together, and
43. then says, "And I don't want any funny business."
44. She opens the next workbook, which is Nicole's.
45. She tells Nicole she is having the same problem
46. that Danny is having, without specifying further.
47. Nicole looks up at her without any expression.
48. She then turns to a third book and says, "Michelle,
49. you're having the same problem." She says,
50. "*Snatch* means to grab. *Beach*, what
51. does it mean?" Michelle doesn't answer.
52. She has her finger in her mouth and
53. looks anxious. The teacher closes
54. the workbook and gives it to Michelle.
55. Michelle takes it and walks away with Nicole.

8:50

56. Teacher then opens the next workbook.

limitations aside, there are few other methods that capture the real-life drama of the classroom as well as the ethnographic record.

Thematic Notes

Thematic notes are facts recorded in traditional outline form, according to predesignated categories of ob-

servation. Much like the detective at the scene of a crime who jots down facts about suspects, motives, times, and places in a notebook, you can use thematic notes to jot down relevant data. Thematic notes are recorded using Roman numerals, *I, II, III,* and so on, representing the major areas to be observed, and letters of the alphabet, *A, B, C,* and so on, representing

EXAMPLE 4.4

I. Learning climate

    A. This is an open classroom with two team teachers.

    B. Teacher speaks in firm voice, encouraging control and obedience. Teacher makes it clear to kids she doesn't want any "funny business."

    C. Teacher exchanges with kids are mostly businesslike.

    D. Atmosphere competitive (workbooks being checked) and independent (individuals reading stories and going over their workbooks).

II. Task orientation

    A. Some students off-task during first ten minutes of class.

    B. Teacher devotes some class time to noninstructional tasks; e.g., "Who lost a quarter?"

    C. Teacher moves from student to student informing them of the correctness of their answers in workbook.

III. Classroom management

    A. Students enter classroom and begin work independently without specific routine (see IIA).

    B. Some feedback for good work; e.g., "Your work was not too bad," but no praise.

    C. Teacher rotates around room monitoring workbook exercises in progress.

    D. Blue Group without supervision or direction (in front of room) while teacher checks work of Green Group.

IV. Student engagement

    A. Some students off-task first ten minutes of class (see IIA).

    B. Students left waiting some of the time; e.g., Blue Group waits in front of room while teacher deals with Green Group.

    C. Teacher chooses not to engage students in extensive recitation or probe about workbook content. Exchanges are brief.

the factual information observed under each of the more general areas. To prepare thematic notes, first determine the precise themes or areas to focus the observation on, and then jot down key facts corresponding to these areas as the action unfolds. Example 4.4 shows what Keiffer might have written if he had chosen to create a set of thematic notes based on the events he observed during Mrs. Tyler's class.

As with the other forms of narrative reporting, the thematic outline has advantages and disadvantages. The advantages of thematic notes include:

1. They preorganize and focus the observer's attention, thereby increasing the depth and accuracy of what is observed.
2. If the themes are chosen thoughtfully, they can relate the events observed to previously established and theoretically sound dimensions of teaching.
3. They are briefer and more concise, and less time-consuming, than most other types of narrative records.
4. They can provide the content outline for a more formal record or report if one is needed later.

Disadvantages of thematic notes include:

1. They provide only general statements that may be too sketchy for recalling the factual events on which they are based.
2. They do not reveal order or sequence; for example, data recorded under Roman numeral *I* does not logically precede data recorded under Roman numeral *II*.
3. They focus attention only in predesignated areas, precluding the observation of other important classroom events that may arise spontaneously.

Visual Maps

Visual maps use pictures instead of words to serve much the same purpose as narratives. Visual maps portray the spatial relationships among physical objects—learning centers, reference libraries, groups at work—that may be important to fully understanding anecdotal reports, ethnographic records, or thematic notes. When you observe events that are clearly related to the spatial layout of a classroom, you'll want to construct a visual map to help you (and any other readers) better understand your narrative record. Often, a visual map can help you evaluate how a particular instructional activity was implemented, or how well classroom discipline is maintained.

For example, in the ethnographic record presented in Example 4.3, it was difficult to know exactly where the Blue and Green reading groups were in the classroom, other than that the Blue Group was told to get their folders and go to the front. Did something physically divide the groups to help foster (or perhaps detract from) their respective assignments? If the observer had provided a visual map with his ethnographic record, we might have better understood the fact that two groups were being taught at the same time, and that Mrs. Tyler was dealing with only one, the Green Group, while leaving the Blue Group somewhere in front of the class awaiting instruction. A visual map corresponding to this record might take the form shown in Figure 4.3.

We learn a number of important details from this picture. For example, neither the Blue nor the Green Group has enough chairs to be seated as a group; Danny is standing, apparently because there is no seat; and the teacher's aide is far removed from the Blue Group, leaving this group almost entirely on its own. Our understanding of the events in this classroom is also increased by seeing that *front*, as it is used by Mrs. Tyler in her instructions to the Blue Group, represents a portion of the classroom unattended by either the teacher or teacher aide. These may be significant details for gaining a complete picture of this classroom, and for properly interpreting the events occurring within it.

Method 2: Rating Scales

Narrative reports allow the observer a great deal of flexibility in choosing which behaviors will be observed; rating scales are more structured and offer you the opportunity to record not only what behaviors you observe, but also the degree of the behavior that you note. In order to use a rating scale, you identify, in advance, the behaviors you want to observe. Rating scales can be used individually or in conjunction with other observation tools such as narrative reports. Two common types of rating-scale formats are checklists and summated rating scales.

Checklists

The simplest type of rating scale is a checklist. Checklists consist of a list of the behaviors to be observed alongside a yes/no or present/absent response scale.

FIGURE 4.3   Visual Map

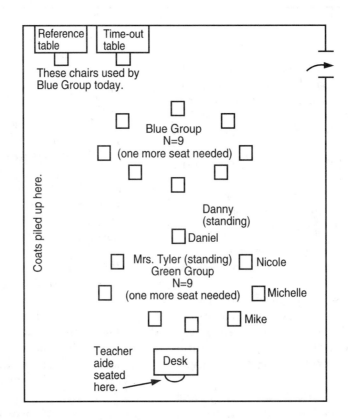

FIGURE 4.4 Checklist for Determining an Individual Student's Group Participation

	Yes	No
Shares information	(Yes)	No
	(+ 1)	(− 1)
Contributes ideas	(Yes)	No
	(+ 1)	(− 1)
Listens to others	Yes	(No)
	(+ 1)	(− 1)
Follows instructions	(Yes)	No
	(+ 1)	(− 1)
Shows initiative in solving group problems	(Yes)	No
	(+ 1)	(− 1)
Accepts and carries out group-determined tasks	Yes	(No)
	(+ 1)	(− 1)
Gives consideration to the viewpoints of others	Yes	(No)
	(+ 1)	(− 1)

Your job as an observer is simply to note the presence or absence of a particular behavior during an observation and mark it on the scale. Simple checklists of this sort are most useful when you are observing behaviors that are difficult to evaluate in degree, but that can be identified as either occurring or nonoccurring.

Checklists can be scored by assigning weights of +1 and −1 to the behaviors rated, depending on whether the behaviors are positively or negatively stated. After summing and averaging the weights across items, a decision can be made as to whether the average score indicates a positive or negative outcome, as noted in Figure 4.4. Notice that this method of coding responses automatically places the concept being observed (for example, group participation) on a −1 to +1 continuum, with 0 as the neutral point. The average of the seven items on this scale would be 4 + (−3) = 1, 1/7 = .14, indicating a slightly positive outcome.

There are times, however, when you may not have the opportunity to observe all the behaviors on a checklist. For example, if you observed a class only while a student was discussing her own ideas, there would be no opportunity to determine if that pupil "Listens to others." Thus, a checklist should indicate whether the observer had the opportunity to observe the behavior, as well as the presence or absence of that behavior. This can be accomplished by using the checklist format shown in Figure 4.5. For this checklist, summation and averaging of codes would be done only for the behaviors that were actually observed. Thus, the average for this set of items would be 3 + (−1) = 2, 2/4 = .50, indicating a fairly positive outcome.

FIGURE 4.5 Checklist and Codes for the Presence or Absence of a Behavior

No Opportunity to Observe	Observed		Code Given
❑	☑	Shares information	−1
❑	☑	Contributes ideas	+1
☑	❑	Listens to others	none
❑	☑	Follows instructions	+1
❑	☑	Shows initiative in solving group problems	+1
☑	❑	Accepts and carries out group-determined tasks	none
☑	❑	Gives consideration to the viewpoints of others	none

Summated Rating Scales

Summated ratings differ from checklists in that more than two degrees of discrimination are possible. Summated rating scales help you focus more closely on the degree of behavior, because they typically describe a behavior at its extremes and at selected intermediate points. As you observe a behavior, you compare what you observe with the scale and choose the degree that best matches your observation. When items represent a common underlying theme, scores across individual scales are summed and averaged, hence the name *summated ratings*. Summated rating scales require an observer to discern not only whether a behavior is present or absent, but at what intensity the behavior is occurring. This means that as an observer, you will need to thoroughly understand the behaviors being rated—and how the rating scale relates to your observations. While summated rating scales require more knowledge on the observer's part, they also provide more specific information regarding the focus of the observation. The most common summated rating scales offer five or seven degrees of discrimination.

Five-Point Scales

Five-point rating scales are customarily referred to as Likert scales. In the Likert scale, five intervals, or degrees of differentiation, are used to distinguish levels of proficiency. Because you may need to construct a summated rating scale to reflect your particular observation interests and questions, we have included a number of examples of how this may be done (see Figure 4.6).

To complete a Likert scale, you check or circle the appropriate alternative. The scale is then scored by assigning weights to each response item: 5 indicates the most positive; 1 indicates the least positive. Scale items measuring a common underlying concept are then summed and averaged. As noted in the examples, scales can be positioned vertically or horizontally, whichever is most convenient. Although verbal descriptions are used on each end and the middle of the scale, they need not be placed at each interval.

Because summated rating scales often include items that require the observation of different classroom events and activities, they may require an extended period of observation before an accu-

FIGURE 4.6   Five-Point Scales

Example 1. Item from a summated rating of teacher clarity.
Teacher informs learners of skills or understanding expected at end of lesson.

_____ Always
_____ Frequently
_____ Occasionally
_____ Seldom
_____ Never

Example 2: Item from a summated rating for lesson preparation.
Quality and accuracy of ideas

1	2	3	4	5
Very limited investigation; little or no material related to the facts.		Some investigation; attention to the facts is apparent.		Extensive investigation; extensive representation of the facts.

Example 3: Item from a summated rating for student cooperation and participation.
Does the student give consideration to the viewpoint of others?

| Never | Infrequently | Sometimes | Frequently | Always |

Example 4: Item from a summated rating of a teacher's oral delivery.
Teacher's enunciation of technical vocabulary

1	2	3	4	5
Very poor	Poor	Adequate	Good	Very good

rate rating can be obtained. For example, it is unlikely that a teacher's clarity, lesson preparation, or speaking ability can be accurately ascertained with a Likert scale from only a few minutes of observation. For many types of behavior, a class period or longer might be needed to observe enough activity to accurately judge the degree to which the general behavior identified on the scale has been attained. For other types of behaviors, days or even weeks of observation may be necessary before an accurate judgment can be made. Generally, the longer the observation period before a rating is made, the more accurate the rating will be. Observations that extend over days, however, may be subject to losses in memory, which could make the rating less trustworthy. Therefore, it is usually desirable to complete a rating at the end of each observation period, and then take an average of the ratings across periods to create an overall rating for an extended period of time.

Seven-Point Scales

Seven-point scales are similar to five-point scales, except that fewer verbal descriptors are used. One of the most popular seven-point scales is the semantic differential, which uses polar, or opposite, adjectives for each end of the scale. By checking one of the seven choices on the scale, the observer indicates the degree to which he feels a particular adjective is representative of the events observed. You completed a semantic differential when you filled out the *General Observation Form* in Chapter 3. Here is another example of a seven-point scale.

This Lesson

Clear	__	__	__	__	__	__	__ Unclear
Unorderly	__	__	__	__	__	__	__ Orderly
Organized	__	__	__	__	__	__	__ Disorganized
Unfocused	__	__	__	__	__	__	__ Focused

Notice that all the adjective pairs focus on a single topic, "This Lesson," thereby creating a homogeneous set of items whose ratings can be averaged. Also, it is customary to alter the lineup of the pairs in a more-or-less random order so that all positively or all negatively worded adjectives do not appear on the same side of the page. This helps keep the rater vigilant. As you read the various descriptors, you'll notice the differences and hopefully avoid generalizing a highly positive or negative rating for one item to the item immediately below it.

Depending upon your interpretation and use, the middle blank can serve two different purposes. In cases where too little information is available, you can mark the middle blank to indicate *no preference for either descriptor*. Or, in the event that you see both positive and negative trends occurring in the same lesson, you can mark the middle blank to suggest that *both ends of the continuum have been evenly exhibited*. If the scale does not include instructions about how the middle blank is to be interpreted, it is a good idea for you to decide, prior to an observation, what it means to you when you mark the middle blank.

As you can imagine, it is often important to go beyond simple polar adjectives to achieve a more detailed description of classroom events. If you want to report behaviors with a greater specificity, you can modify the scale to include phrases or whole sentences. In this case, you replace polar adjectives with opposing concepts expressed in the form of phrases or sentences, providing for a more structured observation and a more detailed judgment. Figure 4.7 provides a modified form of a semantic differential for observing lesson clarity. Notice that considerable detail about lesson clarity is registered with this scale. Item responses are tailored to fit the definition of lesson clarity held by its author. Thus, the observation becomes more structured. The observer looks for finer points of detail that make up the broader concept of lesson clarity, at the same time requiring less subjective judgment or inference.

To score a semantic differential scale, numerical weights are assigned, depending on whether the positive statement is on the left (the extreme positive blank is assigned a 7) or whether the negative statement is on the left (the extreme negative blank is assigned a 1). All the remaining blanks are coded in descending order if the statement on the left is positive, and in ascending order if the statement on the left is negative. The weights for the blanks checked are then averaged. Since 7.0 is the highest attainable average, a score of greater than 3.5 indicates a positive overall rating.

Seven-point scales are preferred over five-point scales when more than five levels of a behavior can be reliably distinguished by a relatively untrained observer. When this is not the case, or when each interval on the continuum that underlies the behavior must be explicitly identified, a five-point scale is a better choice.

The advantages of five- and seven-point scales are:

1. They direct observation toward specific aspects of behavior, and thereby structure what is to be observed.
2. They provide a common frame of reference for comparing all teachers and/or students with the same set of items.
3. They are easy to construct and can be quickly tailored to a specific observation target.

Figure 4.7 A Modified Semantic Differential for Observing Lesson Clarity

1. Informs learners of skills or understanding expected at end of lesson.							Fails to link lesson content to the level of complexity and how the content will be used.
2. Provides learners with an advance organizer that places lesson content in perspective.							Starts presenting content without first introducing the topic in some larger context.
3. Checks for task-relevant prior learning at beginning of lesson, and reteaches when necessary.							Moves to new content without checking understanding of prerequisite facts or concepts.
4. Ends lesson with review or summary.							Fails to restate or review main ideas at end of lesson.
5. Gives directives slowly and distinctly. Checks for understanding along the way.							Presents too many directives at once, or presents them too quickly.
6. Knows learners' ability levels and teaches at or slightly above their current level of functioning.							Fails to recognize that the instruction is under or over the students' level.
7. Uses examples, illustrations, or demonstrations to explain and clarify content in textbooks and workbooks.							Restricts presentation to oral reproduction of textbooks or workbooks.

The disadvantages include

1. They can be easily influenced by the observer's general impression of the person or classroom being rated.
2. Due to their general nature, they allow for only relative judgments (more/less) and not absolute judgments (present/absent).
3. They tend to force ratings toward the middle of the scale when the continuum is large, or when endpoints represent extreme or highly undesirable behavior.
4. They may require the observer to distinguish finer details of a behavior than can be reliably detected in a relatively short observation period (especially true for seven-point scales).

While narrative records and rating scales can provide a wealth of information, sometimes even more specific detail is needed. In such cases, observers turn to classroom coding systems, the most structured of observational instruments.

Method 3: Classroom Coding Systems

Observation systems that help you record the frequency with which various teacher and student behaviors occur are called *classroom coding systems*. They are sometimes referred to as low-inference observation systems because they require fewer judgments or inferences on the part of the observer than summated ratings. Unlike the general concepts measured by rating scales, coding systems measure spe-

FIGURE **4.8**   Summary of Categories in Flanders' System

Teacher Indirect Influence	1. *Accepts feeling*—Accepts and clarifies the tone of the students in a nonthreatening manner. Feelings may be positive or negative. Predicting or recalling feelings is included.
	2. *Praises or encourages*—Praises or encourages student action or behavior. Jokes release tension, but not at the expense of another individual; nods head, or develops ideas suggested by student. As teacher brings more of his own ideas into play, shift to category 5.
	3. *Accepts or uses ideas of students*—Clarifies, builds, or develops ideas suggested by a student. As teacher brings more of his own ideas into play, shift to category 5.
	4. *Asks questions*—Asks a question about content or procedure with the intent that a student answer.
Teacher Direct Influence	5. *Lecturing*—Gives facts or opinions about content or procedures; expresses her own ideas, asks rhetorical questions.
	6. *Giving directions*—Directions, commands, or orders with which a student is expected to comply.
	7. *Criticizing or justifying authority*—Statements intended to change student behavior from nonacceptable to acceptable pattern; bawling someone out; stating why the teacher is doing what she is doing; extreme self-reference.
Student Talk	8. *Student talk–response*—Talk by students in response to teacher. Teacher initiates the contact or solicits student statement.
	9. *Student talk–initiation*—Talk by students that they initiate. If "calling on" student is only to indicate who may talk next, observer must decide whether student wanted to talk. If he did, use this category.
	10. *Silence or confusion*—Pauses, short periods of silence, and periods of confusion in which communication cannot be understood by the observer.

cific and distinct units of behavior, such as "Teacher asks questions" or "Teacher used example," that can be recorded during relatively brief intervals of time. Three frequently used methods for coding patterns of behavior are counting, sign, and event systems.

Counting Systems

With a counting system, the observer counts the number of time intervals in which various teacher and/or student behaviors occur. A time interval (such as every 5 seconds), represents a frame for the observation that is established before the observation begins. Every time the interval or frame elapses, a tally is made to indicate which behavior on the instrument occurred during that interval. Needless to say, the behaviors must be specific enough to be easily recognized during the time interval chosen, and the number of behaviors must be small enough that the observer can remember them and code them as they occur.

Figure 4.8 shows ten behaviors that form a counting system developed by Flanders (1970). The observer using this system records behavior every 3 seconds, or whenever behavior changes. Here is a brief classroom dialogue and how it would be coded using the behaviors and codes specified in Figure 4.8.

Speaker	Dialogue	Code
Ms. Chin:	What system of grids identifies the location of any object on the globe?	4,4
Bobby:	Latitude and longitude.	9
Ms. Chin:	Good, I can see you've been studying. What does longitude mean?	2,4
Bobby:	It's the grid on the globe that . . . goes up and down.	8
Ms. Chin:	What do you mean, "up and down"?	4
Bobby:	They extend north and south at equal intervals.	8
Ms. Chin:	Okay. Now tell me, where do they begin?	4

Speaker	Dialogue	Code
Bobby:	Well, I think they begin wherever it's midnight and end where it's almost midnight again.	8
Ms. Chin:	Let's think about that for a minute. Wouldn't that mean the point of origin would always be changing, according to where it happened to be midnight?	4
Bobby:	Yes, so the grids must start at some fixed point.	8
Ms. Chin:	Anybody know where they begin?	4
Sue:	Our book says the first is one marked "0" and starts at a place called Greenwich, England.	9
Ms. Chin:	How can a grid that runs continuously north and south around the globe start anyplace, Sue?	4
Sue:	I meant to say, it runs through Greenwich, England.	8
Ms. Chin:	Good. Now let's return to Bobby's point about time. Now that we have a fixed line of longitude, marked "0," how might we use it to establish time?	4
Bobby:	Now I remember. Midnight at the "0" longitude—or in Greenwich, England—is called "0" hours. Starting from there, there are timelines drawn around the world, so that when it's midnight at the first timeline, it will be 1 o'clock at Greenwich, England, and when it's midnight at the next timeline, it will be 2 o'clock back at Greenwich, England, and so on.	9,9,9
Ms. Chin:	So what does that mean?	4
Bobby:	Each line equals one hour . . . so . . . so there must be 24 of them!	8
Ms. Chin:	So it should be no surprise that time determined in reference to the "0" grid of longitude is called Greenwich Mean Time.	5,5

Let's use the definitions in Figure 4.8 to interpret this dialogue. Notice that the first statement is coded "4, 4," indicating that this was a question that lasted for two 3-second intervals. The second statement is coded "9" to indicate that Bobby volunteered or initiated a response to the teacher's question. In subsequent statements, Bobby's responses are coded "8" to indicate that the teacher's question is directed specifically to Bobby, and only Bobby was expected to answer. Notice also the "2, 4" code for the third statement. Here the teacher praises Bobby's response, and then goes on to probe with a followup question, which extends into the second 3-second interval. Later, Sue joins the discussion by initiating a response to a teacher question. This is coded "9" because she was not specifically asked to respond. Shortly afterward, a second question is directed specifically to her—that is coded "8." Next, Bobby volunteers some information as a result of a question that takes three 3-second intervals to answer. Finally, the dialogue ends with the teacher giving some facts about the content, coded "5," which extends into a second 3-second interval.

To interpret the sequence of these various behaviors, the numbers corresponding to the behaviors are entered into a matrix. This step is illustrated in Figure 4.9, using the codes from the dialogue. The entries in Figure 4.9 were provided by the sequence of numbers representing the pairs of codes at the left of the matrix. Notice that the sequence of numbers from the dialogue has been marked off in pairs, and that the second number of each pair becomes the first number of the next pair. These pairs are then entered into the matrix by using the first number of each pair to locate the proper row, and the second number of each pair to locate the proper column. Thus, the 4/4 pair is recorded by placing a tally at the intersection of the fourth row and fourth column, the 4/9 pair by placing a tally at the intersection of the fourth row and ninth column, the 9/2 pair by placing a tally at the intersection of the ninth row and second column, and so on, until the last pair is recorded

Notice the two cells with the greatest number of tallies (4/8 and 8/4). These cells indicate that the dialogue was characterized by questions and answers. Six questions were directed specifically to a student (indicated by the 4/8 cell), and five times the student response to the question was followed by another question from the teacher (indicated by the 8/4 cell). Since the majority of questions were directed to specific students and followed by additional questions, we can assume the questions were of short duration (about 3 seconds), and that they were of a factual nature, allowing students to respond with brief answers. Also, we see from the 4/9 cell that only three of these questions required unsolicited or voluntary responses from the class, indicating that the teacher–student questioning during this episode was quickly paced and directed to individual students. In other words, this set of tallies

FIGURE 4.9 Example of an Interaction Analysis Matrix for Interpreting Sequence of Behaviors

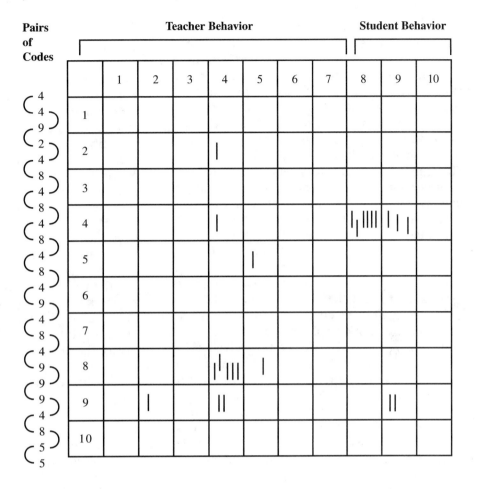

suggests that the students were responding with short answers that could be judged right or wrong. This is also supported by the fact that only three times did behavior extend beyond a single 3-second interval before changing, as indicated by tallies in the 4/4, 5/5, and 9/9 cells. A large number of tallies in any cell in the diagonal of the matrix (i.e., 1/1, 2/2, 3/3, etc.) would indicate a relatively slow or more leisurely classroom pace.

Although only ten categories of behavior are represented, the 10 × 10 matrix permits recording and interpreting a far broader range of behavior by taking into account sequences of events. For example, a matrix like that constructed for the example dialogue could be used to determine whether a teacher was having problems managing the classroom or maintaining order and discipline. If management problems were present, we would expect to find a relatively high number of tallies in the sixth and seventh columns, with perhaps a large number of tallies in the 7/7 cell indicating a large amount of time devoted to giving directions and creating or justifying authority. Severe management problems pertaining to order and discipline would also be in-

dicated by tallies in column 10 and the 10/10 intersection, the latter indicating a high number of intervals characterized by confusion.

Similarly, tallies in the matrix can be used to characterize the type of learning climate in the classroom or the teacher's instructional style. A relatively large number of tallies in Columns 1, 2, and 3, for example, indicates a warm and nurturing attitude on the part of the teacher; a large number of tallies in Columns 4 and 8, and especially in the 4/5 cell, as occurred in our example, might indicate a tightly woven question-and-answer session. A relatively high number of tallies in Columns 5 and 6 and the 5/5 intersection indicates a lecture in which little student participation is solicited or encouraged.

Although Flanders' system was originally conceived with the idea that teachers should increase their portion of Category 1, 2, 3, and 4 behavior (teacher's indirect influence) and reduce their proportion of Category 5, 6, and 7 behavior (teacher's direct influence), research has not supported the advantage of the indirect approach for increasing student achievement. Thus, the use of a once popular theory, represented by the ratio of the number of tallies in the first four categories to the number of tallies in categories 5, 6, and 7 (called the indirect-to-direct ratio) has justifiably fallen into disuse.[*] However, Flanders' system offers many opportunities to study other events in classrooms, and need not be restricted by preconceived theories of what an ideal classroom should be like. This is perhaps why Flanders' system remains one of the most practical and widely used counting systems.

To be practical, counting systems such as the one by Flanders must be simple enough to provide an accurate assessment of classroom behavior with relatively little practice. After a practice session of about 30 minutes, two observers should be able to agree, to within about 75 percent, on the number of tallies they record for a given behavior. If, after practice using an observation instrument, two observers coding the same teacher cannot obtain at least 75 percent agreement, the observers need to formulate a common definition of the behaviors being counted, simplify statements of the behaviors in question, and/or reduce the number of behaviors observed. Due to the simplicity of Flanders' instrument, 75 percent or greater agreement tends to be achieved after a relatively short practice session in which coders watch a videotaped lesson and discuss coding differences when they occur. Appendix A describes a simple procedure for determining observer agreement for a counting system.

The advantages of counting systems include:

1. They provide for a large sampling of behavior.
2. They allow for sequences or patterns of behavior to be conveniently recorded in matrix form.
3. The data derived from them are adaptable to statistical indices, such as ratios and percents.

The disadvantages include:

1. Behaviors must be limited to those that can be divided into specific, discrete units that occur frequently.
2. Coding can be stressful and intense, especially when time intervals are short and/or the behaviors to be coded cannot be quickly and unambiguously recognized in the interval chosen.
3. Some training to acquire a common understanding of the behaviors to be counted and a thorough definition of each behavior is required to achieve satisfactory agreement between observers.

---

[*]Flanders also developed a revised indirect/direct (I/D) ratio, consisting of the proportion of tallies in categories 1, 2, and 3 divided by the proportion of tallies in categories 6 and 7, to more strongly discriminiate between direct and indirect classrooms and to make the earlier (I/D) ratio more independent of subject matter.

Sign Systems

Another procedure for observing patterns of classroom interaction is a sign system. When you use a sign system, you record an event only once, regardless of how often it occurs within a specified time period. Sign systems differ from counting systems in that (a) the interval of observation tends to be considerably longer, 2 to 15 minutes, and (b) the presence of more than one behavior can be recorded during the interval. Each behavior that occurs is given a sign (for example, a checkmark) indicating its presence or absence within a particular block of time. A sign system, using the same behaviors observed with Flanders' Interaction Analysis System, appears in Figure 4.10.

Notice that Flanders' counting system can be converted to a sign system simply by extending the length of the interval from 3 seconds to 5 minutes, and by allowing multiple behaviors to be recorded within the interval. During each of the 5-minute intervals, the observer records which of the behaviors were observed, but not how often they were observed. This typically allows for more categories of behavior to be placed on a sign system than on a counting system, where the demands of rapid coding necessarily restrict one's focus to only a single behavior per time interval. Consequently, sign systems can be lengthy (30 or more behaviors), although they are often focused on a single concept or theme (for example, classroom management, lesson clarity, or student engagement).

One useful sign system for studying the classroom management behavior of teachers was created by Soar and Soar (1983). Some of the behaviors on their instrument appear in Instrument 4.1. Notice that twenty-seven different teacher behaviors pertaining to classroom control are observed. The presence or absence of these behaviors over a 30-minute period indicates the verbal (Items 1–17) and physical (Items 18–27) behaviors used by the teacher to maintain classroom control. Also, within each of these two categories, items are listed in order from least to most obtrusive ("Acknowledges, agrees, complies" to "Scolds, punishes"; "Nods, smiles, facial feedback" to "Ignores, abandons"). Use of these categories in a sign system over several class periods can provide a detailed description of the classroom management style being used. You may want to practice using the sign system in Instrument 4.1.

It is important to note that when you use a sign system to compare the behavior of different teachers, it may not be possible to observe teachers for the same amount of time. For example, if Teacher A were observed once for one hour and twice for two hours, and Teacher B were observed twice for two hours and again for thirty minutes, Teacher A may exhibit

FIGURE 4.10   Sign System

5-Minute Periods										Behaviors
1	2	3	4	5	6	7	8	9	10	
										Teacher accepts feelings.
										Teacher praises or encourages.
										Teacher accepts or uses ideas of students.
										Teacher asks questions.
										Teacher lectures.
										Teacher gives directions.
										Teacher criticizes or justifies authority.
										Student talk — response.
										Student talk — initiation.
										Silence or confusion.

fewer intervals in which a behavior was observed simply because Teacher A was observed less. This problem can be corrected using the percentage of intervals the behavior was observed over the total number of intervals.

For example, let's assume a comparison is being made between Teacher A and Teacher B in Category 2 of Instrument 4.1, and that Teacher A is observed for thirty-six 5-minute intervals (three hours) and Teacher B for fifty-four 5-minute intervals (four and a half hours). If this behavior were observed during eighteen intervals for Teacher A and eighteen intervals for Teacher B, the percentage of intervals for Teacher A and Teacher B would be

$$\text{Teacher A} = 18/36 = 50\%$$
$$\text{Teacher B} = 18/54 = 33\%$$

Converting these to a base rate per hour, we can conclude that Teacher A praises at least six times per hour (eighteen counts/three hours), and that Teacher B engages in this same behavior at least four times per hour (eighteen counts/four and a half hours). Notice that since our intervals are five minutes in duration and only one tally is made per interval, we can only identify the least number of times that each teacher engaged in the behavior per hour. We have created a basis for comparing classrooms when we observe for disproportionate amounts of time, assuming that each classroom is observed a sufficient amount of time under similar circumstances.

The advantages of sign systems include:

1. A larger set of behaviors can be observed than with a counting system due to the longer time interval.
2. Because behavior is coded within a longer time interval, the data tend to be more dependable than with a counting system.

3. Unlike counting systems, sign systems require little or no training.

The disadvantages of sign systems include:

1. They do not indicate the frequency with which a behavior occurs within an interval.
2. Due to the number of behaviors recorded, an overall summary or simple interpretation of a teacher's behavior may not be possible.
3. The tallies recorded cannot be used to establish the sequence of behavior, because the size of the interval may allow intervening events to go unrecorded.

Event Systems

Observers use event systems to record the occurrence of preselected behaviors. Unlike counting and rating systems, however, event systems do not record behavior in intervals of time. Instead, event systems record preselected behaviors in the natural sequence in which they occur. In this sense, event systems are similar to an ethnographic record. For example, suppose you are interested in observing the type of feedback used by the teacher after a student response is given. In this instance, two events may become the focus of your observation: the student's response to a question (right, partially right, wrong, or no answer) and the teacher's reaction to the student's answer (praise, affirm, no reaction, negate, or criticize). You can determine the pattern of feedback provided by the teacher by coding these two events as they occur for individual students. Notice that since no record must be made within a specific period of time (as is the case in both counting and sign systems), you may wait for a long period of time for the event to occur, or you may make many records in a brief period of time.

There are several ways to record classroom events. One of these uses frequency counts to register the

FIGURE 4.11   Record of Frequency Counts

	Event	Frequency of Event
Student Responses	Right	II
	Partially right	JHT
	Wrong	II
	No answer	III
Teacher Reaction	Praise	JHT
	Affirm	III
	No reaction	I
	Negate	II
	Criticize	I

number of times various types of behaviors occur. For example, for our two events, student response and teacher reaction, we could observe and record the number of times variations of each occur. Our first record of the data might take the form shown in Figure 4.11.

While the information in Figure 4.11 helps us see the frequency of responses and reactions, it is limited in several ways. First, it does not tell us which teacher reaction followed from what student response, or what teacher reaction might have caused the next round of student response. Although we can assume that this teacher tends to praise partially right answers more than right answers, we do not know the extent to which some partially right answers may have been negated, criticized, or met with no reaction—because this record makes no attempt to link a particular student response with the teacher reaction that immediately follows it. Nor can we be sure that partially right answers were praised at all. In other words, this format does not indicate the exact sequence or flow of classroom behavior. There's no explanation of the conditions that evoke a certain type of teacher reaction, or the type of teacher reaction that may, in turn, evoke subsequent student responses. To be a true event record, our recording system would need to keep sequences of behavior intact. How could this be accomplished?

Examine Figure 4.12 and compare it to Figure 4.11. What do you notice? The event recording in Figure 4.12 was developed by Good and Brophy (1990) in an effort to capture sequences of events between student and teacher and not simply the frequency with which individual behaviors occur. Figure 4.13 provides definitions for the student

and teacher behaviors observed using this instrument, with codes or symbols for recording them.

Let's examine a brief dialogue to see how these behaviors might occur in the context of the classroom. We will then code the dialogue using the Good and Brophy event record.

Mr. Garza: Today, we will review the order of operations for solving algebraic equations. In a problem involving both addition and multiplication, which should be performed first? David.

David: Don't know.

Mr. Garza: Mark.

Mark: Umm . . . I'd multiply first. That's like squaring and I know you always square first.

Mr. Garza: Good. That's right. And squaring is a form of multiplication. What operation would come next? Anyone?

Susan: Addition.

Mr. Garza: No.

Susan: Well, it must be subtraction then.

Mr. Garza: You're just guessing. You should think before responding. What operation comes next, Diane?

Diane: Multiplication and division go together, so I'd do the division part of the problem next.

Mr. Garza: But if they go together, as you said, why not do the division before multiplying?

Let's return to Figure 4.12. Notice that each exchange with a student response is coded. Five such exchanges occurred during the dialogue. From these codes, we learn that the first student response was a "no answer" (0), followed by no reaction from the teacher (0), who then moves on to ask another student ("Asks Another"). In the second exchange, a right answer (+) is followed by praise (+ +), followed

FIGURE 4.12 Coding Form for the Good and Brophy Event System, With Example Data

Number	Student	Student Response				Teacher Feedback Reaction											
		+	+/−	−	0	+ +	+	0	−	− −	Gives Answer	Explains	Asks Another	Other Calls	Repeats	Clue	New Question
1	Dave				✔		✔						✔				
2	Mark	✔				✔											✔
3	Susan			✔				✔									
4	Susan			✔					✔				✔				
5	Diane		✔				✔									✔	

by a new question ("New Question"). In the third exchange, a wrong answer (−) is followed by an indication that the answer was wrong (−). In the fourth exchange, a wrong answer (−) is followed by criticism (−−), after which the teacher asks another student to respond ("Asks Another"). In the last exchange, a partially right answer (+/−) was neither clearly accepted nor rejected (0). Instead, the teacher appears to give a clue by asking a related question ("Clue").

Overall, this teacher appears to do an effective job of matching the quality of a student's response with the appropriate form and amount of feedback. Unfortunately, we do not know the extent to which this teacher praises students, because so few of the student responses were correct in this brief dialogue. A larger sampling of behavior would no doubt shed some light on this question, which could be an important reason for continuing the observation. From each row of the recording form, however, we do learn the quality of the question-answer-feedback sequence in this classroom. From these codes, we learn exactly what behaviors preceded what other behaviors for both students and teacher, thereby providing an indication of the sequence, not just the presence or absence of the events being observed.

As we noted in the discussion of counting systems, there is always the question of dependability when recording teacher and student behavior, especially when using event systems. To achieve a truly dependable record of classroom events, many observers work in pairs. A reasonable amount of agreement among observers about what to record is a necessary condition for using an event system. If need be, points of disagreement among observers can be discussed, and rules and definitions can be established for increasing the dependability of an instru-

ment. Determining the percentage of agreement—or dependability—for an event system is different than for a counting system, because only the presence or absence of a behavior is recorded after each exchange. Appendix B illustrates a simple procedure for determining percentage of agreement using the Good and Brophy system or a similar event system.

Event systems, such as the Good and Brophy system illustrated here, are used when a specific area of classroom behavior is of particular interest and an in-depth understanding of the antecedents and consequences of behavior is desired. Because event systems are detailed, their use can bring on fatigue quickly. Thus, observers usually reserve them for relatively brief but intensive periods of observation when the events of interest are most likely to occur.

The advantages of event systems include:

1. They keep the sequence of key behaviors intact, indicating the antecedents and consequences of specific actions.
2. They can be used to study interactive sequences involving particular students and special types of learners (more able/less able; male/female).
3. They can focus an observer's attention on only those classroom events relevant to the particular information needed.

The disadvantages include:

1. They can be tiring to use if observation periods are long.
2. To be efficient, the observer must know in advance when and where the behaviors of interest are most likely to occur.
3. They may not be reliable when the events being coded are brief and occur rapidly.

FIGURE **4.13** Revised Good and Brophy (1990) Coding Categories for Question-Answer-Feedback Sequences (The teacher feedback reaction, "Explains," has been added to the original instrument.)

Student Sex

Symbol	Label	
M	Male	The student answering the question is male
F	Female	The student answering the question is female.

Student Response

+	Right	The teacher accepts the student's response as correct or satisfactory.
±	Part right	The teacher considers the student's response to be only partially correct, or correct but incomplete.
–	Wrong	The teacher considers the student's response to be incorrect.
O	No answer	The student makes no response or says he or she doesn't know (code student's answer here if teacher gives a feedback reaction before he or she is able to respond).

Teacher Feedback Reaction

++	Praise	Teacher praises student either in words ("fine," "good," "wonderful," "good thinking") or by expressing verbal affirmation in a notably warm, joyous, or excited manner.
+	Affirm	Teacher simply affirms that the student's response is correct (nods, repeats answer, says "Yes," "okay," etc.).
O	No reaction	Teacher makes no response whatever to student's response—he or she simply goes on to something else.
–	Negate	Teacher simply indicates that the student's response is incorrect (shakes head, says "No," "That's not right," "Hm-mm," etc.).
– –	Criticize	Teacher criticizes student, either in words ("You should know better than that," "That doesn't make any sense—you better pay close attention," etc.) or by expressing verbal negation in a frustrated, angry, or disgusted manner.
Gives Answer	Teacher gives answer	Teacher provides the correct answer for the student.
Explains	Teacher explains after answer	Teacher explains or gives reason why an answer is correct or incorrect.
Asks Another	Teacher asks another student	Teacher redirects the question, asking a different student to try to answer it.
Other Calls	Another student calls out answer	Another student calls out the correct answer, and the teacher acknowledges that it is correct.
Repeats	Repeats question	Teacher repeats the original question, either in its entirety or with a prompt ("Well?" "Do you know?" "What's the answer?").
Clue	Rephrase or clue	Teacher makes original question easier for student to answer by rephrasing it or by giving a clue.
New Question	New question	Teacher asks a new question (for example, a question that calls for a different answer than the original question called for).

Now that you have gained familiarity with some techniques for observing, we will turn our attention to using these techniques as you observe in the classroom. In the following chapters, you will combine your recently acquired knowledge of the instruments of observation with the eight lenses to study and record patterns of effective teaching.

ACTIVITIES*

1. Recall a critical incident you were involved in during your elementary or secondary school years. Write a brief, factual paragraph concerning exactly what happened to you, and a second paragraph giving your interpretation of the incident. Have a classmate read your two paragraphs and make a judgment about your success in separating fact from interpretation.

2. Provide some useful themes for making thematic notes in each of the following classrooms: (1) a tenth-grade algebra class reviewing for a test in a question-and-answer period; (2) a social studies class of low-ability seventh graders involved in a group discussion; and (3) a class of second graders completing seatwork while the teacher monitors and checks their homework. Be sure to change your themes across the three classrooms to reflect special areas of interest that you may have, or that might be consistent with the content and grade level of these classrooms. Explain why you chose the themes that you did.

3. With a group of other students with whom you will be observing this semester or quarter, construct a posterboard-size picture of a classroom that can be altered to show various arrangements of seating and classroom furniture. For example, draw the boundaries of a classroom and, with an additional sheet, cut out different shaped symbols for student seats, tables, the teacher's desk, and other furniture likely to be found in most classrooms. Mount the posterboard on a backing of cork or bulletin-board material that you can pin your symbols on. Use this visual map to illustrate to the class the physical nature of a classroom from which you have collected observation data.

4. Construct a checklist for recording five observable signs that you feel would reflect the climate of a classroom. Be sure to consider whether there will be an opportunity to observe all five of your signs when constructing the format of

your instrument. Using a recent class you have attended, assign responses to your items and score the items to arrive at an overall summary. In your judgment, was the climate of this classroom generally favorable or unfavorable?

5. Construct a five-item Likert instrument suitable for observing instructional variety. Vary the format for your items according to the examples provided in this chapter, but remember to keep all the items focused on instructional variety. To provide practice in scoring your scale, assign responses to each of the five items using a recent class you have attended. Based on the average of the five items, was the instructional variety in this classroom favorable or unfavorable?

6. Using a seven-point scale, write five different polar phrases that could be used to observe a teacher's task orientation. Arrange these on the page exactly as you would want them used by an observer, being sure to write the theme or concept to which your phrases refer at the top of the page. Write some instructions informing an inexperienced observer how to record her responses on the blanks provided. In your directions, make specific reference to how you wish the observer to interpret the middle blank.

7. Construct a sign system for observing whether or not the majority of a class you will be teaching is engaged in the learning process during a class discussion. With the help of a classmate, select ten student behaviors that will indicate whether the class as a group is on-task and actively participating in the instruction ("eyes on teacher," "raising questions," "following assignments," "understanding directions"). Arrange your behaviors into a format suitable for recording their presence or absence for six 10-minute time intervals.

8. Assume that two observers have used a counting system to observe teacher questioning for forty-five minutes. During this time, one observer records forty-five instances of questioning, and the second observer records twenty-five instances of questioning. What is the estimated percentage of agreement between observers, using the formula in Appendix A? Would you consider the percentage of agreement for the observation of this behavior adequate or inadequate? If it is inadequate, suggest some modifications that might increase the percentage of observer agreement for this behavior.

9. Assume that the sign system you have devised in Activity 7 was used to observe student engagement in two different classrooms. The first classroom was observed three times for one hour and one time for 45 minutes. The second

---

*Some of these activities may be grouped into a common activity, divided among classmates, and completed from a single observation.

classroom was observed one time for 1 hour, one time for 2 hours, and one time for 15 minutes. Your observation record shows that the students were engaged for twenty-four intervals in the first classroom, and thirty-two intervals in the second classroom. Compare the students' engagement in these two classrooms, assuming you have chosen 5-minute intervals. What is your conclusion about the similarity of student engagement in the learning process between these two classrooms?

10. Think about your past experiences in school and the resultant expectations you may have developed about education and teaching. List each of the eight lens areas and address your potential strengths and weaknesses in observing each area. For example, under "Instructional Variety" you might reflect on the fact that almost all of your student experience has occurred in teacher-directed classrooms with little cooperative group work. How might you respond when observing in a classroom where students are noisily creating projects in small groups? What assumptions do you have about "good" instruction in each lens area? What do you think might surprise you?

INSTRUMENT 4.1   Sign System With Items From Soar and Soar (1983)

Type	Controlling Behaviors	5-Minute Intervals									Number of Intervals Observed
Verbal Control	1. Acknowledges, Agrees, Complies										
	2. Praises										
	3. Asks for status										
	4. Suggests, guides										
	5. Feedback, cites reason										
	6. Corrects with criticism										
	7. Questions for control										
	8. Questions, states behavior rule										
	9. Directs with reason										
	10. Directs without reason										
	11. Uses time pressure										
	12. Reminds, prods										
	13. Interrupts, cuts off										
	14. Supervises closely, immobilizes										
	15. Criticizes, warns										
	16. Orders, commands										
	17. Scolds, punishes										
Physical Control	18. Nods, smiles, facial feedback										
	19. Uses "body English," waits										
	20. Gestures										
	21. Touches, pats										
	22. Shakes head, eye contact										
	23. Takes equipment, book										
	24. Signals										
	25. Glares, frowns										
	26. Holds, pushes, speaks										
	27. Ignores, abandons										

Chapter 5

CONSIDERING THE LEARNING CLIMATE

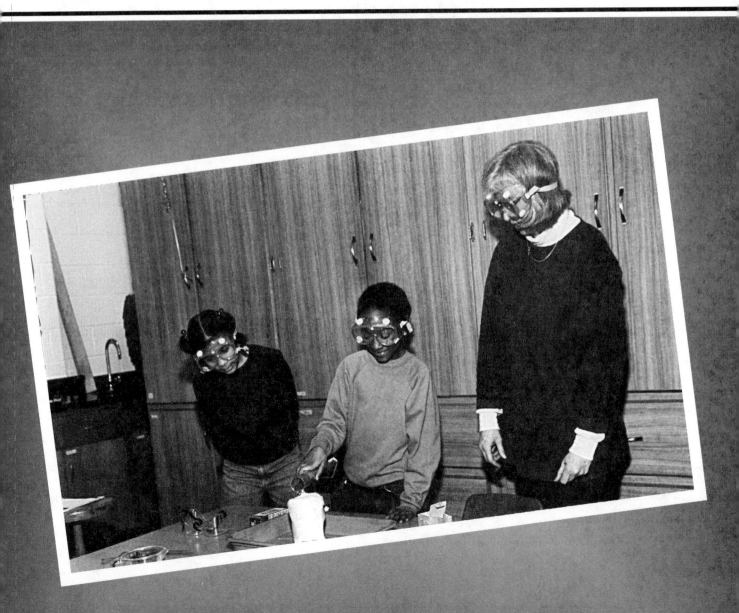

Being Nobody

Have you ever felt like nobody?
Just a tiny speck of air.
When everyone's around you,
And you are just not there.

Karen Crawford (Age 9)

A critical aspect of the classroom relates to how it "feels." Imagine spending several hours every day in a place where you "felt like nobody." How would such feelings affect your learning? Your self-concept? Your belief in your ability? How do teachers create a learning climate that encourages risk-taking and supports development of each individual's abilities? These are crucial questions for observers to consider.

Miracles, selected by Richard Lewis. New York: Simon and Schuster, 1966.

In this chapter, we begin the process of observing by focusing on the learning climate within a classroom. As you will see, learning climate is a multifaceted concept that can be influenced by many different sources. We will study three of these sources—teacher concerns, teacher warmth and control, and social environment—as examples of some of the characteristics of the classroom that can influence and create a positive environment for learning. Let's begin our study by observing in the classrooms of two student teachers—teachers who have taken all of the same university courses together and have done well throughout their teacher preparation program. We'll stop first in Stephanie's class, and then drop in on Jan.

As we enter her classroom, Stephanie greets us with a quick smile, encourages us to make ourselves comfortable on the beanbags and other chairs around the room, and then kneels to talk with Erika. Erika's drooping shoulders straighten as she searches Stephanie's eyes. Suddenly she reaches toward Stephanie's shoulder, touches it lightly, and smiles. Abruptly, she turns to join her six-year-old peers at their table.

Stephanie shares Erika's concern with us: "She's worried that Ms. Martinez will send her out of the room for forgetting her poem. Poor thing. She's so afraid to talk to anyone. I try to show her I want to hear what she says."

A few minutes later, Stephanie joins a reading group on the rug. Seven first- and second-graders read aloud with her, often interrupting the flow to share personal connections to the story, or to ask questions about the text. Expertly, Stephanie weaves their comments into the plot, and then gently resumes the reading. William is a handful—rocking back and forth and tugging at Jennifer's jacket. Stephanie doesn't miss a beat as she hugs him to her side; she never breaks eye contact with José, who spontaneously volunteers what he thinks will happen next in the story.

"Do you think so too, William?" Stephanie asks. Calmed by her touch, William stares down at the pages before him. "I know William has something wonderful to tell us," Stephanie confides to the others. William looks at her, his eyes widening in surprise. "You think . . ." Stephanie prompts. She nods at William, serenely.

"I . . . I . . . I just think Grandma is mean . . ." William offers tentatively.

Stephanie laughs delightedly, hugging William with her right arm—and everyone else in the group with her sparkling eyes. "You know what, William? I've been thinking that very same thing!"

As we leave, we wave good-bye to Stephanie, silently mouthing our thanks. She winks, and we head down the hall to Jan's room. Our short discussion centers on how hard it is to believe that Stephanie has been student teaching for only two weeks. When we enter Jan's classroom, we find a row of chairs placed across the back of the room. Jan is already conducting class, so we quietly file in and take our places along the wall.

Jan presides at the overhead projector, red pen in hand. "Maria?" she intones. "Prewriting." "Kathleen?" "Drafting." One by one each child reports his or her progress within the five-stage writing process. Jan prints each response carefully on a "State of the Class" transparency.

"All right. Time for writing conferences. First student?" Jan scans her clipboard. "Ah yes, Nick. Mario, to the waiting chair. Everyone else to your work." Seated in rigid rows spaced at equal intervals throughout the room, students rummage through their desks for writing materials. Silently, Nick and Mario approach a small table at the back of the room as Jan settles into a chair at its head. Clutching a dog-eared paper, Nick sits beside Jan while Mario slips into the "waiting chair" a few feet away. Turning the pages on her clipboard, Jan queries in a businesslike voice: "Name?"

We wonder if we've heard correctly. Surely Jan knows Nick's name.

"Nick Mariani," Nick answers softly. We strain to hear his voice.

Jan writes Nick's name on a checklist on the clipboard. The form includes spaces for each phase of the writing process.

"Now, let's see. Have you completed a group response sheet?" Nick nods. Jan makes a notation.

"An editing checklist?" Another nod. Another notation.

"Very well then. You may read your piece aloud to me. Wait! What is that word?" Jan points accusingly at the offending letters on Nick's paper. "C-o-o-k-y? Is that how you spell cookie? Perhaps you'd better look this over again before we conference."

Eyes downcast, Nick slides from the chair and slinks toward his desk. At Jan's insistent nod, Mario replaces Nick in the hot seat.

We watch the diminutive fourth-grader crumple into his chair and lay his head on his desk. As we move our eyes toward the floor, we wonder what Nick's story was about.

As you imagine yourself having observed both teachers, what are you thinking about the learning climate in their classrooms? Jan and Stephanie have much in common. Both are twenty-one years old and were raised in middle-class families. They were assigned to the same university cohort and achieved excellent grades in their teacher education courses. For five months, they observed their cooperating teachers and completed practice teaching in the same elementary school. The cooperating teachers working with Jan and Stephanie assist with the same university cohort every year. How, then, do we account for differences between Jan and Stephanie in the classroom? How is it that Stephanie readily connects with her learners—draws them out and draws us in? And how is it that Jan manages to proceduralize all her interactions with her learners to the point that her intended child-centered focus is obscured?

Perhaps Jan and Stephanie simply differ in personality, or in their approaches to children and classroom tasks. Or perhaps they are merely exhibiting different levels of concern associated with the challenges of beginning teaching (Fuller, 1969). As we consider some dimensions of creating a classroom learning climate, perhaps we can also gain insight into the differences we have observed between Jan and Stephanie.

DIMENSIONS OF LEARNING CLIMATE

As you can tell from the climate in these two classrooms, the learning environment is an important lens through which to view life in classrooms because of its effects on how teachers teach and how students learn. We can imagine how students in Stephanie's classroom might respond to the spontaneity and risk-taking required for learning compared to the students in Jan's room. Not surprisingly, researchers have proposed and studied a model of classroom behavior that identifies the climate of the classroom as a cause of many subsequent events that occur within it (Fraser & Walberg, 1991; Getzels & Thelen, 1960). Fraser and Walberg's model, illustrated in Figure 5.1, places classroom climate in an important moderating role in determining classroom behavior.

FIGURE 5.1   Three Dimensions of Classroom Behavior

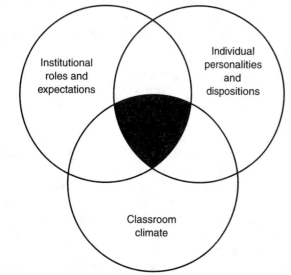

We see from Figure 5.1 that one influence on classroom behavior comes from institutional roles and expectations. *Roles* are partly defined by institutions, such as schools, that bestow on individuals certain obligations, responsibilities, and privileges. Groups, such as students and teachers, interpret and assume these roles, which come with certain expectations that guide their behavior. For example, common role expectations for students are that they come to class, get good grades, conform to the rules of the classroom, and get along with others. For teachers, role expectations include planning lessons that follow the curriculum, managing the classroom, and raising each student's level of achievement during the school year.

A second influence on classroom behavior comes from the individual *personalities* and *dispositions* of the students and teachers within a classroom. Primary elements of this dimension are the abilities and past experiences of individuals that create dispositions, or tendencies to act in a certain way. Cultural beliefs and practices vary from home to home and from student to student, and exert a large influence on what students value and believe to be appropriate. Just as you have developed particular lenses for viewing and understanding your world, so, too, do young learners come to school with personal lenses that affect how they make sense of the world around them. Although students of a particular group may share some (or even many) cultural norms, each individual student's lens will still be unique in many ways. For example, even though two children come from apparently similar cultural and economic backgrounds, one child's world view and resultant disposition may motivate him to volunteer for a class assignment; the other child, placed in the same situation, will choose to skip school rather than be singled out for a particular project.

For the teacher, the influence of classroom climate may be the most important dimension affecting classroom behavior. Unlike institutional roles and expectations and individual personalities and dispositions, which are often beyond a teacher's control, many aspects of the classroom climate can be established and maintained by the teacher's efforts. Indeed, a positive classroom climate can moderate the dispositions and expectations of class members, which in turn can influence the behavior of individuals, as well as of the entire class. This is accomplished by the creation of an atmosphere—or climate—that encourages some classroom behaviors and discourages others, without the aid of formally stated rules or procedures. This is why the learning climate within a classroom has become an important area of research: If properly established, learning climate can promote both high expectations to perform and a commitment to learn.

We will study three different, but related, approaches to classifying and observing the learning climate. One of these will lead us to explore the concerns of the teacher, which can be influential in determining a climate for learning. Research has suggested that whether a teacher is primarily concerned with self ("Can I get through the day?"), the teaching task ("How can I cover the content?"), or her impact on students ("Are my students learning?") makes a difference in establishing an effective learning climate. Next, we will look at the dimensions of teacher warmth and control. Although often expressed as a single dimension, we will present some advantages and ways of observing these elements as two separate but compatible dimensions. Finally, we will explore the interpersonal or social relationships among students, and between students and teacher, that can establish either more or less effective contexts for achieving instructional goals within a classroom.

TEACHER CONCERNS

Before we discuss the influence of a teacher's concerns in establishing an effective learning environment, let's visit Mr. Jenkins' seventh-grade social studies class. Mr. Jenkins, a first-year teacher, was observed during the first month of school. As you read the ethnographic record shown in Example 5.1, think of the kinds of concerns or worries that Mr. Jenkins seems to have. You may want to make some notes in the margin as you read to remind you of what you notice.

What did you notice about Mr. Jenkins and his class? What seems to be the source of greatest concern for this teacher? If you are a typical beginning teacher, your thoughts and concerns, like those of Mr. Jenkins, will probably focus first on your own well being, and then later on the teaching task, and eventually on your students' mastery of material. According to Fuller (1969), a progression from concern about oneself (Will the students like me? Can I control the class?) to concern about the task at hand (Are there sufficient instructional materials? Is there time to cover all the content?), to concern about student understanding (Are the pupils learning? Can they apply what they've learned?) occurs commonly among new teachers—even among student teachers. Fuller speculated that concerns for *self*, *task*, and *pupil* are the natural stages that most teachers pass through, representing a developmental growth pattern extending over months, and even years, of a teacher's career. Although some teachers may pass through these stages more quickly than others and at different levels of intensity, Fuller (1969) suggested that almost all teachers

can be expected to move from one to another, with the most effective and experienced teachers expressing student-centered concerns at a high level of commitment.

Fuller (1969) developed her theory, now known as the *concerns theory*, from a careful analysis of recorded transcripts of interviews with student teachers. Over an extended period of time, these records were used to identify and classify problems that student teachers experienced, and the concerns they expressed about these problems. These expressed concerns, when grouped into developmental and sequential stages, showed that student teachers with the least experience were most concerned about self and self-survival; student teachers with more experience and in-service teachers were more concerned about student achievement and learning.

Stated in its simplest terms, the concerns theory describes the learning process for a prospective teacher as a natural flow from concerns for self (teacher) to task (teaching) to impact (pupil). The physical, mental, and emotional state of the prospective teacher plays an important role in the shift of focus from self to task to impact. Lack of adequate knowledge or emotional support during the critical preteaching and student teaching experience can result in a slower, more labored shift of focus from self to task. This, in turn, can result in a failure on the part of the teacher to reach a concern for his impact on students.

There are several other implications to Fuller's (1969) concerns theory. Some teachers might return to an earlier stage of concern (for example, from a concern for pupils back to a concern for task) as a result of suddenly having to teach a new grade or subject. Or teachers might move from a concern for task back to a concern for self as a result of having to teach in a new and unfamiliar school. Thus, teacher concerns may not always be determined developmentally; they can be context-dependent as well. However, the time spent in a stage the second time is expected to be shorter than the first. Further, the three stages of concern need not be exclusive of one another. A teacher could have several concerns in one area, yet still have concerns of less intensity in one or both of the other stages.

Think back to the descriptions of Jan and Stephanie at the beginning of this chapter. Knowing what you now know about the concerns theory, how might you account for at least some of the differences in the two classrooms? It may help you to consider a list of concerns typically expressed by teachers (and the stages they reflect) and imagine whether Stephanie or Jan would agree with the expressions. Do you see any connections between the predominant areas of concern shown in Figure 5.2

EXAMPLE 5.1

Name of Teacher: Mr. Jenkins

Subject of Observation: A seventh-grade social studies class.

1. Ss (students) have just completed filing in for
2. class. T (teacher) begins class promptly at bell,
3. saying that some parents have called about
4. last week's especially long assignment.
5. T tells Ss not to complain to their parents
6. and that in the future, long assignments will
7. be given extra credit. T picks up with
8. Chapter 6 on who is allowed to vote. Asks
9. the minimum voting age. Class blurts out
10. several different answers in unison. One S
11. says, "When you can drink you can vote."
12. T retorts that only one S is allowed to speak
13. at a time in his class, then calls on Sue. Sue
14. responds that the voting age has nothing to
15. do with the legal age for drinking. Some in
16. the class show disagreement by shaking their
17. heads. T then points out that individual
18. states control the legal age to buy alcoholic
19. beverages, but the federal government
20. sets the voting age. T asks if everyone under-
    stands
21. that. Most of the class nods. T reminds
22. class of a school rule against speaking out,
23. and that the principal listens in on the
24. P.A. system. Two Ss start bickering over the
25. answer, and T tells one to change desks with
26. another S seated in the back of the room.
27. Class quiets down, and T reads from text the
28. constitutional amendment governing the
29. voting age. T explains that there
30. never seems to be enough time for class dis-
    cussion,
31. so that's why he has to read from the textbook.
32. Next, T asks for a show of hands indicating
33. how many Ss really know the procedure for
34. registering to vote. About half the class
35. raises their hands. T says that a pamphlet
36. describing how to register will be placed at the
37. learning center for those who need it
38. to complete their last assignment. T
39. indicates that the text doesn't contain enough
40. information to complete the assignment, but
41. that reference texts from his
42. personal library will be placed at the learning
43. center. Ss are reminded once again that anyone
44. who dislikes the way he is doing things in the
45. class should see him before complaining to
46. their parents. T indicates the class must move
47. on to keep up with Ms. Bennett's class, who
48. will be taking the test at the same time.
49. T continues by asking, "Where do people vote?"
50. One S responds by asking if they can discuss
51. why in some states you're old enough to vote,
52. but not old enough to buy alcohol. T responds
53. that discussions like that will take place only
54. when the class has proved it can behave
55. in a responsible manner and show respect.
56. Someone shouts out, "That's not fair," and T
57. indicates that he will assign punishment
58. for those who speak out. Reminds class of the
59. rule on speaking out mentioned the first
60. class day. T picks up with a presentation of
61. the material in Chapter 6 on places to vote.

---

and the classroom learning climate established by Jan and Stephanie?

A Teacher Concerns Instrument

As you learned in Chapter 4, it is often easier to "see" a psychological construct, such as teacher concerns, when it is in the form of a measuring instrument. Researchers have created an instrument that allows us to measure teacher concerns (Borich, 1997; Rogan, Borich, & Taylor, 1992). Instrument 5.1 applies a five-point rating scale to a series of concerns statements. To acquaint yourself with the concerns theory and the instrument, read each of the items

FIGURE 5.2   Areas of Concern

Self Concerns

I'm worried about whether the students really like me or not.
I'm under pressure a lot of the time.
I worry about doing well when a supervisor (or visitor) is present.

Task (Instructional) Concerns

I lack the freedom to initiate innovative instructional ideals.
I'm concerned about the availability and quality of instructional materials.
I worry about adequately presenting all the material.

Impact (Student Needs) Concerns

I'm concerned about increasing students' feelings of accomplishment.
It's important to me to recognize the social and emotional needs of students.
I'm concerned about challenging unmotivated students.

and ask yourself: When I think about teaching, how concerned am I about this? Use the scale to indicate your level of concern, placing your responses in the boxes to the left. After you complete the scale, we'll show you how to score your responses.

The items representing the dimensions of self, task, and impact are:

Self	Task	Impact
2	1	5
4	3	15
8	6	17
9	7	19
13	10	22
14	11	23
18	12	29
20	16	34
24	21	36
26	25	37
28	27	38
30	31	39
32	33	41
35	40	43
44	42	45

To determine your score, total the number of responses in each of the three categories of concern—self, task, and impact. The higher your score in a category (out of a maximum 75 per category), the more you are identified with that stage of concern. An average rating for each of the three areas can be computed by summing responses to items in each category and dividing by the number of items completed.

The concerns instrument, intended as a self-report, indicates a teacher's level of concern for each of its 45 items. Imagine how helpful it would be to our understanding of their teaching if we could ask Jan, Stephanie, and Mr. Jenkins to complete the

concerns instrument you just filled in. We'd gain important insights into why each teacher acted as he or she did. When you observe teachers, you may wonder how their personal concerns may be influencing the learning climate in the classroom. In most instances, simply asking the teacher in whose classroom you will be observing to complete the instrument will be enough to determine that teacher's predominant stage of concern. The instrument can usually be completed in about 10 minutes, and teachers will often cooperate out of personal interest and curiosity about their concerns.

Knowing about the concerns instrument can be helpful for your own professional development as well. You can complete the concerns instrument at the beginning of and again at the end of your student teaching or field observation experience, noting any changes in the three areas of concern over time. The sum of the scores for each of the three areas of concern (maximum = 75) can be recorded in the format below, shown here with example data.

Stage	Beginning	End	Change
Self	60	45	−15
Task	45	60	+15
Impact	15	30	+15

This example profile indicates a shift of concern from self to task and from self to impact. This is typical of student teachers who spend about a semester in a field experience. Smaller shifts following this same pattern are not uncommon, however, after a semester of in-school observation without practice teaching. Larger shifts, particularly from task to impact, are frequently noted for beginning in-service teachers during their first two to three years of teaching.

Observing Teacher Concerns in the Classroom

Now, let's look more closely at some of the behavioral signs in a classroom that could indicate a teacher's concern for self, task, and impact, and how these concerns can influence the learning climate. For this observation we will return to the ethnographic record of Mr. Jenkins's class. Recall from Chapter 4 that an ethnographic record reports events sequentially as they occur. The observer records everything that occurs, without selecting a specific focus or incident.

As you reread the record of Mr. Jenkins's classroom, your goal will be to identify those lines of the record that indicate a concern for self, task, or impact. Before beginning, go back and label each item on the concerns instrument with an *S, T,* or *I* to remind you of the stage of concern to which each item belongs. Read each set of items (2, 4, 8, etc.; 1, 3, 6, etc.; 5, 15, 17, etc.) as a unit to get a feel for the kind of behaviors that reflect each of the three levels of concern (self, task, impact). Then reread the record, placing an *S, T,* or *I* in the margin when you see any sign of these three areas of concern. You may then want to reread the record with a partner, checking the accuracy of the signs of concerns you noted in the margin and adding others.

Although you may have found others, the following are some of the lines on this ethnographic record the observer indicated contained references to concerns for self, task, and impact. Let's examine these to see if any single stage of concern emerges.

Self	Task	Impact
3–7	29–32	20–21
22–23	35–43	32–34
43–46		
46–48		
52–55		
57–60		

Notice that, according to this observer's judgment, all three stages are represented, but that more entries appear under self concerns than for the other two stages. To substantiate this teacher's predominant stage of concern, the observer might point to three themes in the dialogue related to self: the teacher's need (a) to control the class, (b) to be liked by the class, and (c) to be the final and perhaps only authority. These themes are not uncommon among beginning teachers who, on one hand, may be unsure of their ability to manage the class and, on the other, want to be liked and respected as an authority. These behaviors often originate with a concern for self, which can unintentionally promote a learning climate in which the teacher vacillates be-tween being overly permissive to gain the cooperation of students and overly restrictive to maintain control of the class. There is, therefore, a mixture of climates. Both cooperation and control are being sought, but in different ways. The result, with students attempting to follow in whatever direction (cooperation or control) the pendulum may be swinging at any given moment, can be confusing.

Although our record is too brief to indicate the typical climate that may prevail in this classroom, it does portray a number of contradictions that might spell trouble for this teacher at a later time. Some of the opposing forces that may have been set in motion by this teacher's self concerns are

Leniency vs. rigor
Cooperation vs. obedience
Choral responses vs. individual responses
Teacher facts vs. student opinion

As we consider Mr. Jenkins's class, it appears that the students received little, if any, information about where the teacher stood on these issues. How lenient would the teacher be on difficult assignments? When was disobedience to classroom rules to be taken seriously? When would choral responses to indirect questions be permitted? These are some of the questions left unanswered because this teacher is juggling a need to be liked and respected with a need to be in control. Every teacher has these needs, but it is important that a concern for self be balanced with concerns for task and impact if an optimal learning climate is to be established.

Let's look at another record indicating a different emphasis. Let's imagine that an observer has completed the ethnographic record shown in Example 5.2 of Ms. Chau presenting the same lesson. Again, try to identify and code any lines you believe reflect a concern for self, task, and impact by placing an *S, T,* or *I* beside them.

The following are some of the lines from the ethnographic record that an observer might have indicated contain some reference to a concern for self, task, and impact. Although you may have found some others, let's examine these to see if any single stage of concern emerges.

Self	Task	Impact
8–10	10–13	5–8
	26–30	13–15
	43–45	49–51
	51–55	56–59
	59–62	67–68
	69–71	72–74

Contrary to the previous record, this one has more indications of task and impact concerns. Notice the change from a focus on self to a focus on instructional

EXAMPLE 5.2

Name of Teacher: Ms. Chau

Subject of Observation: A seventh-grade social studies class.

1. Ss have just completed filing in for class.
2. T begins class promptly at the bell. T tells
3. class that today they will discuss who
4. can vote and how votes are cast in a national
5. election. T says this will serve as a
6. review of Chapter 6 and provide an chance
7. to catch up for anyone having trouble with
8. Chapter 6. T acknowledges that last week's
9. homework assignment was difficult, but not to
10. complain to their parents. To help any Ss
11. still having difficulty, a reference library
12. helpful in completing the assignment
13. has been set up at the learning center. T offers to
14. read and make comments on anyone's draft
15. before they turn it in. Calls on Bobby to tell the
16. class what the minimum voting age is for an
17. election. Bobby says he thinks it's 21 because
18. that's the legal age to buy alcohol. T asks
19. if all the laws that govern the behavior of
20. citizens within a state are the same across
21. states. Bobby doesn't say anything. T says,
22. "What about the speed limit?" Bobby then
23. remembers that his family had to
24. drive at different speeds, depending on what
25. state they were in. T then says, "That applies to
26. the legal drinking age, also." Points out a
27. number of examples not in text illustrating
28. the independence of states to establish their
29. own laws; for example, laws pertaining to
30. safety, banking, and purchase of alcohol.
31. T asks another student "When would it be
32. important that the behavior of citizens be the
33. same across all states?" Calls on Betty, whose
34. hand is raised. Betty answers, "When the
35. behavior being governed pertains to the nation
36. as a whole." T responds, "Such as election of
37. the president of the United States." T then asks
38. what the minimum voting age is for a national
39. election. Two Ss start bickering over the correct
40. answer. T then asks one of these students to read
41. a page in the text covering the constitutional
42. amendment pertaining to the minimum voting
43. age. When S finishes, T asks the second student
44. to summarize the two most important points
45. read by the first student. S says that
46. state and federal laws can be different, but
47. laws pertaining to the nation are always the
48. same across states, and that the minimum voting
49. age has been set at 18 for everyone. T praises
50. both students, then moves on to how one
51. registers to vote. T gives students a handout that
52. paraphrases a pamphlet called "How to Vote,"
53. which has been placed at the learning center.
54. T says the handout should make completing last
55. week's homework assignment easier. Goes
56. over six points on handout, and then checks for
57. understanding by asking Ss to recall one
58. point on the handout from memory until all
59. six are covered. T indicates that last
60. week's homework assignment should help
61. in reviewing these six points before the
62. exam next week. T then starts
63. discussion on where to vote in a national
64. election. S interrupts by asking if they
65. can discuss why in some states you're old
66. enough to vote but not old enough to buy
67. alcohol. T acknowledges the question by
68. adding, "Or old enough to go to war but not
69. yet old enough to vote." T says, "Let's cover
70. the section in the text on 'places to vote,'
71. which will be on the test, and then
72. have a class discussion by dividing
73. class into those who see this as a contradiction
74. and those who do not." T picks up with
75. a presentation of material in Chapter 6 on
76. places to vote.

materials, student expression, and student understanding in these two records. The first indication of this change comes when Ms. Chau acknowledges the difficulty of last week's homework assignment. Instead of avoiding the issue by giving extra credit as Mr. Jenkins did, Ms. Chau provides added references to help in the assignment. This shows a concern for task and impact by encouraging more thoroughly completed assignments.

Another indication of a concern for task and impact is Ms. Chau's strategy of staying with a student longer after a wrong or partially wrong response. For example, the teacher follows up a question to Bobby by asking if all the laws that govern behavior of citizens within a state are the same across states. Bobby doesn't respond, so Ms. Chau follows up again with, "What about the speed limit?" This elicits a satisfactory response. These follow-up questions refine the quality of responses, engage the student in the learning process, and encourage the student to think about, work with, or otherwise act on the content presented. This indicates an increasingly student-centered focus.

Notice also how the potential discipline problem involving two students bickering over the voting age question was turned into a constructive activity. This was accomplished by having the first student read from the text, and the second summarize what was read. Both of these simple assignments kept the students task-oriented, quickly directing them back on-task without disrupting the flow of the discussion.

Other events in this record indicate a concern for task and impact. Ms. Chau focused on the quality of the instructional materials by drawing students' attention to the relationship between the previous week's homework assignment and the upcoming exam. She responded to additional student needs by making a future discussion on the contradictions between the voting age and the minimum age for other social behavior possible.

These two ethnographic records, although brief, were intended to illustrate the subtle but important differences in instruction that can be created by a teacher's concerns for self, task, and impact. Every teacher will have concerns in all three areas, but the balance among the three can significantly affect learning climate. In Ms. Chau's class, there was more concern shown toward students by the teacher, leading to a greater degree of spontaneity and response on the part of the students. Also, some aspects of the classroom (the learning center, handout, and reading from text) were directed at fulfilling student, rather than teacher, needs, leading to a greater degree of cooperation between student and teacher. The point of these two records, however, was not to suggest the superiority of one teaching style over another, but rather to show how the balance of concerns can, over time, affect the learning climate in a classroom. By not being aware of a preponderance of self concerns to the exclusion of task and impact concerns, a teacher runs the risk of unintentionally creating a learning climate that may be contrary to the goals of a lesson. Let's explore next how characteristics of warmth and control can influence classroom behavior, as well as the learning environment.

WARMTH AND CONTROL

Another aspect of classroom climate pertains to teacher warmth and control. For many years the dimensions of warmth and control were studied as opposite ends of a continuum. Some teachers falsely believed that before the first day of class they had to choose either to be warm or in control because, in their minds, to be both would be a contradiction.

For example, a teacher who was accepting of student ideas and allowed spontaneity of expression was "warm"; a teacher who was critical of student ideas and allowed little spontaneity or freedom of choice was "cold."

Early research that used Flanders' (1970) classroom interaction analysis system (Chapter 4) to describe the degree to which a teacher was indirect or direct equated warmth with indirectness and control with directness, thereby placing warmth and control at opposite poles of a continuum. Soar and Soar (1983), however, have suggested thinking of teacher warmth and control as two related, but separate, dimensions, as shown in Figure 5.3. This figure illustrates that different degrees of warmth and control may occur simultaneously, and that behavior on one dimension does not necessarily preclude behavior on the other. Four major combinations emerge from this concept of classroom climate.

The first combination is represented by Quadrant A, in which the teacher is characterized as *cold and controlling*. A teacher who falls in the upper left corner of this quadrant might humiliate and criticize students to control all aspects of their behavior. Actions placed in the lower right corner of this quadrant represent a teacher who provides little praise or reward. This quadrant generally represents a classroom climate that is businesslike and almost always task-oriented, with few interchanges with students that are not initiated by the teacher. It also may be a classroom in which motivation for high-level work is inspired more by a fear of punishment, embarrassment, or, in extreme cases, humiliation than by the expectation of praise, reward, or reinforcement.

FIGURE 5.3 Teacher Warmth and Control on Two Separate Axes (from Soar & Soar, 1983)

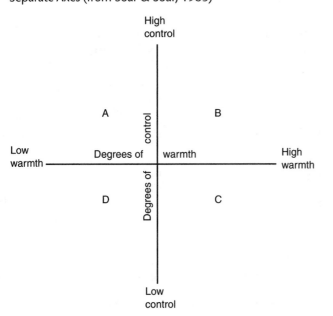

missive. A teacher who falls at the lower right corner of this quadrant praises and rewards students frequently, while providing students almost complete freedom in choosing the limits of their own behavior, which sometimes results in chaos or confusion. A less extreme example of this quadrant would be a classroom in which praise and rewards are apparent, but student spontaneity (for example, calling out) and risk-taking behavior are limited to certain times (group discussion, problem-solving activities) or certain types of content (for example, social studies but not math). During these times, the teacher acts more as a moderator or participant, guiding and directing, but not controlling, classroom behavior. This quadrant represents a classroom climate in which students have considerable freedom in how and when to speak, and in which the teacher's warm and nurturing attitude toward students is for the most part conveyed nonverbally through a mutually agreed upon set of classroom rules.

The fourth quadrant represents a classroom that is *cold and permissive.* A teacher who falls at the lower right corner of this quadrant spends most of the time scolding and criticizing students, but has few classroom rules to control or limit the behavior being criticized. Such an extreme climate sometimes prevails in a classroom taught by a substitute teacher. In these classrooms, selected students may take advantage of the teacher's unfamiliarity with classroom rules and act out, thereby initiating scolding or criticizing by the teacher. Because the classroom rules normally in place are unknown to the substitute, there are no rules to fall back on to prevent misbehavior from recurring continually. The substitute's role is to keep order, not to create or discover the rules; much of his behavior is an attempt to "hold the line" by criticizing, reprimanding, and punishing, if need be, to keep the class under control. A less extreme example of this quadrant would include some coverage of content as a result of student-initiated responses, interspersed with periodic delays for classroom management and misbehavior. This quadrant is characterized by a lack of task orientation and teacher control over the subject matter content, and by frequent scolding, criticizing, and reprimanding.

The second type of classroom climate is represented by Quadrant B, in which the teacher is *warm but controlling.* If warmth were seen as a contradiction of control, as in some early definitions of classroom climate, this quadrant could not occur in practice. However, high degrees of both warmth and control can operate simultaneously. A teacher who falls in the upper right corner of this quadrant associates almost every desirable student behavior with some expectation of reward. The result may well be an almost suffocating climate in which students have little if any room to pursue a behavior or activity on their own. Only those behaviors that have been previously identified by the teacher are eligible for a reward—all others are presumably less worthy. As Soar and Soar (1983) have noted, this may create a classroom climate in which students have little "wiggle room" to pursue any independent behavior because of the tightly managed praise-and-reward system established by the teacher. A less extreme and more desirable portion of this quadrant (toward the lower left) would represent a classroom that balances rewards and consequences, thus promoting a climate of both warmth and control. This quadrant differs from Quadrant A primarily in that motivation for good behavior comes from a well-defined and consistently applied system of *praise and rewards*. In Quadrant A, good behavior results from a well-defined and consistently applied system of *rules and/or punishment.*

The third classroom climate is characterized by Quadrant C, in which the teacher is *warm and per-*

Figure 5.4 summarizes the most obvious characteristics of the four types of classroom climate. A number of unique features can be identified for the dimensions of control and warmth. For the dimension of control, student spontaneity, risk-taking behavior, and student-initiated responses (low control) and teacher talk, task orientation, and teacher authority (high control) are key ingredients. For the dimension of warmth, use of praise and rewards, use

FIGURE 5.4   Four Types of Classroom Climate

A **High Control** **Low Warmth**	B **High Control** **High Warmth**	C **Low Control** **High Warmth**	D **Low Control** **Low Warmth**
High task orientation	Clearly identified and frequent use of rewards for desirable behavior	Frequent use of praise and reinforcement	Frequent scolding and criticizing
Frequent use of punishment or humiliation		Informal classroom rules	Few classroom rules
Lack of praise, reward, or reinforcement	Unsolicited student responses discouraged	Students have say in establishing limits on their own behavior	Students frequently call out
Mostly teacher-initiated interchanges	High task orientation		Teacher talk focuses on minimizing misbehavior
High amount of time devoted to teacher talk	Mostly teacher-initiated interchanges	Student spontaneity and risk-taking behavior allowed	Classroom lacks task orientation
	High amount of time devoted to teacher talk	Teacher acts as moderator or participant	Frequent delays for classroom management and reprimands

of student ideas, and responsiveness to student requests (high warmth) and amount of criticism, scolding and reprimanding, frequent reference to formal rules and procedures, and use of punishment (low warmth) are key ingredients.

Dimensions of Warmth and Control

Instruments 5.2 and 5.3 delineate the dimensions of warmth and control using seven-point rating scales. Each scale item is completed according to how frequently or infrequently the behavior (item) occurs, indicated by the words *high* and *low*, and is scored according to the numbers shown under each blank. The average rating from each scale can be placed on the axes of Instrument 5.4 to determine the quadrant that best represents the climate of the classroom being observed. The two averages, one for control and the other for warmth, are entered as a dot in the proper quadrant. For example, an average rating of 6.6 on warmth and 6.0 on control corresponds to Quadrant B, indicated by the dot on Instrument 5.4. Such a classroom would be characterized as having a high degree of warmth and a considerable degree of control. Verbal descriptions corresponding to the average rating computed for each scale can be used to describe different quadrants. Some example descriptions are shown in Table 5.1.

TABLE 5.1   Verbal Descriptions

Average Scale Rating	Warmth Dimension	Control Dimension
1	No warmth	No control
2	Slight amount of warmth	Slight amount of control
3	Small amount of warmth	Small amount of control
4	Neutral/50-50	Neutral/50-50
5	Fair amount of warmth	Fair amount of control
6	Considerable amount of warmth	Considerable amount of control
7	High degree of warmth	High degree of control

The nearest whole number can be used to determine the best verbal description. For example, a classroom rated 2.1 on the scale pertaining to warmth and 3.3 on the scale pertaining to control could be described as "slightly warm, with a small amount of control." A classroom rated 6.3 and 1.8 on warmth and control, respectively, could be described as "considerably warm, with a slight amount of control."

Behavioral Signs of Warmth and Control

A related approach to observing the dimensions of warmth and control is to look for the presence or absence of specific behavioral signs that indicate these two dimensions. Recall from Chapter 4 that the observation of a large number of specific, discrete units of behavior that could be judged present or absent during a time interval would be recorded using a sign system. Unlike a counting system, which records the presence of a behavior practically each time it occurs, a sign system records a behavior only once—no matter how many times it occurs during the designated interval.

Instrument 5.5 represents a sign system for observing classroom climate using twenty-eight discrete behaviors that correspond to the dimensions of warmth and control. Fourteen behaviors, equally divided between warm and cold, measure the degree of warmth displayed in a classroom; fourteen additional behaviors, equally divided between high and low, measure the degree of control in a classroom. Items for the control dimension were taken from the "Teacher Practices Observation Record" (Brown, 1968). Items for the warmth dimension were written to parallel, in number and type, the items measuring control (Borich, 1994). The result is a 28-item, 4-part sign observation system suitable for measuring classroom climate in terms of both warmth and control. Notice that the behaviors relevant to these two dimensions are recorded in four 15-minute blocks, requiring an hour of observation. This time period is intended to cover a lesson, and can be adjusted by dividing the time allotted to a lesson into four equal parts. One of the advantages of recording classroom climate over several time intervals is the opportunity to note changes from the beginning to the end of a lesson. In this example, four complete records of classroom climate will have been obtained at the end of a single observation period. As you observe how classroom climates vary among teachers, you may find it helpful to complete a sign system instrument like this one. Reading the descriptors and looking for a number of different behaviors can help you look past your own assumptions and expectations to see classroom events in greater detail.

One feature of this sign system is that checkmarks can be tallied for each homogeneous set of seven items (behaviors 1–7, 8–14, 15–21, and 22–28), and the results can be positioned within one of the four quadrants shown in Figure 5.3 to indicate the combination of warmth and control that prevails in a classroom. Here is how it's done.

Within each single 15-minute interval of observation, count the number of checkmarks recorded within each of the four areas (high warmth, low warmth, high control, and low control). Remember that in a sign system only one checkmark can be given for each behavior during the time (15-minute) interval. Add up the number of checkmarks within (*not* across) each 15-minute interval in each of the four categories. Thus, the maximum score for teacher high (or low) warmth or teacher high (or low) control is 7, and the minimum score is 0, for each of the four categories within each 15-minute interval.

Now subtract the number of checkmarks for the low-warmth category from the number of checkmarks for the high-warmth category; subtract the number of checkmarks for the low-control category from the number of checkmarks for the high-control category. Use Figure 5.5 to determine the score that corresponds to each of these differences. These scores can then be used to record this classroom's climate on the warmth and control quadrants shown in Instrument 5.4. If you repeat this for each of the four 15-minute intervals, you will have four dots, one for each 15-minutes, and thus will be able to see shifts in learning climate across the duration of a lesson.

For example, if the difference between the number of high- and low-control items (score for low control subtracted from score for high control) is $6 - 4 = 2$, the proper number from Figure 5.5 to record on the control axis in Instrument 5.4 is 5.0. If the difference between the number of high- and low-warmth items (score for low warmth subtracted from score for high warmth) is $2 - 7 = -5$, the proper number to record on the warmth axis is 2.0. Hence, the learning climate quadrant for this 15-minute interval of observation would be Quadrant A (2 on the control axis and –5 on the warmth axis). Using the verbal descriptions provided previously, the learning climate during this 15-minute period of observation would be described as having a slight amount of warmth (2.0) and a fair amount of control (5.0). A dot can be placed in Quadrant A to mark the climate for further reference. This process can be completed for the remaining intervals of observation, and any shift in climate can be recorded by observing the placement of the second, third, and fourth dots in relation to one another. The climate in different classrooms and over longer periods of time (for example, beginning, middle, and end of student teaching) can be recorded in the same way.

SOCIAL ENVIRONMENT

A third approach to observing the learning climate is to measure the social environment that prevails

Figure 5.5 Converting Numbers From the Sign System (Instrument 5.5) to a 7-Point Scale

Subtract score of low-control items from score of high-control items and find new scale score adjacent to it. Repeat this for the low-warmth and high-warmth scores. Then plot these two new values on the warmth and control axes.

Result of subtracting number of checks in low category from number of checks in high category	New scale score (for placement on axis)
7	7.0
6	6.5
5	6.0
4	5.5
3	5.5
2	5.0
1	4.5
0	4.0
−1	3.5
−2	3.0
−3	2.5
−4	2.5
−5	2.0
−6	1.5
−7	1.0

within a classroom. Unlike the observation of teacher concerns and teacher practices related to warmth and control, this approach focuses on the classroom as a unique social system. This social system includes the interpersonal relationships among students, relationships between students and the teacher, and students' perceptions of the social dimensions of a classroom, such as its activities, organization, and level of cooperation.

The concept and rationale for studying a classroom as a social system are based on the work of Parsons and Shills (1951). Parsons (1959) described two functions of school: socialization and allocation. *Socialization* involves helping a learner translate personal wishes about herself into more realistic adult views and perspectives typical of the world outside the classroom. *Allocation* is the process by which learners are prepared and selected for roles and responsibilities outside the classroom, such as more advanced training and occupations. Parsons (1959) believed that these two functions of schooling could be either stimulated or dampened by the social environment that prevails in classrooms.

One of the earliest research studies based on the work of Parsons was conducted by Walberg and Anderson (1968). Walberg (1966) developed a questionnaire that tapped eighteen dimensions of a classroom's social environment to measure the class as a social system. He then gave the questionnaire to students who were enrolled in a new physics cur-

riculum, called Harvard Physics, in fifty-seven classrooms across the country. The intent of the study was to have the students describe the quality of their class as a social system based on the eighteen dimensions, and then determine the degree of relationship between the dimensions and various measures of student achievement, attitude, and creativity. The results of this early study suggested that there was a significant relationship between the social environment in which learning takes place and important school outcomes related to adult roles and responsibilities, such as creativity and achievement.

Dimensions of Social Environment

Subsequent research has helped expand and improve the Parsons' (1959) social climate concept. Fraser and Walberg (1991) have revised Parsons's work to focus on fifteen dimensions that describe the classroom as a social system. These dimensions are listed in the following paragraphs, with brief descriptions based on work by Fraser, Anderson, and Walberg (1982).

1. *Cohesiveness*—When a group of individuals interact for a period of time, a feeling of intimacy or togetherness develops. Too much cohesiveness within a classroom may separate members of the group from nonmembers, and may also reduce the motivation and willingness of some students to become engaged in the learning process. Too little cohesiveness

may discourage students from an allegiance to group norms and encourage them to focus exclusively on their own personal interests and desires.

2. *Diversity*—the extent to which the class provides for different student backgrounds, interests, and activities is important to learning. Too much diversity in a classroom can make teaching difficult, because students may share little in terms of language, culture, and related expectations. On the other hand, too little *apparent* diversity may encourage teachers to believe students are more alike than they are, and thus overlook individual needs.

3. *Formality*—The extent to which behavior within a class is guided by formal rules can influence the flexibility necessary for both teacher and students to achieve stated goals. A classroom with an extensive, or inflexible, system of rules and procedures might be less productive than a classroom with fewer rules that are changed periodically to accommodate changing goals and conditions.

4. *Speed*—Student commitment to the goals of the class is best achieved when students feel they are learning at the same rate as other students. A pace that is too fast will discourage commitment to group goals on the part of less able learners; a pace that is too slow will discourage commitment from more able learners.

5. *Environment*—The classroom's physical environment, including the amount of space and type of equipment, can influence the structure of the group and the relationships among its members. Generally, the more the classroom reflects the world outside, the more opportunity there is to learn. Further, the placement and storage of instructional materials can send a strong message to students. Students who find it difficult to obtain necessary instructional materials (e.g., textbooks, paper, craft materials) are less likely to enjoy and complete assignments, and may feel they have little control over their own learning. Placement of furniture also sends a message to students: Rows of rigidly spaced desks suggest a very different learning climate than that suggested by small groups of desks turned toward one another.

6. *Friction*—This dimension refers to the extent to which certain students are responsible for class tension and hostility among members of the class. The greater the friction, the more time spent on classroom management and the less the classroom is task-oriented.

7. *Goal direction*—Clearly stated goals and their acceptance by the group orient the class and outline expected roles for class members. Students in highly goal-directed classes reach instructional goals more quickly than students in classes where the goals are unspecified.

8. *Favoritism*—This dimension indicates the extent to which some students and the teacher behave in ways that benefit some class members at the expense of others. A classroom in which there are many "favorites" weakens the self-concepts of those who are not favored, and disengages them from a commitment to class goals.

9. *Cliqueness*—Cliques within a class can lead to hostility among class members and engender alternate norms, which may lead to less than optimal group productivity. A high degree of cliqueness can make some students become distracted or off-task, especially during group work, when students may be more loyal to the clique than to the teacher.

10. *Satisfaction*—Whether or not students gain a sense of accomplishment from completing the events and activities that are assigned affects their learning. Low satisfaction, or sense of accomplishment, leads to greater frustration and less interest in the class, eventually reducing a student's desire to achieve.

11. *Disorganization*—Class disorganization is believed to be related to reduced instructional time, and therefore reduced opportunity to learn. Extreme disorganization can result in classroom management problems and large increases in the time needed to achieve instructional goals.

12. *Difficulty*—Generally, students who perceive the content as easy tend to perform more poorly on measures of achievement than those who do not. A degree of perceived difficulty that is too high, however, will make some students give up and disengage from the learning task.

13. *Apathy*—Students who fail to see the purpose or personal relevance of class activities perform more poorly than those who do see the connections between classwork and their lives. Disenchanted students fail to behave according to the accepted group norms, thereby increasing the rate of misbehavior and time spent on classroom management.

14. *Democratic*—This dimension indicates where the class perceives itself on an authoritarian-democratic continuum. Optimal learning may occur under both extremes, depending on the degree of warmth perceived by students. An authoritarian climate in which the teacher is warm and nurturing may be as productive for learning as a democratic climate in which students have greater control over the learning environment.

15. *Competitiveness*—The effect of competitiveness has been shown to differ widely both within and across classrooms. Too little or too much competitiveness is believed to be detrimental to learning, with repetitive cycles of competition and cooperation being optimal. Competitiveness is also valued differently among students from various cultures.

For example, students from a culture that values group norms and sharing will probably be uncomfortable in an individualistic, competitive classroom (Cazden, 1986; Corno & Snow, 1986; Stallings & Stipek, 1986).

Observing the Social Environment of the Classroom

The original version of the learning environment scale reported by Anderson (1973) comprises 105 items, 7 items for each of the 15 dimensions. The students in a class respond to questions about what their class is like, using a strongly agree, agree, disagree, or strongly disagree response format. The instrument can be administered directly to students at the junior high and high school level in 15 to 25 minutes.

To make this scale more suitable for classroom observation, three items have been selected from the original seven constructed for each dimension and rephrased (with the author's permission) from an observer's point of view in Instrument 5.6. Since students in a class are probably more knowledgeable about their class as a social system than an infrequent observer, this revised observer's version asks for information that might be obtained in the course of a small number of observations. For items with insufficient observation, a "no information" response alternative, which is not scored, has been added. The social environment scale should be administered at the end of a series of observations, or when the observer has gained sufficient familiarity with the class being rated. There are three blocks of fifteen items (items 1–15, 16–30, 31–45), with each block containing one item from each dimension. To acquaint yourself with the social environment scale, read the items in Instrument 5.6, try to associate them with a classroom with which you are familiar, and complete the scale as a practice exercise.

After completing the ratings, the three items for each dimension can be averaged. For example, Items 1, 16, and 31 are averaged for the cohesiveness dimension; Items 2, 17, and 32 for the diversity dimension; Items 3, 18, and 33 for the formality dimension; and so on, until averages for all fifteen dimensions have been computed. Although three items for each dimension would not be sufficient to provide dependable scores for research purposes, the averages obtained can help the observer become aware of the various facets of a classroom's social environment. Using the scales to record changes over time (beginning of school year, end of first grading period, etc.), across units of content that can be expected to stimulate or create different social environments (large class, small class), and across different classes (social studies, math, etc.) can acquaint the observer with the highly variable nature of the classroom social environment.

Finally, note that some of the items are worded negatively. The numbers under these items have been reversed so that a larger number always represents a more positive degree of the concept being measured. For several of the dimensions being measured, however, a higher score is not necessarily better for improving classroom achievement, attitude, creativity, or other desirable school behavior. These dimensions are diversity, speed, difficulty, democratic, and competitiveness. Research has not demonstrated that one end of the scale is necessarily more desirable than the other for these five dimensions. A judgment about the degree of their desirability in a given classroom would depend on one's personal beliefs, the types of students being taught, the goals of the instruction, and the presence of other related circumstances that might make a judgment possible (for example, the speed of the presentation is so fast that it creates friction among students, or the content is so difficult that it makes students apathetic and dissatisfied).

Cultural Diversity and the Learning Climate

One of the first things you will notice when observing in classrooms is the wide variety of learning climates both within and across schools. The variety you will observe—in degrees of teacher warmth and control, in the self, task, and impact concerns of teachers, and in the social interactions of learners—will be influenced by the predominant cultures and ethnicities within a school and classroom. For example, Bennett (1990) points out how interactions among students and between students and teachers are influenced by learning styles that are modified by culture. Cooperative learning, peer tutoring, and collaborative problem solving may establish an effective learning climate in one classroom; discussion, review, testing, and feedback may be equally effective in another. Cushner, McClelland, and Safford (1992) indicate how being a member of a subculture, microculture, minority, or ethnic group can influence the nature of interpersonal relationships within a classroom by increasing its cohesiveness, informality, interpersonal harmony, and cooperativeness. Bowers and Flinders (1991) provide examples of how noise level, use of classroom space, turn-taking, and negotiation vary among races, social classes, and ethnicities to create different, but equally productive, learning climates when properly managed and matched to cultural expectations.

Your role as a classroom observer, therefore, is to consider learning climate in the context of the norms and expectations of the school and school district in which you are observing. Cultural and ethnic information you should become aware of prior to or during your observation includes:

❏ Ethnic, racial, and gender composition of the class and school
❏ Predominant family conditions of the majority students (for example, single-parent vs. two-parent households)
❏ Sense of ethnic identity among teachers and students
❏ Levels of student self-concept and motivation
❏ Teacher perceptions and individual differences related to economic and social class

Another influence on learning climate that you will observe involves language variations and abilities. It is important to learn to listen not only to what teachers and students *say*, but also to what they *mean*. As you visit various classrooms and schools, be sensitive to the contextual characteristics that contribute to learning climate within a classroom and a school. Watch for ways that teachers and students show respect for language differences and for ways that misunderstandings occur. Listen for the tone of voice, the choice of words, the length and cadence of utterances; you'll hear a symphony of communication that can help you develop even greater sensitivity to the verbal orchestration of classroom climate.

It is also a good idea to examine your own background from cultural, ethnic, and economic vantage points. Your experiences and expectations will play an important role not only in what you notice about the culture, ethnicity, and economic status of others, but also in how you value what you see. Observing in a classroom without prior examination of your personal beliefs will be less productive than if you have taken some time to consider your own background and biases, and how these may affect what you interpret during classroom observations. This is not to say that our personal beliefs are somehow wrong or less valuable than the beliefs of those we are observing. It is not necessary, desirable, or even possible for an observer to "leave his world view behind." However, periodic examination of our perspective helps us become aware of the powerful interaction between ourselves and others as we observe, interpret, and discover insights about teaching.

In the following chapters, we will explore several other, equally important, lenses for classroom observation. These lenses—classroom management, lesson clarity, instructional variety, task orientation, student engagement in the learning process, student success, and higher thought processes—are always observed in the context of a particular learning climate, and are therefore inseparable from it. As we turn to our next lens—classroom management—keep in mind the significant impact of the dimensions of learning climate in every classroom and on every teacher and student.

ACTIVITIES*

1. In your own words, list five original concerns that you have in the areas of self, task, and impact. Using the following format and examples as a guide, list one observable sign of teacher behavior corresponding to each of your fifteen concern statements.

Self

Concern: whether the students really like me
Sign: planning lessons that incorporate the interests of the students

Task

Concern: covering required material
Sign: completing lesson plans keyed to the curriculum guide

Impact

Concern: challenging unmotivated, less able learners
Sign: directing less complex questions to unengaged learners

2. If you have not already done so, complete the teacher concerns instrument on page 85 for yourself. Calculate your average score for each of the three stages: self, task, and impact. Plan when you will complete the survey a second time, and predict what you think will happen by then.
3. Read Figure 5.6 with a classmate and agree on the stage of concern with which each sign most closely corresponds. If a consensus cannot be reached, state (a) your reasons for the disagreement and (b) what other signs, if observed, would tend to support the stage of concern you have chosen.

---

*Some of the following activities may be grouped into a common activity, divided among classmates, and completed from a single observation.

Sign	Stage of Concern	Other Signs Needed (if any)
1. Dressing smartly	_____	_____
2. Revising the objectives to fit the class	_____	_____
3. Testing slow learners for learning disabilities	_____	_____
4. Reviewing and sumarizing before a big test	_____	_____
5. Telling students their parents can call you at home	_____	_____
6. Complaining about the time devoted to collecting money for school pictures	_____	_____
7. Spending Saturday night writing the week's lesson plans	_____	_____
8. Telling your students that if they act up, you won't be afraid to call their parents	_____	_____
9. Placing troublemakers in the front of the room	_____	_____
10. Creating a list of extra credit readings for those who have already completed their term papers	_____	_____

	Teacher A (Self-Concern)	Teacher B (Task Concern)	Teacher C (Impact Concern)
1.	_____	_____	_____
2.	_____	_____	_____
3.	_____	_____	_____
4.	_____	_____	_____
5.	_____	_____	_____

4. Identify five behaviors that teachers at the levels of concern listed in Figure 5.7 might perform during the first day of the school year.
5. Teachers A, B, C, and D have the following profiles of scores on the teacher concerns instrument:

	Self	Task	Impact
Teacher A	Low	Medium	High
Teacher B	High	Medium	Low
Teacher C	Low	High	High
Teacher D	High	Low	High

FIGURE 5.8 Classroom Climates and Behavior

	High Control/ Low Warmth	High Control/ High Warmth	Low Control/ High Warmth	Low Control/ Low Warmth
1.	_____	_____	_____	_____
2.	_____	_____	_____	_____
3.	_____	_____	_____	_____
4.	_____	_____	_____	_____

One teacher has been teaching for four months; one has taught the same subject in the same school for eight years; one has taught in the same school for eleven years, but recently has been assigned to teach a subject never taught before; the fourth teacher has taught in the same school for six years, but recently was declared "surplus" and reassigned to the same subject in an inner-city vocational school. Which teacher would most likely have which teaching assignment? Why?

6. Using four different observable signs of teacher and/or student behavior, describe a classroom that reflects each of the climates listed in Figure 5.8.

7. Using the scales identified in Instruments 5.2 and 5.3, an observer assigned the following ratings to each item after a one-hour observation. For the six items measuring control, the ob-

server's ratings were 6, 6, 7, 7, 6, 5. For the six items measuring warmth, the ratings were 2, 1, 4, 4, 3, 3. On the axes in Figure 5.9, place a dot representing the climate of this classroom. What verbal descriptions would you use to communicate the meaning of your numerical ratings?

8. Using the sign system in Instrument 5.5, an observer indicated the presence of the following behaviors during the first 15-minute interval: 1, 2, 4, 5, 7, 10, 13, 18, 22, 24, 25, 27, 28. During the fourth 15-minute interval, the observer indicated the presence of the following behaviors: 2, 6, 9, 10, 11, 13, 14, 17, 18, 19, 21, 26, 28. Following the instructions on page 77 and Figure 5.5, convert the number of observable signs in this system to a seven-point scale. Plot the results for both these intervals on the warmth and control axes in Figure 5.9. How did the

FIGURE 5.9 Axes for Activities 7 and 8

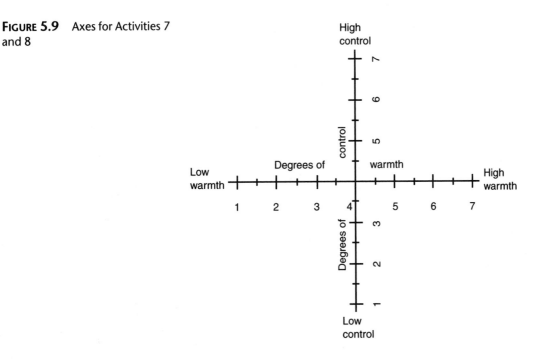

learning climate change across the intervals? What verbal descriptions would you use to describe this classroom at the beginning and at the end of the lesson?

9. For what five dimensions on the social environment scale can either a low or a high numerical rating on a five-point scale represent an undesirable learning environment? For each of the five, describe two learning climates—at opposite ends of the scale—that would be equally detrimental to learning.

10. The following mean scores correspond to ten dimensions of the social environment scale. Interpret their meaning in terms of the degree to which a positive classroom environment is present.

Dimension	Mean Score
1. Cohesiveness	3.5
2. Formality	3.8
3. Environment	2.1
4. Friction	1.2
5. Goal Direction	3.0
6. Favoritism	1.5
7. Cliqueness	4.0
8. Satisfaction	3.3
9. Disorganization	2.5
10. Apathy	3.0

Overall, how would you rate the social environment in this classroom with respect to its potential effect on student achievement, attitude, and creativity?

INSTRUMENT 5.1   Teacher Concerns Instrument

When I think about teaching, how concerned am I about this? Use the scale below to indicate your level of concern

1. Not concerned
2. A little concerned
3. Moderately concerned
4. Very concerned
5. Totally preoccupied

1. ❏   Having insufficient clerical help
2. ❏   Gaining students' respect
3. ❏   Coping with too many extra duties and responsibilities
4. ❏   Doing well when I'm observed
5. ❏   Helping students to value learning
6. ❏   Having insufficient time for rest and class preparation
7. ❏   Getting too little assistance from specialized teachers
8. ❏   Managing my time efficiently
9. ❏   Losing the respect of my peers
10. ❏   Having too little time for grading and testing
11. ❏   Coping with the inflexibility of the curriculum
12. ❏   Having too many standards and regulations set for teachers
13. ❏   Worrying about my ability to prepare adequate lesson plans
14. ❏   Having my inadequacies become known to other teachers
15. ❏   Increasing students' feelings of accomplishment
16. ❏   Dealing with the rigid instructional routine
17. ❏   Diagnosing students' learning problems
18. ❏   Wondering whether the principal thinks there's too much noise in my classroom
19. ❏   Helping each student reach her potential
20. ❏   Obtaining a favorable evaluation of my teaching
21. ❏   Having too many students in my class
22. ❏   Recognizing the social and emotional needs of students
23. ❏   Challenging unmotivated students
24. ❏   Losing the respect of my students
25. ❏   Getting more financial support for my school
26. ❏   Trying to maintain control of the class
27. ❏   Having insufficient time to plan
28. ❏   Getting students to behave
29. ❏   Understanding why certain students make slow progress
30. ❏   Having an embarrassing incident occur in my classroom for which I might be judged responsible
31. ❏   Being unable to cope with troublemakers
32. ❏   Worrying that my peers may think I'm not doing an adequate job
33. ❏   Being able to manage and work with disruptive students
34. ❏   Finding ways to meet students' health and nutrition needs
35. ❏   Appearing competent to parents
36. ❏   Meeting the needs of different kinds of students
37. ❏   Seeking alternative ways to ensure that students learn the subject matter
38. ❏   Understanding cultural differences that can affect students' behavior
39. ❏   Adapting myself to the needs of different students
40. ❏   Coping with the large number of administrative interruptions
41. ❏   Guiding students to intellectual and emotional growth
42. ❏   Working with too many students each day
43. ❏   Getting students to apply what they learn
44. ❏   Teaching effectively when another teacher is present
45. ❏   Motivating students to learn

INSTRUMENT 5.2   Rating
Scale for Classroom Control

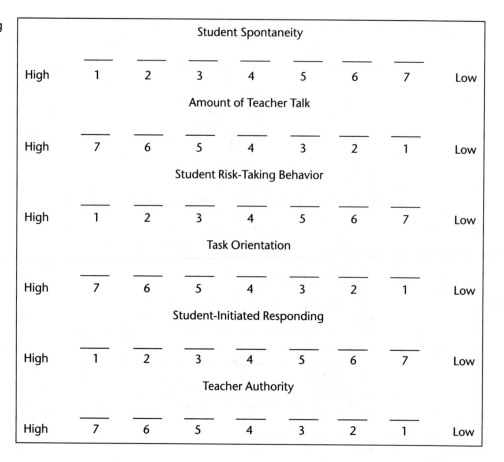

INSTRUMENT 5.3 Rating
Scale for Classroom Warmth

				Use of Praise and Rewards					
	___	___	___	___	___	___	___		
High	7	6	5	4	3	2	1	Low
			Amount of Criticism, Scolding, and Reprimanding						
	___	___	___	___	___	___	___		
High	1	2	3	4	5	6	7	Low
				Use of Student Ideas					
	___	___	___	___	___	___	___		
High	7	6	5	4	3	2	1	Low
			Reference to Formal Rules and Procedures						
	___	___	___	___	___	___	___		
High	1	2	3	4	5	6	7	Low
			Responsiveness to Student Requests						
	___	___	___	___	___	___	___		
High	7	6	5	4	3	2	1	Low
				Use of Punishment					
	___	___	___	___	___	___	___		
High	1	2	3	4	5	6	7	Low

INSTRUMENT 5.4 Classroom Climate for Data From Instruments 5.2 and 5.3

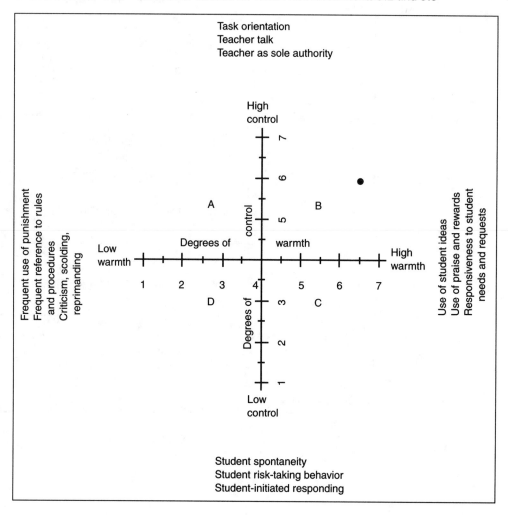

INSTRUMENT 5.5   Sign System for Observing the Dimensions of Classroom Warmth and Control

15-Minute Intervals				Teacher Behaviors Indicating Learning Climate	
1	2	3	4	A.	High Warmth
				1.	Teacher praises or rewards student's behavior.
				2.	Teacher uses student's ideas in presenting lesson.
				3.	Teacher responds to student's expression of need.
				4.	Teacher nods or gestures approvingly.
				5.	Teacher provides clue or hint to student to find right answer.
				6.	Teacher gives encouragement to student after wrong answer.
				7.	Teacher agrees with student or accepts student's feelings.
1	2	3	4	B.	Low Warmth
				8.	Teacher criticizes, scolds, or admonishes.
				9.	Teacher cuts off or interrupts student.
				10.	Teacher calls class's attention to student's deficiencies.
				11.	Teacher ignores student's request to speak.
				12.	Teacher glares or frowns at student.
				13.	Teacher orders or commands student to do something.
				14.	Teacher criticizes wrong answer without giving reason.
1	2	3	4	C.	High Control
				15.	Teacher accepts only one answer as correct.
				16.	Teacher occupies center of attention.
				17.	Teacher expects student to come up with answer teacher has in mind.
				18.	Teacher expects student to know rather than guess answer.
				19.	Teacher asks question that student can answer only by studying the lesson.
				20.	Teacher evaluates work of student by set standard.
				21.	Teacher accepts only answers or suggestions closely related to topic.
1	2	3	4	D.	Low Control
				22.	Teacher organizes learning around student's own problem or question.
				23.	Teacher has student make own selection and analysis of subject matter.
				24.	Teacher has student work independently on what concerns student.
				25.	Teacher makes a wide range of information available.
				26.	Teacher makes doing something center of student's attention.
				27.	Teacher encourages student to put ideas to a test.
				28.	Teacher has student participate actively.

Note: Parts A and B from the author. Parts C and D adapted from *Experimental Mind in Education*, by B. Burton Brown. Copyright © 1968 by B. Burton Brown. Reprinted by permission of Harper & Row, Publishers, Inc.

INSTRUMENT 5.6   Social Environment Scale for Classroom Observers

	Strongly Disagree	Disagree	Agree	Strongly Agree	No Information
1. A student in this class has the chance to get to know all other students (cohesiveness).	1	2	3	4	N/I
2. The class has students with many different interests (diversity).	1	2	3	4	N/I
3. There is a set of rules for the students to follow (formality).	1	2	3	4	N/I
4. Most of the class has difficulty keeping up with the assigned work (speed).	1	2	3	4	N/I
5. The books and equipment students need or want are easily available in the classroom (environment).	1	2	3	4	N/I
6. There are tensions among certain students that tend to interfere with class activities (friction).	1	2	3	4	N/I
7. Most students have little idea of what the class is attempting to accomplish (goal direction).	4	3	2	1	N/I
8. The better students' questions are answered more sympathetically than those of the average students (favoritism).	1	2	3	4	N/I
9. Some students refuse to mix with the rest of the class (cliqueness).	1	2	3	4	N/I
10. The students seem to enjoy their classwork (satisfaction).	1	2	3	4	N/I
11. There are long periods during which the class does nothing (disorganization).	1	2	3	4	N/I
12. Some students in the class consider the work difficult (difficulty).	1	2	3	4	N/I
13. Most students seem to have a concern for the progress of the class (apathy).	4	3	2	1	N/I
14. When group discussions occur, all students tend to contribute (democratic).	1	2	3	4	N/I
15. Most students cooperate rather than compete with one another in this class (competitiveness).	4	3	2	1	N/I
16. Students in this class are not in close enough contact to develop likes and dislikes for one another.	4	3	2	1	N/I
17. The class is working toward many different goals.	1	2	3	4	N/I
18. Students who break the rules are penalized.	1	2	3	4	N/I
19. The class has plenty of time to cover the prescribed amount of work.	4	3	2	1	N/I
20. A comprehensive collection of reference material is available in the classroom for the students to use.	1	2	3	4	N/I
21. Certain students seem to have no respect for other students.	1	2	3	4	N/I
22. The objectives of the class are not clearly recognized.	4	3	2	1	N/I
23. Every member of the class is given the same privileges.	4	3	2	1	N/I
24. Certain students work only with their close friends.	1	2	3	4	N/I
25. There is considerable student dissatisfaction with the classwork.	4	3	2	1	N/I
26. Classwork is frequently interrupted by some students with nothing to do.	4	3	2	1	N/I
27. Most students in this class are constantly challenged.	1	2	3	4	N/I
28. Some members of the class don't care what the class does.	1	2	3	4	N/I
29. Certain students have more influence on the class than others.	4	3	2	1	N/I
30. Most students in the class want their work to be better than their friends' work.	1	2	3	4	N/I

INSTRUMENT 5.6 (continued)

	Strongly Disagree	Disagree	Agree	Strongly Agree	No Information
31. This class is made up of individuals who do not know each other well.	4	3	2	1	N/I
32. Different students are interested in different aspects of the class.	4	3	2	1	N/I
33. There is a right and a wrong way of going about class activities.	4	3	2	1	N/I
34. There is little time in this class for daydreaming.	4	3	2	1	N/I
35. There are bulletin board displays and pictures around the room.	4	3	2	1	N/I
36. Certain students in this class are uncooperative.	1	2	3	4	N/I
37. Most of the class realizes exactly how much work is required.	1	2	3	4	N/I
38. Certain students in the class are favored over others.	1	2	3	4	N/I
39. Most students cooperate equally well with all class members.	4	3	2	1	N/I
40. After an assignment, most students have a sense of satisfaction.	1	2	3	4	N/I
41. The class is well organized and efficient.	4	3	2	1	N/I
42. Most students consider the subject matter easy.	4	3	2	1	N/I
43. Students show a common concern for the success of the class.	4	3	2	1	N/I
44. Each member of the class has as much influence as any other member.	4	3	2	1	N/I
45. Students compete to see who can do the best work.	4	3	2	1	N/I

Chapter 6

FOCUSING ON CLASSROOM MANAGEMENT

Rules

Do not jump on ancient uncles.

Do not yell at average mice.

Do not wear a broom to breakfast.

Do not ask a snake's advice.

Do not bathe in chocolate pudding.

Do not talk to bearded bears.

Do not smoke cigars on sofas.

Do not dance on velvet chairs.

Do not take a whale to visit Russell's mother's cousin's yacht.

And whatever else you do do,

It is better you

Do not.

Karla Kuskin

Rules, rules, and more rules! Is that what you think of when you hear the words *classroom management*? Although effective rules are a part of successful classroom management, by the time you finish reading this chapter, we hope you will associate much more with classroom management than just making and obeying rules.

The Random House Book of Poetry for Children, selected by Jack Prelutsky. New York: Random House, 1983, p. 137.

In this chapter, we continue to explore the process of observing by considering dimensions of classroom management. Classroom management includes many different skills, including the way the teacher arranges the classroom, establishes classroom rules, responds to misbehavior, monitors student activity, selects rewards and reinforcement, and uses daily routines to maintain an efficient and productive learning environment. In this chapter we will introduce some of the most important aspects of classroom management.

If you ask a number of teachers how to handle a particular classroom management issue, you're likely to receive several different, and perhaps even contradictory, responses. Depending upon their own experiences and personal views, teachers approach classroom management from a number of different philosophies. For our purposes, these approaches to dealing with classroom behavior can be grouped into three general traditions.

One tradition emphasizes the critical role of communication and shared problem solving between teacher and students. This approach is called the *humanistic* tradition and is represented by the writings of Ginott (1972) and Glasser (1990, 1986). The second tradition comes from the field of *applied behavior analysis* and is best represented by the writings of Madsen and Madsen (1970), O'Leary and O'Leary (1977), Alberto and Troutman (1986), Jones (1987), and Canter (1989, 1976), who apply behavioristic principles, such as behavior modification, to the classroom. The third approach, which is the most recent, emphasizes skills involved in organizing and managing the classroom. This approach is called the *classroom management* tradition, and its major principles can be found in the writings of Kounin (1970), Doyle (1986), Good and Brophy (1990), and Emmer, Evertson, Clements, and Worsham (1997).

Our discussion in this chapter will emphasize the classroom management tradition. We have chosen to highlight this approach because its principles are derived from research in classrooms, and because it emphasizes the critical role of prevention in managing the classroom.

Successful teachers recognize that research can often provide helpful insights for teaching. In the case of classroom management, a year-long observational study of 27 third-grade teachers in 8 elementary schools yielded several insights about effective classroom management (Emmer, Evertson, & Anderson, 1980). Using the amount of time their students were engaged in the learning process and in off-task behavior after the first three weeks of school, the teachers were classified into two groups: the more effective managers and the less effective managers. Teachers who were categorized as effective classroom managers had significantly higher student engagement rates (more students actively engaged in the goals of the lesson) and significantly lower student off-task behavior throughout the school year. Observation data pertaining to the classroom management procedures of these effective classroom managers were used to compare the two groups.

During the first three weeks of school, observers gathered information on each of the teachers, including room arrangement, classroom rules, consequences of misbehavior, response to inappropriate behavior, consistency of teacher response, monitoring, and praise-and-reinforcement systems. In addition, observers counted the number of students who were on-task or off-task at 15-minute intervals to determine the extent to which students were attending to the teacher.

The more effective managers clearly established themselves as instructional leaders early in the school year. During the first three weeks of school, these teachers spent time working on classroom rules and procedures until students learned them well. Sometimes this decision required teachers to delay content coverage and instead focus on establishing group cohesiveness and socialization and developing a common set of classroom norms. But by the end of the first three weeks, these classes were ready for the rest of the year. In other words, time spent teaching and reinforcing classroom rules and procedures at the beginning of the school year paid off in reduced time spent on management for the rest of the year.

In contrast to the more effective managers, the less effective managers did not work out effective management procedures in advance. This was especially true for the first-year teachers who were observed. For example, the researchers described one new teacher who had no procedures for using the bathroom, pencil sharpener, or water fountain, and as a result, the children seemed to come and go at will, complicating the teacher's instructional tasks.

The poorer managers, like the better managers, had rules, but there was a difference in the way the rules were presented and followed up. In some cases the rules were vague: "Be in the right place at the right time." In other cases they were introduced casually, without discussion, leaving it unclear to most children when and where a rule applied.

The poorer managers were also ineffective monitors of their classes. This was caused, in part, by the lack of efficient routines for pupil activities. In other cases, it was the result of teachers removing themselves from active surveillance of the class to work at length with a single child. The combination of vague and untaught rules and poor procedures for monitoring students frequently left class members lacking sufficient guidance to direct their own activities. Children both need and want specific boundaries for classroom behavior, and the less effective managers failed to define and maintain these boundaries for their students.

Another characteristic of the less effective managers was that the consequences of appropriate and inappropriate behavior were not clear, consistent, or immediate in their classrooms. For example, sometimes teachers issued general criticisms that failed to identify a specific student or a particular event ("*Everyone* needs to get to work now"). Some teachers frequently warned children but did not follow through, even after several warnings ("I've told you several times we're going to lose recess if this continues"). These kinds of comments allowed children to push the teacher to the limits, causing even more problems. Other teachers issued vague disciplinary messages ("You're being too noisy") that were not focused enough to capture the attention of the child, or children, for whom they were intended. Clearly, deficiencies in the areas of creating and enforcing rules, establishing routines, monitoring behavior, and giving consistent praise and reinforcement negatively affected the overall management and organization of the classroom, resulting in a wider range of pupil misconduct, off-task behavior, and disengagement from instructional goals. After only a few weeks had elapsed in such classrooms, there was an established tendency toward undesirable patterns of behavior and low teacher credibility, which persisted throughout the school year.

From this and related studies of classroom management (Emmer, Evertson, Clements, & Worsham, 1997; Brophy 1983), we learn that effective classroom managers possess three broad classes of effective teaching behaviors.

1. They devote extensive time prior to and during the first few weeks of school to planning and organizing their classroom to minimize disruption and enhance work engagement.
2. They approach the teaching of rules and routines as methodically as they approach teaching their subject area. They provide their students with clear instructions about acceptable behavior, and monitor student compliance with these instructions carefully during the first few weeks of school.
3. They inform students about the consequences of breaking the rules, and enforce these consequences consistently.

Not only do effective classroom managers structure the environment to minimize disruptive be-havior, but they present instruction in a format designed to stimulate student interest, establish clear expectations for learning, provide skilled explanations, summarize key ideas, encourage solitary practice, and engage in continuous review. We will study the relationship of these behaviors to classroom management in the chapters ahead. But, first, let's take a closer look at some of the dimensions of classroom management.

DIMENSIONS OF CLASSROOM MANAGEMENT

Figure 6.1 summarizes five behaviors related to effective classroom management.

1. Arranging the classroom to meet instructional goals
2. Preestablishing and communicating classroom rules
3. Developing and communicating instructional routines
4. Establishing a system of incentives and consequences
5. Using low-profile classroom control

PRACTICE OBSERVING CLASSROOM MANAGEMENT: A DIALOGUE

The following dialogue illustrates several dimensions of classroom management. First, review the dimensions in Figure 6.1. Then read the dialogue using the checklist in Instrument 6.1 and looking for signs of classroom management.

Brownwood is a K–8 comprehensive school with a total student body of 850. The school is brand new; in fact, it is in the process of being completed. Workmen move in and out of classrooms daily, painting and adding finishing touches to the carpentry work. Classroom equipment is sparse. Many rooms have an insufficient number of desks. The desks that are available are old and in need of repair. Most of the desks were originally constructed for use in elementary schools. In some of the classrooms, folding chairs are used in place of desks.

The total effect is one of incongruity. The outside of the school building is modern and attractive. It is shaped like a giant doughnut, with classrooms circled around an atrium. Inside, the halls are spacious and carpeted. The brightly painted rooms, which open to the halls, all appear attractive—until the observer notices the desks and chairs. The central office is a large, spacious room that houses the prin-

FIGURE 6.1 Indicators of Classroom Management

Good Classroom Management (Effective Teacher)	Poor Classroom Management (Ineffective Teacher)
1. Arranges the classroom to meet instructional goals (for example, uses appropriate classroom organization to promote lesson goals)	Fails to establish a classroom arrangement that matches the instructional goal
2. Preestablishes classroom rules (for example, in the areas of speaking out, getting out of seat, groupwork, make-up work, in-class assignments, and rule violations)	Fails to inform students orally and visually of expected behavior
3. Develops instructional routines (for example, in the areas of beginning of class, group activities, assignments, instructional activities, etc.)	Fails to develop procedures that guide students through most frequently repeated tasks
4. Establishes a system of incentives and consequences to respond to appropriate and inappropriate behavior	Fails to develop an adequate system of reward, reinforcement, and consequences to promote appropriate behavior
5. Uses low-profile classroom control to maintain instructional momentum	Responds to misbehavior in ways that disrupt the flow of the lesson and increase loss of instructional time

cipal and her secretary. In one corner, large boxes, a key plaque, and filing cabinets line the wall to the right of the counter, which partially shields the principal's desk.

On this morning, several teachers are milling around in the office. Some are talking quietly; a few stand before the bulletin board examining an announcement of coming school events.

Mrs. Towers, a confident and secure-looking woman of about forty-five, stands before the mailbox collecting a sheaf of envelopes and folded papers. She sees Mrs. Gates approaching, and her face lights up in a friendly smile. She moves forward a step.*

Mrs. Towers: Hi, Mrs. Gates. I've been meaning to chat with you ever since the principal introduced you at the faculty meeting last week. I'm Beth Towers. I teach eighth-grade science. [She extends her hand.] Welcome to Brownwood.

Mrs. Gates: [Smiling] Oh, thank you for the welcome. I need it!

Mrs. Towers: How are things going?

Mrs. Gates: Well [ruefully], not so good, really. I'm still a little . . . [she hesitates a moment, then continues] a little disoriented, I guess. Somehow, everything seems so unreal.

Mrs. Towers: [Smiling] Yes, I can imagine. Changing teaching assignments to a completely different school in midyear must be pretty frustrating.

Mrs. Gates: Oh, it is! [She looks around.] There I was last week, in the school where I'd taught for years, where I knew all the children—and their parents, too . . . [Her voice trails off] everything seemed to run so smoothly there. But, here— [She looks around again; this time with a frown on her face] it's all so confused! [With an embarrassed expression on her face she adds, quickly] Oh, I don't mean to imply that this is a bad place to be . . . it's just . . . different. I'm sure I'll feel right at home soon. [She concludes with bravado.]

Mrs. Towers: [With warmth] Yes, I'm sure you will. [She touches Mrs. Gates's arm.] Say, why don't you stop by my room some afternoon before you go home. We'll go to the lounge, have a soda, and talk. I'd like that.

Mrs. Gates: (Smiling) Yes, I'd like that, too! Thank you.

*Based on an excerpt from *Problem Situations in Teaching* by Gordon Greenwood, Thomas Good, and Betty Siegel (Harper & Row, 1971).

The first bell rings. Mrs. Gates collects her keys from the board of keys and starts to go. In her haste she drops a book, which Mrs. Towers retrieves for her.

Mrs. Towers: [Glancing at the title] *The Lives of 10 Great Classical Composers* . . . Are you going to use this with your music class?

Mrs. Gates: Oh, yes. It's so inspirational. My students at Edgewater loved it. They loved reading aloud in small groups about the lives of great composers. We'd arrange our desks in circles, so students could talk to one another without interrupting the other groups. I've arranged my classroom the same way for today's lesson.

Mrs. Towers: [Hesitantly] Do you think the children here will want to read about classical composers without ever having been introduced to classical music?

Mrs. Gates: [Breezily] Sure—they'll love it! You'll see. I've done this at least six or seven times before, and it's always been successful.

Mrs. Gates smiles confidently, gathers her materials, and goes out of the office. She leaves Mrs. Towers standing alone with a slight frown of consternation on her face. Mrs. Towers then shrugs to herself, shakes her head, and turns to go to her classroom.

Mrs. Gates walks down the hall to the music room. Her first class consists of thirty-seven students from the seventh and eighth grades. The ages range from eleven to fourteen. When Mrs. Gates examined the cumulative record of five of the students, she found such teacher comments as "undisciplined," "unruly," "aggressive," "difficult," and "inattentive."

Mrs. Gates enters a small classroom that serves as the music room. The chairs and desks are arranged in haphazard circles around the teacher's desk. Mrs. Gates places her materials on the desk and puts a book on each desk as the last bell rings and the children noisily push and shove their way into the room. Desks are moved about, chairs are pulled across the floor, and books are dropped on the floor. Several students put their other books on top of their music books, or put their music books inside their desks.

Mrs. Gates: [In a firm voice] All right, class, go to your groups. [The talking and the jostling behavior continue. She focuses her attention to one child] Rosalyn!

Rosalyn has been standing in the doorway talking to several boys in the hall. She turns her head momentarily in Mrs. Gates's direction, ignores the admonition to sit down, and then calmly resumes her discussion. Mrs. Gates appears nonplussed by Rosalyn's behavior and turns to Carlos in the back of the room.

Mrs. Gates: Carlos, please sit down. [Carlos is seated on the windowsill.]

Carlos: [Mockingly] But I am sitting down!

Mrs. Gates: [With some frustration] Carlos, you know what I mean. [Firmly] In a chair, this minute! [Then, to the rest of the class] Go to your seats!

The noise and the movement in the room continue as the teacher attempts to direct students to their assigned seats. Rosalyn finishes her conversation with the boys in the hallway and slowly takes a seat.

Mrs. Gates: Adam, please take your seat.

Adam makes a face, picks up a chair, puts it noisily into the corner.

Mrs. Gates: Adam, sit down! [Adam sits, talking to Rosalyn across the room.]

John: [Speaking to Chester across the room.] Hey, Chester! [Chester is watching Rosalyn and Adam; he looks up but does not respond.]

Mrs. Gates: Jeanne, will you come over to the seat where you belong?

Jeanne: I don't know where I sit. [Several students laugh.]

John: Sit next to me.

Mrs. Gates walks over to Jeanne's seat and puts her hand on the desk. Jeanne works her way over to the desk, throws her books on it, and drops into the seat, smiling. The noise in the room continues. Mrs. Gates goes to her desk.

Mrs. Gates: All right! Whoever continues to talk will be assigned to detention! [Pause.] Get into the seats you've been assigned! [Two students come in and slam the door. Mrs. Gates turns to them.] I've warned both of you to be on time. Report to the principal's office. [The two students leave the room, laughing and talking as they go.] Turn to page 138!

Students: We've read that before. We already read that. We done that part.

Mrs. Gates: I'm sorry. Turn to page 139.

Students: Do we have to read again today? Why can't we do anything else? [The noise level begins to build up again.]

Mrs. Gates: That's enough. [Her voice is strident and the students become quiet; then, in a softer voice, she continues] This is a beautiful story about Beethoven's early life as a young musical prodigy. He began composing when he was even younger than you. Now, I want you to take turns reading this story orally. Jodi, will you begin reading first?

As the children take turns reading, they frequently falter and attempt to pronounce words, often with great difficulty. Most of the students appear diffident about the assignment, and some start shuffling papers on their desks. Carlos begins tapping his pencil on his desk in a distinct rhythm. Rosalyn, across the room, looks up, winks at Carlos, and begins to accompany him. The beat is contagious, and Tina and Joan begin to bob their heads. Mrs. Gates turns first to reprimand Tina, and then Joan. The noise fades, but starts up again as soon as another student begins to read. This continues until the bell rings. The students walk in noisy clusters out of the room; a few smile sheepishly, but most talk and laugh loudly as they enter the hallway.

REACTIONS TO THE DIALOGUE

What did you notice about Mrs. Gates's classroom? What advice would you give her to help her manage her classroom better? Did you see any signs of our five dimensions of classroom management—or lack of them—in Mrs. Gate's class? Let's consider her lesson in light of the five behaviors for effective classroom management on our checklist.

Arranging the Classroom to Meet Instructional Goals

The way a classroom is arranged—furniture aligned, partitions placed, walls and bulletin boards decorated, and the environment "softened"—may have as much to do with achieving your instructional and behavioral goals as the rules and routines that you put in place. Psychologists use the term *behavioral setting* to refer to how particular environments elicit specific behaviors, regardless of who is in them. A classroom is an example of a behavioral setting. There are numerous choices to be made about how to arrange a behavioral setting. Each choice encourages certain student behaviors and discourages others. The first step in designing a behavioral setting is to identify what students are to do when they are in it.

Take a moment to think back to one of your favorite classes. What do you remember? How did the classroom arrangement contribute to the fond memories you have of the events in that room? How might the arrangement have been improved? Did your teacher alter the behavioral setting of this classroom often? How did those alterations affect instructional outcomes?

Because behavioral and instructional goals for students will vary from day to day and from month to month as learner needs are identified, behavioral settings should be flexible. Although it may not be possible to create exactly the environment you desire for every instructional activity, often a simple alteration or adaptation will help match your behavioral setting to your behavioral goals.

The physical arrangement of a classroom is important because it communicates the kinds of behaviors expected of learners. For example, the arrangement shown in Figure 6.2 would be more appropriate for acquiring knowledge, rules, and concepts than for developing relationships and learning to cooperate. This so-called traditional arrangement is better suited for a lecture and teacher-led discussion format than it is for more interactive formats. At the beginning of the school year, such an arrangement may make it easier to minimize distractions, monitor students, and hold their attention. But, as students become familiar with classroom rules and routines, and instructional goals require more student-to-student and student-to-teacher interaction and group problem solving, your classroom may change to a more collaborative style, as shown in Figure 6.3.

With this arrangement, more expression of student opinion, increased student talk, and greater spontaneity in student responses can be expected. As the internal features of the classroom evolve from formal to less formal, so will the learning climate (Fraser & Walberg, 1991). Because a less formal arrangement suggests that interpersonal communication and sharing are being encouraged, increased interpersonal communication and sharing will undoubtedly occur, whether it is desired or not. Different classroom arrangements can occur simultaneously, as shown in Figure 6.4, when both individualistic and collaborative activities are frequent instructional goals. Regardless of the arrangement chosen, the social climate created by the classroom's physical arrangement should always match the learning climate intended by the teacher's instructional goals.

It is also important not to take traditional or conventional classroom arrangements for granted. For example, one traditional arrangement involves the teacher standing in front of the classroom lecturing and calling on students seated in neatly ordered rows. The arrangement of space dictates patterns of student involvement; in this case, speaking turns allocated in sequential order, one-to-one involvement with the teacher based on a first-come, first-served basis, and individual seatwork in which the book is treated as a primary source of learning. But some students, due to culture or ethnicity, may be less responsive to classroom arrangements that limit the teacher to calling out to individual students who then must respond in front of the entire group (Phillips, 1983; Erickson & Mohatt, 1982). Thus, classroom arrangement should be responsive to both instructional goals and cultural expectations.

With these ideas in mind, let's consider the behavioral setting in Mrs. Gates's classroom—how she

FIGURE 6.2 A Classroom Arrangement Emphasizing the Acquistion of Knowledge, Rules, and Concepts

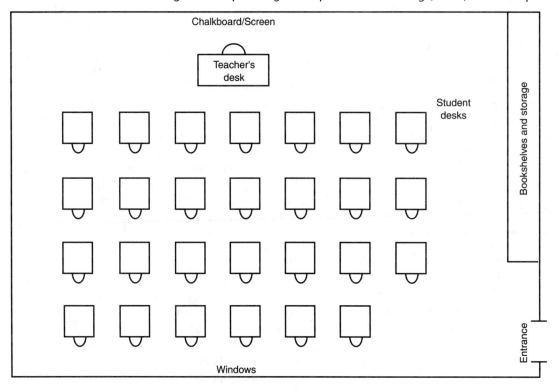

FIGURE 6.3 A Classroom Arrangement Emphasizing Positive Relations and Learning to Cooperate

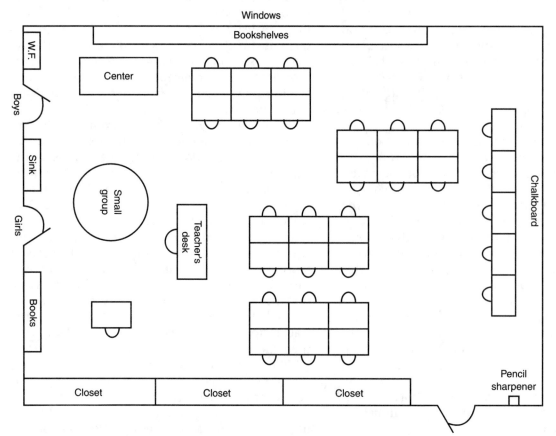

FIGURE 6.4 A Compromise Classroom Arrangement Allowing Independent, Group, and Cooperative Learning

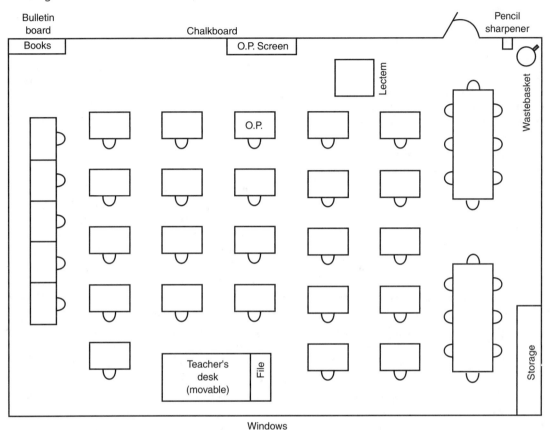

matched the organization of her classroom to her instructional goals. Mrs. Gates began her lesson with the assumption that what worked in the past at another school, would work at Brownwood. However, it soon became apparent that Brownwood isn't the same as her previous assignment. The students and the instructional context are different. Brownwood students may have little or no familiarity with what Mrs. Gates is teaching, and may be less ready for independent reading and group work than her previous classes. Mrs. Gates appears to lack a sense of context and the prerequisites necessary for her students to study the topic at the level of appreciation she is expecting. More than anything, Mrs. Gates's assumption that her students were ready to read, listen, and discuss collaboratively may have been responsible for the disorderly classroom that ensued. It is important for you to quickly come to know your students and to target your instructional objectives to their current level of experience and understanding.

Notice also that Mrs. Gates's assignment to read aloud and to sit in groups appeared inconsistent. Little of the day's lesson actually required group work; small groups scattered throughout the classroom made management of the group of learners even more difficult. Thus, the physical organization of the classroom actually discouraged, not promoted, the purpose of the lesson, which was to acquire an appreciation and understanding of classical music through oral reading. Oral reading is a valuable aid to teaching, but it did not appear to be a good tool with which to begin this lesson. What alternative might you have chosen if you were Mrs. Gates?

Observing the Classroom Arrangement

A behavioral setting can promote certain types of student behavior, with or without the aid of the teacher. As such, the social and physical context of the classroom should be arranged to promote and encourage those behaviors most conducive to the goals of a lesson. Many times this will mean deciding on the best classroom arrangement to promote a competitive, individualistic, cooperative, or combination work environment. Instrument 6.2 provides a format for drawing the arrangement of a classroom with respect to the placement of desks, tables, chairs, and media, as well as students and teacher, to reflect its social and organizational climate. When you observe in a classroom, consider the items in the left margin and then sketch the classroom organization. You can summarize the overall social and organizational message of the classroom by checking the appropriate boxes at the bottom of the instrument. Multiple checkmarks can be used to indicate a combination classroom arrangement. It's a good idea to make a sketch of each classroom you observe, with specific notes on how you believe the behavioral setting supported or challenged the teacher's instructional goals.

Preestablishing and Communicating Classroom Rules

The second behavior for effective classroom management is establishing classroom rules. Just as there is no one behavioral setting or classroom arrangement that's best for all students and every teacher, there is no single set of rules that's best for directing student behavior. Rules make a statement about the type of climate desired in a behavioral setting. They are a message system whereby the teacher's beliefs and philosophy about academic and conduct-related behavior are communicated to students. If an orderly, businesslike, task-oriented climate is desired, rules such as "Speak (or leave your seat) only when recognized" are appropriate. But such a rule may be inappropriate for a classroom (for example, Figure 6.3) where students are expected to discuss, obtain resources in different parts of the room, problem solve, and cooperate with one another. Here are some general guidelines for establishing rules.

First, rules should be consistent with the learning climate. To understand this relationship, review Figure 5.3 which displays quadrants of classroom warmth and control. Does the teacher want the learning climate for a specific instructional task or activity to emphasize control (Quadrant B) or warmth (Quadrant C)? Rules should reflect the degree of warmth and control desired for a particular set of goals, and the classroom's physical arrangement should be chosen to promote it.

Second, rules should be enforceable. A rule that says "No talking or getting out of your seat" may be impossible to enforce when the teacher's personal philosophy or instructional activity encourages independent thinking, problem solving, and group work. Nothing will be more damaging to management of the classroom than unfairness and inconsistency in applying consequences for violations of rules to which the teacher is not fully committed, or that do not match a classroom's instructional goals.

Third, only rules that are necessary should be established. There are four reasons to have rules; if a rule cannot be matched to one of these purposes, it probably is not necessary. Rules should be written to

1. Enhance work engagement and minimize disruption.
2. Promote safety and security.
3. Prevent disturbance to others or other classroom activities.
4. Promote standards of courtesy and interpersonal relations.

Rules should be stated at a level general enough to include a range of specific behaviors. The rule "Respect other people's property and person" covers a variety of problems, such as stealing, borrowing without permission, and throwing objects. Similarly, the rule "Follow teacher requests immediately" may put an end to a variety of off-task, disruptive behaviors that no list of rules could anticipate or comprehensively cover. However, a rule may be stated so generally that the specific problems to which it pertains remain unclear to learners. For example, a rule that simply states, "Show respect" or "Obey the teacher" may be vague enough to be ignored by most learners, and consequently may become unenforceable.

Teachers often ask how many classroom rules are appropriate. If you follow the above suggestions, you'll probably create from six to eight classroom rules. Once you've determined what your classroom rules should cover, it's important to consider how to phrase those rules.

One of the most widely recommended techniques for writing rules is: "State rules positively" (Savage, 1991; Jones & Jones, 1990). Although in general it is better to state what you want to happen rather than what you don't want to happen (``Take notes'' vs. "Don't daydream"), it is sometimes necessary to state rules negatively. If all you want to communicate is not to curse, it is clearer if the rule simply states "No cursing" instead of "Be polite and respectful." The former is to the point; the latter may be interpreted so broadly that most learners will miss the point.

As you know, not all rules are equally important, and rules may have to be added as special circumstances require. But rules about responding and speaking out, getting out of one's seat, communicating during group work, making up work, violating due dates, completing in-class assignments early, and routines for dealing with rule violations are often among the most troublesome for the beginning teacher. Here are some of the issues you'll want to consider in each rule area.

Rule Area	Issues
Responding, speaking out	Must hands be raised? Are other forms of acknowledgment acceptable (e.g., head nod)? What will happen if a student speaks when others are speaking? What will you do about shouting or using a loud voice?
Getting out of seat	When is out-of-seat movement permissible? When can a student come to the teacher's desk? When can reference books or learning centers be visited? What will be done if a student visits another?
Communicating during group work	Can a student leave an assigned seat? How loudly should a student speak? Who determines who can talk next? Will there be a group leader?
Make-up work	Will make-up work be allowed? Will there be penalties for not completing it? Will it be graded? Whose responsibility is it to know the work is missing?
Violation of due dates	What happens when repeated violations occur? Where can a student learn the due dates if absent? What penalties are there for copying another person's assignment? Will make-up work be required when a due date is missed?
Early completion of class assignments	Can work for other classes or subjects be done?
	Can a newspaper, book, or magazine be read? Can the next exercise or assignment be worked on? Can students rest their heads on their desks?
Rule violations	Will names be written on the board? Will warnings be given? Will you have after-class detention? When will a disciplinary referral be made?

Establishing rules for dealing with many possible problem areas will help you feel more secure in your teaching. However, unless the rules are clearly communicated and consistently applied, they will not be effective (Emmer et al. 1997). Also, the choice and expression of rules must be consistent with the culture and ethnicity of the students in order to avoid conflicts with parental values, home-life conditions, and culturally determined participation patterns that can influence assignment completion, speaking out, and interpersonal communication (Bowers & Flinders, 1991).

Rules with clearly established consequences can help prevent awkward pauses while trying to decide what to do, or lengthy interchanges with students to discuss (or even argue about) suitable consequences. Rules prevent minor forms of misbehavior from escalating into bigger problems and, if effectively communicated, can prevent many inappropriate behaviors.

Some researchers suggest that rules are especially effective when students are involved in their formulation (Curwin & Mendler, 1988). While we did not actually view Mrs. Gates's classroom, we can answer the question of whether she had any rules posted, or communicated them in advance, by the events that transpired in her classroom. As you read the dialogue, did you sense that shared classroom norms had been established in her classroom? What led you to believe otherwise? Let's consider how Mrs. Gates might have better applied rules and consequences in her classroom.

On a number of occasions the mention of a rule might have stopped, or at least lessened, the seriousness of a misbehavior in Mrs. Gates's classroom. One such event occurred with Rosalyn standing at the door talking to several boys after the start of class. A rule that requires everyone to be in their seats at the bell may have helped prevent this problem, and a verbal reference to it by Mrs. Gates would have immediately communicated the seriousness of Rosalyn's behavior. Instead, Mrs. Gates seemed to have no ready response, except an expression of displeasure, after which Rosalyn continued to ignore the start of class. Rosalyn is not moved by her teacher's frustration, and may indeed feel a sense of power in being able to upset her.

To be effective, rules must include logical and consistent consequences. Students need to know the consequences of disobeying a rule and must experience those consequences in a predictable manner. For example, Carlos, who fails to sit down after being requested to, not only appears to be unaware of any rule that requires students to be in their seats at the start of class, but also fails to associate his disobedience with any sort of consequence. So naturally Carlos and the others following his lead fail to abide by the teacher's wishes, creating noise and movement long after the start of class. Mrs. Gates's problems escalate as other students speak out freely, continue to move around the room, and finally instigate antagonizing behavior toward one another. Although not all of Mrs. Gates' problems could have been solved with rules, three rules would have been especially helpful at the start of class. These rules might have been stated as

❑ Students must be quiet and in their seats at the start of the bell.
❑ Students must raise their hands and be acknowledged before speaking.
❑ Students must ask permission before leaving their assigned seats.

These rules would have allowed Mrs. Gates to cite an individual's name and the rule at the first sign of misbehavior, with the understanding that a rule violation automatically incurs a predetermined consequence. They also would have helped her avoid relying on personal frustration or disapproval as an unplanned—and ineffective—consequence for unspecified misbehaviors. As you visit classrooms, you'll want to look for evidence of rules, consequences, and the way teachers communicate these to students. You may want to pay particular attention not only to the words a teacher uses, but also to the way in which those words are delivered—and note the apparent effectiveness of the communication.

Observing Classroom Rules

As we have seen, rules help make a classroom an efficient and productive learning environment. Although many rules may be needed for an efficient and productive classroom, only six to eight rules are used frequently enough to warrant visual and/or oral presentation the first day or two of the school year. Many other rules are best left until a particular event that makes the rule meaningful and memorable occurs (for example, when a visitor first comes to the door, or when laboratory equipment is used for the first time).

You can use the form in Instrument 6.3 to record classroom rules that correspond to seven areas. Add at least one rule that you think is particularly important to the list. Did you ever hear or see this rule formally communicated? Do you feel it is broad enough to cover a number of behaviors, and yet not overly vague? What other rules might you want to add to this list and to include in your own classroom?

Developing and Communicating Instructional Routines

The third dimension of classroom management involves instructional routines. As we have discussed in previous chapters, classrooms are busy places. Students and materials must be checked in and out, activities must be begun and ended, learners must be moved through the lessons, and assignments must be given, completed, and evaluated. Groups are formed, disbanded, and rearranged. In the midst of these activities, students need, forget to bring, and borrow things. They get thirsty, hungry, tired, sick, and have to use the bathroom. Handling all this complexity requires a systematic routine. A *routine* is a set of rules organized around a particular time (the beginning of day), a concept (group work), or a place (library, learning center, or playground) that helps guide learners through the day. Well-taught routines can keep learners engaged in learning and the teacher in control.

The amount of time learners spend thinking about, acting on, or working with a learning task is referred to as *engaged learning time* (Savage, 1991). Engaged learning time is different from the time spent teaching a particular lesson or activity. Although a teacher may allocate 35 minutes for a particular activity, students may spend only 15 minutes of that time actively engaged in completing the learning task. What happens to the other 20 minutes? Most likely they are used passing out materials, making announcements, giving directions, dealing with student requests to leave the room or to borrow materials, cleaning up, and handling discipline problems. In the studies of effective classroom managers cited previously, the teachers who were most successful in engaging students in learning were those who communicated routines to their students during the first few weeks of school (Emmer et al. 1997). This research also found a significant relationship between engaged learning time and achievement, suggesting that students achieve more in classes with well-established routines. Let's look at some example routines and how they are established.

Figure 6.5 lists some areas for which routines are commonly established. Each routine has a corresponding set of procedures or informal rules pertaining to specific areas of concern. For example, a beginning-of-class routine includes expectations for what students should be doing while roll is being taken (sit still without talking, check over homework or last assignment, or read silently from text). It must also include how a student should enter the room after the bell has rung (come to the teacher, go

directly to his seat, or see a counselor), and how handouts, tests, and assignments are to be turned in or dispensed (for example, first person in each row collects enough papers for row members from stacks conveniently placed in front and back of room and passes them to the other students). The procedures established for each routine will depend on the classroom's learning climate and teacher's instructional style. They are the procedures most comfortable for the teacher and learners, given the instructional goals and climate of the classroom.

Teaching a routine takes time and energy. But routines established during the first weeks of school will save time later and give students a sense of organization

FIGURE 6.5   Example Areas of Classroom Rountines

Beginning Class Routine
A. Roll call, absentees
B. Tardies
C. Distributing materials

Work Requirement Routine
A. Heading of papers
B. Use of pen or pencil
C. Writing on back of paper
D. Neatness, legibility
E. Incomplete work

Instructional Activity Routine
A. Student attention
B. Obtaining help
C. Student talk
D. Activities to do when work is completed
E. Student movement
F. Bringing materials

Group Activity Routine
A. Expected behavior in group
B. Expected behavior of students out of group
C. Sharing of resources
D. Individual responsibilities
E. Choosing a group leader

Ending Class Routine
A. Putting away supplies, equipment
B. Cleaning up
C. Dismissing class

Interruption Routine
A. Talk among students
B. Turning in work
C. Handing back assignments
D. Getting back assignments
E. Out-of-seat policies

Use of Room/School Area Routine
A. Shared materials
B. Teacher's desk
C. Water fountain, bathroom, pencil sharpener
D. Student desks
E. Learning centers, stations
F. Playground
G. Lunchroom

Assignment Routine
A. Returning in-class assignments
B. Homework assignments
C. Turning in assignments

Checking Assignments In Class Routine
A. Students exchanging papers
B. Making and grading assignments
C. Turning in assignments

Grading Routine
A. Recording grades
B. Grading criteria
C. Contracting with students for grades

Academic Feedback Routine
A. Rewards and incentives
B. Posting student work
C. Communicating with parents
D. Students' record of grades
E. Written comments on assignments

and order. Routines enhance the speed and efficiency with which things get done, especially time-consuming noninstructional activities. Thus, they allow the teacher more time to teach and learners more time to become engaged in the learning process. Routines should be taught with as much planning and thoroughness as learning objectives, and should be followed-up with monitoring (Pasch, 1991; Jones & Jones, 1990).

As we consider Mrs. Gates's experience at Brownwood, we can't help but wonder if having some established classroom routines would have helped. Certainly a beginning-of-class routine that included procedures for taking roll (absentees, tardies) would have brought some immediate structure and order to the start of class by requiring students to be in their assigned seats in order not to be counted *absent* or *late*. Other routines for oral reading and subsequent class discussion might also have been helpful. For example, if Mrs. Gates uses oral reading as an instructional tool often, the steps for completing this routine might have included:

1. Find the pages to be read on the board.
2. Scan the pages to be read to get the main idea.
3. Write down one question to ask about the reading.
4. Be ready to discuss your question with the class at the end of oral reading.

If these instructions were written on the board at the time the students entered the classroom, the signal "Let's go to our reading routine" is all that may have been needed to get the class task-oriented at the very start of class. A routine for when the class gets noisy might also have helped to change the pace and return the class to a quieter state. Such a routine might include the steps:

1. Stop activity.
2. Return to seat.
3. Open book to page ___.
4. Begin reading silently.

Mrs. Gates could have benefited from such a "Stop" or "Time Out" routine as her problems began to escalate. But as you noticed, few, if any, of these types of routines were in evidence in Mrs. Gates's classroom.

Observing Instructional Routines

As we mentioned, a routine is an expected sequence of events that is repeated during a day (or week) to accomplish a given task in the quickest and most efficient manner possible. As noted in Figure 6.5, there are many possible routines for handling specific classroom events, such as beginning of class (roll call, absentees, tardies), managing group activities

(talking, sharing resources, individual responsibilities, choosing a leader), and handling assignments (completing and handing in work). Regardless of the task, however, each routine communicates a set of procedures that must be completed and, when applicable, the order in which they should be followed (for example, raise hand before speaking, and then wait to be acknowledged, or stand by the door when late, be acknowledged, and then go to seat). Established routines help ensure an orderly class day and provide the structure that maintains classroom momentum without repeating verbal messages over and over. The key to avoiding this repetition is to teach routines as a single activity and not as a set of related, but different, activities. This means that you will need to demonstrate before the class each routine you wish your students to follow from beginning to end, not simply communicate it as a set of verbal instructions. In this manner students come to recognize routines as a unit and can reproduce them as a single activity.

While you may not have the opportunity to observe a teacher set up a routine at the beginning of a school year, you can gain a sense of how routines work and what makes them effective through careful observation. Instrument 6.4 provides four different areas for you to consider as you observe routines. Record the step-by-step procedures you observe in each area indicated, and then add one of your own. Indicate how well the students appear to have learned each routine by circling the number *1* if you think the routine was not learned or only minimally learned, the number *2* if some but not all of the students knew the routine, and the number *3* if the routine was learned with efficiency and precision by most of the class. You may find it helpful to ask the teacher how she decided on, introduced, and reinforces a particular routine; include these ideas in your notes.

Establishing a System of Incentives and Consequences

The fourth behavior for promoting effective classroom management involves establishing a system of incentives and consequences. Motivating learners to behave appropriately requires knowing the difference between reinforcement (incentives) and punishment (consequences). In a school setting, it often is natural to set an aversive tone—to say why students *should not do* something rather than why they *should do* something. Recall how frequently you have heard phrases like

If you don't study, you'll flunk the course.
If you don't do the homework, I take five points off.

Do it right the first time, or you'll have to do it over.
If you don't get it today, you'll have to get it on
   your own.
If it's too difficult, you shouldn't be here.

In any environment where a few individuals hold most of the power (e.g., schools), it is natural for those in authority to reinforce the existing structure with penalties. However, when the *only* incentive for good conduct involves avoiding penalties, learners associate school with punishment and their motivation decreases. Learners generally respond far better to rewards for acceptable behavior than to punishment for unacceptable behavior. Unless special circumstances prevail, rewards are more effective than punishment in encouraging individuals to behave appropriately.

Television advertisers learned this lesson when they discovered that the rewards of having fresh, clean teeth persuaded more people to change brands of toothpaste than the negative consequences of tooth decay. When negative consequences (penalties) provoke high levels of anxiety and fear of the consequences, they no longer function to motivate behavior. The implications of advertising research should not be lost on educators: It is more effective to inform learners of the positive consequences of appropriate behavior than to enumerate the negative consequences of misbehavior.

Although both rewards and penalties are necessary, the emphasis on rewards (the positive consequences of the right behavior) should always outweigh the emphasis on penalties. Compare this list with the previous one; it has been rephrased to emphasize reward and not punishment.

Remember to study. It will make the lessons a lot
   easier.
If you do the homework, the tests will be easier.
Save time. Follow the directions.
Listen carefully; it will be easier to understand my
   explanations.
Notice where this assignment is difficult. That will
   indicate what you should study.

Figure 6.6 contrasts phrases that emphasize reward rather than punishment for five strategies for promoting appropriate behavior. Notice how a small change in wording can make the difference between a punishment and a reward.

Other types of incentives can also increase the probability of a desirable response. Some of the most frequently used are

❑ Verbal or written praise
❑ Smile, head nod
❑ Special privileges (for example, visit to the learning center or library)
❑ Time out of regular work to pursue a special project (for example, read)
❑ Permission to choose a topic or assignment
❑ Getting to work in a group, being allowed to select group members
❑ Extra points toward grade
❑ "Smiley face" stickers on assignments
❑ Note to parents on top of a test or paper
❑ Special recognitions and certificates (for example, "most improved," "good conduct award," "neatest," "hardest worker")

Not all of these incentives may be equally reinforcing, however. Some learners may be uncomfortable with verbal praise; others will have no desire to visit the library or learning center. Some students like to be called on; others may be too shy and dislike the personal attention. An incentive that works for one student may be completely irrelevant to another. Finding the right incentive for each student often requires trial and error; if one type of reward does not seem to increase a desirable behavior, try another. Knowing the interests, needs, and aspirations of learners helps in finding the right mix of rewards. Students can be asked for a menu of rewards (for example, readings, music, magazines) that reflect their specific interests, and you can then select the most feasible and desirable from their list.

Unfortunately, incentives for desirable behavior are not always effective. However, there are many ways to deal with misbehavior when incentives fail. On one end of the continuum, you may choose to ignore an infraction if it is brief and not likely to recur (for example, when a student jumps out of and back into his seat to stretch after a long assignment). At the other extreme, you may need to summon outside help (an administrator, a school counselor, or a colleague down the hall) to help resolve a problem. Fortunately, there are many alternatives for handling misbehavior that fall between these two extremes. In approximate order of increasing severity, they are

❑ Looking at the student sternly
❑ Walking toward the student (called *proximity control*)
❑ Calling on the student to provide the next response
❑ Asking the student to stop
❑ Assigning the student to another seat
❑ Discussing the problem with the student
❑ Assigning the student to detention
❑ Calling the student's parents

More important than the variety these alternatives offer is the goal of matching the correct response to the type of misbehavior that has occurred.

FIGURE **6.6** Five Strategies for Promoting Appropriate Behavior

Strategy	Use phrases such as . . .	Avoid phrases such as . . .
Using praise and encouragement	You've got it. Good work. Good try That was quick.	That's a dumb answer. You're being lazy again. I can see you never study. You can never pay attention, can you?
Providing explanations	The reason this is so important is . . . We are doing this assignment because . . . This will be difficult, but it fits in with . . . Experience has shown that without these facts the next unit will be very difficult	Today you will have to learn this, or else . . . Complete this exercise; otherwise, there'll be trouble. This is a long assignment, but you'll just have to do it. We must cover this material, so let's get going.
Offering to help	Should you need help, I'll be here. I'll be walking around, catch me if you have a problem. Don't be afraid to ask a question if you're having trouble.	You should be able to do this on your own. Please don't ask a dumb question. Raise your hand only if you're stuck on a difficult problem.
Accepting diversity	That's not the answer I expected, but I can see your point. That's not how I see it, but I can understand how others might see it differently. This is not something I'm familiar with. Where did you get that idea? That is not a word I've heard before. Tell us what it means.	That's not the kind of answer we can accept around here. I've never heard that expression before—so let's not start something new. Please use ideas that fit in with what I say in class. Don't ever use foreign words in this class.
Providing specific rewards	All homework completed means five extra points. If you get a C or better on all the tests, I'll drop the lowest grade. Those who complete all the exercises on time can go to the learning center. If you have a C average, you get to choose any topic for your term paper.	Five points off for missing homework. If you have less than a C average on all your tests, you'll have to take an extra test. If you don't complete the exercise on time, there can be no use of the learning center. If you don't have a C average, you must choose your term paper topic from a restricted list of difficult topics.

While all rule violations should receive a consistent response, the severity of the punishment can, and should, vary not only according to the students' ethnicity and culture, but also according to the nature of the violation and the frequency with which the violation has occurred in the past. If your re-sponse is too mild when a student has violated a major rule many times before, nothing is likely to change. If your response is too severe when a student commits a minor violation for the first time, you will be perceived as unfair. It helps to be flexible as you seek to resolve discipline problems; take into account both the context in which the violation occurs and the type of misbehavior that has occurred as you determine your response.

Some general guidelines for dealing with mild, moderate, and severe misbehavior are

❑ Talking out, acting out, getting out of one's seat, disrupting others, and similar misbehaviors may deserve a mild response at first. But if they occur repeatedly, a moderate response may be appropriate. In unusual cases, such as continual talking that disrupts the class, a severe response may be warranted.
❑ Misbehaviors like cutting class, abusive conduct toward others, fighting, and failure to complete an assignment may deserve a moderate response at first. But if these behaviors become frequent, a severe response may be warranted.
❑ Misbehaviors such as cheating, plagiarism, stealing, and vandalism usually warrant a severe response. These include major incidents of vandalism, theft, incorrigible conduct, and substance abuse in the classroom, which should be brought to the immediate attention of a school administrator.

As we consider Mrs. Gates's classroom again, we can see clearly the important role of the teacher in assigning certain consequences—mild, moderate, or severe—to rules. In other words, a rule without clearly communicated consequences is an ineffective rule. Consequences can range from a simple warning (a mild response) to withholding privileges (a moderate response), to detention or a visit to the office (a strong response). Whatever alternatives are chosen, they should be made known to students in advance. Mrs. Gates apparently had few alternative consequences in mind, except for detention and a trip to the principal's office. These strong responses may have been unnecessary if a mild or moderate response had been invoked at an earlier time.

Finally, we note that few, if any, incentives were used by Mrs. Gates to promote positive behavior. Instead, most of her attempts to control the class were negatively worded reactions that served only to increase the emotional temperature of the classroom and create an adversarial relationship between Mrs. Gates and her students.

As you observe in classrooms, you'll want to be particularly alert to incentives and positive comments and record them for your own use. As you know, it is far more effective for teachers to focus on offering positive comments and incentives to *prevent* student misbehavior than it is to wait until student misbehavior escalates and then express personal disapproval and frustration. Take every opportunity to observe how teachers redirect student behavior, and consider how you might apply their approaches to your own teaching.

Observing Incentives and Consequences

Incentives and consequences are tools for encouraging appropriate behavior and discouraging inappropriate behavior. Together, they represent a strategy for maintaining a productive learning environment in the midst of what is often a day filled with rapid decision making ("Gosh, they've finished; what do I do now?"), immediacy ("Angela, stop talking back"), administrative disruption ("Who's that at the door?"), and social distraction ("Mark, you can't sit next to Sue"). These and many other features of busy classrooms make a system of incentives and consequences an indispensable tool for managing a classroom.

The manner in which a system of incentives and consequences is applied is important. As we saw earlier, rules should be stated positively wherever possible and made culturally appropriate to students. This same advice goes for incentives and consequences. This means that an incentive to behave appropriately should be something meaningful that is given to the learner, not taken away. Research has long shown that we are more apt to change our behavior to gain something we do not already possess than to protect what we already have (hence, two-for-one sales, cash rebates, and coupons for new products and services). Penalties and/or punishment work best when they are used to motivate one to behave appropriately, not to inflict pain or discomfort. This subtle but important difference can be achieved by incentives and consequences that are thoughtfully worded ("If you don't study, you'll flunk the course," vs. "Let's not forget to do the studying, so we won't have to do extra work"). Punishment in the absence of reward is rarely effective.

The most effective and practical incentives for encouraging appropriate behavior are orally delivered phrases that

❑ Convey praise and encouragement.
❑ Provide explanations.
❑ Offer to help.
❑ Celebrate diversity.
❑ Identify a specific reinforcement or reward.

To help you focus on positive and helpful verbal phrases, Instrument 6.5 provides a form for recording a teacher's oral incentives either to a student or to the class in these five areas. Try to find one example of each during a class observation, and record the teacher's words as you hear them. Afterward, notice whether each statement was positively worded ("I'm here if you need my help") or negatively worded ("If you don't think for yourself, I can't help you"). Which phrasing do you think would encourage *you* to do your best work? How would you reword a negatively phrased comment?

Using Low-Profile Classroom Control

The fifth behavior for promoting effective classroom management is the use of low-profile classroom control. As we have seen, a behavioral setting suited to the goals of instruction, a carefully crafted set of rules and routines, and a system of incentives and consequences are important dimensions of classroom management. Some students, however, may choose not to follow rules and routines, or respond to rewards and consequences, due to a disinterest in school, a lack of skills needed to profit from the lesson, a desire to escape from the tedium of the classroom, or for other personal reasons. Some of these disruptions will be minor, last for only a short time, and resolve themselves. But others will persist. In the face of their persistence, it is important to respond in ways that promote a positive learning climate.

Rinne (1984) used the expression *low-profile classroom control* to refer to strategies used by effective teachers to stop misbehavior without disrupting the flow of a lesson. These techniques are effective for *surface behaviors* (Levin & Nolan, 1991), which include the overwhelming majority of disruptive classroom actions. Examples of surface behaviors are laughing, talking out of turn, passing notes, daydreaming, not following directions, combing hair, doodling, humming, and tapping. They are called *surface behaviors* because they are the normal developmental behaviors of children confined to a small space with large numbers of other children. They are not indicative of some underlying emotional disorder or personality problem, but can disrupt the flow of a lesson and the work engagement of others if left unchecked.

Figure 6.7 depicts several components of low-profile classroom control. Low-profile control for dealing with surface misbehavior is actually a set of techniques that require *anticipation* by the teacher to prevent problems before they occur; *deflection* in order to redirect disruptive behavior that is about to occur; and *reaction* to unobtrusively stop disruptions immediately after they occur. Let's take a closer look at each of these components.

Anticipation

Alert teachers have their antennae up to sense changes in student motivation, attentiveness, arousal level, or excitability. They are aware that at certain times of the year (pre- and post-holidays), week (just before a major social event), or day (right after an assembly, a trip to the playground, or a physical education class) the readiness of the class for doing work will differ from the norm. Skilled classroom managers are alert not only to changes in the groups' motivation or attention level, but also to changes in specific individuals as soon as they enter class.

At these times, anticipation involves scanning back and forth with active eyes to quickly size up the seriousness of a potential problem and head it off before it becomes a bigger problem. For example, a teacher may decide to pick up the pace of the class to counter perceived lethargy in the class after a three-day weekend, or to remove magazines or other objects that may distract the attention of individuals or the group before a long holiday. Some teachers maintain a reserve of activities that are likely to boost the interest of their students during times when it is difficult to stay focused on normal day-to-day activities. Others boost interest by being more positive or eager in the face of waning student enthusiasm; for example, raising and lowering the pitch of their voice and moving to different parts of the room more frequently. At

FIGURE 6.7 Characteristics of Low- and High-Profile Control

Low-Profile Control ◄————————————————————► High-Profile Control		
Anticipation	**Deflection**	**Reaction**
Scanning	Proximity control	Warning
Pick up the pace	Eye contact	Loss of privileges
Remove temptation	Prompting	Time out
Boost interest	Name dropping	Restitution
Change seating arrangements	Peer recognition	Removal

other times it may be necessary to quickly change seating arrangements to minimize antagonism when arguments occur between students. Anticipation involves not only knowing what to look for, but where and when to look for it. It also involves having a technique ready, no matter how small, for changing the environment quickly and unobtrusively to prevent problems from occurring or escalating. The time you invest in observing what to look for, and where and when to look for it, will be well spent in developing a valuable skill—one which will enhance your ability to anticipate problems in your own classroom.

Deflection

As we have noted, good classroom managers sense when disruption is about to occur. They are attuned to verbal and nonverbal cues, called *antecedents* or *precursors*, that have preceded disruptive behavior in the past. Such cues may involve a student who abruptly closes a textbook, sits and does nothing, squirms, asks to be excused, ignores a request, sighs in frustration, or makes a facial expression of annoyance or anger. Although not disruptive by themselves, these behaviors may signal that more disruptive behavior is about to follow.

Some teachers who are aware of the significance of these antecedents deflect many problems by simply moving nearer to the student who may be about to misbehave, thus preventing a more disruptive episode. Other teachers may make eye contact with the learner, combined with certain facial expressions like raised eyebrows or a slight tilt of the head, to communicate a warning. Both these techniques are effective nonverbal signals to deflect a potential problem. But verbal signals are also effective. Verbal deflection techniques include prompting (the teacher reminds the class of the rule or says, "We are all supposed to be doing math now"), name dropping (the target student's name is inserted into the teacher's explanation or lecture; for example, "Now if Angela were living in Boston at the time of the Boston Tea Party, she might have . . . , and peer recognition (the teacher notices a student engaged in appropriate behavior and acknowledges this to the class). As the potential for the problem to escalate increases, the effective manager shifts from nonverbal to verbal techniques to keep pace with the seriousness of the misbehavior that is about to occur.

Reaction

Anticipation and deflection can efficiently and unobtrusively prevent behaviors that disrupt the flow of a lesson. These techniques allow students the opportunity to correct themselves, thus fostering the development of self-control. However, the classroom is a busy place, and there may be many demands on a teacher that make problem behavior difficult to anticipate or to deflect.

When disruptive behavior occurs that cannot be anticipated or deflected, the teacher's primary goal should be to end the disruptive episode as quickly as possible. An effective reaction requires a class rule that corresponds with the behavior in question and specifies the consequences for violating the rule. Glasser (1990) points out that an effective consequence for breaking a rule is temporary removal from the classroom—provided the classroom is a place where that student wants to be—or loss of a privilege, such as recess, time at a learning center, or other activity the learner would miss.

When disruptive behavior occurs, a suggested anticipation-deflection-reaction sequence would include the following:

1. As soon as a student disrupts, acknowledge a nearby classmate who is performing the expected behavior: "Chris, I appreciate how hard you are working on the spelling words." Then wait 15 seconds for the disruptive student to change her behavior.
2. If the disruption continues, say, "Clara, this is a warning. Complete the spelling assignment and leave Carrie alone." Wait 15 seconds.
3. If the student doesn't follow the request after this warning, say, "Clara, you were given a warning. You must now leave the room for 5 minutes (or you must stay inside during lunch, or you cannot go to the resource center today). I'll talk to you about this later."

The low-profile techniques of anticipation, deflection, and reaction, when used skillfully, promote lesson flow. When these techniques do not work for a particular student or group of students, it may occasionally be a signal that the needs of the student are not being met, and a school counselor or school psychologist should be consulted. We will look at other patterns of low-profile classroom control in the chapters ahead.

As we consider the application of low-profile control in Mrs. Gates's lesson, it appears that Mrs. Gates failed to anticipate, deflect, and react appropriately to surface behaviors in her classroom. In fact, almost all of Mrs. Gates's problems stemmed from minor infractions of unspoken rules that could have been handled easily with low-profile control. Scanning, picking up the pace, boosting interest through intriguing questions or instructional variety, removing temptation, and changing seating arrangements might have diminished, if not eliminated, the minor forms of misbehavior Mrs.

Gates was experiencing—had they been used early enough. If these techniques were not effective, Mrs. Gates could have employed physical movement (walking near a misbehaving student), eye contact, prompting, name dropping, and peer recognition to avoid escalating problems. And finally, warnings or loss of privilege could have been invoked, if necessary. Mrs. Gates's only response, regardless of offense, seems to have been detention or a visit to the office—two of the strongest reactions possible. When these are used immediately, there are few other, stronger responses available. Being quick to use strong responses can make a teacher look ineffective in the eyes of students—and may send a message that the teacher is not in control. This is why low-profile control is so important: It provides the opportunity for the teacher to help correct misbehavior with a mild response, and to prevent the behavior from escalating.

Observing Low-Profile Classroom Control

Remember that the purpose of low-profile control is to respond to small incidents of misbehavior (laughing, talking, passing notes, daydreaming, not following directions), called *surface behaviors*, without losing the rhythm and momentum of your instruction. Dealing with a single student's behavior at length can encourage reactions from other students and promote acting-out behavior that halts the forward movement of a lesson—sometimes irretrievably. Recall that low-profile control comprises three separate behaviors—anticipation, deflection, and reaction—any one or combination of which may be used to deal with misbehavior quickly and unobtrusively. To focus an observation on low-profile classroom control, use the form provided in Instrument 6.6. Place a checkmark in a box each time you observe an example of any of the types of anticipation, deflection, and reaction listed. Add examples of your own as you see them. In your opinion, were the examples culturally appropriate? Did the teacher consistently choose a response that matched the misbehavior? Why?

As you observe teachers and consider how to apply these concepts to your own teaching, it is important to remember that the largest part of effective classroom management involves anticipation. Wise teachers anticipate the types of problems that are most likely to occur in a given class or during a particular lesson, and then plan, in advance, how they will respond when problems do occur. For example, imagine the first week of school during your first teaching assignment. How do you envision your classroom? Will students do more listening or talking? Should they be calm and quiet or excited and talkative? Is conversation to be encouraged or discouraged? Will an atmosphere of independence and self-study, or one of cooperation and group problem solving, prevail? How will you arrange the physical spaces in your classroom to encourage the kinds of behavior you hope to see? How will you establish and maintain rules, routines, and procedures? As you observe experienced teachers, keep these questions in mind—you'll build a useful repertoire of plans and interventions.

Our reactions to Mrs. Gates's lesson are summarized in Figure 6.8. We gave Mrs. Gates poor marks for her management of this classroom. Comments on the checklist indicate some of the most noticeable problem areas that might be observed on a subsequent visit. For example, the observer may want to see if Mrs. Gates uses low-profile control techniques, refers to classroom rules, and has incentives to help make her rules effective.

Cultural Diversity and Classroom Management

One of the most difficult problems in maintaining effective classroom discipline is deciding on a response that is culturally appropriate and well matched to the severity of the behavior. The effectiveness of some responses to misbehavior may differ significantly, depending upon a student's culture and ethnicity. Ekman and Friesan (1967) point out that humans send messages through their body language; indeed, the body can be read as a "fluid text." For members of some cultural or ethnic groups, a stern look at a student may be interpreted as a more severe response than asking the student to stop a particular behavior—especially depending on how the same action is used at home. Calling on a student who is misbehaving may not only send a message to stop misbehaving, but also serve as a punishment for students who don't want to be spotlighted during large-group instruction. Thus, research suggests that a teacher's response to misbehavior should match the student's cultural and ethnic background as well as the offense. Tharp and Gallimore (1989), Dillon (1989), and Bowers and Flinders (1991) present convincing arguments that different cultures react differently to nonverbal and verbal classroom management techniques, including proximity control, eye contact, warnings, and classroom arrangement. Furthermore, these authors cite numerous examples of how teachers of different cultures interpret disruptive behaviors and children differently.

For example, facial expressions during a reprimand have been found to communicate different messages concerning the importance of the reprimand (Smith,

FIGURE 6.8   Checklist for Observing Mrs. Gates's Classroom

Behavior	Observed	Not Observed	No Opportunity to Observe
1. Arranges classroom to match instructional goals		Collaborative seating did not match oral reading goal ✓	
2. Has preestablished classroom rules in place		Failed to cite rules or have rules posted ✓	
3. Exhibits use of instructional routines for most frequently performed activities		Did not have routine for most frequent activities (e.g., beginning of class) ✓	
4. Uses incentives and consequences to promote appropriate behavior and discourage inappropriate behavior		Used mostly negative phrases and consequences to encourage desirable behavior ✓	
5. Uses low-profile classroom control to maintain instructional momentum		Did not use anticipation, deflective, or reaction techniques ✓	

1984). Research by Dillon (1989) has pointed out that many actions of teachers may diminish participation among minority students and/or build resentment, because the actions are culturally incongruent. One of Dillon's suggestions is that teachers examine their own value and belief systems to become more aware of how different these systems may be from their students', and use the social organization of the classroom to bridge cultural gaps by

❑ Establishing an open, risk-free learning environment where students can feel good about themselves.
❑ Planning and structuring lessons that meet the interests and needs of students.
❑ Implementing lessons that allow all students to be active learners through activities and responsibilities that are congruent with the learner's culture.

These will be important considerations during your observation of classroom management.

In the following chapters, we will turn our attention to several other equally important lenses through which to observe classrooms. These lenses—lesson clarity, instructional variety, task orientation, student engagement in the learning process, student success, and higher thought processes—are always observed in the context of the dimensions of classroom management. As we turn now to our next lens—lesson clarity—keep in mind the significant impact of the dimensions of classroom management studied in this chapter.

ACTIVITIES*

1. Use the checklist in Instrument 6.1 to observe a lesson for signs of classroom management. At the end of your observation, add a brief description to each box, highlighting at least one specific reason why you placed each of your checkmarks as you did. Using your written descriptions as a guide, write a paragraph describing some of the reasons for the level of classroom management you observed.
2. Following the examples of five-point scales in Chapter 4, convert the positively stated indicators of classroom management listed in Figure 6.1 into a Likert scale. Consider the vertical and horizontal placement of each indicator on the page, whether words will be affixed to all or only some of the response blanks, and what

*Some of the following activities may be grouped into a common activity, divided among classmates, and completed from a single observation.

verbal response alternatives will be best suited to each question. Show your scale to a classmate who also has constructed a five-point scale. Together, create a single revised version incorporating the best features of each.

3. Using the seven-point polar scale shown in Chapter 4 as an example, convert the positive and negative indicators in Figure 6.1 into this scale format and observe a lesson for signs of classroom management. At the end of your observation period, complete the scale by indicating with a checkmark the degree to which the lesson achieved each dimension of classroom management. Use the code "N/O" for any item you didn't have the opportunity to observe, or that was inappropriate for the lesson being observed. Reflecting on your experience, return to each item and place an *X* on the blank that, in your opinion, represents the degree of classroom management found in most classrooms. Cite the reasons you scored this lesson the same, higher, or lower on each dimension.

4. Using the format provided in Instrument 6.2, draw the arrangement of a classroom you have recently observed. Indicate whether the arrangement of this classroom is best suited for group projects, independent work, lecture and discussion, or some combination of these approaches. How could this classroom most easily be changed to match another instructional goal?

5. Using the format provided in Instrument 6.3, create one rule of your own for each of the seven rule areas. Indicate the order in which your rules would be listed on a handout to your students, and which rules you believe may be culturally sensitive.

6. Using the format provided in Instrument 6.4, detail the steps or procedures you would in-clude in routines for the beginning of class, handing in assignments, transitions, and the violation of rules. Indicate how you would demonstrate each routine to the class at the beginning of the school year.

7. With the aid of Instrument 6.5, create an incentive for each of the five areas listed that would encourage appropriate behavior and discourage inappropriate behavior. Indicate how different cultural groups might respond to your incentives.

8. For the following misbehaviors, identify a response that you believe would match the severity of the problem.

Talking back
Sleeping in class
Leaving seat
Provoking or arguing
Taking another's property
Defacing books or materials

9. Use the format provided in Instrument 6.6 to observe low-profile classroom control. Record each occurrence you observe of anticipation, nonverbal deflection, verbal deflection, and reaction techniques. Write down any other responses that you believe represent low-profile classroom control. Add up how many times you observed each example of low-profile classroom control. Which was used most often; which were used least often or not at all?

10. Work with a classmate to create a number of positive phrases, other than general statements like "Good," you could use to provide a greater incentive to a student who is behaving appropriately.

INSTRUMENT 6.1 Checklist for Observing Dimensions of Classroom Management

Behavior	Observed	Not Observed	No Opportunity to Observe
1. Arranges classroom to match instructional goals			
2. Has preestablished classroom rules in place			
3. Exhibits use of instructional routines for most frequently performed activities			
4. Uses incentives and consequences to promote appropriate behavior and discourage inappropriate behavior			
5. Uses low-profile classroom control to maintain instructional momentum			

INSTRUMENT 6.2   Drawing the Classroom Arrangement

Placement of items to consider:

- Teacher's desk
- Student desks/tables
- Blackboard
- Media (for example, overhead projector)
- Reference books/shelves
- Learning center
- Worktable(s)
- Rugs and visual texture
- Space dividers

The social and organizational context of this classroom is best suited for (check all that apply):

☐ group projects

☐ independent work

☐ lecture and discussion

☐ other _____

INSTRUMENT 6.3   Observing Rules in Some Frequently Occurring Areas

1.   Getting out of seat: _____

   _____

   _____

   _____

2.   Responding, speaking out: _____

   _____

   _____

   _____

3.   Communicating during group work/discussion: _____

   _____

   _____

   _____

4.   Makeup work: _____

   _____

   _____

   _____

5.   Violating due dates: _____

   _____

   _____

   _____

6.   Assignment completion: _____

   _____

   _____

   _____

7.   Rule violation: _____

   _____

   _____

   _____

8.   Other: _____

   _____

   _____

   _____

INSTRUMENT 6.4   Observing Routines in Some Frequently Occuring Areas

Beginning of class routine   1   2   3
Steps: _____

_____

_____

_____

Handing in assignments routine   1   2   3
Steps: _____

_____

_____

_____

Transition to next activity routine   1   2   3
Steps: _____

_____

_____

_____

Violation of rule routine (disciplinary)   1   2   3
Steps: _____

_____

_____

_____

Other   1   2   3
Steps: _____

_____

_____

_____

INSTRUMENT **6.5** Recording Examples of Orally Delivered Incentives

1. Using praise and encouragement: _____

   _____

   _____

   _____

2. Providing explanations: _____

   _____

   _____

   _____

3. Offering to help: _____

   _____

   _____

   _____

4. Accepting diversity: _____

   _____

   _____

   _____

5. Providing reinforcement or reward: _____

   _____

   _____

   _____

INSTRUMENT 6.6   Observing Low-Profile Classroom Control

			Times observed			
	1	2	3	4	5	6
Anticipation						
back-and-forth scanning	❏	❏	❏	❏	❏	❏
faster pace	❏	❏	❏	❏	❏	❏
louder voice/high pitch	❏	❏	❏	❏	❏	❏
greater movement	❏	❏	❏	❏	❏	❏
change to other activity	❏	❏	❏	❏	❏	❏
other _____	❏	❏	❏	❏	❏	❏
Deflection						
Nonverbal						
moving closer to student	❏	❏	❏	❏	❏	❏
personal eye contact	❏	❏	❏	❏	❏	❏
facial expression	❏	❏	❏	❏	❏	❏
other _____	❏	❏	❏	❏	❏	❏
Verbal						
rule reminder (prompting)	❏	❏	❏	❏	❏	❏
name dropping	❏	❏	❏	❏	❏	❏
peer recognition	❏	❏	❏	❏	❏	❏
other _____	❏	❏	❏	❏	❏	❏
Reaction						
warning	❏	❏	❏	❏	❏	❏
incentive	❏	❏	❏	❏	❏	❏
loss of privilege	❏	❏	❏	❏	❏	❏
punishment (detention)	❏	❏	❏	❏	❏	❏
other _____	❏	❏	❏	❏	❏	❏

Chapter 7

LOOKING FOR LESSON CLARITY

Beside the Line of Elephants

I think they had no pattern
When they cut out the elephant's skin;
Some places it needs letting out,
And others, taking in.

(Author unknown)

Just as an accomplished seamstress creates a garment well fitted to the intended wearer, so too do wise teachers develop lesson objectives and plans that fit instructional goals—resulting in seamless instruction tailored to particular learners. In this chapter, we'll focus on seven dimensions of lesson clarity that will enable you to create optimal learning environments for your students.

Imagine a scene from an old spy movie. The mission leader says to the others, "Is that clear?" The others nod solemnly, synchronize their watches, and prepare to enter the dangerous world of espionage and intrigue.

What does it mean to be "clear"? How important is clarity when it comes to instructional design and delivery? In the old movies, the value of clarity was crucial: Agents who misunderstood secret codes or other important information risked their lives. While it's unlikely that our students will encounter life-and-death situations as a result of lesson clarity, our choices as instructors will certainly influence the rate at which students learn in our classrooms. In this chapter, we will consider ways of looking for lesson clarity.

For a lesson to be clear, its focus should be readily apparent. Learning activities should be understandable and easy to connect to one another—and to the overall lesson focus. As you observe lessons for clarity, some aspects will probably stand out immediately. For example, does the teacher explain concepts in a logical, step-by-step order that students are able to follow? Is the teacher's oral delivery audible, intelligible, and free of any distracting mannerisms? Are the points the teacher is making at the students' current level of understanding? Do students know how particular learning activities relate to the overall lesson objective?

Classroom research indicates that teachers vary considerably in their clarity. Not all teachers are able to communicate clearly and directly to their students without wandering, speaking over students' heads, or using speech patterns that confuse listeners. Teachers who fail to achieve lesson clarity often exhibit one (or more) of the following language patterns (Land, 1987; Smith & Land, 1981):

1. They rely on vague, ambiguous, or indefinite language (e.g., "might probably be," "tends to suggest," "could possibly happen").
2. They use overly complicated sentences (e.g., "There are many important reasons for the start of World War II, but some are more important than others, so let's start with those that are thought to be important but really aren't").
3. They give directions that are frequently followed by student requests for clarification (e.g., "Which center do we go to first?" or "What did you want us to do again?").

Clarity is a complex behavior because it extends beyond a teacher's oral presentation to many other cognitive behaviors, such as how a teacher organizes the content, uses media and illustrations, and delivers the content to learners (e.g., using examples, discussion, questions and answers, recitation, or cooperative group work). Indeed, teachers vary in both cognitive

and oral clarity. This variation can produce differences in student achievement as measured by test performance. Generally, teachers who teach with a high degree of clarity (both oral and cognitive) help students focus on specific learning objectives. This allows students to answer questions correctly the first time through a lesson, to experience a high degree of success, and to spend more time engaged in instruction.

DIMENSIONS OF LESSON CLARITY

Take a moment and recall a lesson that was clear and specific. What did the teacher do to create this lesson? List some of your ideas below.

Figure 7.1 summarizes seven teaching behaviors that contribute to lesson clarity. Which of the behaviors in Figure 7.1 match those on your list?

_____

_____

_____

As you reviewed Figure 7.1, did you notice that three behaviors occur at the *beginning* of a lesson, and the remaining four are implemented *during* a lesson? The three behaviors for achieving lesson clarity that occur at the beginning of a lesson are

1. Informing learners of the objective.
2. Providing learners with an advance organizer.
3. Checking for task-relevant prior learning and reteaching, if necessary.

Let's examine each of these behaviors teachers use to enhance the clarity of their lessons as they begin instruction. Then we will practice looking for them in a classroom dialogue.

Informing Learners of Lesson Objectives

At the start of a lesson, most students will not know what behaviors, skills, or concepts they are expected to learn, or how they may be expected to show their understanding. Not knowing what to expect can produce unrealistic fears in learners' minds, fears that may be worse than reality. Anxiety shortens learners' attention spans and may block their ability to focus on lesson content. Informing students at the beginning of a lesson how they will be expected to show their understanding of the subject matter can replace unrealistic fears and uncertainty with realistic expectations. This is most easily accomplished by translating the expected outcome of a lesson into some of the ways it might be used; for example, presenting a short oral summary, taking a multiple-choice or essay test, participating in a class discussion or question-and-answer period, or recording and sharing results of a cooperative group activity

FIGURE **7.1**   Indicators of Clarity

High Level of Clarity (Effective Teacher)	Poor Clarity (Ineffective Teacher)
1. Informs learners of the lesson objective (describes what behaviors will be tested, used orally, or required on future assignments as a result of the lesson).	Fails to relate lesson content to how and at what level of complexity the content will be used.
2. Provides learners with an advance organizer (places lesson in perspective of past and/or future lessons).	Starts presenting content without first introducing the subject in a broader context.
3. Checks for task-relevant prior learning at beginning of the lesson (determines level of understanding of prerequisite facts or concepts and reteaches, if necessary).	Moves to new content without checking for the facts, concepts, or skills needed to acquire the new learning.
4. Gives directives slowly and distinctly (repeats directives when needed, or divides them into smaller pieces).	Presents too much clerical, managerial, or technical information too quickly.
5. Knows learners' performance levels and teaches at or slightly above their current level of understanding (knows students' attention spans).	Fails to know that instruction is under or over students' levels, or when most students have "tuned out".
6. Uses examples, illustrations, and demonstrations to explain and clarify (uses visuals to help interpret and reinforce main points).	Restricts presentation to routine verbal reproduction of text or workbook.
7. Provides review or summary at end of lesson.	Ends lesson abruptly without repackaging key points.

with other class members. One way to accomplish this translation is to write examples of expected behaviors on the blackboard at the beginning of a unit; each day, place a checkmark beside the ones that most apply to that day's activities. For example, a teacher introducing a unit on the environment might list the following behaviors for the class, explaining that, by the end of the unit, students will be expected to accomplish all four.

☑ Recite a definition of global warming.
❑ Draw a picture of some of its possible effects on the Earth.
❑ Explain how it works.
❑ Using the map, identify which parts of the world may be affected most.

Notice that these behavioral outcomes range from repeating a simple definition to drawing, explaining, and using information. Knowing at which of these levels they are expected to perform, students will have a way to select and focus their attention on those parts of the instruction most relevant to the desired outcome for that day. Additionally, the other listed outcomes provide a guide to show students what will be expected in subsequent discussions and assignments.

Another way teachers inform learners of the objective is to use verbal statements at the beginning of a lesson that indicate how the content will be needed in a future assignment, such as

"Remember the four definitions of power that will be presented today. Tonight, you will need to complete an assignment using these definitions." (general science)
"Today, I want you to be able to use the possessive form to express ownership. Later, I am going to ask each of you to orally express ownership in a sentence to the class." (English)
"At the end of class today, I will ask you to identify a mystery specimen of lower animal life using the microscope." (life science)
"As a result of our discussion today, each of you should be able to state an opinion about our laws dealing with pornography." (social studies)

Simple statements such as these help learners organize and focus attention on the most important components of the day's lesson. If the students know that they are expected to be able to recall four definitions of power at the end of a lesson on energy, they will be more likely to focus their search, retrieval, and retention processes on the various definitions or categories of power presented during the lesson. Informing the learner of the objective enables her to be selective about how the lesson information should be organized and remembered and, most importantly, to know when the proper level of expected behavior has been attained. Effective teachers formulate such statements carefully, however, knowing that students may overlook important information that is not highlighted. Who among us has not asked, "Will this be on the test?" As you observe teachers communicate lesson objectives, you may want to consider what happens to important, but unemphasized, concepts, as well as to those the teacher stresses.

Observing Lesson Objectives

Instrument 7.1 provides a way for you to record whether learners have been informed of the objective, how they were informed of it, and the level of performance expected. In the first part of the record, you record if the learners were informed of the objective, and if not, why not. This is important because not every lesson will require informing learners of the objective (for example, when the lesson is a continuation of a series of related lessons for which the objective is already well known to learners, or when the lesson is devoted entirely to a review, in which case many different objectives may be touched on but not taught directly). After recording this information, indicate whether the objective(s) stated is (are) cognitive, affective, psychomotor, or some combination thereof. If possible, indicate the highest level of performance expected of the learner by selecting the expected outcome that comes closest to the action verbs listed on the form. If you cannot determine the intended level of performance at the start of a lesson, you'll usually be able to infer it at, or near, the end of the lesson by considering the nature of the content and/or exercises provided. Don't be surprised if you find yourself listing several objectives during one lesson. It is not unusual for lessons to have multiple objectives within, and even sometimes across, the cognitive, affective, and psychomotor domains, for which multiple marks should be entered.

Providing Advance Organizers

Another behavior for achieving clarity involves the use of advance organizers. Advance organizers are concepts presented orally or in visual form (charts and diagrams), usually at the beginning of a lesson, that give an overview of the day's work and of topics to which it will subsequently relate. An advance organizer (Mayer, 1987; Ausubel, 1968) gives the learner a conceptual preview of what is to come and helps prepare the learner to store, label, and package the content for retention and later use. In this sense, an advance organizer functions as a treelike structure with main limbs that act as pegs, or placeholders, for the branches that are to come. Without the limbs on which to hang content, important distinctions can easily become blurred or lost. An advance organizer helps the student focus her thinking in advance of the lesson by providing mental "hooks" on which to hang key ideas. This activates the learning process and focuses it in the direction that is most efficient for obtaining the expected outcome. Examples of advance-organizing activities provided at the beginning of a lesson would be

Listening to examples of both vowels and consonants before teaching the vowel sounds (reading)

Discussing the origins of pollution before describing its effects (social studies)

Showing a chart illustrating the skeletal evolution of humans prior to explaining the skeletal relationships between forms of animal life (life science)

Drawing examples of, and showing the similarity among, different types of triangles before introducing the concept of a right triangle (plane geometry)

Showing and explaining the origins of the periodic table of elements before introducing any of the elements found within it (chemistry)

Each of these examples presents a general concept as well as the specific related concept that is the subject of the day's lesson. Advance organizers are not designed to review content taught at some earlier time, but to present a concept (the alphabet, or origins of pollution, human evolution, triangular shapes, an organized system of atomic weights) into which fits not only the content to be taught that day, but also the content for all related lessons in a unit of study. Advance organizers lay the groundwork for expanding the present lesson topic, prevent every lesson from being seen as something entirely new, and integrate related concepts into larger and larger patterns and abstractions that later become unit outcomes (reading words with vowel and consonant blends in complete passages, planning an antipollution campaign, knowing the evolution of skeletal forms, or drawing different types of triangles). An advance organizer indicates the highest level of behavior or understanding expected to result from a sequence of lessons, and illustrates graphically how the present lesson will contribute to achieving that behavior or understanding.

As you observe teachers, you'll discover that one of the most frequently used advance organizers is a simple *verbal marker* that tells students what to watch for or what behaviors will be expected of them at the end of the lesson. These verbal markers often look like, and sometimes are embedded within, a statement that informs the learner of the objective for the lesson. Categories and examples of verbal markers providing advance organization include:

1. Relating content to past learning ("Today we will apply what we learned yesterday to a real laboratory experiment involving saline solutions.")
2. Verbally (and/or visually) summarizing what is to come ("The main points of today's lesson will be (a)_____, (b)_____, and (c)_____.")
3. Relating content to future learning ("We will conduct a debate in which each half of the class will participate, but first I will give each side the facts they will need to win.")
4. Providing clues about what to look for ("Today our topic is ways of measuring weight. I want you to watch carefully as I use these instruments in front of me to adjust and balance a scale for measuring weight.")
5. Providing and describing a written handout at the beginning of class ("This sheet outlines what we will cover and the order in which we will cover it. Take a minute and look over each of the points identified.")

More elaborate types of advance organization may be called for when the complexity of the behavioral outcome requires learners to fit many dissimilar pieces, or segments, of a lesson or unit together. Typically these more elaborate forms of organization are used to introduce units of instruction, but they may occasionally be required at the lesson level. These advance organizers typically take the form of charts (for example, of the periodic table of elements), pictures (of the skeletal structure of the human anatomy), or illustrations (a flow diagram indicating the steps to be followed in conducting a debate). Advance organizers can be verbal, visual, or both, and can be presented at the beginning of the lesson, during the lesson, or continually throughout the lesson. The teacher can turn to the advance organizer at each appropriate place in the lesson, reminding students where they are in the larger unit of content.

Observing Advance Organizers

There are many varieties of advance organizers; Instrument 7.2 offers you a way to catalog, or list, the advance organizers that you see being used across different content areas, grade levels, and learners. To complete this record, you observe several different classes and teachers to obtain the broadest sampling of advance organizers possible. Place a checkmark under beginning, middle, and/or end, depending on whether the organizer was introduced and/or used during the first, second, or last third of the lesson. A checkmark under all three time periods indicates the advance organizer was woven into the lesson content and referenced repeatedly. Place a checkmark in the last column each time the organizer is referenced during the lesson. Finally, include a short description of each advance organizer to help you remember what you saw. This will allow you to engage in more meaningful discussion about your observations, and will provide a more complete reference list to draw from in your own teaching. You may want to keep a card file that lists the most interesting advance organizers you encounter and how they are used. Include the reference number found in the second column of the form on your card to help you remember where you saw the organizer used. Keep these cards on file, organized according to subject and grades, for future reference. You'll find this list to be a valuable source of ideas as you plan your own lessons.

Connecting Task-Relevant Prior Knowledge to New Topics

Learning is enhanced when students are able to connect new ideas with what they already know. Thus, a third behavior for achieving lesson clarity involves helping students to focus on relevant content or to review prerequisite material (Hunter, 1994, 1982). Sometimes students have prerequisite knowledge, but fail to retrieve it or to connect it to new ideas. Effective teachers incorporate into their lesson plans some method of reviewing, summarizing, restating, or otherwise stimulating in students' minds previously acquired key concepts that are instrumental for achieving the goals of the present lesson. For example, if the goal is to read vowel–consonant blends, students must have acquired the proper pronunciation of vowels and consonants. If the goal is to have learners use a microscope to differentiate an amoeba from other animals, then facts, concepts, and skills acquired previously will have to be used to achieve this new outcome. Definitions of single-celled animals, unique characteristics of an amoeba that distinguish it from other one-celled animals, and skill in using the microscope represent just some of the task-relevant prior knowledge that has to be retrieved to attain the goal of the present lesson. Stimulating the recall of the most relevant aspects of this knowledge at the beginning of the lesson will prepare learners for the task of combining old and new content.

To help students retrieve and connect relevant information to the task at hand, teachers generally condense key aspects of prior learning into a brief and easily understood format. Not all of what has gone before can be summarized in a few brief minutes of preparatory comments, so thought-provoking and stimulating techniques are needed to bring sizable amounts of prior learning into focus in a short period. Choices range from informal questions asked randomly of a few students to a formal check of workbooks and a review of a previous assignment. Reviewing components of a previously introduced advance organizer may also help students recall and connect ideas.

Another useful technique for activating prior knowledge involves the use of oral questions that bring into focus unique or memorable events that enable students to recall earlier content simply and quickly. For example, the teacher might ask the class, "Who can remember what Johnny did to see the amoeba in the microscope?" (he turned it to high magnification); "Do you remember Betty Jo's description of how fast the reproduction cycle of an amoeba is?" (she equated cell division with waking up one morning to find a new baby in the family); "How many of you recall the picture Juan drew of the cellular structure of an amoeba?" (everyone had commented on how lifelike the picture was). Such questions help students retrieve task-relevant prior learning, not by summarizing the learning, but by tapping into a *mental image* created in an earlier lesson. Once the image is retrieved, students can search for details nestled within it and bring forth still greater recall. When extensive deficiencies in task-relevant prior learning are apparent from oral questioning or checking of assigned work, reteaching prerequisite content will be more important than teaching the new content scheduled for the day's lesson.

Based on our discussion, you might think that beginning a lesson by activating previously learned task-relevant knowledge and adjusting new content to learners' understanding would be a common practice, especially among experienced teachers. Yet Good and Grouws (1979) found that only 50 percent of experienced teachers began a lesson in this fashion. This is surprising, because daily checking and review at the beginning of a lesson can be accomplished in many ways, which include:

1. Having students correct each other's assignments at the beginning of class.
2. Having students identify especially difficult concepts during a question-and-answer session.
3. Orally sampling the understanding of those students who are indicators of the range of knowledge possessed by the entire class.
4. Explicitly reviewing the task-relevant information necessary for the day's lesson.

Some teachers avoid review at the beginning of lessons because they fear they will be wasting the time of the students who understand the material. To address this concern, Dahllof and Lundgren (1970) proposed that teachers check the understanding of a *steering group* comprised of lower performing learners in a class to determine the extent to which review and reteaching may be needed. If the steering group idea is expanded to include a small number of lower, average, and higher performing learners, teachers can question these students (who are changed from day to day) at the start of class on the task-relevant prior knowledge needed for the day's lesson, and thus gain an idea of the relative understanding of class members (Rosenshine & Stevens, 1986). When high performers miss a large proportion of answers, extensive reteaching for the entire class may be necessary. When high performers answer questions correctly, but average performers do not, some reteaching may need to occur before a new lesson begins. Finally, if most of the high and average performers answer the questions correctly, but most of the low performers do not, then individualized materials, extra reading and worksheets, or a tutorial arrangement may be needed to support the low performers in addressing new material. Checking understanding across a steering group can be done quickly and ensures that large amounts of class time are not devoted to review and reteaching that may benefit only a small number of students.

Observing Connections Between Task-Relevant Prior Knowledge and New Topics

As you can imagine, it is important to know not only if a teacher checks for task-relevant prior knowledge, but also what prior knowledge is required for the day's lesson and what future knowledge may depend on it. For any class you observe, make arrangements to consult the text, curriculum guide, and/or the unit plan to determine the facts, skills, or concepts that should have been learned prior to a lesson, and that will become task-relevant prior learning for subsequent lessons. Past and future learnings can be recorded in the following format, followed by the reason for placing the content of the day's lesson between them in this curriculum.

1. Using the text, curriculum guide, or unit plan, list any facts, skills, or concepts that need to be attained for learners to achieve the objectives of today's lesson.
   Facts _____
   Skills _____
   Concepts _____
2. Using the text, curriculum guide, or unit plan, list any facts, skills, or concepts to be taught in future lessons that may be dependent upon the content of today's lesson.
   Facts _____
   Skills _____
   Concepts _____
3. Cite the reason, as you see it, for placing the content of today's lesson at this point in the curriculum as it applies to any of the following:
   Facts _____
   Skills _____
   Concepts _____

The final question on the record is designed to help you discern why these facts, skills, or concepts have been placed in today's lesson (for example, are they steps that will be used to solve problems in a subsequent lesson, or examples that illustrate the concepts taught in a previous lesson?). You can test the validity of this placement by observing future lessons.

So far, we've discussed three teaching behaviors that can be performed at the start of a lesson to increase lesson clarity. Now let's consider four additional behaviors (see Figure 7.1) for achieving lesson clarity during a lesson.

4. Giving directives slowly and distinctly.
5. Knowing students' previous performance levels and teaching to them.
6. Using examples, illustrations, and demonstrations to explain and clarify text and workbook content.
7. Providing a review or summary at the end of the lesson.

Giving Directives Clearly

If learners are to understand a message (or lesson concept), they must be ready to receive it. As we have already discussed, informing the learner of what is expected, providing advance organization, and checking for and reteaching task-relevant prior learning all help to prepare learners to receive the message. In addition to these important behaviors, however, the message itself must be clear. It must be presented in ways that make it intelligible to learners, so that they not only hear, see, and interpret what is being taught, but also retain it long afterward. Thus, an important aspect of message clarity involves how students are directed during learning tasks.

One of the most frequently heard excuses from students for poor performance is that they "weren't told (or didn't understand) what to do." Students who do not understand the directions given often remain silent. As a result, directives about completing workbook exercises, engaging in learning center and group work, and completing reading assignments, homework, and handouts should be communicated with the same deliberateness as lesson content.

An effective teacher deliberately slows the pace when conveying instructions, divides directives into steps if necessary, and then checks to see that each step is understood. Combining verbal, visual, and kinesthetic input helps support student understanding, so effective teachers also summarize instructions in writing (e.g., on an overhead, a chalkboard, or in printed copy form), in another visual form (e.g., an example of the desired end-product), or physically (modeling a behavior and having students follow along).

Along the same lines, Evertson and Emmer (1982) found differences in the way effective and ineffective teachers handled assignments, particularly homework. Giving assignments appeared almost effortless for the effective teachers; for ineffective teachers the normal classroom routine sometimes came to an abrupt halt, the noise level went up, and there was much commotion and fuss as they attempted to make assignments. What accounts for the differences?

These effective teachers attached assignments directly to the end of an in-class activity, avoiding awkward pauses or even the need for a transition. The assignment appeared to students as a logical extension of what was already taking place, which in fact it should be. The practice of giving the assignment immediately after the activity to which it most closely relates, as opposed to mentioning it at the end of class, at the end of the school day, may be much like getting an injection while the physician is smiling and engaging you in a friendly conversation: If the conversation is engaging enough, you might not feel the pain. Consider how the following assignments might be received by learners.

Teacher A: I probably should assign some homework, so do problems 1 through 10 on page 61.

Teacher B: For tonight, do the problems under Exercise A and Exercise B—that should keep you busy.

Teacher C: We're out of time now, so I guess you'll have to finish these problems on your own.

In each of these statements, there is the question of whether the homework is really needed, or whether it is being given mechanically or as some sort of punishment. Why this homework is being assigned may be a mystery to most students. The teacher requests make no mention of either the in-class activities to which the homework relates, or of the future benefits that may accrue from completing the assignment. These explanations are important if anything other than a mechanical or begrudging response is expected. Most students will appreciate knowing why an assignment is made before they are expected to do it.

Consider the same assignments again, this time with an explanation added.

Teacher A: Today we have talked a lot about the origins of the Civil War and some of the economic unrest that preceded it. But some other types of unrest were also responsible for the Civil War. These will be important for understanding the real causes behind this war. Problems 1 through 10 on page 61 will help you understand some of these other causes.

Teacher B: We have all had a chance now to try our skill at forming possessives. As most of you have found out, it's a little harder than it looks. So let's try Exercises A and B for tonight, which should give you just the right amount of practice in forming possessives for tomorrow's lesson.

Teacher C: Well, it looks like time has run out before we could complete all the problems. The next set of problems we will study requires a lot of what we have learned here today. Let's complete the rest of these for tonight to see if you've got the concept. This should make the next lesson go a lot easier.

Keep in mind that effective classroom teachers give assignments that

❑ Follow closely in time the lessons or activities to which they relate.
❑ Provide explanations about why the assignment is, or will be, of value.
❑ Avoid unnecessary negative connotations (for example, "that should keep you busy") that may make the assignment look more like a punishment than an instructional activity.

Observing Clarity of Directives

Figure 7.2 provides a format for recording clarity of directions. Use this instrument to record each student response–teacher reaction sequence after directions have been given for any one of the several types of classroom assignments listed (for example, homework, an in-class activity, or a test). The purpose of this observation form is to help you determine how

FIGURE 7.2 Coding Form for Recording Student Response–Teacher Reaction During Instructions

Student or Number	Assignment							Student Response				Teacher Reaction						
	wb	hw	oas	hand	test	proj	other	rpt	specif	uncert	other	crit	rpt	ans	restate	check	ignore	other
John	✓							✓				✓	✓					
Betty	✓								✓				✓			✓		

FIGURE 7.3 Coding Symbols and Categories for Observing Clarity of Directions

Direction or Instructions Pertaining to:

Workbook	wb
Homework	hw
Oral assignment	oas
Handout	hand
Test	test
Extended project or paper	proj
Other type of assignment	other

Student Responses

Student asks teacher to repeat directions or instructions.	rpt
Student asks specific question for clarification.	specif
Student expresses uncertainty orally (for example, "I don't understand") or physically (for example, frowns shrugs).	uncert
Student uses some other measure to indicate directives or instructions were not understood.	other

Teacher Reactions

Teacher criticizes student for not understanding.	crit
Teacher repeats directive or instruction.	rpt
Teacher answers student question about directive.	ans
Teacher restates instructions in different words.	restate
Teacher checks for understanding (for example, asks student to repeat or asks student a question).	check
Teacher ignores student response.	ignore
Teacher reacts in some other way.	other

clearly a teacher's instructions are received by the students and what, if any, reaction the teacher has to a learner's difficulty in receiving them. A description of the categories and codes to be recorded is provided in Figure 7.3, and a form for recording the actual student response–teacher reaction sequences is given in Instrument 7.3.

Figure 7.2 provides data from a student response–teacher reaction sequence. The marks in the first row of Figure 7.2 indicate that some instructions about an assignment in the workbook (wb) have been given. John then asks the teacher to repeat (rpt) the instructions. The teacher criticizes (crit) John and repeats (rpt) the instructions. Next, Betty, in response to the same instructions about the workbook, asks a specific question (specif). The teacher answers (ans) and then checks (check) to see if Betty understands.

In this manner, student response–teacher reaction sequences are recorded to assess the clarity of the teacher's original instructions and the teacher's response to any misunderstanding on the students' part. Patterns across individual students and assignments might reveal, for example, more problems with directions pertaining to one type of assignment (for example, homework) than another (a workbook), or that the teacher tends to criticize when students ask for the directions to be repeated, but not when students ask specific questions for clarification. These types of patterns are often the most revealing because they explain the differences in the clarity of instructions (and sometimes the academic performance of students) across classrooms. For example, some teachers repeatedly criticize student requests for more information with expressions such as "You weren't listening," which may discourage some students from asking for clarification again. Also, it is important to check the uniformity with which the teacher responds to different students (for example, higher and lower levels of previous performance or experience, or students of a particular culture or ethnicity) who express difficulty in understanding the directions given. These and other student characteristics can be entered beside, or instead of, a student name on the coding form, and later analyzed to reveal biases or preferences that may be unintentionally limiting the opportunity for certain groups of students to complete assignments properly.

Knowing Students' Previous Performance Levels and Teaching to Them

The fifth behavior for achieving clarity is knowing your students' previous performance levels and teaching to them. Because several levels of achievement are likely to be present in your classroom, it will be important to package your instructional message in the form of oral presentations, visual messages, exercises, written assignments, readings, and group interactions at the current level of understanding of all students. To accomplish this, learning centers, reference libraries, different types of pictorial displays, and alternate texts and exercises that tap into performance levels above and below the average learner are needed to provide a range of instructional stimuli at the current level of functioning of each student.

Regardless of the level of difficulty at which a lesson begins, a lesson may be too difficult for some learners, and not difficult enough for others. Unit and lesson planning in a heterogeneous classroom is largely a game of averages in which the teacher attempts to provide *most* of the instruction at the current level of understanding of *most* of the learners. There are, however, some procedures that can help address the range of prior achievement and experience within a classroom through individualized and self-directed learning activities. Alternatives for individualizing instruction and providing students a degree of control over the pace of their own learning include:

1. *Task ability grouping*—A class can be subdivided according to particular skills required for learning specific lesson content. For example, higher performing readers may be asked at the beginning of a lesson to read ahead and work independently on advanced exercises while the lesson is directed to lower performing readers. Similarly, a lesson's objectives, activities, and instructional materials, as well as assessment, can be divided into difficulty levels and targeted to different groups, depending on the range of previous performance and experience within the classroom.

2. *Peer tutoring*—Some students can be assigned to help other students who have not yet acquired specific task-relevant prior knowledge. Since some students may require remediation, peer tutors can begin at a particular student's current level of understanding and bring it to the level required for a subsequent lesson.

3. *Learning centers*—At times, some students will profit more from working at learning centers or workstations than from exercises and workbooks above their current level of understanding. When a learning center contains media, supplemental resources, and exercises that present content in alternative formats (for example, visual or auditory), it should be included as an integral part of the lesson. A learning center can help individualize a lesson for those students who lack the prerequisite knowledge or skills required by the lesson entry level, and who need to catch up before any new learning is possible.

4. *Review and follow-up materials*—As noted previously, a lesson can begin with a review of task-relevant prior knowledge. A summary with supplementary handouts, in which the critical or most complex aspects of a previous lesson can be looked up as needed, may be sufficient to bring some students up to the required level while not boring others for whom a review may be redundant. Brief supplementary handouts provided to each student can cover the prerequisite knowledge, thereby taking the minimal amount of time away from the presentation of new content and limiting an oral review for the entire class to only the essentials.

5. *Self-paced, programmed texts*—Programmed texts break content into small segments and present the learner with immediate feedback about the correctness of the response to each piece. Although higher performing students typically find programmed texts boring because of their slow and repetitive pace, these texts are often successful in helping lower performing learners master basic facts and understandings that would not have been acquired through full-class instruction. Also, self-paced materials can contribute to a high level of motivation by providing a nonthreatening, individualized context in which catch-up learning can take place.

6. *Games, simulations, and role-playing*—Games, simulations, and role-playing provide still other opportunities for individualized and self-directed learning. With the large-scale availability of computers and prepackaged activities from publishers, games and simulations take on added importance as instructional activities that can elicit the direct involvement of students in the learning process at

their current level of understanding. These activities can become important aids to achieving clarity in heterogeneous classrooms where students are allowed to independently pursue instructionally relevant goals using interactive activities and software. Role-playing opportunities can allow students to "practice" content in the guise of another character, "trying on" and "testing out" ideas in a safe environment.

Observing Level of Instruction

During observations, you can determine the extent to which the instruction is being delivered at the students' current level of understanding by recording signs of student behavior. For example, at least some of the student behaviors in Figure 7.4 have been observed when instruction directed to the entire class is (a) below, (b) at or slightly above, and (c) considerably above the learners' current level of understanding.

Circle one entry from each of the three columns in Instrument 7.4 to record the approximate percentage of learners in a class for whom the content appears below, at or slightly above, or above the learners' current level of understanding. Use the list provided in Figure 7.4 as your guide. You can describe the behavioral signs that were most obvious in making your choices by filling in the blanks in the following questions, selecting from and adding

to the previous list of behaviors as needed. (Notice how this format can be used to identify additional behaviors related to small-group work and cooperative learning activities, resulting in a chart similar to Figure 7.4).

1. What observable signs led you to believe that the lesson content (or group activity) was below the current level of understanding of ____ percent of the class (if other than 0)?
2. What observable signs led you to believe that the lesson content (or group activity) was at or slightly above the current level of understanding of ____ percent of the class (if other than 0)?
3. What observable signs led you to believe that the lesson content (or group activity) was above the current level of understanding of ____ percent of the class (if other than 0)?

The patterns in Figure 7.5 are typical of most classrooms during direct or expository instruction to the entire class. Percentages for Classroom A indicate that the instructional materials, media, and procedures used may have been boring, or may have contained previously learned content. Here, an upward adjustment in curriculum materials and outcomes to a higher level of behavioral complexity might be the target of future lessons. Percentages for Classroom B represent a fairly typical classroom in which materials, media, and procedures are gener-

FIGURE 7.4 Student Behaviors Observed at Different Levels of Instruction

Instruction Below Level of Learners	Instruction at or Slightly Above Level of Learners	Instruction Above Level of Learners
Students talking among themselves.	Students' eyes focused on teacher.	Students off-task and inattentive.
Students don't hear questions when asked.	Students volunteer answers.	Students answer questions incorrectly.
Students working on other coursework.	Students cooperate with teacher requests.	Students don't understand questions when asked.
Students challenge teacher's authority and knowledge.	Students ask leading questions.	Students' posture and eyes not in tune with instruction.

FIGURE 7.5 Typical Patterns of Distribution

	Below (%)	At or Slightly Above (%)	Above (%)
Classroom A	75	25	0
Classroom B	25	50	25
Classroom C	0	25	75

ally on target but, because of the heterogeneous grouping of students, may be above or below the current level of functioning of some students. This set of percentages indicates the value of integrating both remedial and alternative learning materials into the existing curriculum in either an independent study, small group, or learning center format to accommodate differences in prior knowledge and ability among students. Finally, Classroom C indicates that a downward adjustment in the curriculum materials might be made to teach prerequisite skills and better match the ability level of the majority of students (Gagne, Briggs, & Wagner, 1992).

Using Examples, Illustrations, and Demonstrations

The final two behaviors for achieving clarity—using examples, illustrations, and demonstrations, and reviewing and summarizing—have several things in common: Both behaviors occur well into the lesson, and both are intended to expand and clarify lesson content that may not be understood completely or uniformly without some reorganization and elaboration.

The content organization found within most texts, workbooks, and curriculum guides has been created for the purpose of communicating content intended to be read, not for the purpose of presenting content that must be explained orally within the time frame of a specific lesson. Chapter titles, subheadings, or Roman numerals in curriculum outlines are often too broad to cover in a single lesson. Some teachers stick tenaciously to these formal headings without considering the volume of content that falls within them, or the time it takes to orally explain, illustrate, and practice this content. More effective teachers realize that some texts require reorganization to better fit the needs of students and class schedules. As a result, they learn to subdivide text material for their students, often independently of chapter headings and other markings. When effective teachers reorganize content, they often share the pattern they followed with their students. For example, they might ask students to read for a list of rules ("Here are some rules to follow"), steps ("We will do 'this', and then 'that'"), or practices ("Here is the first of five things we will cover") that reorganize content into smaller pieces. These teachers then provide examples, illustrations, or demonstrations, as well as practice and feedback, for these smaller pieces of information within the context of a single lesson.

Think of a teacher who made a particular subject come alive for you. What did he do to accomplish that? Did the teacher offer interesting oral examples? Visual illustrations? Practical demonstrations? Did he

allow for plenty of group discussion and sharing of personal insights and opinions? Any of these forms can increase the clarity of a lesson by repackaging its content and affording students with diverse backgrounds or learning styles the opportunity to relate it to their own levels of experience and understanding. Audiovisual media, worksheets, problem sets, and study aids, especially when used in the context of group activities, discussion, and question-and-answer sessions, can help make textbook content meaningful to the learner.

Observing Use of Examples, Illustrations, and Demonstrations

Since teachers may use examples, illustrations, and demonstrations many times during a lesson, it is important to record how often they are used during an observation period to enhance the lesson's clarity. Instrument 7.5 illustrates an observation record in which you can record various types of visual and oral examples, illustrations, and demonstrations each time they occur. The purpose of this instrument is to determine the preferences a teacher may have for various techniques and how they are used. For this record, checkmarks are placed each time an example, illustration, or demonstration is presented visually, orally, or both. A relatively large proportion of checkmarks in any one row may indicate an overreliance on one form of example, illustration, or demonstration. Few or no marks in the visual categories, for example, can indicate a lack of lesson interest or appeal, especially for learners who may favor the visual modality. Because there are many visual and oral ways of providing examples, illustrations, and demonstrations in addition to those listed, you should add other clarity-enhancing techniques to the "Other" category when you see them.

Reviewing and Summarizing

Reviews and summaries at the end of, or interspersed throughout, a lesson can have much the same effect as examples, illustrations, and demonstrations. A review or summary need not be a simple parroting of what was taught in an abbreviated form. Instead, an effective review or summary recasts content into a slightly different form than the one in which it was originally presented, thereby elaborating on and reorganizing earlier content for efficient storage and retrieval.

One of the most effective ways of accomplishing this recasting is to undertake *transmediation* (Siegel, 1983). Transmediation is the expression of an idea across media forms. For example, students who explore the properties of triangles in written form during a lesson might review these properties by creating a simple musical jingle. Students who read about the exploits of a particular explorer in social studies might summarize these exploits in a dramatic presentation or in an artistic mural. Determining key concepts and how to best present them in another medium can add freshness to a review or summary—as well as help students better retain the information.

Planning for review and summary activities provides learners the opportunity to plug into the content at a different time and in a different manner. Content not learned or misunderstood during the lesson can be learned and clarified during summaries and reviews, if the summary and review go beyond simple repetition of content to a repackaging of the lesson and unit concepts. Another way of accomplishing this is by combining or consolidating key points into a single overall conclusion, as in this example.

Teacher: Today we have studied the economic systems of capitalism, socialism, and communism. We have found each of these to be similar, because some of the same goods and services are owned by the government. We have found them to be different, however, with respect to the degree to which various goods and services are owned by the government, with the least number of goods and services owned by a government under capitalism, and the most goods and services owned by a government under communism.

This teacher is drawing together, or highlighting, the single most important conclusion from the day's lesson. To do this, the highest level of generalization or conclusion that can be made from the lesson is expressed, without reference to any details that were necessary to arrive at it. This teacher consolidates many different bits and pieces by going to the broadest, most sweeping conclusion that could be made, thereby capturing the meaning and essence of all that has gone before.

Another procedure for summarizing and reviewing is to reiterate the most important content that has been presented. Here the teacher repeats the most important content to be sure that it is understood. Obviously, not all of the content can be repeated, so some selection is in order.

Teacher: Before we end, let's look at our two rules once again (writes on board as she speaks): Rule 1: Use the possessive form when an "of" phrase can be substituted for a noun. Rule 2: If the word for which we are denoting ownership already ends in an "s," place the apostrophe after, not before, the "s."

This teacher is consolidating by summarizing, or touching on, each of the key elements of the lesson. The teacher's review is rapid and to the point, pro-

viding students with an opportunity to fill in any missing gaps about the main features of the lesson.

Still another method for reviewing and summarizing provides learners with a structure by which key facts and ideas can be remembered, without a review of them. With this procedure, facts and ideas are reorganized into a framework for easy recall.

Teacher: Today we studied the formation and punctuation of possessives. Recall that we used two rules—one for forming possessives whenever an "of" phrase can be substituted for a noun, and another for forming possessives for words ending in *s.* From now on, let's call these rules the *of rule* and the *s rule,* keeping in mind that both make use of the apostrophe.

By giving students a framework for remembering the rules (the *of rule* and the *s rule*), the teacher reorganizes the content and indicates how it should be stored and remembered. The key to this procedure is to provide students with a *code* or *symbol* system by which the contents of the lesson can be more easily stored and recalled for later use.

These examples suggest that reviewing or summarizing means more than just calling attention to the end of a lesson. In the first instance, the highest level generalization that could be made was restated; in the second, the content at the level at which it was taught was summarized; and in the third, students were helped in remembering each of the important categories of information with codes or symbols. Each is a valuable means of increasing lesson clarity.

Observing Review and Summary Techniques

If a lesson ends with a review or summary, you can record the type of the review or summary using the following format.

❑ Reviews key points, which are _____

_____

❑ Provides symbols, codes, or mnemonic devices, which are _____
❑ Other (for example, handout). Describe: _____

_____

The purpose of this record is to observe how a summary or review can, and many times does, go beyond a simple regurgitation of the facts as they were presented. This format can be used to describe how any one, or a combination, of the summary and review methods discussed previously were applied in a lesson. If you, as an observer, can identify a generalization, key point, or symbol used in conducting the summary or review, you can gain valuable insight into the review's clarity.

Cultural Diversity and Lesson Clarity

One of the most recent developments in the area of cultural diversity and lesson clarity involves the concept of *social framing*. Social framing refers to the context in which a message, such as a lesson, is received and understood. Tannen (1986) defines a frame as a taken-for-granted context that delimits the sources from which meaning can be derived. When a teacher announces that "Today's lesson will expect you to know how to 'borrow' when subtracting two-digit numbers," the teacher has implicitly set a frame for the lesson that conveys to the learner what he is expected to learn. Recent research has examined how best to frame a lesson so that learners can derive a common understanding from the content presented, or how to alter the frame of a lesson so that it will be more understandable to cultural or ethnic groups that may be accustomed to an alternate frame. For example, Michaels and Collins (1984) report an example of an Anglo teacher who framed a story with linear, topic-centered patterns (for example, "Today I will read you a series of events that happened in the lives of three characters"), while her African-American students framed the task according to topic-associating patterns (for example, "She's going to tell us the kinds of things that can happen to people"). While one group primarily looked for a sequential list of events that unfolded from the beginning to the end of the story, the other group made notes about the events and the memories they evoked. Thus, frames that are ambiguous or less appropriate to one group than another can alter how and what content is learned.

Bowers and Flinders (1991) make a case for understanding the context in which different cultures expect information to be transmitted. They recommend that the teacher (1) present content from the frame most dominant to the classroom, (2) make explicit what the frame—the context—through which learners must see the content is (for example, facts to be learned, skills to be performed, or concepts to think about), and/or (3) negotiate, when necessary, the frame with students at the start of the lesson.

Bowers and Flinders (1991) suggest three ways of establishing a frame at the start of a lesson that encourage students to respond in like manner. These approaches involve self-disclosure, humor, and dialogue.

❑ *Self-disclosure* involves being open about your feelings and emotions that lead up to the lesson. "I've been struggling to make this topic meaningful and here's what I've come up with." This will encourage similar statements of self-disclosure from students, which can be used to frame the lesson.

❑ *Humor* at the start of a lesson establishes a flexible, spontaneous, expressive mood from which frames can become established. "Here's a funny thing that happened to me about what we're going to study today" will encourage students to share other personal episodes that can be used to provide a context for the lesson.

❑ *Dialogue*, the back-and-forth discussion of lesson content, involves random and simultaneous responding. Here every student can expect to be heard, and lesson content is expressed idiosyncratically in the words of the learners. The responses of students are then used to further structure and elaborate lesson content.

Each of these framing techniques is believed to enhance lesson clarity across cultural and ethnic groups, some of whom can be expected to be less responsive to the traditional frames of prepackaged lesson plans and textbooks. As you would expect, sensitive framing also encourages a warm and supportive classroom environment and encourages students to take the risks involved in learning new material and grappling with unfamiliar ideas.

PRACTICE OBSERVING LESSON CLARITY: A DIALOGUE

A dialogue illustrating several aspects of lesson clarity that have been presented in this chapter follows. To prepare for evaluating the dialogue, review the seven dimensions of lesson clarity presented in Figure 7.1. Then read the dialogue and look for the dimensions of clarity—or lack thereof. Keep a record of your observations using the checklist in Figure 7.6.

Ms. Raskin teaches computer literacy, a state-mandated requirement for all students in her state. Her classes tend to be large (about 34 students) and heterogeneous in ability. Today she is introducing the components of a microcomputer system, in preparation for teaching how to use the word processing software that the students will be expected to master later in the course. Today's lesson follows several introductory lessons on "What Is a Computer?" and precedes a unit entitled "How a Computer Works." We peek in on Ms. Raskin's first class of the day during the second week of school.

Ms. Raskin: [at the bell] Okay, let's settle down. No one should have their computer on. We have only a few more lessons on the basics before we will begin working with the computer, so let's be patient. Last week we introduced what a computer is and related it to our own abilities to select, remember, and process various types of information. We associated the kinds of processing a computer does with filing information, much like a manual system in a filing cabinet; subjecting information to statistical procedures, much like

FIGURE 7.6   Checklist for Observing Lesson Clarity

Effectiveness Indicators	Observed	Not Observed	No Opportunity to Observe
1. Informs learners of skills or understandings expected at end of lesson.			
2. Provides learners with an advance organizer that places lesson content in perspective.			
3. Checks for task-relevant prior learning at beginning of lesson and reteaches if necessary.			
4. Gives directives slowly and distinctly. Checks for understanding along the way.			
5. Knows learners' ability levels and uses media, materials, and procedures at or slightly above their current level of functioning.			
6. Uses examples, illustrations, or demonstrations to explain and clarify content in text and workbooks.			
7. Provides review or summary.			

using a hand calculator; and creating symbols and codes, much like writing music or creating graphics in the form of pictorial representations. These indicate the variety of functions a computer can serve, but also that computers do essentially the same things that we humans do—only faster and more efficiently. Today we will turn our attention to those other things a computer needs to help it perform these functions. We will group these other things into two categories, called *hardware* and *software*. As you can see, I've written these two categories on the board. Under hardware, I have the components [points to each word in turn with pointer]: *monitor, printer, keyboard, disk drive*. These are some of the most common components of a microcomputer system that fall under the category of hardware. At the end of today's class, I will expect you to be able to describe what each of these components does, and to identify some of the differences that exist among various types of monitors, printers, keyboards, and disk drives. Now, let's see how much you remember from last week. Quann, what's missing from our list of hardware to make our microcomputer system complete?

Quann: Remember, Ms. Raskin, I transferred in late, so I missed most of last week.

Ms. Raskin: That's right. Libby, can you help us?

Libby: I think so. It's the CPU that's missing.

Ms. Raskin: And, Alberto, what's a CPU?

Alberto: It's the central processing unit—or the heart of the whole system.

Ms. Raskin: Keisha, you had your hand up, too.

Keisha: It's the part that does the computing.

Alberto: That's what I said!

Ms. Raskin: Alberto, remember to raise your hand. That's correct—you are both right. Can anyone remember from last week what part of our body is like the CPU? Ralph, you can give us the answer, can't you?

Ralph: It's like our brain—it's the part of the computer that does the thinking.

Ms. Raskin: Remember, we don't want to say "thinking" but . . .

Ralph: Oops, I mean processing, because humans do the thinking, and then they program the computer to do the processing.

Ms. Raskin: Yes. Does everyone remember the argument we had last week on whether computers—or CPUs—can really think? [Most of class nods in agreement.] Keisha, what was our conclusion?

Keisha: Well, we all had a good laugh because I thought HAL, the computer in the movie *2001* we saw, was actually doing his own thinking—I forgot that someone had to program him to think like a human. Also, I guess I forgot that the movie was only science fiction, and that we haven't been able to make computers come that close to thinking yet.

Ms. Raskin: Good, now let's begin today's lesson, in which we will describe and show how each of these components of hardware [points to board again] are used by the CPU to carry out its various functions. Notice I have the word *software* written up here as another category, but I have nothing listed under it. For now, I just want you to be aware that a microcomputer system requires both hardware and software. Tomorrow when you come in, there will be some components of software written under this category, which will be the topic of our next lesson. For tonight, think about what some components of software might be, write them down, and when you come in tomorrow, see if your list is similar to mine. Pages 31 to 34 in the text will give you some hints about what to put on your list. Now, let's begin with the first component under hardware [points to word *monitor*]. This one's easy because we see one every day. Debby, what is a monitor like in our everyday lives?

Debby: Our TV set at home.

Ms. Raskin: Of course. And what function does it serve?

Debby: It lets us see pictures.

Ms. Raskin: And what else? Danny.

Danny: Well, it could show us words, too, if we wanted.

Ms. Raskin: Yes, and this is particularly important for using word processing software. Oops, I just gave you one entry for your list of software tonight. Some of you may even choose to write the book report you will be doing for your English class this grading period on the computers in front of you. For that, you will need to have monitors that show the words you write. Now, let me demonstrate various types of monitors to show that not all monitors are alike. [Teacher clicks on three monitors, one after another, positioned in front of the class facing the students. Each monitor has been programmed to read "Hello, my name is HAL. What is different about me?" Some members of the class laugh as each screen lights up.]

Student: But, Ms. Raskin, I thought HAL couldn't think.

Ms. Raskin: Let's remember to raise our hands before speaking out. [Keisha raises her hand feverishly.]

Keisha: You told the CPU to show those words.

Ms. Raskin: That's right, I wrote those words and programmed them to appear on the screen. Now, what about the answer to HAL's question. Anyone? David, you haven't said anything so far. What's the answer?

David: Well, in the first HAL, the letters are black and white—like the old TV sets. In the second, the letters are green. And in the third, the letters are all different colors—red, green, and blue.

Ms. Raskin: That points up one of the most important differences in monitors—some are only black and white, some are what are called *green phosphorous*, and some are color. So, how many of you like the color monitor the best? Raise your hands. [Most students raise their hands.] How many like the green phosphorous? [A few students raise their hands.] And how many like the black and white? [No hands are raised.] I see all of you have gotten used to your color TV sets at home. A color monitor is most appropriate when a lot of graphics or pictures will be shown on the screen; a green phosphorous monitor is most appropriate when a large amount of text must be read from the screen. A black-and-white monitor is the hardest to read and the least interesting when graphics or pictures are to be displayed. Anybody notice any other differences? Trevor.

Trevor: The printing on the black-and-white monitor is harder to read. It's kind of fuzzy.

Ms. Raskin: Yes. This is because the black-and-white monitor is actually an old TV set; they are often used as monitors because they are inexpensive. But notice that a screen made for a TV is not as clean looking, especially in displaying fine print, as might be required in reading a book report or term paper from the monitor. This aspect of a monitor is called its resolution: The easier to read, the higher the resolution. Color and green phosphorous monitors can differ in resolution as well, but black-and-white TVs used as monitors have the poorest resolution. Any other differences? [No response, so teacher calls on Alberto.] Alberto.

Alberto: Well, this may be silly, but the screen on the black-and-white monitor is bigger than the other two.

Ms. Raskin: That's right. And that brings up another point: The bigger the screen, the poorer the resolution, or clarity, of the picture. Since computer monitors are always adjacent to a keyboard, large screens are unnecessary, so small screens, about 12 to 16 inches, are used to create high-resolution pictures. Has anyone ever seen one of those very small portable TVs? [Alberto raises his hand.] Alberto.

Alberto: My uncle in California got me one last Christmas.

Ms. Raskin: And what's the clarity of the picture like?

Alberto: It's unbelievable! Especially compared to our large TV in the living room.

Ms. Raskin: That's my point—the smaller the screen, the higher the resolution, and the clearer the picture. [Skipping to near the end of the lesson now, after completing similar discussions for printer, keyboard, and disk drive.] Now it's time to look back at some of the things we have said today. [Teacher turns on overhead projector with the columns and rows shown in Figure 7.7 predrawn on transparency.] Let's try to fill in this chart from our earlier discussion. Recall that our discussion pointed to several differences among our three HALs. One of the differences was the purpose for which each might be used, another was their cost, and a third was their resolution.

Quann, if I recall correctly, we began today's lesson with you. Despite your absence last week, let's see how well you've caught on to today's lesson. Tell me what to place in the Black and White column?

Quann: Okay, I think I can. Let me start with cost, since that's the easiest. [Teacher nods.] Black-and-white monitors are the least expensive, especially if they're a TV being used as a monitor.

Ms. Raskin: Good. [Teacher writes in *least expensive* on transparency.]

Quann: Now, for resolution . . . the resolution will not be as good if it's just an ordinary TV or if the screen is very large. [Teacher writes *lowest* in the appropriate place on the transparency.] And, finally, well for uses . . . I guess it can be used for graphics and pictures as well as for reading words, since it doesn't favor either one. [Teacher writes *Both text and pictures equally* on transparency.]

Ms. Raskin: That was good, Quann. Looks like you're all caught up with us. Tim, what about our next column, pertaining to our second HAL monitor.

Tim: Well, a green phosphorous screen is best suited for reading large amounts of text, but costs more than a black-and-white monitor and has better resolution. [Teacher writes each response on transparency.]

Ms. Raskin: Very good. Keisha, would you like to take our last column?

Keisha: HAL 3, that's the color monitor, is best suited when a lot of graphics or pictures will be displayed; it's the most expensive and has good resolution—I guess the same as the green phosphorous screen, if both were the same size. [Teacher fills in third column with Keisha's answers.]

Ms. Raskin: This chart shows some of the most important characteristics of monitors, so be sure to copy it into your notebooks. Let's summarize our earlier discussion about printers in the same way with this next transparency. Who'd like to begin?

REACTIONS TO THE DIALOGUE

Take a look at your checklist. Which of the seven dimensions of lesson clarity did you observe in this dialogue? Recall that lesson clarity involves explaining concepts in a logical step-by-step order; presenting content at the students' current level of understanding; and communicating lesson content in specific, unambiguous language. Two of the most important dimensions of clarity that help ensure a lesson is understandable and can be followed in a logical step-by-step order are informing the learner of the objective and providing advance organizers.

Recall that Ms. Raskin began by reviewing what had occurred in several previous lessons. This approach is sometimes called *overlapping*, where the beginning of one lesson repeats or overlaps with the end of the preceding lesson. This helps students place the content of the day's lesson in the perspective of previously learned content, emphasizing the continuity and relationships that exist among lessons within the same unit. Thus, each new lesson is seen as an expansion or extension of content already mastered. It was in this context that Ms. Raskin informed learners of the lesson topic and the level of performance that would be expected of the students at the end of class.

Next, Ms. Raskin established some divisions of content that would serve as advance organizers for this and the following lesson, and wrote these on the board to emphasize their importance. The words *hardware* and *software* thus became touchstones for labeling, storing, and later retrieving discrete pieces of information that would be presented under each category—monitor, printer, keyboard, disk drive—to which would be added a list of software in a subsequent lesson. At this point, more overlapping occurs when Ms. Raskin asks what component is missing from those listed on the board. The teacher's goal turns from providing advance organization to checking for task-relevant prior knowledge and reviewing this knowledge. She asks Quann what is missing from the list to see if the topic of a previous lesson can be recalled and correctly described. Although Quann was unable to answer because he transferred into the class late, Libby responds correctly with, "It's the CPU that's missing." Although we can't be sure, Ms. Raskin could have intentionally called on Libby to respond because she was a

FIGURE 7.7 Ms. Raskin's Transparency for Overhead Projector

	HAL 1 **Black and White**	HAL 2 **Green Phorphorous**	HAL 3 **Color**
Uses	Both text and pictures equally	Text more than pictures	Pictures more than text
Cost	Least expensive	More expensive	Most expensive
Resolution	Lowest	Higher	Highest

member of a steering group, which would give the teacher an indication of how the rest of the class may have responded to this question. Recall that a steering group consisting of a few students performing below average, average, and above average can be used to estimate the level of attainment of the entire class by asking group members to recall task-relevant knowledge with a few sample questions at the start of class. In this instance, if Libby was a lower achieving learner within the steering group, chances are that most of the class had the task-relevant prior knowledge needed for the day's lesson. Alberto, Keisha, and Ralph also provided knowledgeable answers to similar questions, indicating that most, if not all, of what had been taught in an earlier lesson had been mastered by most of the class.

Finally, to reinforce but not reteach an important previous point, Ms. Raskin asks Keisha to recount a memorable incident, which occurred during a previous lesson, that underscored the important distinction between processing and thinking: Keisha is asked to share with the class her mistaken notion that HAL in the movie *2001* was actually thinking rather than mimicking the words and logic programmed into it. For those in the class who remembered, this may have conjured up a mental image (for example, of HAL talking to his creator) that could be used to remember and better understand this distinction for a long time to come. The teacher checked for task-relevant prior knowledge and reinforced it before proceeding with the day's lesson.

Recall that another behavior for achieving lesson clarity involves the use of examples, illustrations, and demonstrations. Were any of these evident in Ms. Raskin's lesson? Although not all lesson content can be conveniently demonstrated in the classroom as it appears in the real world, Ms. Raskin did not fail to utilize the opportunity provided by the real-life nature of her content. Monitors, printers, keyboards, and disk drives exist not only as concepts, but as devices in our everyday lives. Ms. Raskin could have chosen to discuss computer monitors abstractly, simply referring to the fact that they come in different colors, shapes, and sizes. But would her lesson have had the same impact on her students? Probably not. Pictures and lifelike models used in the context of the classroom are often far more conducive to remembering key concepts than are words alone. Ms. Raskin's lecture, if composed only of words, could not possibly have related all that was being seen and recorded by her students. Thus, this teacher's demonstration of distinctions in color, size, and resolution helped increase the clarity of the lesson. This did not come, however, without some extra work on Ms. Raskin's part, as each of her three monitors had to be programmed to display the intended message.

An important underlying theme among teachers whose lessons routinely exhibit high levels of clarity is that they prepare examples, illustrations, or demonstrations to reinforce each key aspect of the lesson. Verbal or visual examples of lesson content, illustrations of how what is taught applies to the real world, and demonstrations of how devices and concepts work are especially effective means of reinforcing major ideas and themes, and therefore of increasing lesson clarity. Ms. Raskin's online demonstration had some of each of these qualities, increasing the likelihood that her presentation would be understood and remembered.

Finally, we note that Ms. Raskin's lesson contained at least one other dimension for achieving clarity: It ended with a summary or review. This summary neatly encompassed all the relevant distinctions in a 3×3 table consisting of the three types of monitors classified by use, cost, and resolution. This was a succinct way of hitting the high points of the lesson without having to go back over large portions of content. Each relevant piece of information was translated into a coordinate position on the table, which was conveniently displayed on a transparency for the whole class to see. Here again, advance preparation was necessary to have a transparency ready-made in the exact format for the review. By using the responses of only three students, the review was kept short and to the point.

There are, of course, some aspects of Ms. Raskin's clarity we do not learn from this dialogue. We do not know, for example, the clarity of her instructions to the class. Few directives about how to complete an assignment were required for this lesson. Although we can presume that Ms. Raskin knows the ability level of her students and is generally teaching to it, she still could be teaching above or below the levels of at least some of her students. The use of alternative texts and assignments, as well as individualized, small-group, or self-directed learning activities for those who may be more advanced or in need of prerequisite skills or knowledge, could indicate that this dimension of clarity is being achieved. Presumably, these aspects of clarity would be evident to an observer after additional observations later in the year, when differences in student skills and understanding also might be more evident.

These reactions to Ms. Raskin's lesson are summarized in the checklist in Figure 7.8. How does our checklist compare with the one you made? We believe that Ms. Raskin did an effective job of achieving most of the seven dimensions of clarity. Notice how we placed comments adjacent to each entry on the checklist to remind us of important points for later discussion, provide useful content for review prior to a subsequent observation of the

Figure 7.8 Checklist for Observing Ms. Raskin's Classroom

Effectiveness Indicators	Observed	Not Observed	No Opportunity to Observe[a]
1. Informs learners of skills or understandings expected at end of lesson.	✓ To describe and identify differences.		
2. Provides learners with an advance organizer that places lesson content in perspective.	✓ Overlapped present with previous content.		
3. Checks for task-relevant prior learning at beginning of lesson and reteaches if necessary.	✓ May have used steering group.		
4. Gives directives slowly and distinctly. Checks for understanding along the way.			✓ Gave only a small homework assignment.
5. Knows learners' ability levels and uses media, materials, and procedures at or slightly above their current level of functioning.			✓ Too early in year to tell.
6. Uses examples, illustrations, or demonstrations to explain and clarify content in text and workbooks.	✓ Demonstration effective!		
7. Provides review or summary.	✓ Used preorganized transparency.		

[a]Including inadequate opportunity or irrelevance to the format of the lesson.

same classroom, and focus our attention in certain unfinished areas of observation. You'll probably want to annotate your checklist when you observe in actual classrooms. For example, our questions (if we return to Ms. Raskin's class) center on whether a steering group does in fact exist; whether directives before an assignment are clear; and if individualized, self-directed, and/or cooperative learning materials or activities are available to meet individual learning needs.

In the following chapters, we will turn our attention to several other important lenses through which to observe classrooms. These lenses—instructional variety, task orientation, student engagement in the learning process, student success, and higher thought processes—are always observed in the context of the dimensions of lesson clarity. As we turn now to our next lens—instructional variety—you'll want to keep in mind the significant impact of the

dimensions of lesson clarity studied in this chapter on all other lenses we'll discuss.

Activities*

1. Using the checklist shown in Figure 7.6, observe the presentation of a lesson and look for signs of clarity. At the end of your observation, add a brief description to each box, highlighting at least one specific reason why you checked that box. Using your written descriptions as a guide, write a paragraph about the reasons for the lesson clarity, or lack thereof, you observed in this classroom.

---

*Some of the following activities may be grouped into a common activity, divided among classmates, and completed from a single observation.

2. Using the five-point scales shown in Chapter 4 as an example, convert the positive and negative indicators in Figure 7.1 into this format and then observe a lesson for signs of clarity. Consider the vertical and horizontal placement of each indicator on the page, whether words will be affixed to all or only some of the response blanks, and what verbal response alternatives will be best suited to each question. Show your scale to a classmate who has also constructed a five-point scale. Together, create a single revised version incorporating the best features of both scales.

3. Using the seven-point polar scale presented in Chapter 4, observe the presentation of a lesson for signs of clarity. At the end of your period of observation, complete the scale by indicating with a checkmark the degree to which this lesson achieved each dimension of clarity. Use the code "N/O" for any items that you did not have the opportunity to observe or that are inappropriate for the content being observed. Reflecting on your experience as a student and on previous classroom observations, return to the scale and place an *X* on the blank corresponding to each scale item that, in your opinion, represents the degree of clarity found in most classrooms. Note the difference between your ratings for this lesson and what might be the typical or average lesson clarity across classrooms. Cite the reasons this lesson was the same, higher, or lower on each dimension.

4. Observe a lesson using the procedure and format provided in Instrument 7.1 to determine if learners are informed of the objective.
   a. If the teacher informed learners of the objective, paraphrase the written or oral statement with which the objective was communicated to the class. In your opinion, was it communicated clearly, and perceived accurately by the students?
   b. If the teacher did not inform learners of the objective, indicate the domain (cognitive, affective, and/or psychomotor) and action verb(s) that, in your opinion, best describe this lesson's objective. Using the content of the day's lesson, write a sentence or two that could be used to inform learners of the lesson objective.

5. Obtain a package of 5″ × 8″ index cards and, if possible, a small plastic file for storing and organizing the cards. Bring several of these index cards to each observation you make during this semester or quarter. During, or at the completion of, each observation, describe any advance organizer that was used, and when and how it was used in the context of the lesson. Number the card and place it in your file. Using the format shown in Instrument 7.2, record (a) the reference number assigned to the advance organizer, (b) the grade level and subject matter with which it was used, and (c) its placement in the lesson (beginning, middle, end). Arrange to exchange your advance organizer cards with other observers to collect more organizers in areas of interest to you. When completing a lesson plan, scan your master list and index cards for any advance organizers that might fit the lesson you are planning.

6. Using the assigned text or curriculum guide for a lesson you will be observing, list any prior facts, skills, or concepts that are needed to attain this lesson's objective. Explain why you believe the objective for the lesson you will be observing requires this prior learning, and why it may represent prior learning for a future lesson.

7. Using the categories in Figure 7.2 and the coding form in Instrument 7.3, observe and record the student response–teacher reaction sequences for clarity of directions that occur during a class period. Write a narrative description of the sequence of events that occurred in this classroom with the data from each row of the coding form.

8. After observing a class period, indicate the approximate percentage of learners for whom the content appeared to be (a) below, (b) at or slightly above, and (c) above their current level of understanding. Assign percentages to these categories so that they add up to 100 percent. Using the list of verbal descriptions in Figure 7.4, describe the behavior of the students in this classroom. Which, in your opinion, creates the greatest threat to an efficient and productive classroom: students for whom the content is below their current level of understanding, or those for whom the content is above their current level of understanding? How would you expect the behavior of these two categories to differ?

9. Using the event record in Instrument 7.5, observe the same classroom for at least three lessons and look for examples, illustrations, and/or demonstrations that explain and clarify content. Add any additional types of examples, illustrations, and demonstrations to the instrument as they are observed. Analyze the frequency of marks you have placed for each row of the instrument. Can you detect any preferences or cultural and ethnic biases in the way this teacher likes to frame content? In your opinion, is this teacher's pattern of framing a strength or a weakness in conveying lesson content?

10. Using the three observations from Activity 9, indicate those for which a summary or review of lesson content was provided at, or near, the end of the lesson. If a summary or review was provided, how was the lesson content repackaged? Did you find (a) a restatement of the highest generalization reached during the lesson; (b) a review of key points; or (c) the use of symbols, codes, or mnemonic devices? In your opinion, which of these or other techniques most helped learners to remember and store the content learned?

INSTRUMENT 7.1 Format for Recording Information Pertaining to Informing
Learners of the Objective

Place a check in the appropriate boxes.
Teacher *did* inform learners of objective. If so, how?
❏ verbally ❏ on board or overhead ❏ with handout ❏ other _____
Teacher *did not* inform learners of objective. If not, why?
      ❏ Learners knew objective from previous lesson. (lesson continuation)
      ❏ Not relevant to goals and purposes of lesson. (review)
      ❏ Other (identify) _____
      ❏ No reason apparent.

Cognitive	*Affective*	*Psychomotor*
❏ Recall, name, or identify	❏ Listen, attend, notice	❏ Repeat, follow from visual model
❏ Explain, summarize, paraphrase	❏ Comply, obey, participate	❏ Repeat, follow from verbal directions
❏ Use, solve, demonstrate	❏ Prefer, convince, value	❏ Perform accurately, proficiently
❏ Relate, differentiate, distinguish	❏ Formulate, systematize, theorize	❏ Perform with speed, timing
❏ Create, design, compose	❏ Display, internalize, exhibit	❏ Perform effortlessly, automatically
❏ Judge, justify, defend		

INSTRUMENT 7.2   Cataloging Advance Organizers

Type	Reference Number	Advance Organizer		Time in Lesson Used			Number of Times Referred To
		Grade	Subject	Beginning	Middle	End	
Verbal	1			❑	❑	❑	
	2			❑	❑	❑	
	3			❑	❑	❑	
	4			❑	❑	❑	
	5			❑	❑	❑	
Visual	6			❑	❑	❑	
	7			❑	❑	❑	
	8			❑	❑	❑	
	9			❑	❑	❑	
	10			❑	❑	❑	

INSTRUMENT 7.3   Coding Form for Recording Student Response–Teacher Reaction During Instructions

Student or Number	Assignment							Student Response				Teacher Reaction						
	wb	hw	oas	hand	test	proj	other	rpt	specif	uncert	other	crit	rpt	ans	restate	check	ignore	other

Direction or Instructions Pertaining to

Workbook	wb
Homework	hw
Oral assignment	oas
Handout	hand
Test	test
Extended project or paper	proj
Other type of assignment	other

Student Responses

Student asks teacher to repeat directions or instructions.	rpt
Student asks specific question for clarification.	specif
Student expresses uncertainty orally (for example, "I don't understand") or physically (for example, frowns shrugs).	uncert
Student uses some other measure to indicate directives or instructions were not understood.	other

Teacher Reactions

Teacher criticizes student for not understanding.	crit
Teacher repeats directive or instruction.	rpt
Teacher answers student question about directive.	ans
Teacher restates instructions in different words.	restate
Teacher checks for understanding (for example, asks student to repeat or asks student a question).	check
Teacher ignores student response.	ignore
Teacher reacts in some other way.	other

INSTRUMENT 7.4   Percentage of Learners at Each Level of
Instruction

Observation 1

Content Appears Below Students' Level (%)	Content Appears At or Slightly Above Students' Level (%)	Content Appears Above Students' Level (%)
0	0	0
25	25	25
50	50	50
75	75	75
100	100	100

Observation 2

Content Appears Below Students' Level (%)	Content Appears At or Slightly Above Students' Level (%)	Content Appears Above Students' Level (%)
0	0	0
25	25	25
50	50	50
75	75	75
100	100	100

Observation 3

Content Appears Below Students' Level (%)	Content Appears At or Slightly Above Students' Level (%)	Content Appears Above Students' Level (%)
0	0	0
25	25	25
50	50	50
75	75	75
100	100	100

INSTRUMENT 7.5 System for Recording the Use of Examples, Illustrations, and Demonstrations to Explain and Clarify Content

	Indicator	Number of Occurrences									
		1	2	3	4	5	6	7	8	9	10
V i s u a l	Writes on board										
	Uses overhead										
	Points to or holds up visual										
	Shows slides or film										
	Demonstrates with model or equipment										
	Other										
O r a l	Provides or asks for example										
	Tells illustrative story										
	Recalls personal experience										
	Relates to past learning										
	Poses problem										
	Compares and contrasts										
	Other										

Chapter 8

VERIFYING
INSTRUCTIONAL VARIETY

Daddy Fell into the Pond

Everyone grumbled. The sky was gray.
We had nothing to do and nothing to say.
We were nearing the end of a dismal day,
And there seemed to be nothing beyond,
THEN
Daddy fell into the pond!

And everyone's face grew merry and bright,
And Timothy danced for sheer delight.
"Give me the camera, quick, oh quick!
He's crawling out of the duckweed." Click!

Then the gardener suddenly slapped his knee,
And doubled up, shaking silently,
And the ducks all quacked as if they were daft
And it sounded as if the old drake laughed.

Oh, there wasn't a thing that didn't respond
WHEN
Daddy fell into the pond!

Alfred Noyes

Who among us hasn't experienced a dull lecture—or a boring afternoon in class? At such times, no matter what our intention, it can be difficult to focus, and perhaps even to stay awake! The same can be true of classrooms when routines are so entrenched that *everything* is predictable and mundane. Wise teachers understand the value of instructional variety for enhancing student engagement and learning. Let's explore how variety can truly be the "spice of life" in the effective classroom.

The Random House Book of Poetry for Children, selected by Jack Prelutsky. New York: Random House, 1983, p. 156.

Instructional variety refers to a teacher's variability and flexibility in delivering instructional content. It includes the planned mixing of different instructional activities, such as discussion, facilitation of small-group work, demonstration, explanation, questioning, and recitation within the context of a single lesson, as well as variation in physical movement and gestering, eye contact, and voice intonation. Instructional variety also includes the use of learning materials, equipment, displays, and classroom space that encourages student involvement in the lesson. All these components of the classroom contribute to instructional variety, which, in turn, has been found to influence both student achievement and student engagement in the learning process. Classroom research studies have reported less disruptive behavior in classrooms with a greater-than-average variety in classroom activities and materials (Emmer, Evertson, Clements, & Worsham, 1997); other studies have shown variety to be related to student attention (Lysakowski & Walberg, 1981).

DIMENSIONS OF INSTRUCTIONAL VARIETY

Think back to classes you have enjoyed and felt you learned a lot from. What were some of the ways your teachers got and kept your attention? Figure 8.1 summarizes teaching behaviors that contribute to instructional variety, which include:

1. Using attention-gaining devices.
2. Showing enthusiasm and animation.
3. Varying the activities with which instruction is presented.
4. Mixing rewards and reinforcers.
5. Varying types of questions and probes.
6. Using student ideas.

It is important to recognize that not all the indicators of instructional variety listed in Figure 8.1 will—or should—occur for every lesson. Depending on the purpose or content of the lesson (for example, a lesson devoted entirely to review, or new content that is taught in a lecture format, precluding the use of student ideas), some indicators may not be relevant to a lesson. Whenever you seek to verify instructional variety, you should note when the purpose and/or content of the lesson does not afford the teacher an opportunity to exhibit the behavior.

PRACTICE OBSERVING INSTRUCTIONAL VARIETY: A DIALOGUE

Let's practice verifying instructional variety by visiting Mr. Marks's class and using the checklist in Figure 8.2 to help consider six key behaviors related to instructional variety.

Today Mr. Marks is teaching a social studies lesson to his class of thirty-three culturally diverse

FIGURE 8.1 Indicators for Variety

Using Variety (Effective Teacher)	Poor Variety (Ineffective Teacher)
1. Uses attention-gaining devices (for example, begins with a challenging question, visual, or example)	Begins lessons without full attention of most learners
2. Shows enthusiasm and animation through variation in eye contact, voice, and gestures (for example, changes pitch and volume; moves about during transitions to new activity)	Speaks in monotone, devoid of external signs of emotion; stays fixed in place for entire period or rarely moves body
3. Varies mode of presentation (for example, lectures, asks questions, and then provides for independent practice)	Rarely alters modality through which instructional stimuli are received (for example, seeing, listening, doing)
4. Uses mix of rewards and reinforcers (extra credit, verbal praise, independent study)	Rarely reinforces student behavior; tends to use same rewards every time
5. Varies types of questions (divergent, convergent) and probes (to clarify, to solicit, or to redirect)	Always asks the same type of question (for example, What do you think about . . . ?) or overuses one type of question
6. Incorporates student ideas or participation in some aspects of the instruction (for example, uses indirect instruction or divergent questioning)	Assumes the role of sole authority and provider of information; ignores student contributions

FIGURE 8.2 Checklist for Observing Instructional Variety

Behavior	Observed	Not Observed	No Opportunity to Observe
1. Uses attention-gaining devices			
2. Shows enthusiasm and animation through variation in eye contact, voice, and gestures			
3. Varies activities with which the instruction is presented; for example, lecturing, explaining, questioning, discussion, practicing			
4. Uses mix of rewards and reinforcers			
5. Various types of questions and probes — Questions: Convergent, Divergent			
5. Various types of questions and probes — Probes: To clarify, To solicit, To redirect			
6. Uses student ideas and participation to foster lesson objectives when appropriate to goals of instruction			

students. His lesson focuses on regulatory tariffs during the time of the Civil War, which is a natural transition from a previous lesson on the geography of the South. We peek in on Mr. Mark's class during the fourth month of the school year.

Mr. Marks: All desks clear. Today, I need to present some . . . [Interrupting himself.] June, put the math book away. We're on social studies now . . . some information about taxes and tariffs and how they are sometimes used to control commerce—or the kind of business that goes on between states and nations. This isn't going to be as interesting as our discussion of the battles of the Civil War last week, but pay attention anyway. As I said, our topic is taxes and tariffs used to regulate commerce. Does anyone know what a tariff is? [Silence.] Anyone? [Silence again.] Okay. A tariff is simply a tax imposed by a government on goods imported—or brought into a country—and in some instances on goods exported—or sold outside a country. Why would a government place a tax on goods coming into its own country, and who would want such a thing? Anyone? [Silence.] I can see some of you are not taking this lesson seriously. This topic will be on the test next week. [At this point, Mr. Marks sits down at his desk. Carlos, sitting in the first row directly in front of Mr. Marks, raises his hand.]

Okay, Carlos is ready to work. [Points to Carlos to respond.]

Carlos: I don't understand why anybody would want to tax themselves.

Mr. Marks: Give us the answer to my question.

Carlos: Well, what I meant is, it would seem people would complain if they had to pay more for something they wanted just because someone else wanted to place a tax on it.

Mr. Marks: And actually they did complain—just before the Civil War. At that time, in 1862, the government placed taxes on domestic manufacturers and duties on imports for two reasons. Can you think of one of these reasons?

Carlos: Well, to raise money to run the government, I suppose, and maybe—like we said last week—to get ready for a war.

Mr. Marks: Okay, so a tariff on manufactured goods, whether created in this country or another, raises lots of money that could be used to run a government. What about another reason? Angel [who is sitting next to Carlos in the front row], what do you think?

Angel: It seems to me that taxes to run a government and taxes on goods coming into the country are two completely different things. If products that are made in this country are taxed, what's the point of taxing imported products, which might make TV sets and cars coming from Japan too expensive?

Mr. Marks: And then what? [Nodding to Angel to continue.]

Angel: Everyone will stop buying them because they won't be able to afford them.

Mr. Marks: And then what? [Nodding to Angel again, but now Angel looks confused.] Okay, Carlos.

Carlos: Now I get it! Sure, we'll stop buying, or at least buy fewer of these imported products, forcing us to buy ones made in the United States.

Mr. Marks: Now, this is an interesting point Carlos is raising. Who can summarize it? [Angel nods in anticipation of being called on.] Angel?

Angel: What he's saying is that, as the price of imported products goes up, we are being forced to buy similar products made in our own country. And because things like cars and TVs are taxed by our own government, money would be raised for running the government. Is that right?

Mr. Marks: Right. And who knows what we call tariffs on imported goods to encourage us to buy U.S. goods? [Silence.] Okay, I'll give you a hint. What do such tariffs protect?

Carlos: U.S. businesses who are having trouble selling their products because of foreign competition.

Mr. Marks: And that's called . . . ? [Waits for Carlos to respond, and then looks at Angel, but still no response.] It's called *protectionism.* About the time of the Civil War, large tariffs were placed on goods imported from Europe—goods that were also being manufactured in the North. To increase the market for these American products in the South, and to encourage the development of a strong industrial base, located primarily in the North, taxes were placed on things like textiles, leather, paper, iron, and lead products being imported into this country. By 1864, these taxes had risen to an average of about 50 percent of the price of the product being imported. So what do you think the people in the South felt about these tariffs? Angel?

Angel: Well, if they had to pay more for these products, I suspect they'd be pretty mad, especially at the North, who gained from selling all these products to the South.

Mr. Marks: Well, class, do you think Carlos and Angel know what a tariff is? [Some class members respond favorably in low voices; others nod. Carlos and Angel turn around to look at the class and check on the extent of the admiration.] Okay, now I'm going to pass out this fact sheet on tariffs, which is what you'll need to know for the test. Angel, would you see that everyone gets one? [Teacher remains at desk, pushing a stack of handouts toward Angel.] As you will see from the handout, it's a bit more complicated than our discussion this morning. We're going to spend the rest of the period going over the facts on this handout. I'll

ask you questions, and you look on the handout for the answers. [The handout is organized into brief explanations under the following headings: *Definition of a Tariff; Some Examples of Tariffs; Tariff Act of 1816, Tariff Act of 1828, Tariff Act of 1842, Tariff Act of 1862,* and *1864 and After.*]

Mr. Marks: Okay, let's begin. Ricky [who is seated behind Angel in the front row], what's a definition of *tariff*?

Ricky: [Quickly glancing over handout, and then reading directly from it.] A list or schedule of customs duties imposed by a government on imports and also, in some instances, on exports. Originally, such imports were levied for . . . .

Mr. Marks: [Interrupting] Okay, that's sufficient. Tim, give me an example of a tariff.

Tim: Which one?

Mr. Marks: Any one. Pick one from the sheet.

Tim: Is the Tariff Act of 1862 okay?

Mr. Marks: Any one.

Tim That was when tariffs on imported products were raised an average of 50 percent.

Mr. Marks: Which products? [Tim scans the paragraph nervously for clues.] What do we cover ourselves with every day?

Tim: [Hesitating] Clothes?

Mr. Marks: Of course. Under the Tariff of 1862, you'll see the word *textile*, which is yarn or cloth used in making clothes. Were any other products included under the Tariff Act of 1862? Angel, let's come back to you.

Angel: Well, I see a whole lot of products listed here . . . glass, iron, hats, leather, coffee, tea, sugar. . . .

Mr. Marks: But go on. What else does it say about coffee, tea, and sugar?

Mark: They're taxed, too.

Mr. Marks: Amanda, can you add anything?

Amanda: It says the import taxes were the least, and were eventually reduced, for items such as coffee, tea, and sugar.

Mr. Marks: Why?

Amanda: Okay, now I see. Because these types of things did not really compete with U.S. products.

Mr. Marks: And that means . . . ?

Amanda: That we don't produce them in this country, so there was nothing to protect . . . there was no need for pro . . . tex . . . tionism.

Mr. Marks: Very good. Did the rest of you hear Amanda's answer? Can you summarize your answer for the class, Amanda?

Amanda: I guess I could say that tariffs work best when they apply to foreign products that compete with similar products made in the United States. Otherwise they just drive up the price of things that everyone needs and can't get anywhere else. That's why import taxes are low for some products and high for others. But there's one thing I don't understand. [Mr. Marks nods for Amanda to go on.] Wouldn't placing taxes on imported goods allow the manufacturers in this country to raise their prices unfairly?

Mr. Marks: That's a good question. Think about it for tomorrow, and then write down how you believe a tariff could work to make prices on domestic goods rise, as Amanda suggests, and how a tariff might work to lower prices on domestic goods. I'll have some of you read your answers at the beginning of class tomorrow.

REACTIONS TO THE DIALOGUE

Which of the six dimensions of instructional variety did you see in this dialogue? Obviously, not all of these dimensions of variety can be observed from this brief dialogue, but some can. Let's explore each of the six dimensions as it appeared in Mr. Marks's classroom—and as it might ideally occur in our own teaching. We'll also consider some observation instruments that can help us consider particular behaviors in greater detail.

Using Attention-Gaining Devices

One of the most obvious dimensions of instructional variety is the use of attention-gaining devices. These are used at the beginning of a lesson (and sometimes during it) to stimulate the learners' receptive modalities and the cognitive processes associated with them. Attention-gaining devices can take many forms, such as pictures, audiovisual media, and live demonstrations. They can also take less dramatic forms, such as posing a challenging question, presenting a dilemma or a bewildering situation, or even bringing about silence to accompany a unique visual display. Whether dramatic or subtle, attention-gaining devices wake up the receptive modalities of sight and sound, and stimulate the cognitive processes associated with them (Goetz, Alexander, & Ash, 1992; Mayer, 1987). Without this conscious change from the mood and tempo of an earlier activity or class, your learners' attention may never be fully focused on the lesson. Attention-gaining devices help create natural cycles of highs and lows that make life in classrooms more interesting and less regimented.

One of the most common attention-gaining devices is to arouse students' curiosity. This can be accomplished by asking a thought-provoking question, such as "Have you ever wondered how we got the word *horsepower*?" (from a lesson on units of measurement), "Can anyone think of a popular automobile with the name of a Greek god?" (from an introductory lesson on mythology), or "Have you ever wondered how some creatures can live both in the water and on land?" (from a lesson on amphibious animals). These questions are called *openers*. They are not designed to have a single correct answer, or even to accurately reflect the fine details of what is to follow, but to amuse, stimulate, and sometimes even bewilder students so that they will be receptive to the more detailed content and questions that follow. Other ways questions work as openers are

- ❑ *To surprise and astound*—"How many realize that our sun will eventually exhaust all its energy and our planet will be completely dark?" (from a lesson in science)
- ❑ *To promote controversy*—"Some storytellers believe that the individual should always be in a struggle with the society in which one lives. Others believe the individual is meant to live in harmony with society. Which is true?" (from a lesson in reading)
- ❑ *To present a contradiction*—"Why do you think the Greek empire collapsed when it was at its strongest?" (from a lesson in history)
- ❑ *To promote curiosity*—"Who thinks he can see lower forms of animal life with the naked eye?" (from a biology lesson)

How did Mr. Marks begin his lesson? How did he stimulate the receptive modalities of his learners? Like many teachers, Mr. Marks relied on an opening statement that simply told the students what would be covered ("Some information on taxes and tariffs and how they are sometimes used to control commerce . . ."). This statement presented the topic of the lesson, but did little to make it exciting or to whet the appetites of his students to learn more. Students who had never heard the word *tariff* might not even have understood what the lesson was about. A verbal question or statement to promote curiosity (for example, "How many of you paid a tax on something you bought this week?"), to present a contradiction ("Do you know that the tax placed on some products helps some people at the expense of other people?"), to create controversy ("Should a group of people who think they are taxed unjustly pay their taxes?"), or to surprise or astound ("Do you know that some products imported from another country are taxed at more than 100 percent of their worth?") might have awakened the receptive modalities of some—if not most—students.

Diagrams, pictures, lifelike models, films, and interactive video are other aids for gaining the learners' attention. These devices are used to appeal to the students' sense of vision while the accompanying oral presentation appeals to their sense of hearing. These kinds of openers may include samples of materials to be used in the day's lesson, or equipment which students may touch and feel before a lesson begins (for example, scales, buttons, or meters). Graphics, visuals, or equipment of almost any kind can be particularly effective openers, especially with students who are known to be more responsive to visual than to auditory presentations.

You're probably thinking that Mr. Marks could have used other, perhaps more creative, attention-gaining devices in his lesson, such as a picture of a tariff that was handwritten in the nineteenth century, a cartoon from an early American newspaper making fun of tariffs, or a brief excerpt from a speech by a congressman against (or for) a tariff—all items that are readily available from general reference works. It's likely that Mr. Marks would have captured the attention of more of his students had he put a little more effort into his opening. Instead, the price Mr. Marks paid for his unimaginative beginning was that no one wanted to answer his questions. Most of his opening questions were met with silence, until the only alternative left was to change to a lecture format ("Okay, I'll tell you").

Observing Attention-Gaining Devices

As you seek to verify instructional variety in classrooms, you can enhance your investigation by using the form provided in Instrument 8.1. This record can help you consider attention-gaining devices in more detail, because it divides them into four categories: verbal statements and questions, visuals, media, and *realia* (real or lifelike examples of the topic to be presented). You will likely observe teachers using more than one of these four categories at the same time, as when a lesson begins with a question intended to promote curiosity ("How long did it take Columbus to reach America?") followed by a photograph of a captain's log and a scale model of a sextant used by early mariners to cross the ocean. In a case like this, you would place three checkmarks in the row corresponding to this lesson topic. You can note the repeated use of attention-gaining devices during a lesson by placing ditto marks under Lesson Topic. If you use this checklist to observe the same teacher over a number of lessons, your record will show the variety of attention-gaining devices used repeatedly in a classroom, those used infrequently or seldom, and those used to complement one another within the same lesson (for example, the teacher tends to follow up verbal statements with a visual to promote curiosity). Total frequencies and/or percentages can be tallied in the last row. As you observe the various attention-gaining devices used by particular teachers, you'll want to watch closely for their effect on students. Such observations will help you make your own teaching decisions.

Showing Enthusiasm and Animation

Once a teacher has piqued the students' curiosity, interest, and excitement through successful openers in a lesson, the momentum can be maintained by learning to vary voice, eye contact, and body movement. This is the second behavior of instructional variety. Although teachers are not actors, there is a lot they can learn from the field of dramatics. Lessons, like plays, should have opening and closing acts with a main story in between, which may have many climaxes and anticlimaxes to keep the audience's attention. How well a teacher plans the script—or lesson—will have a lot to do with its attention-getting quality. There should be natural variety in the topics and instructional activities that a lesson contains. That variety can be enhanced by a teacher's willingness to accent high points and bolster low points with changes in voice, eye movement, and body movement. Simply put, a teacher's voice inflection, eye contact, and positioning in the classroom should change often during a lesson, especially during its high points (for example, lively group discussion) and low points (for example, rote recitation from the workbook). These small but consistent changes are easily felt by students, who will be looking for signs that the teacher is aware of, and responsive to, the natural rhythm of the classroom.

What did you notice about Mr. Marks's enthusiasm and animation? Recall that he began the lesson by conveying a feeling to his students that, if not required by the curriculum, he might not even be teaching the lesson. Phrases such as "I need to present some information," "This isn't going to be as exciting as our discussion of battles of the Civil War last week, but pay attention anyway," are not lost on perceptive students, who quickly see that the teacher is less than enthusiastic about teaching the topic. The message, if the teacher is not enthusiastic, is that students need not be concerned about the topic either.

Mr. Marks's lack of enthusiasm might be even more apparent if we could examine his eye contact and body movement. Recall that, for almost the entire length of this dialogue, Mr. Marks interacted with only two students, Carlos and Angel, both of whom are seated directly in front of his desk. Later in the lesson when Ricky (who is seated behind Angel) joins in, Mr. Marks is still talking to only a small percentage of his class. Later exchanges include Mark and Amanda, but even so only five students are included in the discussion; three are seated in the front and center portion of the classroom closest to the teacher. This effectively excludes most others from participating, and may convey the impression that the opinions of others are not valued as highly as those of Carlos, Angel, and Ricky.

Although we have no way to be certain, Mr. Marks's eye contact may have been limited to a small part of the classroom as well, since eye movement often follows the same path as verbal exchanges. Adding to this was the teacher's decision to remain seated throughout most of the lesson. Although sitting behind a desk may be appropriate when students are completing assignments in workbooks or reciting answers to problems in a drill-and-practice format, it is generally not suited to the kind of informal, spontaneous exchanges desired during question-and-answer sessions or group discussion. Staying in a single position in the classroom for long periods of time, removed spatially by the physical barrier of a desk, can detract from student interest and engagement in the lesson content.

Kounin (1970) coined the word *withitness* to refer to a teacher's ability to keep track of many different signs of student behavior simultaneously and thereby convey a sense of physical presence—or vigilance. Eye contact that scans the whole classroom is one of the most important ingredients in conveying withitness, animation, and liveliness, which can add variety to a classroom.

Teachers limit their withitness to only a portion of the classroom when they

Talk only to the middle-front rows.
Talk with their backs to the class when writing on the chalkboard.
Talk while looking toward the windows.
Talk while some students block their view of other students.

When teachers engage in the above behaviors, they lose contact with the remaining parts of the classroom. One of the simplest and most effective ways for a teacher to increase withitness and physical presence is to remember to look around the room from time to time, and to vary voice, eye contact, and body movement at intervals of rising and falling action throughout a lesson.

Kounin (1970) noted that one of the most important distinctions between effective and ineffective classroom managers is the degree to which they exhibit withitness. Effective classroom managers are aware of what is happening in all parts of the classroom. More important, these effective classroom managers are able to communicate this awareness to their students through variations in voice, eye contact, and body movement. How would you rate Mr. Marks's withitness in this dialogue? What suggestions for positive change might you offer him?

Observing Enthusiasm and Animation

To look more closely at a teacher's enthusiasm and animation, we can focus on four behaviors: body movement, eye contact, voice intonation, and gesturing. These four behaviors can be rated on a Likert scale like the one in Instrument 8.2. Notice that this Likert scale has been changed to the horizontal position, and descriptive labels are provided only for the middle and ends of the scale. This format allows you to place a checkmark anywhere along the continuum, including between vertical marks, to represent the degree of the behavior you are observing. For scoring purposes, the numerical code for the scale point closest to the checkmark may be used, or fractional parts may be estimated. Also note that the middle point represents the most appropriate degree of behavior for the scale measuring body movement. To average the scores from scales such as this with others that place the most desired behavior at one end, the middle point is assigned a numerical code of 5, both extreme endpoints are assigned a code of 1, and both intermediate points are assigned a code of 3.

Variation in Instructional Activities

Another behavior that can be utilized to achieve variety involves using a mix of instructional activities. Although many general types of activities can be defined by what the *teacher* does (e.g., questioning, discussion, guided practice, and recitation), instructional activities may also be categorized by considering what is required of the *student*. According to Doyle (1983), an instructional task involves determining a product to be formulated, selecting an operation to create the product, and obtaining and/or providing the resources to create the product. Even though the word *product* is used here, it need not always refer to a tangible item. Task products may vary from subvocal thoughts composed by students while a teacher is explaining or lecturing to an oral response in the form of an answer to a question from the teacher or text, to a written response in the form of a multiple-choice answer, short answer, or paragraph/essay, to a project or model of a concept. Typical operations required to create these products include recognition and discrimination, application and practice, problem solving, and discovery. The resources consulted include orally delivered content as well as content drawn from the text, a workbook, the blackboard, handouts, or other media. These elements are shown in the form of an activity structure checklist in Instrument 8.3. You can use this checklist to look more closely at the variety of tasks utilized in a lesson.

Observing the Variation in Instructional Activities

As you observe variations in instructional activities, complete Instrument 8.3 by considering what products, operations, and resources are required by a particular task. Place a checkmark in each column next to the combination, thus breaking a more general instructional activity into three separate components. For example, if the task is to follow along with new content presented for the first time in the context of a lecture, you might place checkmarks alongside subvocal thought, recognition and discrimination, and oral content. If you find it difficult to determine which entries to check, it may mean that the task has no formal structure for which student engagement is being elicited. Checkmarks consistently repeated within the same rows across tasks may represent a bias on the part of the teacher for only a certain type of product, operation, or resource, restricting the variety of instructional activity in the classroom. One of the more interesting uses of this instrument is to determine when one task has ended and another has begun. A new task might be defined as the point at which the product, operation, or resource changes, requiring the start of a new column. Using this or a similar rule, you can determine the total number of tasks that make up an activity structure for a lesson.

Another useful categorization of instructional tasks and activities is the sensory modality (or modalities) in which lesson content is being constructed by the learner. At least four different modalities may be used interchangeably to engage learners with lesson content: auditory, verbal (involving the written word), visual, and tactile (performing). Lesson content can be communicated by speaking, writing, showing, touching, or any combination of these. Figure 8.3 identifies some of the most common ways these modalities are used in the classroom.

Instructional variety within a classroom is increased when instructional tasks include all of these modalities or combinations of them. Wise teachers plan for activities that involve different modalities in different combinations. Changes across two or three modalities, or channels of communication, may be required to keep most students attending to and engaged in the learning process. The frequency with which changes in a lesson should be made will depend on the age of the student; younger learners in the early elementary grades or lower achieving learners may often require a greater range of sensory stimuli and more changes across channels than higher achieving or older students. The record in Instrument 8.4 places these four modalities in a sign observation system. As you observe a lesson, you place a checkmark after each 5-minute interval to indicate the mix of channels through which learners are constructing their understanding of lesson content.

If channels are used simultaneously during the interval, place multiple checkmarks in each row in Instrument 8.4. This might indicate, for example, that a teacher delivers content orally while pointing to a chart or illustration. The final rows can be used to total the intervals checked within a channel and to determine the percentage of intervals in which that channel was being used. The total number of intervals should correspond to a lesson. If instruction occurred for 50 minutes and four 5-minute intervals were checked under visual, the percentage entered for visual would be $(4/10)100 = 40\%$, indicating that during approximately 40 percent [or $.40(50) = 20$ minutes] of the lesson the visual channel was in use. Such percentages should be used as estimations, however, since individual checkmarks do not indicate that a given channel was in use during the entire interval. If you desire more accurate percentages, you can shorten intervals to one or two minutes. But the most important information involves the changes, if any, that occur from column to column, or from one interval to the next. Checkmarks appearing consistently in one column for large portions of a lesson may indicate a lack of instructional variety.

With these thoughts in mind, let's consider how using a variety of instructional tasks might have affected Mr. Marks's lesson. Although Mr. Marks lacked attention-gaining devices and enthusiasm at the beginning of his lesson, the tone of his lesson did change from an exclusively oral presentation to one that included both oral and written stimuli when he introduced the handout. In this sense, Mr. Marks demonstrated the value of variation in instructional activities. By altering the instructional format, Mr. Marks was on the right track.

Researchers and experienced teachers alike agree that effective teaching involves many different classroom activities. A teacher who does nothing but talk for an entire period, engages students only in prolonged seatwork, or only exposes students to attention-gaining devices will have difficulty achieving outcomes at the desired level of performance. Although it is true that some lessons should emphasize a single activity, it is important to realize that the majority of lessons must offer variety and a mix of instructional tasks that make different cognitive demands on the student. For example, lectures should be followed by guided practice (at individual, small-group, and whole-group levels) in which learners make their first attempts at responding at different

FIGURE 8.3 Presentation Modalities Used to Create Variety[a]

Oral	Verbal[b]	Visual	Tactile
Teacher explaining	Teacher writing on board	Teacher using charts, graphs, illustrations	Students examining specimen
Teacher/students asking questions	Teacher writing on transparency	Students looking at diagrams, pictures in text or on board	Students using equipment
Teacher playing audiotape or record	Students reading text	Students watching film/videotape	Students building/constructing (pasting, gluing, cutting out, drawing)
Students reciting	Students working in small groups with text	Students seeing lifelike or scale models	Students arranging/ordering material
Students discussing in small groups	Students writing		

[a] The olfactory modality, the sense of smell, is another channel through which the learner may receive instructional stimuli.
[b] As a receptive modality, this is not distinguishable from the visual. Since it has special significance for the presentation of content, we will consider it as another channel through which learning occurs.

levels of engagement (following along, responding subvocally, or providing a written response) in a supported way. Guided-practice activities should be planned so that students engage with the material in different ways—by listening (lectures, listening to tapes and other media), seeing (reading textbooks and tradebooks, viewing videos and other media), and doing (experiments, writing, workbooks)—and with different levels of responding that provide learners with a sense of control over their own learning (Marx & Walsh, 1988). Students should also be asked to vary the products they create (e.g., oral responses vs. written answers), the operations they use to generate a product (memory vs. application), and the resources they use to produce a product (oral response of another student vs. a textbook example; magazines, tradebooks, and electronic media vs. traditional encyclopedias). Therefore, a lesson plan that includes some combination of lecture, discussion, question and answer, guided practice, and independent seatwork is generally preferable to one that emphasizes only a single task and a single way of responding.

Activity structures that vary the tasks learners are expected to perform and the products to be produced can add an important dimension to instructional variety in a classroom. Mr. Marks could have included even greater variety in his instructional plans to actively involve more students in the content, and could have provided appropriate changes of pace for those students already engaged.

Mr. Marks could also have planned instructional activities designed to help his students become aware of their own thinking and of ways to enhance their problem-solving strategies. Several researchers (Brown, 1987; Wang & Jones, 1982) have investigated the cognitive demands placed on the learner by different classroom activities. One result of this research is a concept known as *metacognition*. Meichenbaum (1983) explained metacognition as the "debugging" devices used to think through a problem, including *cognitive* (thinking) processes such as self-interrogation, self-checking, self-monitoring, analyzing, and mentally scanning alternative strategies for solving a problem, as well as the use of memory aids (*mnemonics*) and classifying incoming information for better comprehension (Barel, 1991). Palincsar and Brown (1987) have explored ways to teach students to become more metacognitive—to think about their thinking. They suggest that teachers seek to help students to

1. Become aware of and develop an understanding of their own cognitive (internal thought) strategies for solving learning problems.
2. Select and use appropriate mental strategies to accomplish a particular task.

3. Monitor their own use of effective thinking strategies through internal self-questioning as they proceed through a learning activity.

Teachers can follow a series of instructional steps to assess students' metacognitive abilities and then encourage students to become more metacognitive. These steps include:

❏ Providing a new learning task (for example, reading a short text selection that will be used as the basis for an essay) and observing how the student approaches the task.
❏ Asking the student to explain how she approaches the task of learning the textual information in preparation for the essay. (This helps the student analyze her own cognitive approach.)
❏ Describing and modeling more effective procedures for organizing and accomplishing the task: explain and demonstrate how to use the study questions at the end of a selection to help focus reading; highlight the main ideas in each paragraph of the selection with a fluorescent felt-tip pen; and write outline notes of key points on a separate sheet or notecards as a study guide for later review. (This gives the student new strategies for cognitively organizing the learning task.)
❏ Providing the student with another, similar learning task to practice the new cognitive strategies and observing as the student proceeds with the task, giving reminders and corrective feedback.
❏ Modeling self-questioning behavior aloud while analyzing a similar problem. For example: "How will I begin this task?" "What are the key questions I will need to answer?" "What is the main idea in this paragraph?" These questions can be written on an index card for the student to use as a reminder.
❏ Providing opportunities for the student to practice the skills using self-regulation rather than ongoing teacher monitoring.
❏ Checking the result of the learning task by questioning for comprehension and by asking the student to recall the learning strategies that were used.

As students learn to regulate their own problem-solving behavior effectively, they will be better able to profit from active exchanges with peers and the instructional variety teachers present. Armed with an understanding of these steps, Mr. Marks could have encouraged more active metacognition among his students when he introduced the handout. For example, he could have asked questions that required his students to *go beyond* the facts given, and he could have modeled various ways to accomplish this goal. He could have challenged students to determine relationships, compare and contrast, or make judgments about information to integrate the material included on the handout and previously learned information. Indeed, when considering instructional variety, the possibilities for extending and expanding learning seem almost limitless. Selecting appropriate and challenging learning activities is one of the delightful aspects of effective lesson planning.

Another consideration in selecting instructional tasks is the need to teach adaptively. *Adaptive teaching* involves seeking to achieve a common instructional goal with learners whose prior achievement, aptitude, or learning styles differ. This means that teachers select different learning activities and strategies designed to aid various groups of students in learning the same content. Two different approaches to adaptive teaching—the remediation approach and compensatory teaching—have been effective (Rohrkemper & Corno, 1988; Corno & Snow, 1986).

The first approach to adaptive teaching, sometings called the *remediation approach,* is to provide the prerequisite knowledge, skill, or behavior to those who may need it to benefit from the planned instruction. This will be successful when the prerequisite information, skill, or behavior required to overcome a deficiency can be taught within a reasonable period of time. Teachers using a remediation approach will plan a learning activity designed to help students fill in missing information before moving on to the new content to be learned. This is a good choice when content can be easily reviewed or presented; however, sometimes remediation is not possible or requires a great deal of classroom time. In those cases, another approach to adaptive teaching is warranted.

Compensatory teaching is an instructional method that attempts to circumvent or compensate for deficiencies in information, skills, or ability. In compensatory approaches, teachers engage students with content using different communication modalities (for example, pictures vs. words) or by supplementing the content with additional learning resources (games and simulations) and activities (cooperative learning groups, self-regulated learning materials). The idea is that the activity is structured to compensate for missing information on a student's part. For example, students who are poor at reading comprehension and lack a technical vocabulary might be taught a math unit almost exclusively with visual handouts that portray mathematical concepts graphically to emphasize the visual modality. Other students with an adequate vocabulary level and reading comprehension might be allowed to skip this more time-consuming approach and learn about the same concepts from the text, thereby emphasizing the verbal modality.

Notice that with adaptive teaching, the variety of instructional activities provided helps all students achieve the same goal, regardless of their individual, cultural, or ethnic differences, by using alternative instructional methods to maximize their strongest learning modalities (for example, visual vs. auditory). A menu of strategies (different teaching methods, slide presentations, and instructional materials) is indispensable for adapting instruction to different levels of ability, achievement, and learning styles. Instructional alternatives that adapt instruction to the current level of understanding of different learners and add variety to a lesson include:

Visually/verbally oriented materials
Inductive/expository presentation
Rule-example/example-rule ordering of content
Group discussion/lecture
Teaming/pairing
Lecture/question and answer
Inductive/deductive presentation
Teacher-moderated discussion/student-moderated discussion
Doing (trying)/seeing (watching)
Programmed/conventional text

Each of these pairs represents teaching methods or styles of presentation that are more effective for some types of learners than for others (Wang & Lindvall, 1984; Cronbach & Snow, 1977) and therefore can be used alternately within a lesson to teach adaptively and provide instructional variety. Take a moment to consider Mr. Marks's lesson. How might he have structured his activities to support learners using different modalities?

Mixing Rewards and Reinforcers

One of the first things you will notice when observing in classrooms is the teacher's interaction with students. Most obvious among these interchanges will be those concerning rewards and reinforcement, the fourth behavior for verifying instructional variety. The effectiveness of rewards depends on the variety with which they are administered and the types of reinforcement with which they are associated. For example, nothing is less reinforcing than the phrase "That's good" or "That's correct" if it's repeated in the same tone of voice hundreds of times for different problems and learners and without further comment (Costa, 1984; Brophy, 1981). The phrase soon becomes meaningless and loses its ability to reinforce a behavior. It is important, therefore, that verbal praise, like all rewards, vary in type, amount, and intensity, and that it be associated with other, more durable types of reinforcers (for example, "Would you like to tell the class how you got the right answer?"). In Chapter 6 we presented a list of incentives that, like verbal praise, could be used to increase the probability of a desired response. These rewards varied from a simple smile or head nod to allowing a student to work in a group, to posting an exam or homework for others to see. Other types of rewards that can be particularly effective in reinforcing desired behavior include using a student's answer as a model for others to follow, having a particular student retrace for the class how he obtained the correct answer, and having peers comment on the correctness of a student's answer.

Not all rewards are equally reinforcing. Some learners may dislike working in a group. Others will have no need for, or intention of, ever visiting the library or a learning center. Some students like to be called on; others may be too shy to appreciate the added attention. What is a reinforcement to one student may be irrelevant to another. Finding the right reinforcer for a student is often a matter of trial and error: If a reward does not seem to increase the probability of a desired behavior, it should be changed for another until success is obtained. Knowing the interests, needs, and aspirations of your students can save valuable time in finding the right mix of reinforcers. For example, students who are visually oriented might enjoy time for looking at maps, charts, or models at a learning center; for others, extra time to read may be equally appealing as a reward for desirable behaviors. Students can be asked which rewards are in tune with their specific interests, or can select the rewards they like best from a list you prepare at the beginning of the school year. This latter approach has the advantage of ensuring that what is chosen will be practical within the context of a given classroom and relevant to the culture and ethnicity of individual students.

Finally, it is important to note that, in a dominant-subordinate environment such as school, it is natural for those in authority to reinforce the existing structure with penalties for failing to comply with it. When this is the only form of incentive for good conduct, however, it can be detrimental to the motivation of learners. Learners will generally be far more responsive to rewards for producing acceptable behavior than to punishment for not producing it.

Let's think back to Mr. Marks's use of rewards and reinforcement. From his responses to students' ideas, it appears that Mr. Marks has not established a consistent pattern of reward and reinforcement (at least in this lesson), although some informal types of reinforcement are evident (gives verbal praise, uses student answer as a model, asks peers to show admiration). We would need to observe Mr. Marks's classroom for a longer time to discern the use of any long-term rewards (such as extra credit, group work, special duties, or use of special resources), which, when properly varied, also contribute to instructional variety in a classroom.

Observing the Use of Rewards and Reinforcers

You can use the event record shown in Instrument 8.5 to divide rewards and reinforcements into informal (which can be expected to occur frequently within a lesson) and formal (which tend to occur less frequently across lessons) categories. The top half of the form is intended for use on a daily basis; the bottom half of the form can be used with repeated observations over intervals of a week or longer. Some teachers will use a particular reinforcer on a daily (informal) basis; others may use the same one on a less frequent (formal) basis. Although we have included common reinforcers in both categories, make changes to the list according to the situation you observe.

Although you'll probably observe fewer formal than informal rewards, the absence of checkmarks in this category over time, or the repeated use of only a single type of reward, can indicate an inadequate variety of rewards. The repeated use of only a single informal reward, such as "gives verbal praise" or "smiles and nods," suggests a superficial reward system, which students may soon come to ignore for lack of more enduring and sincere reinforcement. Again, you'll want to consider the connections between a teacher's behaviors and student responses carefully to inform your own teaching decisions.

Varying Types of Questions and Probes

A fifth source of variety felt by students in a classroom is the teacher's use of questions and probes. The purpose of these two related techniques is to draw out a response, sometimes *any* response, that can then be refined and developed into a better or more complete response. Questions and probes provide a vehicle for engaging a student in the learning process by getting the learner to think about, work with, and act on the material being presented.

To achieve variety, questions can alternate between convergent and divergent (Gall, 1984; Flanders, 1970). *Convergent* questions have a single or limited number of right answers, and are most commonly associated with the goals of direct instruction. *Direct instruction* occurs when the teacher is the major provider of information (e.g., giving a lecture as opposed to assigning a group discovery project); the teacher's role is to pass on facts, rules, or action sequences in the most direct way possible. Teachers often use convergent questions to facilitate direct instruction, because they want to direct students to the correct answers as efficiently as possible. You'll likely observe many convergent questions when teachers undertake recitation, drill and practice, or briskly paced question-and-answer sessions with their students.

Examples of convergent questions having a single or limited number of right answers are

What is 20 divided by 5?
What is a definition of *democracy*?
What is the chemical composition of the atmosphere on the moon?
What are four literary devices that can make a story interesting?

Convergent questions involve the recall of facts, the summarization or paraphrasing of learned knowledge, or the application of knowledge to a context similar to that in which it was learned. Convergent questions often place heavy reliance on text or workbook content that resembles the desired response ("Look at this word and then say it." "Watch me form a possessive and then do the next one." "Read the instructions, and then focus the microscope."). The task for the learner is to produce a response that resembles, as closely as possible, the form and content of a stimulus provided by the text or teacher.

Divergent questions, on the other hand, may have many right answers and are most commonly associated with the goals of *indirect instruction*, which are to help students use their own knowledge and experiences to actively construct an understanding of particular concepts and related information. A question for which there is no single best answer or for which there are many correct answers would be an indirect question because some choice in the content and form of the response resides with the students, providing learners with a degree of control over their own learning. Divergent questions usually take place in the context of inquiry, problem-solving, or discovery-type activities in which the control of the form and content of the instruction is shared between students and teacher.

Examples of divergent questions having many right answers are

What are some examples of things that are divisible by 5?
Who would like to start by telling us what the word *democracy* means to them?

What might be some ways life could be sustained on the moon?
What types of things make a story interesting?

These questions do not require the answer to a specific problem; rather, they are asked in such a way that almost any student can search for and find an answer that would be at least partially correct. By inserting a phrase such as "means to you," "What might," or "What types of things," a teacher can encourage a response from every student.

The purpose of divergent questions is not to quiz or to teach directly, but to focus student attention on particular ideas or issues and to promote inquiry, problem solving, and discovery. By accepting many different answers, the teacher can use student responses from divergent questions to formulate subsequent questions that shape more accurate responses. The purpose of divergent questions, then, is not to arrive at a correct answer in the quickest and most efficient manner, but to begin a process of search and discovery whereby successively more acceptable answers are constructed.

Classroom researchers who have studied the effects of convergent and divergent questions on student achievement (Dillon, 1988; Gall, 1984; Redfield & Rousseau, 1981) have found that almost five times more convergent than divergent questions occur in classrooms. Yet the rationale given for using higher level, divergent-type questions includes promotion of thinking, formation of concepts and abstractions, and development of decision-making and judgment skills. While research has not clearly substantiated that the use of higher order questions is related to gains in student achievement, at least not as measured by tests of standardized achievement, some educators believe that more divergent questions should be used in teaching. Research does indicate, however, that higher order questioning tends to encourage students to use more complex thought processes in composing a response. Research presented by Gall (1984) and Redfield and Rousseau (1981) indicates that teachers who ask questions requiring analysis, synthesis, and evaluation elicit these types of behaviors from their students more frequently than do teachers who use fewer higher level questions. These process behaviors are desirable whether or not their effects show up on standardized tests of student achievement. Therefore, the effects of higher level questioning on the process of thinking may be justification alone for applying higher level questions consistently at moderate rates. As you observe, pay special attention to how and when teachers utilize divergent questioning techniques in the classroom.

Both convergent and divergent questions are tools for engaging students in the learning process, and therefore you will observe them often. To make the content relevant and meaningful to learners, convergent and divergent questions should be posed in a coherent series of carefully timed questions that are at, or slightly above, the students' current level of understanding. To help make questions more meaningful and to elicit thoughtful responses, both convergent and divergent questions can be followed up with probes that attempt to pierce the glib, superficial, or inadequate responses that are given initially. *Probes* are questions that follow questions and are carefully crafted to deepen, enrich, and extend an earlier response. Probes can be used to elicit a clarifying response to an earlier question, solicit new information related to an earlier question, or redirect the learner into a more productive area. Each of these uses can be a source of instructional variety, encouraging learners to act on and reshape their responses and, most importantly, their thinking.

Another important characteristic of probes—questions that follow other questions—is the time allowed for a student to respond. Rowe (1986) determined that the normal wait time between asking a question and following up with another question was one second or less. By observing teachers who increased their wait time to three or more seconds, Rowe found a number of consequences directly related to the problem-solving behavior of students, which included

❑ The length of student responses increased, on average, between 300 and 700 percent.
❑ More student inferences were supported by evidence and logical argument.
❑ The number of questions asked by students increased.
❑ Student-to-student exchanges increased and teacher-centered behavior decreased.
❑ The number of students failing to respond decreased.
❑ Misbehavior decreased.
❑ More students volunteered to respond.

Rowe (1986) also reported that students use the teacher's wait time to determine the level of thoughtfulness they will devote to an answer: The greater the teacher's wait time, the more the student will attempt to respond in a thoughtful and logical manner.

As you consider the use of questions and probes, what are your thoughts about Mr. Marks's lesson? Looking at the way the lesson improved over time, we believe that Mr. Marks's use of questions, probes, and student ideas was critical. After he introduced the handout, Mr. Marks posed a convergent question to Ricky ("What's a definition of a *tariff*?"). Although the correct answer could be expressed in different ways and could include different examples, the range of correct answers is limited by the nature of the question, making it convergent. The question evokes little cognitive activity on Ricky's part—he simply reads the answer from the handout. So the teacher follows up with another question, this time directed to Tim ("Give me an example of a tariff"). Tim is asked to choose an example from the handout and summarize his choice. He decides to respond by choosing the Tariff Act of 1862: "That was when tariffs on imported products were raised an average of 50 percent." The teacher responds "Which products?" and gives the hint "What do we cover ourselves with every day?" This exchange continues, with the teacher following up each student response with a probe for further clarification ("Can you summarize your answer for the class?"), additional information ("What else does it say about coffee, tea, and sugar?"), or redirection ("Were any other products included under the Tariff Act of 1862?"). Some of the other probes—or follow-up questions—to student responses during the last part of the dialogue were

"Any other products included . . . ?"
"Can you add anything?"
"Why?"
"And that means . . . ?"

Notice that, unlike the beginning of the lesson, Mr. Marks is now engaging his students in the learning process not with rote or mechanical questions, but with questions that force them to go beyond the words on the handout and paraphrase, summarize, and extend crude or incomplete answers. These probes, and the questions that preceded them, added variety to the lesson. But even more important, they were imbedded in an activity structure that engaged learners in the lesson and required them to formulate a product (response to the question) and use several cognitive operations (recognition, application, and problem solving) with the aid of a resource (handout). This activity had the dual effect of maintaining student involvement and evoking responses that went beyond parroting back content in the precise form in which it was presented.

Observing Types of Questions and Probes

You can use Instrument 8.6 to observe the sequence of teacher questions, student responses, and teacher probes as they occur in the classroom. For each question asked by the teacher, determine whether the question is intended to have a single or limited number of correct answers (convergent) or many different correct answers (divergent). Next, record the student's response to the question as *accepted*, *partially accepted* (with qualifications or reservations), *not accepted* (wrong or irrelevant), or as a lack of response (doesn't know). Finally, record the nature of the follow-up probe, if one occurs. In recording the probes, determine whether the teacher's probe (1) asks the student to clarify or expand the answer given, (2) asks a related question to solicit additional information and lift the original answer to a more complete state, (3) redirects the student by giving hints, or (4) asks the same question of another student. The pattern of checkmarks across each row of the instrument indicates the sequence of questioning and responding for individual questions. An analysis of checkmarks down the columns will reveal the variety of questioning, responding, and probing occurring in the class, as

well as how meaningful the particular series of questions and probes is. Definitions for the terms used in this event system appear in Figure 8.4. Some of the more frequent patterns to watch for are

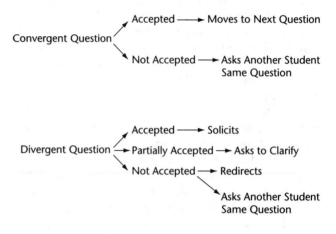

Another way to distinguish types of questions is to consider the degree of behavioral complexity—or

FIGURE 8.4 Definitions for Question-Response-Probe Sequential Event System (Instrument 8.6)

Teacher Question	Convergent	Teacher asks question that has one correct answer. ("What's 6 times 6?" "Who can name each of the main characters in *Huckleberry Finn*?")
	Divergent	Teacher asks question that has more than one correct answer. ("What household products contain the element sodium?" "What did you like about *Of Mice and Men*?")
Student Response	Accepted	Teacher accepts answer as stated through verbal affirmation ("That's right," "Good," or "Okay") or expressive behavior (nods head).
	Partially Accepted	Teacher tells student that response is incomplete. ("That's not quite right, "You're on the right track.")
	Not Accepted	Teacher informs student that answer is not acceptable. ("Next," "Wrong," "No")
	No Response	Student fails to respond. Teacher may try to get student to respond, but to no avail.
Teacher Probe	None	Teacher fails to follow up student's response. Moves to new question or other activity.
	Clarify	Teacher asks student to clarify, expand, or restate answer in other words. Teacher wants to better understand what student said.
	Solicit	Teacher tries to uplift or extend student response by getting student to supply new information.
	Redirect	Teacher attempts to change direction of student response by giving hints or clues about what direction to take.
	Asks Other	Teacher ignores student response or lack of response and asks another student the same question.

thinking—they require of the learner. Bloom et al. (1994, 1984) identified six levels of behavioral complexity that can be applied to questions. These levels are referred to in many curriculum guides and teaching materials, so you'll want to be familiar with them. Definitions for these six levels appear in Figure 8.5. You'll notice that the levels are divided into lower and higher order questions, depending on the relative amount of cognitive processing (thinking) they require on the part of the student. Although you might expect that teachers would rely on higher order questions often, some research data suggest that 70 to 80 percent of all questions teachers ask are lower order, with most of these at the knowledge level (Brown & Edmundson, 1984). There are reasons for asking questions at the knowledge, comprehension, and application levels, but there seems to be little explanation for why such a large percentage of these questions are asked to the exclusion of higher order questions, which are believed to more actively engage students in the learning process.

The recording form in Instrument 8.7 will help you distinguish among various types of questions as you observe in classrooms. When you first observe questioning procedures, you may find that distinguishing among question types in a quickly paced lesson can be difficult. We suggest that you use the middle two columns of this record, labeled *LO* (lower order) and *HO* (higher order), until you gain a sense of the teacher's questioning style. After you've heard several question-response sequences, you'll be able to make finer distinctions, and can gradually begin placing checkmarks in the appropriate boxes representing specific levels of questions. The last row can be used to total the number of questions in each category. A good guideline is to try to identify the first 15 questions or so only as LO or HO. Then you can attempt finer levels of discrimination.

To help you focus on wait time, use the last column to record whether the wait time allowed for a student response was less than (or more than) approximately three seconds. Minus or plus signs can be used to

FIGURE 8.5 Six Levels of Question Complexity

	Question Level	Expected Teacher Behavior	Expected Student Behavior	Instructional Process	Key Words
Lower Order	Knowledge (Remembering)	Teacher intends student to recall specific information for which there is only one correct answer.	Student remembers or recalls information and recognizes facts, terminology, and rules.	Repetition Memorization	Define Describe Identify
	Comprehension (Understanding)	Teacher intends student to translate, paraphrase, or summarize given material.	Student changes the form of a communication by translating what has been read or spoken.	Explanation Illustration	Summarize Paraphrase Rephrase
	Application (Transferring)	Teacher intends student to apply the information to a situation that is different from the situation in which it was learned.	Student applies the information learned to a context other than the one in which it was learned.	Practice Transfer	Apply Use/Employ
Higher Order	Analysis (Relating)	Teacher intends student to separate, compare, or determine relationships among concepts, information, or ideas.	Student breaks a problem down into its component parts and draws relationships among the parts.	Induction Deduction	Relate Distinguish Differentiate
	Synthesis (Creating)	Teacher intends student to combine previously learned information, opinions, or concepts into an original, creative response.	Student combines parts to form a unique or novel solution to a problem.	Divergence Generalization	Formulate Compose Produce
	Evaluation (Judging)	Teacher intends student to make a choice or decision, to judge, or to select from a number of alternatives.	Student makes decisions about the value or worth of methods, ideas, people, or products according to expressed criteria.	Discrimination Inference	Appraise Decode Justify

record these two alternatives, or a timepiece can be used to determine exact values. Rowe (1986) found that most teachers' wait times are about a second instead of the more appropriate three or more seconds. Questions directed to culturally different students can be coded with an asterisk in the Wait Time column.

After you complete an observation, you may want to compare your findings with those of previous research. Research suggests that teachers sometimes ask as many as four lower order questions (knowledge, comprehension, application) for every higher order question (analysis, synthesis, evaluation). Knowledge questions are generally the most prevalent among the lower order questions; analysis questions are generally the most prevalent among the higher order questions. What do you notice about the teachers you observe? What implications do you see for your own teaching?

Using Student Ideas

The final behavior for achieving instructional variety involves the use of student ideas. Palincsar and Brown (1989), Duffy and Roehler (1989), and Flanders (1970) describe five different components of this behavior.

Acknowledging—using the student's idea by repeating the logical connectives expressed by the student.

Modifying—using the student's idea by rephrasing it or conceptualizing it in the teacher's own words.

Applying—using the student's idea to teach an inference or predict the next step in a logical analysis of a problem.

Comparing—using the student's idea by drawing a relationship between it and ideas expressed earlier.

Summarizing—using what was said by an individual student or a group of students as a summarization of concepts.

Consider a brief dialogue that incorporates some of these behaviors.

Teacher: Tom, what is the formula for the Pythagorean theorem?

Tom: $c^2 = a^2 + b^2$ [At this point the teacher could have simply said "Good!" and gone on to the next question. Instead, this teacher continues.]

Teacher: Let's show that on the board. Here is a triangle. Let's do exactly as Tom said. He said: Squaring the altitude, which is *a*, and adding it to the square of the base, which is *b*, should give us the square of the hypotenuse, which is *c*. Would someone like to come up and measure the hypotenuse of this triangle with a ruler, and show us that it equals the square root of c^2?

Which, if any, of the five ways of using student ideas are present in this dialogue? First, by putting Tom's response graphically on the blackboard, this teacher *applied* Tom's answer by taking it to the next step, constructing a proof. Also, by repeating what Tom said, the teacher *acknowledged* to the entire class the value of Tom's contribution. And by having someone come to the blackboard to show the correctness of Tom's response, a *summary* of the concept was provided. All this was accomplished from Tom's simple (and only) utterance, "$c^2 = a^2 + b^2$."

There may be no greater variety than that which occurs in student responses to divergent questions. This diversity can be a problem as well as a benefit, however, when unexpected or difficult-to-evaluate responses put the teacher on the defensive. A common response of some teachers is to invent a correct answer on the spot and end the awkward pause that frequently follows an unusual and unexpected answer. This is not a proper use of divergent questioning because two of the reasons for posing divergent questions are to incorporate student ideas and encourage participation in the lesson. The key to eliciting individual student ideas and opinions is to make the ideas and opinions useful to the goals of the lesson, thereby creating a greater understanding for all students. Rowe (1986) found that by increasing wait time after asking a question and after a student's response, teachers showed

Greater flexibility in responding to student comments.

Greater variety in number and kind of questions asked.

Higher expectations for certain students.

This was accomplished, in part, by

❑ Encouraging students to use *examples* and *references* from their own experience.

❑ Asking students to seek *clarification* of, draw *parallels* to, make *predictions*, and draw *associations* from what they already know.

❑ Encouraging understanding and retention of ideas by relating them to the students' own sphere of *interests*, *concerns*, and *problems*.

We will return to these behaviors in Chapter 12 to show how each can be used to promote higher thought processes.

Let's consider Mr. Marks's use of student ideas in the class discussion. Recall that student ideas can be used by acknowledging, modifying, applying, comparing, or summarizing a student's contribution. We believe that Mr. Marks was somewhat effective in motivating students to use the contributions of other students, thereby according respect and status to student contributions and providing content for further discussion. For example, Mr. Marks says, "Now, this is an interesting point Carlos is raising. Who can summarize it?" "Well, class, do you think

Carlos and Angel know what a tariff is?" "Very good. Did the rest of you hear Amanda's answer? Can you summarize your answer for the class . . . ?" Each of these statements acknowledged and/or summarized a student idea, giving these students a sense of pride in the development of the lesson content.

While Mr. Marks often capitalized on his students' ideas, there were times when he chose not to acknowledge or use certain student responses, perhaps because they lacked the quality or depth needed for the discussion. Remember when he said, "Give us the answer to my question" or "Okay, that's sufficient"? In these examples, Mr. Marks fails to leave sufficient wait time to allow the student to clarify an answer that could be better or complete an answer already begun, possibly leaving these students feeling a lack of pride and sense of failure. Such curt or controlling responses, if applied consistently, can discourage students from volunteering or participating again (Noddings, 1992; Belenky, et al., 1986). This may be particularly true when the teacher and student are members of different cultures or genders.

Observing the Use of Student Ideas

To better understand how to utilize student ideas in classroom activities, use the event system in Instrument 8.8. Recall that five teacher behaviors are associated with the use of student ideas: *acknowledging* (repeating a student response), *modifying* (rephrasing a student response), *applying* (using a student response to take the next step), *comparing* (drawing a relationship between a student response and other responses), and *summarizing* (using a student response to recapitulate). To use this observation record, place a checkmark in the appropriate box under each column each time the teacher acknowledges, modifies, applies, compares, or summarizes a student's response, according to the definitions provided. To illustrate, let's return to the brief dialogue earlier between the teacher and Tom. To code this dialogue using the observation record, we would place checks in the first column after applying, acknowledging, and summarizing, indicating that these three behaviors occurred. When the action turns to another student, or the same student is provided the opportunity to respond again, the next column is coded, and so on through the lesson. Not all student responses can—or should—be integrated into the lesson with one or more of these behaviors. However, the infrequent use of student ideas or the consistent use of student ideas employing the same teacher behavior (for example, acknowledging) can indicate a lack of variety in a classroom.

Notice that tallies can be summarized in two ways on this record. The first, indicated by the final row of the record, shows the total number of teacher behaviors used in response to a single idea. A second total can be identified by noting, across the top, the last number checked for each specific type of teacher behavior. Each view can provide information about ways to use student ideas in the classroom.

Cultural Diversity and Instructional Variety

A number of authors have studied the effects of various forms of instructional variety on student behavior. For example, Hall (1977) found a connection between spatial distance and involvement in the classroom: The greater the spatial distance between teacher and students, the more some students became passive listeners and the teacher's talk was perceived as a lecture. As the teacher moved closer to students, communication tended to become more interactive, with more student-to-student and student-to-teacher communication. Hall observed that standing closer to individual students can promote involvement, since these students will be drawn into nonverbal forms of communication, such as eye contact and changes in voice and body movement, that send a message of involvement.

Scollon (1985) found that the use of space also can communicate a sense of power and control, which can promote involvement or uninvolvement. For example, a person who is standing expresses more power than one who is seated, and a person who speaks from a distance expresses more authority than one who is talking up close. Accordingly, teachers who stay behind their desk separated from students are expressing control and authority, which in turn can send a message that students are expected to be passive, subservient, and nonparticipatory. Such decisions clearly affect the warmth (or lack of warmth) of the classroom learning climate. Teachers are often creative in their approaches to space and classroom climate. For example, Bowers and Flinders (1991) report a case of a teacher who moved from student to student checking work while seated on a swivel chair with casters. In this manner the teacher was able to elicit more spontaneous and relaxed student responses, resulting in greater student involvement. Clearly, a teacher's animation and proper use of spatial variety can foster a sense of trust and sharing among students who, by virtue of their language, culture, or ethnicity, may not wish to be spotlighted in the traditional teacher-dominated manner.

In considering instructional variety, it is important to realize that interaction patterns are often related to particular cultural expectations. For example, students from one culture may feel threatened by the close proximity or penetrating eye contact common in another culture. Further, cultural patterns that are unfamiliar to Anglo teachers may provide misleading signs of involvement and uninvolvement. For example, Erickson (1982, 1979) reports a case in which African-American students were viewed as inattentive and an Anglo counselor was perceived as demeaning because the head nodding, gaze, eye contact, and body cues of the two groups did not correspond. Specifically, Anglo speakers tend to look at a listener only occasionally, but when in the role of listener they look continuously at the speaker. On the other hand, African-American speakers tend to look continuously at the listener, and when in the role of listener look at the speaker intermittently.

The speech patterns of ethnic and cultural groups also must be taken into consideration when allocating the proper amount of wait time between questions and after a question. For some cultural groups, particularly those who may be Limited English Proficient (LEP), Rowe (1986) suggested that a 3-second wait time may be insufficient to elicit a response and promote active participation. Although little is known about this facet of cultural diversity, wait times considerably greater than those used for the majority of students may be appropriate for some cultural groups. One finding is clear: Wait times of less than about 3 seconds seem to inhibit thoughtful responses on the part of all students.

The results from these and other studies of cultural diversity and instructional variety suggest that

- ❑ A closer spatial distance when asking questions and responding will be more appropriate for learners who, due to culture, language, or ethnicity, do not wish to be spotlighted in the traditional manner.
- ❑ For some cultural groups, looking at the speaker only intermittently can indicate full attention and engagement in the lesson, despite the dominant cultural pattern.
- ❑ Speech patterns of some cultural groups, especially if Limited English Proficient, may require a substantially longer wait time (greater than 3 seconds) after a question.
- ❑ A closer spatial distance tends to convey a less formal learning climate, to promote more relaxed and spontaneous responses, and to increase participation among all students.

As you observe in various classrooms, you'll want to learn about the accepted interaction patterns in schools and communities—especially before making judgments about what you see. Such an understanding will help you view interactions with a much clearer lens.

In the following chapters, we will turn our attention to several other important lenses through which to observe classrooms. These lenses—task orientation, student engagement in the learning process, student success, and higher thought processes—are always observed in the context of the dimensions of instructional variety.

ACTIVITIES*

1. Using the checklist provided in Figure 8.2, observe the presentation of a lesson looking for signs of instructional variety. At the end of your observation, add a brief written description to each box highlighting at least one specific reason why you chose to place each of your checkmarks as you did. Using your written descriptions as a guide, write a paragraph describing some of the reasons for the instructional variety, or lack thereof, in this lesson.

2. Using the examples of five-point scales shown in Chapter 4, convert the positively stated indicators of instructional variety listed in Figure 8.1 into a Likert scale. Consider vertical or horizontal placement of each indicator on the page, whether words will be affixed to all or only some of the response blanks, and what response alternatives will be best suited to each question. Show your scale to a classmate who has also constructed a five-point scale. Together, create a single revised version incorporating the best features of each.

3. Using the seven-point, polar scale presented in Chapter 4 as an example, convert the positive and negative indicators in Figure 8.1 into this scale format and observe a lesson for signs of instructional variety. At the end of your observation, complete the scale by indicating with a checkmark the degree to which this lesson achieved each dimension of instructional variety. Use the code *N/O* for any items that you did not have the opportunity to observe. Reflecting on your experience as a student and previous classroom observations, return to the scale and place an *X* on the blank corresponding to each scale item that, in your opinion, represents the degree of instructional variety found in most classrooms. Note the difference between your ratings for this lesson and what might be the typical or average instructional variety across most classrooms. Cite the reasons why this lesson was the same, higher, or lower on each dimension.

---

*Some of the following activities may be grouped into a common activity, divided among classmates, and completed from a single observation.

4. Using the form shown in Instrument 8.1 for recording attention-gaining devices, observe several lessons in different classrooms. In each classroom, be sure to record any verbal statements/questions, visuals, media, and realia used to capture student attention that do not fit the predesignated categories on the record. With these other attention-gaining devices included, add the tallies in each column and enter the totals in the last row. Do your data suggest any one category is used more frequently than the others? If so, what do you believe accounts for this result?

5. Using the Likert scales provided in Instrument 8.2 for observing a teacher's body movement, eye contact, voice intonation, and gestures, place a checkmark along the precise point on each continuum that in your judgment best reflects the behavior of a teacher you have observed. Assign a numerical value from 1 to 5 to each checkmark, and use fractional scores when your marks fall between major divisions on the scale. Be sure to note the direction of each of the scales before assigning numerical values. Overall, how would you describe this teacher's enthusiasm and animation?

6. Using Instrument 8.4, record the channels through which content is transmitted by observing the presentation of a lesson lasting for 40 to 50 minutes. At the end of each 5-minute interval, indicate whether the oral, verbal, visual, and/or tactile modalities, as described in Figure 8.3, are used by the teacher to convey lesson content. Calculate the approximate number of minutes and percentage of time each of these modalities is in use. Rank the use of the four modalities in this classroom according to percentage of time. Do you believe this pattern is typical of most classrooms? What, in your judgment, would be the most desirable pattern for this lesson?

7. Using the event record for observing informal and formal types of rewards presented in Instrument 8.5, observe several days, as close together as possible, in the same classroom. Complete a new record each day, entering a checkmark each time an informal or formal teacher response/activity that serves as a reward or reinforcement occurs. Keep a list of any other rewards that do not fit the categories listed, classifying them as formal or informal. Total the number of entries within categories on each form, and then sum the totals for each category across forms (days). Which categories of formal and informal rewards were used most often? Which were used least?

8. Observe a class for which there is scheduled a question-and-answer session or group discussion in which student questioning is likely to occur. Complete Instrument 8.6 for recording the sequence of teacher questions, student responses, and teacher probes. Continue observing until a sufficient number of both convergent and divergent questions has been recorded. Total the number of entries in each column separately for convergent and divergent, as indicated in the final two rows. Using these totals, identify the most frequent student response to a convergent question and the most frequent teacher probe to a student response following a convergent question. Do the same for a divergent question. In this class, how did student responses and teacher probes differ across types of questions?

9. Using Instrument 8.7 for observing lower order and higher order questions at the six levels of behavioral complexity, observe another class session in which teacher-student questioning is likely to occur. For the first 15 or so teacher questions, record only whether the questions are lower or higher order. Then identify questions as knowledge, comprehension, application, analysis, synthesis, or evaluation, according to the definitions given in Figure 8.5. Total the number of entries in each column. How do your results, including wait time, compare with what classroom researchers have found?

10. Observe a class discussion, using Instrument 8.8 to record the teacher's use of student ideas. Complete the final row by adding the number of entries for each column. How many times did each of the five teacher behaviors for using student ideas occur in this classroom? Can you cite any unique ways in which this teacher used student ideas?

INSTRUMENT 8.1   Checklist for recording Use of Attention-Gaining Devices

Date	Lesson Topic	Verbal Statements and Questions					Visuals				Media			Realia			
		To Promote Curiosity	To Present a Contradiction	To Create Controversy	To Surprise/ Astound	Other	Diagrams/Charts	Blackboard	Photographs/Pictures	Other	Audio	Film/TV/Video	Computer	Living Things	Scale Models	Technical/Laboratory Equipment	Other
	Totals																

INSTRUMENT 8.2   Likert Scale for Observing Four Behaviors of Teacher Enthusiasm

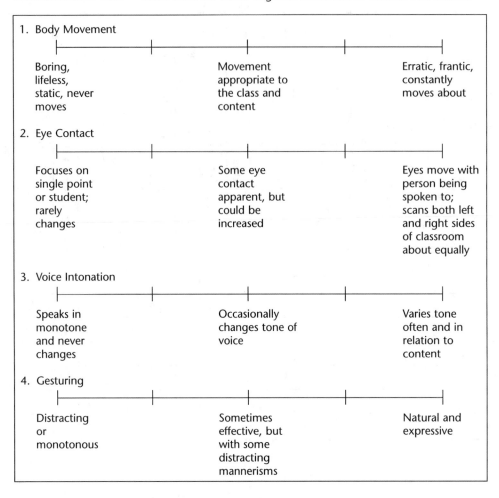

1. Body Movement

| Boring, lifeless, static, never moves | Movement appropriate to the class and content | Erratic, frantic, constantly moves about |

2. Eye Contact

| Focuses on single point or student; rarely changes | Some eye contact apparent, but could be increased | Eyes move with person being spoken to; scans both left and right sides of classroom about equally |

3. Voice Intonation

| Speaks in monotone and never changes | Occasionally changes tone of voice | Varies tone often and in relation to content |

4. Gesturing

| Distracting or monotonous | Sometimes effective, but with some distracting mannerisms | Natural and expressive |

INSTRUMENT 8.3   Activity Structure Checklist

Task Components		Tasks									
		1	2	3	4	5	6	7	8	9	10
Task Products	**Subvocal thought**										
	Oral response										
	Written response										
Task Operations	**Recognition and discrimination**										
	Application and practice										
	Problem solving										
	Invention, discovery										
Task Resources	**Oral content**										
	Text/workbook										
	Blackboard										
	Handout/media										

INSTRUMENT 8.4   Sign Observation System for the Four Modalities

Five-Minute Intervals	Oral (Speaking, Hearing/ Listening)	Verbal (Written)	Visual (Showing, Viewing)	Tactile (Touching)
1				
2				
3				
4				
5				
6				
7				
8				
9				
10				
Total				
Percent				
Minutes (approx.)				

INSTRUMENT 8.5 Event Record for Informal and Formal Types of Rewards

	Teacher Response/Activity	Times of Occurrence									
		1	2	3	4	5	6	7	8	9	10
Informal (Daily)	Gives verbal praise only ("good"), smiles, nods head only										
	Gives verbal praise with reason why response is correct										
	Uses student answer as model (puts on board)										
	Has student help/tell others how to do it										
	Asks peers to show admiration ("Isn't it good")										
	Allows work in groups										
	Allows use of the learning center										
	Allows independent study time										
	Other										
Formal (Weekly, Monthly)	Gives extra credit, writes on assignment										
	Allows use of games, simulations, or special materials										
	Allows work in groups										
	Selects student for special duty										
	Gives recognition certificate										
	Allows use of learning center, library, or reference desk										
	Allows independent study time										
	Posts assignment/exam										
	Writes message to parents										
	Other										

INSTRUMENT **8.6**   Event System for Recording Student–Teacher Interaction

Question Number	Teacher Question		Student Response				Teacher Probe				
	Convergent	Divergent	Accepted	Partially Accepted	Not Accepted	Don't Know/No Response	No Probe	Solicits More Information	Asks to Clarify	Redirects (Hints, Gives Clues)	Asks Another Student Same Question
1											
2											
3											
4											
5											
6											
7											
8											
9											
10											
11											
12											
13											
14											
15											
Totals	Convergent										
	Divergent										

INSTRUMENT 8.7 Form for Distinguishing Among Six Types of Questions

Question Number	Question Level								Wait Time
	Knowledge	Comprehension	Application	LO	HO	Analysis	Synthesis	Evaluation	
1									
2									
3									
4									
5									
6									
7									
8									
9									
10									
11									
12									
13									
14									
15									
Totals									

INSTRUMENT 8.8   Event System for Observing Use of Student Ideas

Teacher Behavior	Times Student Ideas Are Used														
	1	2	3	4	5	6	7	8	9	10	11	12	13	14	15
1. Acknowledging	✓														
2. Modifying															
3. Applying	✓														
4. Comparing															
5. Summarizing	✓														
Totals															

Chapter 9

Observing Task Orientation

Helping

Agatha Fry, she made a pie,

And Christopher John helped bake it.

Christopher John, he mowed the lawn,

And Agatha Fry helped rake it.

Zachary Zugg took out the rug,

And Jennifer Joy helped shake it.

And Jennifer Joy, she made a toy,

And Zachary Zugg helped break it.

And some kind of help

is the kind of help

That helping's all about.

And some kind of help

Is the kind of help

We all can do without.

Shel Silverstein

What kinds of tasks and what kinds of help are effective in classrooms? How do teachers formulate, introduce, and monitor learning tasks in classrooms? How do they increase the chances that a learning task will be the "kind of help that helping's all about?"

Where the Sidewalk Ends. New York: Harper and Row, 1974, p. 101.

Task orientation refers to the degree to which the teacher provides students with the opportunity to learn. Patterns of this behavior include the amount of time the teacher spends covering the assigned topics and encouraging students to think about the material taught, and the amount of intellectual or cognitive emphasis given an assigned topic by the teacher's activity structure. Most researchers agree that classrooms in which most of the interaction between students and teacher focuses on subject matter rather than administrative and clerical tasks are likely to have higher rates of achievement than those that do not. It is also probable that teachers in content-oriented classrooms are more familiar with the material likely to appear on end-of-year achievement tests, so that their instruction parallels the curriculum that guided the construction of these tests. In short, teachers with a high degree of task orientation are goal-oriented; that is, they organize instruction around their goals and stick to those goals in the midst of distracting, irrelevant activities that reduce students' opportunity to learn. Most important, a task-oriented teacher has high, but realistic, expectations for student performance.

DIMENSIONS OF TASK ORIENTATION

Figure 9.1 summarizes five behaviors for achieving task orientation. These behaviors include:

1. Developing unit and lesson plans that reflect the curriculum.
2. Performing administrative and clerical tasks efficiently.
3. Preventing and correcting misbehavior with a minimum of class disruption.
4. Selecting the most appropriate instructional strategies for the objectives being taught.
5. Establishing cycles of review, feedback, and testing.

PRACTICE OBSERVING TASK ORIENTATION: A DIALOGUE

Let's practice observing signs of task orientation by visiting Mrs. Libby's class and using the checklist in Figure 9.2 to consider the five key behaviors related to task orientation.

FIGURE 9.1 Indicators for Task Orientation

Task Oriented (Effective Teacher)	Poor Task Orientation (Ineffective Teacher)
1. Develops unit and lesson plans that reflect the most relevant features of the curriculum (each unit and lesson objective can be referenced back to curriculum guide or text)	Develops lessons almost exclusively from personal or student interests; breadth and depth of lesson content fails to distinguish between primary and secondary content in the curriculum guide and text
2. Handles administrative and clerical tasks (visitors, announcements, collection of money, dispensing of materials and supplies) efficiently by anticipating and preorganizing some tasks and deferring others to noninstructional time	Attends to every administrative and clerical task in detail during the time normally devoted to instruction.
3. Prevents and corrects misbehavior with a minimum of class disruption (has preestablished academic and work rules to prevent intrusions into instructional time)	Attends to specific misbehavior at length; singles out individual students for punishment and lectures on the offense during instructional time
4. Selects the most appropriate instructional strategy for the objectives taught	Uses inefficient instruction methods for achieving lesson objectives (frequently attempts to teach facts through discussion, or concepts through drill and practice)
5. Builds toward unit outcomes with clearly definable events (weekly or monthly review, feedback, and testing sessions)	Has no systematic milestones (progress checks, reviews, individual assignments or projects) to keep the class on schedule and moving toward a clearly defined goal

FIGURE 9.2 Checklist for Observing Task Orientation

Behavior	Observed	Not Observed	No Opportunity To Observe
1. Develops unit and lesson plans in accordance with text and curriculum guides			
2. Handles administrative and clerical interruptions efficiently			
3. Stops or prevents misbehavior with a minimum of disruption to the class			
4. Selects the most appropriate instructional strategy for the objectives taught			
5. Builds toward unit outcomes with clearly defined events (weekly and monthly reviews, feedback, and testing)			

Today Mrs. Libby is teaching her students about reproductive systems, a topic required by the curriculum guide and covered in Chapter 3 of the adopted textbook. This lesson is intended to be a transition to a unit on the reproductive systems of higher life forms to be taught the following week. This lesson occurs during the first month of the school year.

Mrs. Libby: Okay, everyone settle down. Tricia, get to your seat. [At the bell.] You, too, Mark.

Alexa: You want my homework now?

Mrs. Libby: I'll collect everyone's homework at the end of class.

Alexa: But some haven't got it, and they're just gonna do it during class.

Mrs. Libby: Alexa, let me make the decisions. You just worry about getting a good grade.

Alexa: But . . . .

Mrs. Libby: [Notices Kyoko walking in late.] And where have you been?

Kyoko: My locker got jammed and I had to get Mr. Tiller to open it for me.

Mrs. Libby: Did he give you a late pass?

Kyoko: Nope.

Mrs. Libby: You can't just walk in late without a pass. [Some murmuring is heard among the other students.]

Kyoko: I guess he forgot.

Mrs. Libby: Please get one and then come back. If I let you walk in late, everyone will do the same.

Kyoko: I'd have to interrupt his class. He's probably already teaching.

Mrs. Libby: I'm marking you absent until you come back with a pass or a note from a counselor. [Kyoko whispers something, which the teacher chooses to ignore, and then leaves the room. By this time, a few students are out of their seats visiting friends, and loud talking can be heard.] Okay, that's enough. [Claps hands to restore order.] Some of you may feel sorry for Kyoko, but he's got to learn that being on time is a mark of a responsible person. Life is a series of hurdles we all have to cross, and one of them is being on time. Are we all settled down now and ready to go to work? [A few students nod; the others remain passive.] Okay, then, I can begin presenting today's lesson. It's about the reproductive cycle. [Some snickering can be heard in the back of the room.] This is serious, class, and I don't want any laughing. Who remembers from our previous discussion some of the ways lower forms of animal life reproduce? [Sudia raises his hand. The teacher nods.]

Sudia: Well, one way we studied is by dividing in half.

Mrs. Libby: Okay, this is called *reproduction by fission*. That's when the parent organism splits into two or more organisms and loses its original identity. It is the way most single-celled animals reproduce. Now, this process can only be seen under a microscope. How many of you have ever used a microscope?

Milo: [Shouting out.] I have one at home.

Mrs. Libby: [Ignoring Milo.] Those who have used a microscope before, raise your hand. [Teacher counts five hands.] Okay, well a few of you know that, with a microscope, things can be seen that cannot be seen by the naked eye.

Milo: [Shouting out again.] Yeah, I used to put little bugs under mine and watch 'em squirm. [Class laughs.]

Mrs. Libby: [Looking at Milo.] You're not supposed to call out. First of all, you spoke without raising your hand. Second, we're talking about lower forms of animal life that cannot be seen by the naked eye. So let this be a warning. Let's see now, where were we?

Kathy: [Calling out]. Single-celled animals that reproduce by dividing up.

Mrs. Libby: Yes. But I wanted to say that, later, we will have an opportunity to use microscopes to see single-celled animals. These microscopes are expensive and can be damaged easily if they are not used correctly. I might as well let you know that each of you will have to pass a test before you can use our microscopes. These microscopes are new this year, and the principal is concerned about their safety. There just isn't money to replace any of them if they should be broken through carelessness. I don't know if you heard about the new rule, but those students who break equipment through their own carelessness have to pay for it. So that's a warning in advance. Can anyone think of any other means of reproduction? [Silence. Shelena looks uncertain, but captures the teacher's eye.] Shelena.

Shelena: Sometimes an egg—or something like an egg—gets fertilized.

Mrs. Libby: We're talking about lower forms of animal life. Bill. [Who is waving his hand.]

Bill: Isn't there a way that new life can be created by parts of other things coming together?

Mrs. Libby: Good. You must be talking about a process called *conjugation*. This occurs when two similar organisms fuse, exchange nuclear material, and then break apart, taking two different identities. Now, can anyone think of a way higher forms of animal life reproduce?

Milo: [Calling out.] You mean like dogs and cats?

Mrs. Libby: This is your second warning about calling out. One more time and I'll have to assign you extra homework. [Class snickers with delight at Milo getting in trouble.] Well, now . . . [Catching the thought again.] Many multicellular forms of animal life reproduce by having male and female reproductive cells that unite to form a single cell called a *zygote*, which then divides to form a new organism. The word that describes the union of male and female cells is *fertilization*. In this form of reproduction, half the genes in the zygote come from one parent and half from the other.

Mark: [Calling out.] That's what sex is all about.

Mrs. Libby: [Pointing to Mark.] That will be an extra assignment for tonight for calling out. Answer all the questions under A, B, and C at the end of Chapter 3 for tonight. Barbara, tell Mark what we are talking about.

Barbara: We're talking about zygotes!

Mrs. Libby: Yes. Now in higher animals—including humans—single species are either male or female, according to whether they produce male or female reproductive cells. Somewhere there's a picture of male and female cells in your text. Does anyone remember seeing it? [Some students shake their heads yes, and others no.] Can someone find the page it's on? [Class starts thumbing through pages of book noisily, while teacher goes to her desk and looks, too.]

Bobby: I found it. It's on page 72.

Mrs. Libby: [Turning to page 72 in her book.] No. That's not what I'm thinking of.

Kathy: Here it is on page 63!

Mrs. Libby: [Turning to page 63 now.] No. That's not it either. Maybe I remember seeing it in one of my books. [Mrs. Libby grabs a thick book from the reference shelf behind her desk and renews the search. Class gets noisier.] Well, here's one kind of like what I was thinking of. [Holds page of book up to class.] Can everyone see it? [Students in front look at picture with curiosity; students in back shout out "no." Some get up from their seats and walk to the front for a better look.] Okay, let's stay in our seats. I'll make a transparency of this tonight and we will take a better look at it tomorrow. [Closes reference book; some students moan for effect.] For those who didn't see it, the picture shows a typical male reproductive cell—called a *sperm*—and a typical female reproductive cell—called an *egg*, or . . . [Students start smiling and looking at each other with embarrassment. A click can be heard, indicating an announcement is about to be made over the P.A. system. Mrs. Libby goes to her desk and sits down to await the message. The noise level goes up as students talk among themselves, trying to anticipate what the rest of the lesson will be about.]

Principal: [Over the P.A. system.] Teachers, I'm sorry to interrupt, but I have an important announcement. Orders for individual class pictures must be in no later than 3:00 P.M. today. Failure to place your order by that time means you will not receive pictures this year. While I have your attention, I would like to tell students to remind their parents that tonight is Parent-Teacher Night. We would like a good turnout, so be sure to remind Mom and Dad. Thank you. [Some students have gotten out of their seats to talk to others.]

Mrs. Libby: Class isn't over. Open your books to the questions at the end of Chapter 3. Let's see if you know the definitions of these words from our discussion. Some of these will be on the test next week. Damon, you take the first one. What is *fission*?

REACTIONS TO THE DIALOGUE

What examples of task orientation did you see in this dialogue? Recall that *task orientation* refers to the degree to which the teacher provides students with the maximum opportunity to learn, and includes the amount of time the teacher spends covering the assigned topics and the emphasis placed on the content of the lesson, as opposed to the administration and management of the classroom. It also includes the appropriate selection of teaching strategies and student tasks to help students learn selected materials.

Preparing Unit and Lesson Plans That Reflect the Curriculum

The first dimension in Figure 9.1 pertains to unit and lesson plans that reflect the most relevant features of the curriculum. A task-oriented lesson begins with objectives that are based on the curriculum guide and text. Without unit and lesson objectives derived from an adopted text and curriculum, a teacher may be tempted to translate or extend content into topics of personal interest about which she is more knowledgeable, or those which the students appear most eager to learn, regardless of the prescribed curriculum.

We learn in the introduction to Mrs. Libby's lesson that the topic to be presented, reproductive systems of lower forms of animal life, has been taken from the curriculum guide and coincides with the content in Chapter 3 of the adopted text. This topic is task-relevant prior learning for a subsequent unit on the reproductive systems of higher forms of animal life. Thus, Mrs. Libby's lesson appears to follow the prescribed curriculum for this grade and time of year.

There is, however, a more subtle aspect to task orientation: How much does the teacher revise, elaborate, or otherwise add to the curriculum to present it at students' current level of understanding? The interest, motivation, and ability level of the students in Mrs. Libby's class may have indicated that elaboration of the content and instructional resources beyond those in the text might be required. For example, given the apparent lack of student interest and participation in the topic, some elaboration of why this topic is important in this class, what significance it may have in subsequent courses or the world outside the classroom, or even some historical account of how it was first discovered and studied in the laboratory might have piqued student interest.

While task orientation can be enhanced by elaborating and extending content, digressions irrelevant to the immediate goals of the lesson should be avoided. For example, Mrs. Libby's digression into the topic of microscopes, which included references to their expense, the principal's concern about them, and procedures for replacing them, seems irrelevant. Even her reference to an exam on the use of microscopes was premature, since they would not be used for some time. At a different time and in another context these issues might have been relevant and deserving of coverage. But was this the time? Without the immediate event to which the comments apply, it is unlikely that many students would retain the information conveyed. This is perhaps the trickiest part of developing unit and lesson plans. Units and lessons must not only reflect the curriculum, but must also stress content at the most relevant time.

While curriculum guides at the department and school-district levels usually are explicit about the content to be covered in a specified period of time, they may be far less explicit about the behaviors that students are expected to acquire during this time, leaving considerable judgment to the teacher. For example, a typical excerpt from a curriculum guide for English language instruction might be

1. Writing concepts and skills. The student shall be provided opportunities to learn
   A. The composing process
   B. Descriptive, narrative, and expository paragraphs
   C. Multiple-paragraph compositions
   D. Persuasive discourse
   E. Meanings and uses of colloquialisms, slang, idioms, and jargon

Notice from this excerpt the specificity of the content to be taught, but the lack of specificity concerning the level of behavioral complexity at which the content is to be learned. This is typical of many curriculum guides. Recalling the taxonomy of behavior in the cognitive domain presented in Figure 8.5, the teacher may ask, "For which of these content areas will the simple recall of facts be sufficient? For which areas will a comprehension of those facts be required? For which areas will an application of what is comprehended be expected? For which areas will higher level outcomes involving analysis, synthesis, and decision-making skills be desired?" These decisions involve selecting the level of behavioral complexity at which an instructional unit or lesson will be taught, and the level at which student behavior will be tested. Curriculum guides seldom provide this level of specificity.

The teacher's interpretation of the curriculum guide will depend on the unique behavioral characteristics of the students, the time that can be devoted to a specific topic, and the overall behavioral outcomes desired at the unit level. A knowledge of instructional aims and goals at the state level, the curriculum guide at the school-district level, and adopted text at the subject or grade level can help ensure that the interpretations made at the classroom level result in lesson plans that are task-oriented. A close relationship among general aims at the state level (as expressed by laws and policies), goals at the school-district level (as expressed by the curriculum guide), and objectives at the classroom level (as identified by the teacher and curriculum materials) is necessary for maintaining task orientation, as illustrated in Figure 9.3

Observing How Unit and Lesson Plans Reflect the Curriculum

We can also use the format in Figure 9.4 to more closely observe how a teacher relates unit and lesson plans to the curriculum guide and adopted text. Item 6 in Figure 9.4 can provide an explanation for why some—or all—of the lesson content may not correspond to the curriculum guide or text. For example, it is not unusual for local priorities to supplant the established curriculum when crucial learning needs or academic deficiencies become known unexpectedly. Or significant current events (the election of a president, an important Supreme Court decision, a new scientific discovery, or a moral dilemma being faced by the local community), which have no immediate counterpart in the curriculum guide or text, may be used as the basis for instruction. Capitalizing on such events by occasionally seizing the instructional opportunities they present may reflect a task orientation, if the topic is relevant to the grade and ability levels of the students. Progress tests at the district level, or mandated competency tests at the state level, may reveal critical learning needs that require immediate reteaching of task-relevant prior learning.

Performing Administrative and Clerical Tasks Efficiently

A second behavior for maintaining a task orientation is performing administrative and clerical tasks efficiently. As noted in Chapter 6, this behavior was found to be among the most important in determining a teacher's task orientation for the entire class period. Emmer, Evertson, and Anderson (1980) found that it is difficult to return to an instructional task (for example, a group recitation) from a noninstructional activity (passing out materials or checking for supplies) without devoting

FIGURE 9.3 Flow of Teaching Content From the State Level to the Classroom Level

State Curriculum Framework
- Provides philosophy that guides curriculum implementation
- Discusses progression of essential content taught from grade to grade; shows movement of student through increasingly complex material
- Notes modifications of curriculum to special populations (gifted, bilingual, challenged)

District Curriculum Guide
- Provides content goals keyed to state framework
- Enumerates appropriate teaching activities and strategies
- Gives outline for unit plans; lists and sequences topics
- Reflects locally appropriate ways of achieving goals in content areas

Teacher's Unit and Lesson Plans
- Describes how curriculum-guide goals are implemented daily
- Refers to topics to be covered, and materials and activities to be used
- Identifies evaluation procedures
- Notes adaptations to special populations

Teacher's Grade Book
- Records objectives mastered
- Identifies need for reteaching and remediation
- Provides progress indicators
- Guides promotion/retention decisions

time to getting students back on task. Not only was time spent on the noninstructional activity, but just as much or more time was spent getting learners to return their attention to the instructional content.

Although unexpected interruptions such as a messenger at the door or an unscheduled announcement

FIGURE 9.4 Format for Studying Relationship Between Unit/Lesson Plans and Curriculum Guide/Text

1. Subject and grade: _____

2. Topic or main objective of lesson to be observed: _____

3. Title of adopted text and, if applicable, accompanying workbook: _____
   _____

4. Chapter and/or workbook subheadings and pages pertaining to the objective(s):
   Text: _____ pages: _____
   Workbook: _____ pages: _____

5. Lesson activities observed:
   ❑ Media: _____
   ❑ Manipulative: _____
   ❑ Student collaboration: _____
   ❑ Teacher lecture/demonstration: _____
   ❑ Group discussion: _____
   ❑ Other tasks or assignments: _____

6. If a correspondence between lesson activities and text and/or workbook is not apparent, suggest the reason why, if evident (teacher is off-task, compensatory remedial materials are being used, critical local priorities are being addressed instead, students are unable to grasp textbook content):
   _____
   _____

on the public address system cannot be avoided, rules about what students will do when these events occur can be established beforehand. For example, simple procedures such as taking messages but responding to them after class, or continuing to move about the classroom silently in a businesslike fashion during unexpected announcements, can prevent off-task behavior and the loss of valuable minutes of instructional time. Less effective classroom managers often spend great amounts of time returning a class to normal after interruptions because they have not planned in advance what to do when these events occur.

Effecting smooth and efficient transitions can also lessen a teacher's administrative responsibilities. In studies by Emmer et al. (1997) and Evertson (1997), less effective classroom managers found it difficult to keep students' attention during a transition from one instructional activity to another. Switching from lecture to seatwork, from discussion to explanation, or from seatwork to discussion is a time when some students become distracted. Moving the entire class from one activity to another in a timely and orderly manner can be a major undertaking. Problems during these transitions often occur for two reasons: a lack of readiness on the part of the learners to perform the next activity, and unclear expectations about appropriate behavior during the transition.

When students are uncertain about, or unaware of, what is to come next, they naturally become anxious. This is when transitions get noisy. Some individuals feel more comfortable with the previous activity and do not want to make the change to the next; they are not likely to rush headlong into a new activity for which they feel unprepared. In this sense, transitions are as much psychological barriers as they are actual divisions in time between activities. Students must adjust their psyches for the next activity, just as they may fumble through their books and papers (or guess which ones will be needed) at the beginning of a lesson. As we saw in Chapter 6, it will help if students are taught, at the start of the year or of the semester, the daily routines that are expected of them. These may be second nature after a few weeks, but they deserve special mention and practice during the first days of school.

Figure 9.5 shows ways in which effective classroom managers responded to problems during transitions, increasing their task orientation, in the studies by Emmer et al. (1997) and Evertson (1997).

Finally, these teachers displayed prior assignments openly so that students who missed an assignment could conveniently look it up. The teacher did not have to waste valuable class time finding an assignment that may have been days (or even weeks) old. A simple 2′ × 2′ sheet of art board, divided into days of the month and covered with plastic to write

FIGURE 9.5 Effective Responses to Problems During Transitions

Problem	Solution
Students talked loudly at the beginning of transitions.	Teachers established a rule that no talking was allowed between transitions, acknowledging that it is difficult to allow a small amount of talking and then keep it at a small amount.
Students socialized during the transition, delaying the start of the next activity.	Teachers allowed no more time than was necessary between activities (for example, to close books, gather up materials, select new materials).
Students completed assignments before the scheduled time for an activity to end.	Teachers made assignments in terms of the time that was to be filled, not exercises to be completed, and assigned more than enough exercises to fill the allotted time.
Students continued to work on the preceding activity after a change.	Teachers gave time warnings (for example, at five minutes and at two minutes) before the end of any activity, and used verbal markers such as "Shortly we will end this work" and "Let's finish this up so that we can begin . . ." They also created definite beginning and end points for each activity, such as "Okay, that's the end of this activity. Now we will start . . ." or "Put your papers away and turn to . . ."
Some students lagged behind others in completing the previous activity.	Teachers didn't wait for stragglers. They began new activities on time. When a natural break occurred, they spoke privately with students still working on previous tasks to tell them that they must stop and change. They also noted the reason some students did not finish (material too hard, lack of motivation, off-task behavior).

on, is a convenient and reusable way of communicating past assignments on a monthly basis.

What did you think of Mrs. Libby's handling of administrative and clerical tasks? We noted at least two instances in which class time was lost. The first was Mrs. Libby's unpreparedness in presenting an illustration of the male and female reproductive cells, which was relevant to the content being presented but appeared to be more of an afterthought than a planned visual aid. This led to a time-wasting game to see who could find the picture in the text. As some students searched for the illustration, others became distracted and off task. Realizing the momentum of the class had been broken, these students seized the opportunity to disengage themselves from the instruction. Valuable instructional time was lost searching for an illustration that should have been ready in advance. Other examples of inefficient administrative or clerical procedures, although not seen in Mrs. Libby's classroom, include stopping class to collate and staple handouts before passing them out, getting needed materials out of a file cabinet or drawer while the class is left waiting, and dispensing materials and supplies that could be placed at students' desks in advance.

The second event that consumed class time was the P.A. announcement. Although such distractions are annoying, especially when the teacher is trying to maintain momentum, they can seldom be avoided. Plans can be made, however, to minimize their potentially harmful effects. Visitors at the door, disturbances outside the classroom, and announcements over the P.A. all can have disorienting effects on even the most well-planned lessons if classroom rules or procedures have not been formulated and communicated in advance. Rules or procedures may simply remind students that talking and moving about are not permitted during these times. Mrs. Libby may have promoted some of the talking and disorder by retreating to her desk and shifting to a more leisurely style during the announcement, unintentionally communicating a less businesslike attitude. Continuing to circulate around the classroom and indicating a readiness to return to the instructional routine at the last word of the announcement might have communicated that this was only a momentary pause, not the end of the day's work or a transition to a new activity.

Observing Administrative and Clerical Tasks

To get a closer look at this task-oriented behavior, you can record the percentage of time the teacher is on task, or pursuing activities relevant to the objectives identified in the lesson plan. The teacher's task-oriented activities may include a formal presentation of content, review, questions and answers, group discussion, collaborative activities, recitation, guided practice, seatwork, or any other activities reflecting the content of the lesson. A somewhat simpler approach is to record the number of minutes during a class period devoted to interruptions from (a) administrative and procedural duties, (b) transitions, and (c) student conduct. A timepiece with an easy-to-read minute hand can be used to record the approximate number of minutes spent on various off-task activities in these three areas. A format for recording, with some example entries, is provided in Figure 9.6.

The minutes of off-task behavior are added, divided by the total number of minutes for the lesson, and multiplied by 100 to arrive at the percentage of the class period devoted to noninstructional events. Rounding to the minute on a digital display (or to the minute closest to the secondhand) will be sufficient for this record. For the example 50-minute observation period shown in Figure 9.6, 48 percent of the class was devoted to noninstructional events

$(6 + 5 + 1 + 4 + 2 + 1 + 3 + 2 = 24$ minutes; $24/50 = .48 (100) = 48\%$). This may appear to be a large amount of off-task behavior, but in fact it is not. Notice that the definition of off-task behavior includes activities that may be necessary for instruction to proceed smoothly, but are not a direct part of it. Returning papers so students can learn from their mistakes, reprimanding a student so the student then pays attention during the remainder of the class, and talking to a counselor about the special learning needs of a student all are vital, though indirect, instructional events. Some of these indirect events are unavoidable and necessary. The effective teacher cannot eliminate these events entirely, but can minimize the time allocated to them. The percentage of time for each type of noninstructional activity can be determined in a similar manner. For our example, this teacher appears to be efficient at handling misbehavior and transitions, but somewhat less efficient at handling some administrative chores, particularly taking roll and collecting homework, to which 11 minutes, or 22 percent of the class time, was devoted. Instrument 9.1 can be used to record the results of your own observations.

FIGURE 9.6 Record for the Approximate Number of Minutes Spent on Noninstructional Activities

Time		Noninstructional Activities		
		Administrative/Procedural	**Transitions**	**Student Conduct**
9:05	Minutes			
:05-:11	6	Takes roll		
:12-:16	5	Collects homework		
:24-:24[a]	1			Reprimands a student
:35-:39	4		Transition to workbooks	
:40-:42	2	Counselor at door		
:43-:44	1			Puts student's name on board
:49-:52	3	Passes back papers		
:53-:55	2		Class waits for bell to ring	
9:55	end			
Totals	24	16 minutes	6 minutes	2 minutes

[a]Counts as one minute.

You may also average off-task teacher behavior over several class periods and compare percentages across classes and classrooms. In making these comparisons, you can specifically choose classes and teachers that might exhibit differences in the degree of off-task teaching behavior; for example, regular vs. advanced, first period morning vs. first period after lunch, or Mondays vs. Fridays. These comparisons can be made either within different periods taught by the same teacher or among different teachers.

Preventing and Correcting Misbehavior

The third behavior for maintaining task orientation involves preventing and/or stopping misbehavior with a minimum of class disruption. Although typically a classroom-management concern, this behavior also has much to do with the task orientation of the teacher. Intrusions into teaching time due to misbehavior can be devastating to lesson objectives. Not only are large amounts of instructional time lost in administering warnings, handing out punishments, and otherwise maintaining control of a classroom, but such activities can also drain the teacher so that, when the disruption is over, he lacks the stamina and enthusiasm to pick up where he left off. Misconduct can be expected in every classroom, but how it is handled often makes the difference between a classroom that is task oriented and one that is not. In the classroom studies of Emmer et al. (1997) and Evertson (1997), effective classroom managers deemphasized the significance of misbehavior at the time it occurred and dealt with it at a later, noninstructional time chosen by the teacher. Several classroom procedures helped make this possible.

First, academic and work rules, both posted and delivered orally, set a tone of classroom organization that deterred many incidents of misbehavior. Besides establishing rules, however, effective teachers tended to defuse the misbehavior and absorb it into the normal flow of activities by quickly dealing with the misbehavior and moving back into the main flow of instruction. When procedures concerning misbehavior were established and communicated to students beforehand, the teacher was able to return to a task orientation almost immediately by identifying the misbehaving student and the rule pertaining to the misconduct. Effective task orientation therefore requires establishing an efficient system of rules for dealing with misbehavior so that only the rule must be cited at the time of the misbehavior; lengthier deliberations about consequences or related circumstances, if required, can be deferred to a time when the teacher's attention is undivided. The time and the arena for discussing the misbehavior can then be of the teacher's choosing.

As noted in Chapter 6, establishing rules and procedures in anticipation of misbehavior is one of the most important classroom-management activities a teacher can perform. These rules and procedures reflect a commitment to providing an ounce of prevention rather than a pound of cure. Although many rules and procedures are necessary to manage a classroom effectively, they can be divided into two general categories: academic work and classroom conduct. Classroom-management rules for these two areas are shown in Figure 9.7. For the elementary grades, most of these rules should be presented orally, provided in the form of a handout, and posted for later reference by the students. In these grades, students forget oral messages quickly or choose to ignore them if there is no physical representation of the rules to serve as a constant reminder. In the later elementary grades and in junior high, the teacher can recite the rules while students copy them into their notebooks; for high school students, simply hearing the rules may be sufficient, as long as they are posted for later reference. Notice also that the rules in each of these categories need not be communicated to the students at the same time or in the same way. Some rules are best held until the right opportunity to reinforce the rule presents itself (for example, when a visitor comes to the door); others should be communicated the first day of class (how to respond or speak out) or shortly thereafter (when to complete makeup work). The rule areas listed in Figure 9.7 provide examples of the types of rules that are normally needed the first day of class, shortly thereafter, or during the first week of class. Keep in mind that rules communicated orally should also be communicated in at least one other form, such as in a handout, on the bulletin board, or on an overhead projector.

Consistency is one of the most important reasons why some rules are effective and others are not. If a rule is not applied consistently, a loss of respect for the person who has created the rule is sure to follow. There are many reasons why a particular rule is not applied consistently. Emmer et al. (1997) suggest that among the most frequent reasons are

- ❏ The rule is not workable or appropriate. It does not fit a particular context or is not reasonable, given the nature of the individuals to whom it applies.
- ❏ The teacher fails to monitor students closely enough, so that some individuals violating the rule are noticed, but others are not.
- ❏ The teacher does not feel strongly enough about the rule to be persistent about its implementation, and thus makes exceptions to the rule.

FIGURE 9.7 Classroom Rules for Conduct and Work

	Rules for Classroom Conduct	Rules for Academic Work
Rules Normally Communicated the First Day	❏ Where to sit ❏ How seats are assigned ❏ What to do before the bell rings ❏ Responding, speaking out ❏ Leaving at the bell ❏ Drinks, food, and gum ❏ Washroom and drinking privileges	❏ Materials required for class ❏ Homework completion ❏ Makeup work ❏ Incomplete work ❏ Missed quizzes and examinations ❏ Determining grades ❏ Violation of rules
Rules Normally Communicated the First Week	❏ Tardiness/absences ❏ Coming up to teacher's desk ❏ When a visitor comes to the door ❏ Leaving the classroom ❏ Consequences of rule violation	❏ Notebook completion ❏ Obtaining help ❏ Note taking ❏ Sharing your work with others ❏ Use of learning center and/or reference works ❏ Communication during group work ❏ Neatness ❏ Lab safety

Keep in mind that no one likes rules, and almost all students would prefer not having any, but that does not mean a rule is not working or not necessary. A rule should be modified, however, when it no longer achieves its original purpose or is inappropriate for a particular group of students or classroom situation. The inability to enforce the rule over a reasonable period of time is the best sign that a change is needed. Repeated misbehaviors of a similar nature also indicate the need to revise a rule or to create a new one.

What did you notice about Mrs. Libby's handling of misbehaviors? We wondered about the long discourse by Mrs. Libby after Kyoko walked in late, which used valuable class time. Since her students often come in late, Mrs. Libby should have foreseen the need for a rule. Rules indicating acceptable behaviors and the consequences if they are not followed prevent many forms of misbehavior. Simply informing Kyoko that he was late is all that may have been required. Unfortunately, Mrs. Libby engaged Kyoko in an interrogation, and then preached about the significance of his tardiness. Such extended comments provide an opportunity for misconduct to pop up elsewhere in the classroom. The teacher's exclusive focus on a single individual diminishes her vigilance toward other parts of the classroom: While Mrs. Libby was focusing on Kyoko, other students talked and moved about until the teacher finally had to clap her hands to regain the attention of the class. This might have been avoided with a shorter, more direct, preplanned response.

Observing the Prevention and Correction of Misbehavior

Since new teachers often cite classroom management as their biggest challenge, you'll want to observe how teachers minimize disruptions from misbehavior. As noted previously, some off-task behavior (for example, passing back papers) is unavoidable because it indirectly serves the teaching task. The greatest portion of off-task behavior that can be controlled or minimized by the teacher, however, is the time spent responding to misbehavior and getting the class back on task afterward. This is why the discussion of low-profile classroom control in Chapter 6 was so important. The effective teacher responds to misbehavior in the manner that is least disruptive to the momentum or flow of classroom activity. One of the simplest ways to minimize disruption is to have a system of classroom rules that makes clear (a) what behaviors are unacceptable, diminishing the likelihood that misconduct will occur in these areas, and (b) the consequences for the various types of misbehavior that are likely to occur, so that these consequences do not have to be communicated during instructional time. One of the greatest benefits of a system of carefully thought-out rules is the reduction in class time devoted to classroom conduct.

To determine whether or not a system of rules has been communicated, compile a list of rules pertaining to academic work and conduct appearing on bulletin boards or in handouts. Since rules are not always displayed openly, you may have to request a list of rules from the teacher. Record the rules in the form they have been given to students, and indicate the manner in which they have been communicated. Use the format shown in Instrument 9.2. Check the appropriate boxes to record how each rule has been communicated to students. Generally, and especially for younger students, the most important rules should be displayed, provided in a handout, or transcribed by students into their notebooks as well as given orally.

Another method for determining the effectiveness of a system of rules is to note the number of interruptions caused by misbehavior; for example, time spent warning, reprimanding, explaining the rule, making a new rule, or assigning punishment. Time to the nearest second will be the most accurate indicator, because many interruptions for misbehavior take less than a minute of class time. Again, a timepiece with an easy-to-read second display that can be started and stopped will be helpful for recording this behavior. Figure 9.8 illustrates the recording format. Instrument 9.3 can be used to record the results of your own observations.

As soon as a misbehavior that requires a stop in the normal classroom routine occurs, the timepiece is started and kept running until the classroom is back to normal. The total number of minutes and seconds for this interval is placed in the last column of Figure 9.8. The misbehavior is described briefly, and the type of response is recorded by placing a checkmark in any one or a combination of boxes. The amount of time is then tallied for all misbehaviors, converted to minutes, and divided by the total number of minutes of class observed to determine the percentage of time devoted to classroom conduct during the period of observation.

How the checkmarks are distributed across the record indicates the way the teacher prefers to deal with misbehavior at different levels of severity. After approximately ten or more responses to misconduct have been recorded, the observer should group off-task student behaviors by the teacher response most frequently used. The goal is to produce a list of student behaviors requiring a nonverbal warning, a verbal warning, rule reminders, and so on. If accumulated over a variety of different classrooms, these lists can provide a general guide to what types of responses are likely to be most appropriate to student behavior in your own classroom.

Selecting the Most Appropriate Strategy for the Objectives Taught

The fourth behavior for maintaining task orientation involves using instructional time efficiently. Inefficient instructional strategies can be waste as much instructional time as administrative chores and misbehavior. Unless considerable thought is explicitly given to the match between a teacher's objectives and the instructional activities used to

FIGURE 9.8 Recording Format for Observing Time Spent on Dealing With Misbehavior

Misbehavior	Gives Look or Gestures	Verbally Warns, Scolds	Reminds/Recites Rule	Establishes New Rule	Assigns Punishment	Other	Time
1. Jumps out of seat	☑	☑	☐	☑	☐	☐	1:20
2. Talks out	☐	☐	☑	☐	☑	☐	0:10
3. Throws object	☐	☐	☐	☐	☑	☐	0:30
4. _____	☐	☐	☐	☐	☐	☐	____
5. _____	☐	☐	☐	☐	☐	☐	____
						Total	____

Teacher Response

achieve those objectives, it is easy to be misled into thinking that the desired outcomes are being achieved.

For example, it is possible to observe in some classrooms a lesson that attempts to teach *concepts* in the context of a drill-and-practice exercise and *facts* in the context of an inquiry or problem-solving discussion. Although both outcomes might eventually be achieved in either context, the teaching of concepts by rehearsing facts (memorizing parts of the body to learn about living systems, memorizing the names of the branches of government to understand what it means to live in a democracy, or memorizing a poem to learn to appreciate poetry) would be inefficient. The teaching of facts rarely allows for the generalizations and discriminations required for concepts to be acquired, and the teaching of concepts often fails to emphasize the mental processes required for the acquisition of facts. Therefore, matching the type of learning outcome to be achieved with the instructional strategy that most efficiently accomplishes that outcome is important for establishing task orientation.

The teaching of facts, rules, and action sequences will be most efficiently achieved through a process known as the *direct-instruction model*. Direct instruction (also called *expository* or *didactic teaching*) is a strategy in which the teacher is the major provider of information. In the direct instruction model, the teacher's role is to pass on facts, rules, or action sequences to students in the most direct way possible; this usually takes the form of explanations, examples, and opportunities for practice and feedback that recur in cycles.

Under the direct-instruction model, the behavior required of the learner is limited to (a) learning units of the stimulus material (such as facts, rules, or examples) in some meaningful way so that they can be remembered, and (b) arranging parts of the stimulus material into a whole so that a rapid and automatic response can occur. Learning at the lower levels of the cognitive domain (knowledge, comprehension, application) relies heavily on these two processes. Both can be put into action efficiently with stimulus material that closely resembles the desired response (for example, "Read this word and then say it." "Watch me form a possessive and then do the next one." "Follow the instructions, and then focus the microscope."). The desired response does not need to go much beyond what is provided. The learner's task is to produce a response that resembles, as closely as possible, the form and content of the stimulus provided. A great deal of instruction involves behaviors at the lower levels of complexity, which require learning units of content and arranging the units into a whole so that a rapid and

automatic response can occur. Thus, the direct-instruction model tends to be most efficient when the behavioral outcomes are at the knowledge, comprehension, and application levels.

But not all learning is limited to the lower levels of behavioral complexity. In fact, if all (or even most) lessons used only direct instruction, students would be unlikely to function successfully in subsequent grades or in the world outside the classroom. Most of the jobs, responsibilities, and roles performed outside of school—analysis, synthesis, and decision-making behaviors—require more behavioral complexity. These behaviors are not learned the same way as behaviors at lower levels of complexity. (In Chapter 12, we will study how to observe these higher thought processes, and how to achieve them in your classroom.) Let's look at a model of instruction that can be used to efficiently promote these higher forms of behavior.

When sets of stimuli are presented and learners are asked to go beyond the stimuli to form concepts and relationships, the *indirect model of instruction* is being employed. The learner acquires a behavior indirectly by transforming stimulus material (for example, facts) into a response or behavior that differs from both (a) the stimulus used to present the learning and (b) any previous response given by the student. Because the stimulus material can be added to and rearranged by the learner during this process to make it more meaningful, the elicited response or behavior can take many different forms. Therefore, in contrast to direct instruction, there is seldom a single best answer in the indirect model of instruction. Instead, the learner is guided to an answer that goes beyond the problem or stimulus presented.

Indirect instruction is inefficient and even ineffective for teaching many types of facts, rules, or action sequences for which the desired response is almost identical to the learning stimulus presented. Rules for punctuation and capitalization, for example, are most efficiently taught by giving students the rules and asking them to practice applying them. Here, knowledge acquisition and application are taught with a direct-instruction strategy because the stimulus material (written rules and examples) already contains the correct answers in the form most desired. The purpose of the lesson is to apply the rules—not to discover them or to invent new ones.

Generally, task orientation will be most efficiently maintained when the teaching functions associated with direct instruction are applied in the context of knowledge, comprehension, and application objectives, and the teaching functions associated with indirect instruction are applied in the context of analysis, synthesis, and evaluation objectives.

Although these models and the associated functions are seldom implemented in any pure form and may be used interchangeably within a lesson, the degree to which they are effective depends on whether the intended outcomes are primarily lower or higher order. Figure 9.9 summarizes some of the teaching functions associated with the direct and indirect models of instruction. Figure 9.10 provides example activities and expected outcomes for each teaching function listed in Figure 9.9.

FIGURE 9.9 Direct and Indirect Teaching Functions

Direct-Instruction Functions[a]	**Indirect-Instruction Functions**[b]

1. Reviews, checks previous day's work, and reteaches, if necessary:
    Checks homework.
    Reteaches areas where there were student errors.
	1. Provides a means of organizing content in advance.
	    Provides advance organizers and conceptual frameworks, which serve as "pegs" on which to hang key points that guide and channel thinking to the most productive areas.

2. Presents and structures new content:
    Provides overview.
    Proceeds in small steps (if necessary), but at a rapid pace.
    New skills are phased in; old skills are measured.
	2. Provides conceptual development of content using inductive and deductive methods.
	    Focuses generalization to high level of abstraction by
	        Inductive methods (selected events are used to establish concepts or patterns).
	        Deductive methods (principles or generalization are applied to specific instances).

3. Provides for guided student practice:
    High frequency of convergent questions and overt student practice (from teacher and materials).
    Prompts are provided during initial learning (when appropriate).
    All students have a chance to respond and receive feedback.
    Teacher checks for understanding by evaluating student responses.
    Continue practice until responses are firm.
    Success rate of 80 percent or higher during initial learning.
	3. Uses examples and nonexamples:
	    To define criterial attributes and promote accurate generalizations.
	    To gradually expand set of examples to reflect the real world.
	    To enrich concept with understanding of noncriterial attributes.

4. Gives immediate feedback and correctives (and reteaching, if necessary):
    Feedback to students, particularly when they are correct but hesitant.
    Student errors provide feedback to the teacher that corrections and/or reteaching is necessary.
    Corrections by simplifying question, giving clues, explaining or reviewing steps, or reteaching last steps.
    When necessary, reteach using smaller steps.
	4. Uses higher-order questions to guide the search-and-discovery process.
	    Uses questions to:
	        Raise contradictions.
	        Probe for deeper level responses.
	        Extend the discussion.
	        Pass responsibility to the class.

5. Assigns independent practice so that student responses are firm and automatic:
    Seatwork.
    Practice to overlearning.
    Need for procedure to ensure student encouragement during seatwork (i.e., teacher or aide monitoring).
    95 percent correct or higher.
	5. Encourages students to use examples and references from their own experience to seek clarification, and to draw parallels and associations that aid understanding and retention.
	    Relates ideas to past learning and to students' own sphere of interests, concerns, and problems.

6. Schedules weekly and monthly reviews (reteaching, if necessary).	6. Allows students to evaluate the appropriateness of their own responses, and provides guidance when necessary. Provides cues, questions, or hints as needed to call attention to inappropriate responses.
	7. Uses discussion to encourage critical thinking and help students to examine alternatives, judge solutions, make predictions, and discover generalizations.

[a]Entries in this column are based on Rosenshine (1983)
[b]Entries in this column are based on Borich (1996)

FIGURE 9.10   Example Activities and Expected Outcomes for the Direct and Indirect Models of Instruction

Direct-Teaching Functions	Example Activities for Students	Expected Outcomes	Indirect-Teaching Functions	Example Activities for Students	Expected Outcomes
Reviews, Checks	Recites answers from workbook or homework	Recall, recognition	Provides conceptual framework	Reproduces mental or graphic representation of framework	Comprehension, synthesis
Presents new content	Listens, takes notes	Comprehension	Develops content inductively and deductively	Asks questions that draw relationships to past knowledge	Analysis
Presents guided practice	Responds orally or in workbook	Application	Gives examples and nonexamples	Makes proper distinctions on handout or in workbook	Analysis, synthesis
Gives feedback	Corrects verbal or written response	Application, analysis	Asks higher-order questions	Responds orally or in writing to problem situation	Evaluation
Assigns independent practice	Completes homework or extended seatwork	Application	Encourages student ideas	Discusses own experience with class	Application, analysis
Reviews, reteaches	Asks questions, takes notes, and listens	Recall, recognition, comprehension	Allows for self-evaluation	Examines correctness of own and other's response	Analysis, synthesis
			Guides discussion to promote critical thinking	Extends prior content to new ground	Evaluation

Let's consider Mrs. Libby's use of instructional strategies. As you know, inefficient instructional strategies can be as damaging to a student's opportunity to learn as the presentation of irrelevant or poorly timed instructional content. Recall that our discussion of instructional strategies encompassed the direct and indirect models of instruction. The former included six teaching functions that are generally believed to be most efficient for teaching objectives at the knowledge, comprehension, and application levels of behavioral complexity; the latter included seven teaching functions that are generally believed to be most efficient for teaching objectives at the analysis, synthesis, and evaluation levels of behavioral complexity. Although seldom implemented in a pure form (and sometimes used interchangeably within a lesson), these models are guides for attaining a desired level of outcome most efficiently.

Review Figures 9.9 and 9.10 to find out which model Mrs. Libby's lesson reflected. If you think it was the indirect model, you are right. But she also used the direct model. This brief dialogue, in a fashion typical of most classrooms, represented both models. In fact, Mrs. Libby seemed to alternate between models, perhaps indicating she did not make a conscious attempt to use either model or to combine them in any meaningful fashion. Instead, the lesson format seemed to be pulled first in one direction and then in another. Let's return to the beginning of the dialogue to examine Mrs. Libby's behavior on this dimension.

After the commotion with Kyoko has ended, Mrs. Libby begins to review and check for task-relevant prior knowledge. She asks, "Who remembers from our previous discussion some of the ways in which lower forms of animal life reproduce?" Sudia answers correctly, and his answer is rephrased by the teacher—providing a review of previous content for those who may have missed it. After her digression about microscopes, Mrs. Libby returns to the content of the lesson and asks, "Can anyone think of any other means of reproduction?" Shelena responds first, but with too broad an answer about higher forms of animal life, which is a topic to be presented later. So the teacher refocuses with the comment, "We're just talking about lower forms of animal life." Bill then responds by asking, "Isn't there a way that new life can be created by parts of other things coming together?" The teacher uses Bill's response to expand the discussion by introducing the word *conjugation*.

To determine which model of instruction these exchanges represent, we must ask what level of outcome the teacher wants to attain with this series of questions. Are these questions asked to provide guided practice with outcomes at the knowledge, comprehension, or application level (direct-instruction model), or are the questions asked to promote a search-and-discovery process with outcomes at the analysis, synthesis, or evaluation levels (indirect-instruction model)? If students are combining pieces of previously learned information (analysis) that has not been combined previously in any meaningful way (synthesis), then higher-order outcomes are being sought and the teacher would be well advised to employ the indirect model (advance organizers, induction and deduction, examples and nonexamples, student ideas). If the students recall knowledge from an earlier lesson and parrot it in a slightly different form (comprehension), or apply it in a new context (application), then lower order outcomes are being sought, and the teacher would be well advised to employ the direct-instruction model (more correctives and feedback, guided practice, and independent seatwork). Either of these approaches might have been Mrs. Libby's goal, but until one or the other is strengthened by the addition of appropriate teaching functions, neither will lead to the desired behavioral outcomes. Mrs. Libby's lesson, at least the part we saw, seemed to lack follow-through, as well as a sequence of teaching functions that converged on a common goal. It is difficult to tell what level of behavioral complexity she was asking of her students. Task orientation involves knowing where you are heading, and then implementing the most efficient mix of teaching functions to get you there.

Observing the Most Appropriate Strategy for the Objectives Taught

We have observed some of the behaviors that can reduce the time a teacher devotes to instruction and reduce student opportunity to learn. But a teacher's task orientation also involves efficiently using the instructional time that *is* available. This means that there must be correspondence between intended behavioral outcomes and the teaching strategies used to achieve them.

Generally, objectives at the knowledge, comprehension, and application levels are most efficiently taught with direct instruction; objectives at the analysis, synthesis, and evaluation levels are most efficiently taught with indirect instruction. The learning of certain facts, rules, and action sequences must often precede the learning of concepts, patterns, and abstractions, requiring a sequence of lessons within a unit plan leading from least to most behavioral complexity. Instrument 9.4 illustrates a method of recording the relationship among behavioral outcomes at different levels of complexity and some of the direct and indirect teaching functions that might be used to elicit them.

The behavioral outcomes listed across the top are divided into two types: lower order and higher order. The phrase *lower order* is used to describe knowledge, comprehension, and application outcomes; the phrase *higher order* is used to describe outcomes at the analysis, synthesis, and evaluation levels.

The teaching functions listed on the left side of Instrument 9.4 are divided into direct- and indirect-instruction functions. Recall that in direct instruction the teacher is the primary provider of information, passing on facts, rules, and action sequences to the learner in the most direct way possible so that information can be recalled rapidly and automatically. In indirect instruction the students are active providers of content and acquire, through search and discovery, concepts and abstractions that differ from the stimulus used to present the learning and any previous responses given by the student.

For the recording form in Instrument 9.4, a checkmark is placed in the appropriate box *each time there is a change* in function or behavioral outcome. Multiple checkmarks may appear across rows for the same strategy (for example, when a guided-practice exercise changes from knowledge to application content) and down columns for the same behavioral outcomes (for example, when application is taught in a lecture format and then in an inquiry-oriented group discussion). The majority of checkmarks may appear in the first three columns; by some estimates, as much as 80 percent of school instruction takes place at these levels. With a sufficient number of observations, however, checkmarks should appear in the upper left quadrant (lower order/direct) and lower right quadrant (higher order/indirect) because direct-instruction strategies tend to be more efficient for teaching outcomes at the lower level of behavioral complexity, and indirect-instruction strategies tend to be more efficient for teaching outcomes at the higher levels of behavioral complexity. As other direct and indirect teaching functions are observed, they should be added to the record under "Other."

Establishing Cycles of Review, Feedback, and Testing

The final behavior for achieving task orientation involves establishing a schedule of activities built around clearly definable end products (a test, review session, or assignment). These end products represent visible student goals toward which classroom activities build with increasing intensity and expectation. They also serve to create cycles of rising and falling intensity, with the high point of the cycle just before the expected event and the low point, which marks the beginning of a new cycle, immediately afterward. In the upper grades, several different cycles may occur concurrently; for example, some classroom activities prepare students to complete a term paper due next week, and other classroom activities prepare students to take a test at the end of the month. Thus, different cycles may be in place for tests, assignments, and major projects, and these cycles may be staggered so that one is near its highest point when another is near its lowest. This ensures that high levels of intensity, enthusiasm, and expectation pertaining to a clearly defined end product are always present. Figure 9.11 illustrates several concurrent cycles: a book report due every month, increasingly comprehensive reviews conducted weekly, and a cycle of exams given every six weeks.

One of the most important activities for establishing cycles of rising and falling action in a classroom is a review. The primary purpose of periodic review is to ensure that all task-relevant information for future lessons has been taught, and to identify areas for which reteaching of key objectives may be necessary. Without periodic review prior to testing, there may be no signal to the teacher that the instruction has been successful, and no signal to the student that further study may be necessary. Thus, periodic review serves to task-orient and reorient both teacher and students.

Periodic review has long been a part of almost every instructional strategy. During direct instruction, for example, periodic review and the recycling of instruction are important because of the brisk pace at which the instruction is conducted. The teacher usually establishes the proper pace by noting the approximate percentage of errors occurring during guided practice and feedback; 60 to 80 percent correct responses usually indicates a satisfactory pace during didactic or expository teaching (Rosenshine & Stevens, 1986). Weekly and monthly reviews provide opportunities to determine if the pace is appropriate and to make necessary adjustments before too much content has been covered. When student responses to questions posed in weekly and monthly review sessions are correct, quick, and firm about 95 percent of the time, the pace is adequate (Bennett et al., 1981). Independent practice and homework should increase the per-

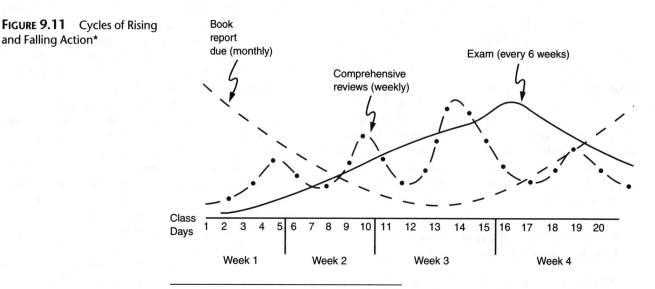

FIGURE 9.11 Cycles of Rising and Falling Action*

*Height of cycles indicates relative amounts of instructional focus and student intensity.

centage of correct responses from between 60 and 80 percent during guided practice and feedback to approximately 95 percent on weekly and monthly reviews. When results are below, and especially when they are substantially below, these levels during didactic or expository teaching, the pace has been too fast. Weekly and monthly review sessions can be used to give some learners a second chance to grasp material that was missed or only partially learned the first time through, and to strengthen correct but hesitant responses of those who may not have thoroughly mastered the material the first time. Review sessions are often welcomed by students as a chance to go over material that will be covered on unit tests.

What did you notice in Mrs. Libby's lesson regarding cycles of review, feedback, and testing? Did her cycles include projects, papers, major assignments, and informal but regularly scheduled question-and-answer sessions? Unfortunately, we know little about these sequences in Mrs. Libby's class, other than that a departmental test is scheduled. Cycles may have helped focus and give greater meaning to the lesson for some students. Other events would also need to be scheduled to keep students working toward a common goal with increasing expectation. Multiple milestones help establish momentum if they are planned so that expectations about one event begin as another event is completed. We must reserve judgment on this dimension, pending a more detailed examination of how Mrs. Libby has scheduled and sequenced cycles over the course of an entire grading period.

Observing Cycles of Review, Feedback, and Testing

We can observe how teachers establish a schedule of activities built around clearly identified end products such as reviews, tests, and major assignments (term papers, book reviews, projects) on a weekly basis using the format shown in Instrument 9.5. A checkmark is used to indicate the end products scheduled for a given day. The absence of checkmarks indicates that a schedule of end products may not have been determined, or that some end products are emphasized to the exclusion of others. It is important, however, that the end products checked on this record represent those that have been communicated to students ahead of time or that are part of the normal instructional routine (test every Friday; major review every other Thursday). Several students can indicate end products for which they see themselves responsible, and their responses can be checked for agreement. This can be one indica-

tion of how clearly the end products have been communicated to the class.

The number of checkmarks across the columns for limited (daily and weekly) and cumulative (monthly) reviews and tests will indicate the degree to which students are working toward end products that they see as meaningful intermediate steps toward achieving long-term outcomes. For example, the absence of any cumulative reviews as end products may indicate a lack of task orientation over the long term, even though task orientation in the short term may be indicated by limited reviews that focus on content taught the same day or week. Such a profile may mean that students see limited reviews and tests as isolated events that have no larger purpose; hence, they may feel no need to discover relationships that bridge areas of content, or to accumulate learning from one topic to the next. Each of these outcomes will impair the task orientation of both students and teacher.

We have summarized our observations about Mrs. Libby's lesson in Figure 9.12. Notice that three of the five dimensions for achieving task orientation were not observed, and that instructional time was lost to administrative interruptions, misconduct, and a poorly defined instructional strategy. Recall, however, the hard-to-handle nature of this class and the sensitive nature of the subject matter, which, together, would make this a particularly challenging lesson for experienced and inexperienced teachers alike.

Cultural Diversity and Task Orientation

Throughout much of the history of education in America, the traditional classroom could be characterized as teacher-centered and text- and workbook-dominated. Today, the teacher's role in the classroom has widened considerably, and texts and workbooks have evolved to provide a variety of orientations to the teaching task, including materials and activities for cooperative learning, peer tutoring, self-regulation, programmed learning, and interactive instruction. Stimulating this evolution has been recent research on the effects of individual differences, and cultural and ethnic expectations, on learning. Some of this research has focused on the cognitive styles of learners (Castaneda & Gray, 1974), the structure of the learning task (Doyle, 1983; Hunt, 1979), and variations in teaching styles (Hill, 1989; Hilliard, 1976).

Studies by Castaneda and Gray (1974) found that learners could be distinguished on the basis of the cognitive processes they use to learn and whether

FIGURE 9.12   Checklist for Mrs. Libby's Classroom

Behavior	Observed	Not Observed	No Opportunity to Observe
1. Develops unit and lesson plans in accordance with text and curriculum guides	✓ Lesson topic covered in text		
2. Handles administrative and clerical interruptions efficiently		✓ Lost task orientation while searching for picture in text	
3. Stops or prevents misbehavior with a minimum of disruption to the class		✓ Focused attention at length on single misbehaving student	
4. Selects the most appropriate instructional strategy for the objectives taught		✓ Instructional strategies did not converge on single approach or clearly defined outcome	
5. Builds toward unit outcomes with clearly defined events (weekly and monthly reviews, feedback, and testing)			✓ Difficult to tell; only one test was mentioned

they are presented a task *in a way that allows them the opportunity to use their preferred cognitive style.* Two of the cognitive styles they studied were field independence and field dependence (Figure 9.13).

Research by Ramirez and Castaneda (1974) suggests that certain cognitive styles tend to predominate among certain cultures; for example, bilingual learners tend to be both field independent and field dependent.

The implications of field independence and dependence have been related to students' need for structure by Hunt (1979), who identified some of the characteristics of students who need more or less structure to maximize their opportunity to learn. Some of Hunt's characteristics, which have implications for how and in what medium content is presented, are listed below.

Those needing more structure

❑ Have shorter attention spans and like to move through material rapidly

❑ Are reluctant to try something new and don't like to appear wrong
❑ Tend not to ask questions
❑ May need reassurance before starting a task
❑ Want to know facts before concepts
❑ Usually give only brief answers

Those needing less structure

❑ Like to discuss and argue
❑ Want to solve problems with a minimum of teacher assistance
❑ Dislike details or step-by-step formats
❑ Are comfortable with abstractions and generalities
❑ Emphasize emotions and are open about themselves
❑ Tend to make many interpretations and inferences

Hunt (1979) goes on to suggest specific ways teachers can orient themselves to the teaching task

FIGURE 9.13 Field-Independent Learners and Field-Dependent Learners

The Field-Independent Learner	The Field-Dependent Learner
1. Perceives content as discrete parts; easily sees details	1. Perceives content globally; easily sees the whole
2. Is attracted to abstract and analytical problem solving; likes to think in terms of cause and effect	2. Avoids analytical problem solving in favor of a more holistic approach; likes to think in terms of associations, relationships, and codependent actions
3. Is self-reliant and prefers individualistic, rather than cooperative, strategies of inquiry	3. Is sensitive and attuned to the social environment; prefers cooperative over competitive strategies of inquiry
4. Favors inquiry and independence; provides own structure for learning	4. Favors discovery and a participant approach to learning; likes to observe, reflect, and react to others
5. Is intrinsically motivated and less responsive to social reinforcement	5. Is extrinsically motivated and more responsive to social reinforcement

to promote particular cognitive styles. For example, for students who require more structure, he suggests the teacher

1. Have definite and consistent rules
2. Provide specific, step-by-step guides and instructions
3. Make goals and deadlines short and definite
4. Change pace often
5. Assess problems frequently
6. Move gradually from seatwork to discussion

For students who require less structure, the teacher can

1. Provide topics to choose from
2. Make assignments longer, with self-imposed timetables
3. Encourage the use of resources outside the classroom
4. Use group work, with the teacher serving as a resource person
5. Use and encourage interest in the opinions and knowledge of others
6. Provide an opportunity for extended projects and assignments

Although little is known about how these aspects of a teacher's task orientation relate to specific groups of learners, Hill (1989) suggests that some cultural and ethnic groups tend to benefit more and adapt better to a task orientation that is less structured and more field dependent. Researchers provide alternatives to the notion that the most effective task orientation for the teacher is to stand in front of the classroom, lecturing or explaining to students seated in neatly arranged rows, who have

little or no expectations about, or experiences with, the content being taught. Recent findings suggest that not only may some task orientations (for example, cooperative vs. competitive) be more appropriate for some groups than others, but many of today's content objectives (especially multidisciplinary and interdisciplinary objectives) may require frequent variation in task orientation. Watch especially for those teachers who seem to move easily between providing lots of structure to offering students a number of choices. You'll also want to discover which students appear most comfortable and productive—and in which settings. These insights will be important to you as you make instructional decisions in your own classroom.

In the following chapters, we will turn our attention to other lenses through which to observe classrooms. These lenses—student engagement in the learning process, student success, and higher thought processes—are always observed in the context of task orientation, as well as in the context of the other lenses discussed in previous chapters.

ACTIVITIES*

1. Using the checklist in Figure 9.2 as your guide, observe a lesson, looking for signs of task orientation. At the end of your observation, add a brief written description to each box, highlighting at least one specific reason why you

---

*Some of the following activities may be grouped into a common activity, divided among classmates, and completed from a single observation.

chose to place each checkmark where you did. Using your written descriptions, write a paragraph describing some of the examples of task orientation (or lack thereof).

2. Using the examples of five-point scales shown in Chapter 4, convert the positively stated indicators of task orientation listed in Figure 9.1 into the form of a Likert scale. Consider the vertical or horizontal placement of each indicator on the page, whether words will be affixed to all or only some of the response blanks, and what value will be assigned to each response. Show your scale to a classmate who has also constructed a five-point scale. Together, create a single, revised version incorporating the best features of both scales.

3. Using the seven-point polar scale described in Chapter 4 as an example, convert the positive and negative indicators in Figure 9.1 into this scale format and observe a lesson for signs of task orientation. At the end of your observation, complete the scale by indicating with a checkmark the degree to which this lesson achieved each dimension of task orientation. Use the code N/O for any items that you did not have the opportunity to observe. Reflecting on your experience as a student and previous classroom observations, return to the scale and place an *X* on the blank corresponding to each scale item that, in your opinion, represents the degree of task orientation found in most classrooms. Note the difference between your ratings for this lesson and the average task orientation in most classrooms. Cite the reasons why this lesson was the same, higher, or lower on each dimension.

4. Ask the teacher of a lesson you wish to observe for her objective(s). Then ask for a copy of the text and student workbook (if applicable) for this class, and obtain a copy of the state or district curriculum guide if available. Using Figure 9.4, determine whether the lesson plan reflects the curriculum. If it does not, or does so only partially (some objectives correspond with content in the text and curriculum guide, but others do not), suggest reasons why. In your opinion, does the lesson content represent instructional goals that can be justified in another way (for example, local priorities or critical learning needs)?

5. Using the form provided in Instrument 9.1, observe a classroom for a complete lesson or class period. Record all noninstructional activities (administrative procedures, transitions, and student conduct) and the approximate number of minutes devoted to each. Total the number

of minutes for each area and find the percentage of time each area contributes to the total amount of noninstructional time. Which area consumed the most time? The least? If you were to advise this teacher on how to improve task orientation, what noninstructional activity would you bring to his attention? What suggestions would you provide for reducing the time devoted to this activity?

6. Select one pair of observations to complete from the following list:

Less able/more able class
Early A.M./after lunch class
Discussion/lecture class
Social studies/math class

For the pair you have chosen, use Instrument 9.1 to determine the percentage of noninstructional time devoted to administrative procedures, transitions, and student conduct. Compare the percentages in your two classes in each of these three areas. Describe and explain any large differences. Comment on how representative you feel the activity in each classroom is in relation to what normally might occur at these times during the school year.

7. Arrange a brief interview with a teacher whose classroom you would like to observe. Using Instrument 9.2, ask the teacher to identify the rules communicated to students with regard to academic work and student conduct. Enter these rules on the record, indicating the manner in which the teacher communicated them to students (on display, in a handout, orally). Be sure to note any unique or unusual means of communicating or creating rules (student handbook, group consensus). Ask the teacher which rules would be required the first day of class, the second through fifth days of class, and later. If this were your classroom, what rules would you have chosen for the first day of class, the second through fifth days, and still later?

8. If possible, observe a class that might be expected to exhibit misbehavior frequently. Your own intuition, knowledge of the school, and teachers' conversations with teachers can lead you to such a class. Using a timepiece with a second hand that can be started and stopped, complete Instrument 9.3. Place a checkmark after each misbehavior, indicating whether the teacher responded to it with a warning, a reminder, a new rule, punishment, or another response. Keep track of the approximate number of minutes and seconds of class time devoted to the misbehavior. Continue observing for the full lesson, or longer if only a small number of

entries have been made. Separate the misbehaviors you have listed into two groups: Those for which response time was less than the median value, and those for which response time was more than the median value. What types of teacher response characterize these two groups of misbehavior? Do you believe the different types of response representing these two divisions are the most effective for returning a class to normal?

9. Use Instrument 9.4 to record the relationship between teaching functions and levels of behavioral complexity over a series of observations. (Several observations may be required to obtain a sufficient number of tallies indicating a pattern between functions and levels of behavioral complexity.) Write down any functions not identified on the record that indicate the teacher pursues the goals of either direct or indirect instruction. At the end of your observations, inspect the tallies in each of the four quadrants: Direct/Lower Order, Direct/Higher Order, Indirect/Lower Order, and Indirect/Higher Order. Count the total number of entries in each of the four quadrants to find a pattern. Are more tallies found in the Direct/Lower Order and Indirect/ Higher Order quadrants, as would be expected, or has some other pattern emerged? If your data reflect the unexpected, explain why you believe the results turned out as they did. If your data reflect the expected, explain why lower order outcomes tend to be associated with direct instruction and higher order outcomes with indirect instruction.

10. Choose a classroom that you have observed often (or with which you are familiar). Using Instrument 9.5 for recording end products, place a checkmark under each end product (review, test, homework, and project) according to the date on which it is to occur or was due. Complete this assignment and activity schedule for one month, about twenty consecutive school days. Include any other scheduled end products that are not listed, and the day they occur. From an inspection of the record, explain in what ways and how often the teacher uses (a) reviews, (b) tests, (c) homework, (d) major assignments, and (e) other end products to create cycles of expectation. How might this teacher improve her task orientation by scheduling other end products or using those listed more frequently?

INSTRUMENT 9.1 Record for the Approximate Number of Minutes Spent on
Noninstructional Activities

Time	Noninstructional Activities		
	Administrative/Procedural	**Transitions**	**Student Conduct**
Minutes			
____ ___	_____	_____	_____
____ ___	_____	_____	_____
____ ___	_____	_____	_____
____ ___	_____	_____	_____
____ ___	_____	_____	_____
____ ___	_____	_____	_____
____ ___	_____	_____	_____
____ ___	_____	_____	_____
Totals	minutes	minutes	minutes

INSTRUMENT **9.2**   Checklist for Observing How Rules Are
Communicated to Students

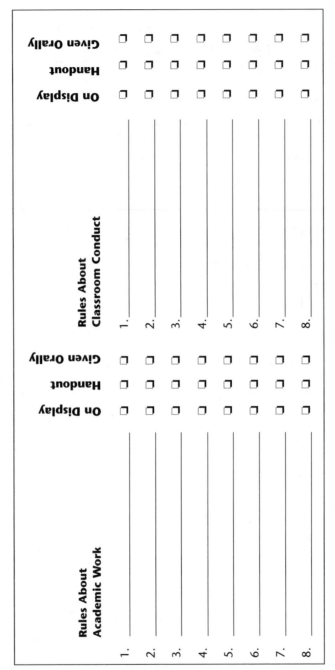

INSTRUMENT 9.3   Recording Format for Observing Time Spent on Dealing With Misbehavior

	Teacher Response						
Misbehavior	**Gives Look or Gestures**	**Verbally Warns, Scolds**	**Reminds/Recites Rule**	**Establishes New Rule**	**Assigns Punishment**	**Other**	**Time**
1. _____	❏	❏	❏	❏	❏	❏	_____
2. _____	❏	❏	❏	❏	❏	❏	_____
3. _____	❏	❏	❏	❏	❏	❏	_____
4. _____	❏	❏	❏	❏	❏	❏	_____
5. _____	❏	❏	❏	❏	❏	❏	_____
6. _____	❏	❏	❏	❏	❏	❏	_____
7. _____	❏	❏	❏	❏	❏	❏	_____
8. _____	❏	❏	❏	❏	❏	❏	_____
9. _____	❏	❏	❏	❏	❏	❏	_____
10. _____	❏	❏	❏	❏	❏	❏	_____
						Total	_____

INSTRUMENT 9.4 Form for Recording the Relationship Between Levels of Behavioral Complexity and Teaching Functions

		Lower Order			Higher Order		
	Teaching Functions	Knowledge	Comprehension	Application	Analysis	Synthesis	Evaluation
Direct Functions	Reviews, checks previous day's work						
	Presents new content, lectures						
	Provides guided practice, drill and practice						
	Asks convergent, closed questions having a single right answer						
	Assigns independent practice, workbook						
	Reviews previously learned content						
	Other						
Indirect Functions	Organizes content in advance and provides advance organizers						
	Uses induction and deduction to arrive at desired outcomes						
	Presents examples and nonexamples to identify critical attributes						
	Asks divergent, open questions having more than a single right answer						
	Provides for group discussion						
	Allows students to respond from their own experience or point of view						
	Other						

INSTRUMENT 9.5   Record for Identifying End Products

Week	Day	Review, Limited	Review, Cumulative	Test, Limited	Test, Cumulative	Major Assignment (Book Review, Paper, Problem Set, Notebook)	Other (Feedback on Test, Question-and-Answer Session)
1	Mon.						
	Tues.						
	Wed.						
	Thurs.						
	Fri.						
2	Mon.						
	Tues.						
	Wed.						
	Thurs.						
	Fri.						
3	Mon.						
	Tues.						
	Wed.						
	Thurs.						
	Fri.						
4	Mon.						
	Tues.						
	Wed.						
	Thurs.						
	Fri.						

EXAMINING
ENGAGEMENT IN THE
LEARNING PROCESS

Halfway Down

Halfway down the stairs
Is a stair
Where I sit.
There isn't any
Other stair
Quite like
It.
I'm not at the bottom,
I'm not at the top;
So this is the stair
Where
I always
Stop.

Halfway up the stairs
Isn't up,
And isn't down.
It isn't in the nursery,
It isn't in the town.
And all sorts of funny thoughts
Run round my head:
"It isn't really
Anywhere!
It's somewhere else
Instead!"

A. A. Milne

As you glance at the students, all eyes are on the work on their desks. Not a sound invades the engrossed silence. "Ah, the students are working," you think to yourself. Or are they? When Roberto is looking at his science book, where is his mind? Is he, like the child in the poem "somewhere else instead"? How do effective teachers engage students in their learning? And how do we know, as observers and teachers, when that engagement is occurring?

Favorite Poems Old and New, selected by Helen Ferris. Garden City, New York: Doubleday and Company, Inc., 1957, p. 10.

In Chapter 9, we saw that one of the ways teacher behavior influences student achievement is through the amount of instructional time devoted to a subject. This relationship can be strengthened by a teacher's task orientation. In this chapter, we will present a related, but different, way of looking at learning time.

Separate from the teacher's task orientation is the time students are engaged in thinking about and learning the presented material (Savage, 1991). This way of measuring learning time is called *student engagement in the learning process*, and represents the amount of time during a lesson that students are thinking about, acting on, or otherwise using the presented content.

Engagement in the learning process is expressed as the percentage of time allocated to instruction that the student is on task or engaged with the instructional materials and activities. For example, if 45 minutes are devoted to content coverage, and most of the students are engaged in the learning process (participating in discussion, completing a workbook assignment, or otherwise looking alert and attentive) for 30 minutes during this time, the engagement rate would be (30/45) 100 = 67 percent. Engagement rates tend to vary considerably from student to student, and are therefore often calculated for individuals in a class; the average rate is taken as an approximate indication of the engagement rate of the entire class.

The key to understanding engagement rate is that, even though a teacher can be task-oriented and provide maximum content coverage, the students may not be engaged all of this time (Hosford, 1984; Fisher et al., 1980). This disengagement can involve an emotional or mental detachment, or both, from the lesson, which may or may not be obvious to an observer. Students who jump out of their seats, talk, read a magazine, or leave for the restroom are obviously not engaged in instruction, no matter how task-oriented the teacher is. Students may also be disengaged in more subtle ways, such as looking attentive while their thoughts are many miles away. Correcting—and even observing—this type of nonengagement is a difficult task. Several studies have contributed useful information for increasing student engagement. From these studies, it was possible for Rosenshine and Stevens (1986) and Copple, Siegel, and Sanders (1984) to assemble the following suggestions for increasing student engagement in the learning process.

❑ Teachers should have a system of rules flexible enough to allow students to attend to their personal and procedural needs (obtaining reference books, handouts, and resources) without having to obtain the teacher's permission.

❑ Teachers should move around the room at regularly scheduled intervals to monitor students' seatwork and to communicate an awareness of student progress.

❑ Teachers should avoid timing errors by using low-profile classroom control to prevent off-task behavior before it spreads to and influences other learners.

❑ When students work independently, teachers should ensure that the assignments are interesting and easy enough to be completed by each student working without teacher direction.

❑ Teachers should minimize activities such as giving directions and organizing the class for instruction by writing the daily schedule on the board. This will ensure that pupils know what activities will be expected and the order in which they will be performed.

❑ Teachers should make abundant use of group work, activity books, self-directed assignments, and projects that are at, or slightly above, a student's current level of understanding.

❑ Teachers should choose classroom activities that are congruent with ethnic and cultural expectations.

In this chapter we will take a closer look at these and other suggestions for engaging students in the learning process.

DIMENSIONS OF STUDENT ENGAGEMENT IN THE LEARNING PROCESS

Figure 10.1 summarizes the behaviors related to student engagement. Effectively engaging students in the learning process involves

1. Eliciting the desired behavior.
2. Providing an opportunity for feedback in a noncritical atmosphere.
3. Using individualized and self-directed learning activities to maintain interest and promote attention during the learning process.
4. Using meaningful verbal praise.
5. Monitoring and checking for progress.

PRACTICE OBSERVING STUDENT ENGAGEMENT IN THE LEARNING PROCESS: A DIALOGUE

Let's use the checklist in Figure 10.2 to observe the following class for evidence of student engagement in the learning process.

FIGURE 10.1 Indicators for Engaging Students in the Learning Process

Engaging Students Effectively in the Learning Process (Effective Teacher)	Engaging Students Ineffectively in the Learning Process (Ineffective Teacher)
1. Elicits the desired behavior after presentation of instructional stimuli (provides exercise or workbook problems with which the desired behavior can be practiced)	Fails to ask learners to attempt the desired behavior
2. Provides opportunities for feedback in a noncritical atmosphere (asks students to respond as a group or subvocally the first time through)	Evaluates initial student responses in ways that could be threatening or embarrassing
3. Uses individual and self-directed activities (performance contracts, programmed texts, games and simulations, learning centers, and reciprocal learning) as instructional strategies	Fails to use alternative instructional methods to accommodate the learning needs of special students (less able or remedial learners)
4. Uses meaningful verbal praise to get and keep students actively participating in the learning process	Fails to provide praise that is timely and meaningful to the student (never says why something is correct)
5. Monitors seatwork and frequently checks progress during independent practice	Does not evenly monitor students progress during seatwork (spends too much time with some students and fails to observe work of others)

FIGURE 10.2 Checklist for Observing Student Engagement in the Learning Process

Behavior	Observed	Not Observed	No Opportunity to Observe
1. Provides for guided practice			
2. Provides feedback to guided practice			
3. Uses individualized or self-directed materials and activities to promote learning, when appropriate			
4. Uses meaningful verbal praise			
5. Monitors seatwork by circulating and frequently checking progress			

For this dialogue, we peek into the beginning of an elementary math lesson. The lesson for today is about ratios and proportions. The teacher, Mr. Swade, has noticed that math interest is not high among most members of his class. His students have been noticeably anxious about an upcoming math test, and some may not have grasped all that they should have from earlier lessons.

Mr. Swade: Today we will study ratios and proportions, but we'll use more real-life problems than in previous lessons. Some of you have had trouble calculating ratios, so let's back up and review our skills in division. Who can tell me why division is so important in computing a ratio? [Marcus raises his hand.]

Marcus: It's because ratios are nothing but division problems.

Mr. Swade: Yes, that's right, in the sense that ratios can be expressed as one number over another, like this [writes *4/8* on board]. Now let's look at some other expressions. I'll write them on the board, and you see if you can identify which ones are expressed as ratios and which ones are not. [Mr. Swade writes the following: *8, 1/2, 6 × 6, 5/10.*] Okay, which ones are expressed as ratios? Remember what Marcus just said. Think about the first one. Is it a ratio, yes or no? Class?

Class: [With most members responding.] No.

Mr. Swade: And why not, Marcus?

Marcus: It doesn't show division.

Mr. Swade: Okay, let's take the next one.

Class: [Again with most members responding.] Yes.

Mr. Swade: Right again. Notice how easy it is to spot a ratio; it's because of the division. Ratios are the result of one number being divided by another. Today we will study a special type of ratio called a *proportion*, in which one number is always divided by a bigger number. But before we get to these problems, let's finish our last two. [Mr. Swade points to *6 × 6* on board.]

Class: No.

Mr. Swade: And . . . [Mr. Swade points to the last one, *5/10.*]

Class: [In almost perfect unison.] Yes.

Mr. Swade: Good. Now you see that ratios are often expressed as one number over another, like this [points to *4/8* on the board]. Now let's look at this cereal box. Calley, take the box in your hands and tell me how full it is.

Calley: Well, I don't exactly know. It feels pretty heavy—I mean . . . it's kind of full.

Mr. Swade: What if I asked you to tell me how much "kind of full" is?

Calley: I'd say kind of full means almost full—well, maybe a little less than almost full. [A few members of the class laugh.]

Mr. Swade: I think some of the class may have thought your answer was funny because they would like to know what "a little less than almost full" means. Now, since this is a typical problem—the kind people face every day at home and at work—it would be nice to express some things more accurately without the use of words, which can be imprecise when describing amounts of things. How might we be more precise, Tomas?

Tomas: Maybe we could express it as a ratio.

Mr. Swade: Okay. But how do we go about forming a ratio to describe the amount of cereal in this box? Can you tell us some more?

Tomas: Well, we need to know how much the box holds.

Mr. Swade: That's right. You've got the first step. Now, Tim, what's the next step?

Tim: I don't know.

Mr. Swade: Maria? [Silence. After 10 seconds.] Britta? [Silence. Addressing the class.] I know you can do it. Think about our earlier examples and Marcus's answer.

Britta: [Catching the hint.] I think we should divide by comparing how much it has in it with how much the box holds.

Mr. Swade: So, our second step, Britta, is . . . ?

Britta: To measure how much is in the box.

Mr. Swade: That's right. You have just given us the form of a proportion without actually saying it. The form is [writes on board]:

$$\frac{\text{what is}}{\text{what could be}} = \frac{\text{a little less than half full}}{\text{full}}$$

Now comes the hard part. How will we find numbers to put in the top and bottom of this division problem? Any suggestions? [Danny waves his hand.]

Danny: I have an idea. Let's see how many glasses of water the box holds and then see how many glasses of water it takes to fill the box to where the cereal is.

Mr. Swade: That's a pretty clever idea, but it may have a few problems. Bobby, you look like you want to say something—what about Danny's idea?

Bobby: The box isn't going to hold water long enough to do the counting.

Mr. Swade: Right. And what if the box doesn't fill up exactly at a full glass? Let's look on the box and read how this food company measured what's inside. [Hands box to Terri.]

Terri: It says, "Six 8 ounce servings measured by volume."

Mr. Swade: So, how many ounces does the whole box contain? Let's review. You supply the answers as I go down the list. [Writes] *1 × 8 =*
[Class responds.] 8
$2 \times 8 = 16$
$3 \times 8 = 24$
$4 \times 8 = 32$
$5 \times 8 = 40$
$6 \times 8 = 48$

So, 48 ounces is our total. Now, let's go back to Danny's original idea about the water, but let's measure the contents of the box using ounces instead. I happen to have an 8 ounce measuring cup. Marcus, you pour while the rest of us count.

Class: One. [As the cup is filling.]

Marcus: Where do I empty it?

Mr. Swade: Let's put it in this empty box.

Class: [As the remaining contents are poured out.] Two . . . three . . . four . . . five . . .

Marcus: The sixth one's not full.

Mr. Swade: Okay. Read on the side of the cup how full it is.

Marcus: It's right at "2" on the cup.

Mr. Swade: That means 2 ounces. Let's do a little arithmetic. What's our total? Who wants to do this problem? [Maria raises her hand.]

Maria: Well, we had five full cups, so that's 8 plus 8 equals . . . 16, plus 8 equals . . . 24, plus 8 equals . . . 32.

Class: One more.

Maria: Yeah, I guess that's only four, so 32 plus 8 equals . . . 40, and then the 2 at the end makes . . . 42.

Mr. Swade: Okay, now we have all that we need to form a proportion that can tell us exactly how full the box was. What does the form of this proportion look like, class?

Class: [With most responding.] Forty-two divided by forty-eight. [Now Mr. Swade writes on board]:

$$\frac{42}{48} = \frac{\text{what is}}{\text{what could be}}$$

Mr. Swade: Now let's practice what we've learned. Britta and Tom, would you pass these sheets around? [Gives stack to Britta and Tom, who are on opposite sides of the room.] On the sheet, you'll find ten word problems similar to our cereal example. Each problem gives you all the information you will need to form a proportion that represents "what is" over "what could be." [Points to words on the board.] Work on these for the next 15 minutes by yourselves, and I'll come around to check your work. Be sure to read the problems carefully. Form a ratio just as we did with the cereal example, and then do the division. Show your work in the space provided, and place your answer on the blank at the right. Your answer will be in the form of a proportion that will require the use of a decimal. If you're having trouble, raise your hand. I'll come to those having difficulty first. [After a few minutes Alex raises his hand, and Mr. Swade moves over to help him.]

Alex: [Quietly to Mr. Swade.] This first one confuses me. [Mr. Swade draws a circle around the words representing "what is" and "what could be" in the word problem and draws arrows to the top and bottom of a line to the right, indicating division. Mr. Swade then moves to the back of the room to check Niko's paper. He finds Niko's second answer is incorrect and places an X beside it.]

Niko: What did I do wrong?

Mr. Swade: What always goes on the bottom?

Niko: What could be.

Mr. Swade: How large is the can of fruit?

Niko: Oh. I get it. [Mr. Swade moves to front of class, spot-checking answers from Marcus, Britta, and Calley. Mr. Swade scans Marcus's paper and nods approvingly; he then says "Good" to Britta after reviewing her first three answers, but finds two errors among Calley's responses.]

Mr. Swade: [To Calley] Problems 2 and 4 are wrong. Think some more about these after you've finished the rest. I'll be back to check on these. [Mr. Swade goes back to his desk to grade papers until the class finishes. As students finish, noise picks up. A few students start to laugh and giggle at a note passed around by Alex, who finished in about half the allotted time.]

REACTIONS TO THE DIALOGUE

What dimensions of student engagement did you see in this dialogue? Recall that student engagement involves the amount of time in which students are thinking about, acting on, or otherwise using the content presented. Student engagement differs from a teacher's task orientation. A teacher can be task-oriented and provide maximum content coverage, but the students may not be engaged all of this time. Although student engagement in the learning process may not always be obvious to an observer, our description of student engagement in this chapter focuses on observable teacher activities that encourage students to think about, act on, and use the content presented.

Eliciting Desired Behavior

The first dimension for promoting student engagement involves eliciting the desired behavior after the presentation of new content. Did you see any examples of this in the dialogue? If you said yes, you are correct. In fact, Mr. Swade does an effective job of arranging his lesson so that students can practice the behaviors as they are taught. This is accomplished with the use of prepared examples and exercises. Notice how Mr. Swade is able to catch his students' attention and focus them on the content by inserting a question, problem, or exercise at regular intervals throughout the lesson.

The first example of this comes at the outset of the lesson, when Mr. Swade asks his class if the expressions placed on the board are examples of ratios. Four expressions are written on the board, only two of which are ratios. Mr. Swade guides his class through the initial problem by saying, "Remember what Marcus just said." In this brief series of problems, Mr. Swade's purpose appears to be getting his students to make their first crude association between the process of division and ratios. With each of the four problems presented, students are asked to determine its correctness in their own minds. Critical judgments of any one student's response, which might dampen a student's willingness to respond to the next problem and remain engaged in the lesson, are avoided. Although Mr. Swade's behavioral goal is simple, he accomplishes it not by telling or showing students ratios involving division, but by having his students think about the distinction and identify examples placed on the board.

Next, notice how Mr. Swade actively involves the class in the lesson after Terri reads from the cereal box. Instead of simply providing the answer—that 6 × 8 = 48 ounces—or calling on a student to provide the answer for the entire class, the teacher has the class calculate the total themselves by reviewing multiplication by 8. Here, Mr. Swade composes, probably on the spur of the moment, six multiplication problems (1 × 8 = , 2 × 8 = , and so on) and requires the class to provide the correct answers. This also helps focus class attention, which may have begun to drift by this time. Inserting these small exercises that require the immediate response of students at the end of important segments of the lesson is particularly effective for engaging learners—especially young learners—in the learning process and keeping them engaged throughout the lesson.

Finally, Mr. Swade assigns a practice exercise so that he may evaluate the responses of individual students by checking their answers to the problems on the handout. Recall that one of the purposes of guided practice is to motivate students to make a crude first response, sometimes any response, and then to refine it gradually by trial and error. The earlier guided practice activities motivated some students to begin thinking about and formulating a response; this last activity adds an evaluative component that helps to revise and refine earlier responses. It provides still more opportunity for practice that requires all students to respond overtly, and thereby makes evaluation possible.

As we have seen, engagement in the learning process begins when the learner is given the opportunity to practice using the content that is taught. Without immediate practice to engage the student in the learning process, learning rarely occurs. Some teachers, however, teach as they themselves were taught in the college classroom, without realizing the vast differences that separate the adult from the elementary-school or secondary-school learner. At the college level, where considerable independence and motivation are expected, the instructor may appropriately assume that engagement in the learning process will take place at the convenience of and on the initiative of the individual student as she works through the lecture material in the privacy of the study room or library.

At the elementary- and secondary-school level, however, content presentation and practice go hand-in-hand, separated by minutes, not days. Engagement in the learning process must be an integral part of the instruction itself, because the learner at this age is not likely to know how to make the leap from content presentation to practice without the active and direct guidance of the teacher. In Chapter 12 we will study eliciting activities that promote student engagement by challenging learners to go beyond the content presented to develop higher thought processes. In this chapter, we will study eliciting activities that encourage students to make a first crude response from which higher thought processes can develop.

Oral questions, workbook exercises, problem sets, activity handouts, and discussion, under the guidance of the teacher, are some of the ways students may be encouraged to think about, act on, or otherwise practice content. This practice should be provided as soon as possible after the instruction to which it relates, and for complex material should be interspersed at intervals throughout the lesson, creating cycles of presentation and practice.

The primary ways of accomplishing this integration of instruction and practice include the use of workbooks, handouts, textbook study questions, verbal and written exercises, and oral questions in which students are asked to immediately apply what was learned, if only in the privacy of their own minds. The idea is to position a classroom activity as close in time as possible to the presentation of new material to encourage an immediate response. It is important that the eliciting activity be noncritical, to encourage a response unhampered by anxiety and a fear of failure, which can occur in a test-taking situation. The goal of the eliciting activity is to encourage the learner to organize a crude first response that strives for, but may not attain, the intended behavior. Sometimes these activities can be inserted at the end of each unit of information throughout the lesson, which adds variety. In other instances, the activities can occur toward or at the end of the presentation of new material. In either case, the eliciting activity that brings forth the response is brief, noncritical, and focused on posing a condition (such as a question, problem, or exercise) for which the learner must organize and produce a response. The response may be written, oral, or subvocal (for example, when the teacher poses a question and the students answer to themselves).

Rosenshine and Stevens (1986) have suggested several different types of eliciting activities.

- ❑ Preparing a large number of oral questions beforehand
- ❑ Asking many brief questions on main points, supplementary points, and the process that is being taught
- ❑ Asking students to summarize a rule or process in their own words

❑ Having all students write their answers (on paper or the chalkboard) while the teacher circulates through the room

❑ Having all students write their answers and check them with a neighbor (frequently used with older students)

❑ Writing the main points on the chalkboard at the end of a lecture/discussion, and then having the class meet in groups to summarize them (especially helpful for older students)

Observing Eliciting Activities

Eliciting the desired behavior involves guided practice. The goal of guided practice is to elicit from the learner a crude first response, and then to keep the learner responding in trial-and-error fashion until initial responses are gradually refined into correct, quick, and firm responses. Typical methods for eliciting learner responses include oral questions, exercises in the text or workbook, problems presented in handouts, and problems or questions written on the board or on an overhead. These and other eliciting activities can be recorded with the format shown in Instrument 10.1.

For this record, a checkmark is placed in the appropriate box each time an eliciting activity occurs during a lesson. Notice that the proximity of the practice activity to the presentation of lesson content is recorded simultaneously. Guided practice is most effective when it is interspersed throughout, or immediately follows, the presentation of content. Also notice that five different alternatives (from *Interspersed* through *Indefinite*) are provided to record when the eliciting activity recurs. The more immediate the eliciting activity is to the presentation of content, the greater the chance that feedback and correctives will improve the learner's initial response and keep the learner responding until responses are correct, quick, and firm. The longer the time between the presentation of content and the questions, problems, or exercises of the eliciting activity, the less effective the activity becomes.

Providing Feedback in a Noncritical Atmosphere

A second behavior for engaging students in the learning process is providing feedback about the correctness of the elicited response. At this point in the learning process, it is important that feedback be given in a noncritical context to encourage response. Crude and often inadequate initial responses are refined, through repetition, into slightly less crude and more adequate responses, which in turn provide the basis for finely tuned responses at a high level of accuracy. If behaviors related to the acquisition of knowledge are being sought (direct instruction), the feedback must help the learner recall individual units of content and put them together to create a smooth and automatic response. If behaviors related to inquiry or problem solving are being sought (indirect instruction), the feedback must go beyond the examples given and separate examples from nonexamples. In either case, the feedback must unambiguously inform the learner about the adequacy of any response and must be given in a manner that will not embarrass or humiliate the learner, or lower the learner's own expectations. Because initial responses to a guided-practice exercise may be crude, sometimes illogical, and occasionally funny (in the teacher's eyes), the potential for emotional harm is greatest during this phase of learning. The teacher's job is not to pass judgment, but to provide nonjudgmental feedback so that the learner can judge his own work. This is accomplished by having students respond in unison, showing answers on a transparency after each problem is completed individually, or simply supplying the correct answers at the end of a designated work time, and may also include requesting that students write out their responses or orally respond so that the teacher may be certain that students are engaged in the problem solution and do not simply wait for the answer to be given.

Opportunities for feedback should always be closely connected in time and substance to the eliciting activity. An eliciting activity will promote learning if the learner can determine the correctness of the attempted response, whether oral, written, or subvocal, immediately after the response has been given. Although the response itself must be an individual's attempt to recall, summarize, paraphrase, apply, or solve an aspect of the new learning, the feedback that follows can be directed to the entire class to create immediacy for everyone. For example, the teacher may either reveal his answer to a problem or question, or choose a student's answer. A wrong response by a student, however, should be responded to with encouragement to maintain the noncritical flavor of the learning activity. Responses such as "That's a good try," "That's not quite what I'm looking for," or "Keep thinking" can switch the focus to more useful responses without penalizing the student for attempting and producing a crude initial response. Other ways of confirming correct responses would be to

❑ Read aloud and correct answers from the workbook.

❑ Provide a handout with the correct answers.

❑ Show the answers one by one on a transparency after students complete each question.

FIGURE 10.3 Methods of Providing Feedback

Individual Students	Small Groups	Class
Nod while walking past	Sit with group and discuss answers	Place answers on a transparency
Point to correct answer in workbook or text	Have one group critique another group's answers	Provide answers on a handout
Show student the answer key	Give each group the answer key when finished	Read answers aloud
Place X beside incorrect answers	Assign one group member the task of checking the answers of other group members	Place answers on the board
Have students grade each other's papers, using the text or assigned reference as a guide		Have selected students read their answers aloud
		Have students grade each other's papers as you give answers orally

❏ Nod or smile to indicate the correctness of an individual performance or to encourage the revision of a wrong response.

These and other ways of providing feedback to individuals, small groups, and the full class are summarized in Figure 10.3.

What did you notice about how Mr. Swade provided correctives? Did you notice that Mr. Swade's practice opportunities at the start of the lesson were oriented toward the entire class, avoiding any potential embarrassment to individual students whose initial responses might have been crude, funny, or illogical? In the first two guided-practice activities, students responded in choral fashion, thereby avoiding altogether an evaluation of individual responses. The teacher provided the correct response with which students could evaluate their own answers. When students have difficulty grasping a concept, and large numbers of initial responses are likely to be incorrect, choral responses or responses made privately can minimize potentially embarrassing answers and possible humiliation to individual students. Mr. Swade may have known that some of his students did not learn all that they should have from earlier lessons; this may be the reason he decided to start his lesson with class-corrected rather than individually corrected exercises. Class-corrected exercises and choral responses are no guarantee, however, that all students will participate. More formal feedback also will be necessary to check the accuracy of earlier choral and private responses.

Mr. Swade's final exercise seems to provide the individual student evaluation that the earlier practice activities lack. Notice that even though this last activity is evaluative, it too is relatively nonjudgmental. The teacher responds to students individually, not in the presence of other students. Notice also that, for the most part, Mr. Swade's feedback is immediate, with the shortest possible time between the generation of a response and information about its correctness. This tends to strengthen a correct response, reinforcing its value for the learner and making it more likely that the response will be remembered.

Since oral questions are an important eliciting activity, Mr. Swade's responses to these kinds of questions deserve examination as well. Recall that a teacher's response to a student question can be categorized as *praise, affirm, negate, criticize,* or *no response.* A teacher's corrective response to a student answer can be categorized as *gives answers, repeats question, explains, rephrases question,* and *gives clue* (See Chapter 4, Figures 4.12 and 4.13 and Chapter 11, Instrument 11.1). Using these categories of teacher answer and feedback, which alternatives do you think were most typical of Mr. Swade's reactions to student responses? Let's look at just a few of these exchanges to see how he engages his students in the learning process with feedback and correctives.

Mr. Swade's first question is typical of his questioning strategy throughout the dialogue. He asks, "Who can tell me why division is so important in computing a ratio?" Marcus replies, "It's because ratios are nothing but division problems." The teacher responds, "Yes, that's right, in the sense that ratios can be expressed as one number over another, like this (writes 4/8 on board)." Notice that the teacher first affirms that the student response is correct—or partially correct. Then the teacher rephrases or elaborates on the question for both the student and the rest of the class. In other words, this teacher's response takes the student's answer and rephrases it in a manner useful for moving to the next part of the lesson. For example, the teacher extends Marcus's response "nothing but division problems" to "one number over another" to provide a transition. Indeed, we find the idea of "one number over another" plays a key role throughout the lesson as the teacher develops the model "what is/what could be" to communicate the notion of a proportion—and to respond to problems on the handout. Thus, the feedback provided to Marcus's answer not only evaluated his response, but also lifted his answer to a new level.

This question-answer-feedback strategy appears throughout the dialogue in several different forms. For example, at another point the teacher asks, ". . . how do we go about forming a ratio to describe the amount of cereal in this box?" Tomas replies, "Well, we need to know how much the box holds." The teacher responds, "That's right. You've got the first step. Now, Tim, what's the next step?" Here, the teacher affirms the correctness—or partial correctness—of the response, and then goes on to use the answer as a springboard for additional content. Each student response lays the groundwork for additional content added by the teacher or provided in the form of a new question to another student. This type of feedback uses student responses as transitions to new content. It is characterized by more praise and affirmation than negation and criticism, because most student responses are interpreted as partially correct, with some usable content for a transition to the next idea.

Observing Feedback

Although the recording format in Instrument 10.1 indicates the nature of the guided-practice activity, it does not indicate whether any correctives are being provided to individual students. When practice activities are interspersed throughout the presentation of content, provided immediately afterward, or saved until the end of the lesson, correctives may or may not be provided. Even oral questions interspersed in the presentation of content may or may not be corrective. The teacher may pose a question and then immediately answer it without giving students time to respond, indicate that a response is wrong but give no indication why, or not expect any answer at all. Also, because meaningful verbal praise is a significant component of the teacher's feedback, it, too, can be an important aspect of engaging students and keeping them engaged in the eliciting activity.

After gaining a familiarity with eliciting activities using the recording format in Instrument 10.1, you may want to shift to the student response–teacher reaction instrument (see Figures 4.12 and 4.13 and In-

strument 11.1) to obtain a more detailed account of the specific interactive sequences during an eliciting activity (Good & Brophy, 1990). Recall that this instrument records whether the teacher praises, affirms, negates, criticizes, or gives no reaction to a student response that is right, partly right, or wrong. It also records the nature of the corrective provided by the teacher (gives answer, asks another student, explains answer, repeats question, rephrases question, or gives clue). Thus, the instrument provides an opportunity for you to record the teacher's use of both correctives and verbal praise.

With this record, unintended gender or cultural biases can become obvious after coding only a brief sequence of student–teacher exchanges. For example, a teacher may selectively criticize partly right answers and then move to another student, or affirm correct answers without providing feedback about why the answer was correct, thereby preventing the response from being used as a model for others to follow. On the other hand, a teacher who frequently finds opportunities to praise and affirm and uses a variety of correctives (for example, explains answer, repeats or rephrases question, and gives clue) in response to partly right or wrong answers exhibits a balanced and culturally appropriate profile of feedback.

Using Individual and Self-Regulated Learning Activities

The use of individual and self-directed activities is the third behavior for engaging students in the learning process. For some students, guided practice and noncritical feedback will not be sufficient. These learners need additional incentives to become sufficiently energized or excited about learning to attempt even a crude initial response to practice opportunities. Individualized instruction and self-directed learning, which give students a degree of control over their own learning, can be useful in getting these students, who may represent a sizable portion of a class, engaged in the learning process.

Teaching to different groups (or even a single group) of special learners in addition to the regular class is not a matter of choice in many of today's heterogeneous and mainstreamed classrooms. Yet many teachers may not have the time or the flexibility to apply different instructional methods to those who may have different learning needs. A collection of appropriate individualized materials (including performance contracts, programmed texts, games and simulations, activity books, and learning centers) for challenged, at risk, and culturally and ethnically different learners can allow different learning needs to be met in the midst of a heterogeneous class of learners, engaging those who might otherwise be left unengaged.

The lower achieving learner will be one of those most frequently disengaged from the learning process. Many of these learners have difficulty learning at an average rate from the instructional resources, texts, workbooks, and learning materials that have been designated for the majority of students in the classroom. These students will benefit from special instructional pacing, frequent feedback, corrective instruction, and/or modified materials, all administered under conditions flexible enough to engage them in the learning process. These learners may also require more than the usual amount of variation in method of presentation (direct/indirect), instructional materials (films, workbooks, games, and simulations), and learning activities (oral questioning, group discussion, and tutoring) to keep them actively engaged in the learning process. These learners respond favorably to the frequent reinforcement of small segments of learning typically found in interactive media and similar materials. Also, some students may learn more efficiently by seeing and hearing than by reading. Incorporating films, video, and audio into learning centers can help accommodate instruction to the learning modalities that are strongest among these learners.

In addition to these formal approaches to individualizing instruction, some group tasks can be presented in a form that gives learners the opportunity to self-regulate the pace and complexity of their responses. For example, cooperative group activities and tasks can employ self-directed learning activities (e.g., position papers, research reports, or debates) to gradually transfer control over the learning process to students, thereby increasing each student's responsibility for his own learning. Using self-directed learning activities in the context of cooperative groups can be particularly helpful when the variety of student abilities, interests, and motivation in a classroom is so great as to preclude the use of any prepackaged set of materials intended for a homogeneous subgroup.

Self-regulated tasks can also provide flexibility in the pace and manner in which individual students learn. For example, after all learners complete a common set of problems, they can be given the opportunity to select from several activities that vary in cognitive complexity. Students whose performance (or confidence) in completing the common exercise falls below expectations can choose from an exercise at a lower level of cognitive complexity; students whose performance falls above expectations can choose an exercise at a higher level of cognitive complexity. The teacher can also vary the amount of

time given to complete the problem sets. In this manner, self-directed assignments transfer a degree of control over the learning process to the student, who is monitored by the teacher. This can be a motivating force in getting a heterogeneous class of learners engaged in the learning process.

Another important ingredient in self-directed learning is the variety of task demands that are made (Doyle, 1983). To be effective, self-directed learning activities must make varying cognitive demands so that students can tap into them at their current level of understanding. For example, some tasks might be chosen to emphasize knowledge and comprehension; others to emphasize comprehension, application, and analysis; and still others to emphasize analysis, synthesis, and evaluation. Also, tasks that allow easy transitions between levels must be chosen to encourage self-initiated movement up and down the ladder of behavioral complexity for both lower and higher achieving learners.

What did you observe about Mr. Swade's use of individualized and self-regulating activities to promote engagement in the learning process? This dialogue may have been too brief to provide sufficient information. But subsequent observations might focus on what Mr. Swade does with those students who cannot grasp the concepts on his guided-practice handout—perhaps as evidenced by a large proportion of incorrect responses after two or three cycles of monitoring and checking. We can focus on how Mr. Swade handles Alex and students like him, who seem more advanced than the rest of the class. To keep these special types of students engaged, individualized activities in the form of self-regulated tasks, programmed texts, games and simulations, computer software, audiovisual media, peer tutoring, group work, teams, and independent projects might well be in order.

Observing Individual and Self-Regulated Learning Activities

As we have seen, lower achieving students may need remedial instruction; higher achieving learners may prefer a learning modality that does not correspond to the needs of the majority of the class. At other times, the teacher may want learners to assume some of the responsibility for their own learning. Many activities and materials that transfer a degree of control of the pace and complexity of learning to the student are available. The use of some of these activities and materials in a classroom can be recorded by categorizing them as shown in Instrument 10.2.

Because the use of these activities and materials must be recorded over time, Instrument 10.2 is intended for use in your cooperating teacher's classroom or another classroom in which you will spend a considerable amount of time. The category *Other* may be used to describe any written self-regulating class assignments (homework or practice activities) that provide students with a degree of control over the pace and/or behavioral complexity of their responses.

Using Meaningful Verbal Praise

The fourth behavior for engaging students in the learning process is the use of meaningful verbal praise. Verbal praise provided frequently in the absence of genuine accomplishment may be seen by students as mechanical and devoid of reinforcing value. Between glib responses such as "Correct," "Okay," or "Yep" and overly emotional responses such as "That's wonderful," "Fantastic," or "Brilliant" lies a range of verbal praise that neither passes by nor embarrasses a student in the eyes of others. Meaningful verbal praise links a student's response to the level of accomplishment attained. For example, instead of simply being informed that the response is correct, the learner can be told that the response is correct because the directions were followed carefully, the correct sequence of events was chosen, or care was taken to consult the text. Instead of just informing the learner that a response is correct, the teacher can explain the higher level thought processes that may have been used to produce the response (for example, the answer shows the ability to find relationships between information in different chapters). In each of these instances, the desire to keep engaged in the learning process is enhanced because verbal praise is provided in the context of a successfully accomplished operation. In other words, if praise is to be effective it should be

- ❑ Specific to the particular behavior being reinforced.
- ❑ Applied immediately after the behavior occurs.
- ❑ Varied according to the situation and the student being reinforced.

Meaningful verbal praise is especially important in the case of partially correct or correct-but-hesitant responses. Here, praise must be tempered with a sign that a better or less hesitant response is desired. To ignore the inadequacy or hesitation in favor of a simple okay may give an indication to others that they, too, can provide a less than satisfactory response. In this case, the praise must be proportional to the adequacy of the response, such as "That's partly correct, but now let's see if you can put it all together" or "Good try. Now change one

thing and you'll have it." Examples such as these point out the subtle differences between a partially correct answer and a wrong answer, which is often a matter of judgment. The effective teacher chooses to praise with qualification a partially correct answer. Figure 10.4, from a review by Brophy (1981), provides guidelines for using praise effectively.

Praise occupies surprisingly little class time for most teachers (Brophy & Good, 1986). Wragg and Wood (1984) report that, on average, only about 2 percent of a teacher's day is devoted to any kind of praise. Yet there is little doubt among behavioral psychologists that a reward contingent on an appropriate behavior increases the frequency of that behavior. A positive verbal response tells the student that the reward is contingent on appropriate performance. More important, it tells learners that by producing the correct response, they can control the flow of rewards.

When meaningful praise is consistently applied, the link between the performance and the praise is strong enough to create a need to achieve. This link becomes internalized by the learner and directs her to anticipate the next reward. Praise is a strategy that is always available to the teacher. It is one of the most effective means of engaging students in the learning process when it is specific, applied immediately, and varied according to the situation and student being reinforced.

Finally, it can be noted that verbally punishing students for responding thoughtlessly or carelessly (for example, "I'm ashamed of you," "That's a dumb mistake," "I thought you were brighter than that") rarely teaches them to avoid the mistake in the future. Reminders to study harder, pay more attention, think some more, or go over mistakes are often desirable stimulants to engaging students in the learning process and should not be confused with phrases that ridicule, demean, or draw the class's attention to someone's abilities. The latter rarely, if ever, lead a learner to change the behavior that led to the careless response.

What did you think of Mr. Swade's feedback to the students? You may have noticed that Mr. Swade's style of feedback closely matches our definition of meaningful verbal praise. *Meaningful verbal praise* occurs when a teacher's response to a student answer is specific, applied immediately after the answer is given, and varied according to the student being reinforced. The teacher's response is tailored to fit the specific answer given by the student and the characteristics of the student giving the answer. Effective praise often explains the value of a learner's response and extends or picks up on the response for further discussion.

FIGURE 10.4 Guidelines for Effective Praise

Effective Praise	Ineffective Praise
1. Is delivered contingently	1. Is delivered randomly or unsystematically
2. Specifies the particulars of the accomplishment	2. Is restricted to global positive reactions
3. Shows spontaneity, variety, and other signs of credibility; suggests clear attention to the student's accomplishment	3. Shows a bland uniformity, which suggests a conditioned response made with minimal attention
4. Rewards attainment of specified performance criteria (can include effort criteria)	4. Rewards mere participation, without consideration of performance processes or outcomes
5. Provides information to students about their competence or the value of their accomplishments	5. Provides no information at all, or gives students little information about their status
6. Orients students toward better appreciation of their own task-related behavior and problem solving	6. Orients students toward comparing themselves with others and competition
7. Uses students' own prior accomplishments as the context for describing present accomplishments	7. Uses the accomplishments of peers as the context for describing students' present accomplishments
8. Is given in recognition of noteworthy effort or success at particularly difficult tasks	8. Is given without regard to the effort expended or the meaning of the accomplishment
9. Attributes success to effort and ability, implying that similar successes can be expected in the future	9. Attributes success to ability alone, or external factors such as luck or ease
10. Fosters endogenous attributions (students believe that they expend effort on the task because they enjoy the task and/or want to develop task-relevant skills)	10. Fosters exogenous attributions (students believe that they expend effort on the task for external reasons—to please the teacher or win a competition or reward)
11. Focuses students' attention on their own task-relevant behavior	11. Focuses students' attention on the teacher as an external authority figure who is manipulating them
12. Fosters appreciation and desirable attributions about task-relevant behavior after the process is completed	12. Intrudes into the ongoing process, distracting attention from task-relevant behavior

How often did Mr. Swade's responses do this? Notice that Mr. Swade's response to correct or partially correct answers did not stop at neutral affirmation, but went on either to explain the value of the response to the class or to use the response to move the discussion to a new or different level. Mr. Swade's affirmation of a correct response took forms such as

"Yes, that's right, in the sense that . . ."
"Right again. Notice how easy it is to spot . . ."
"Good. Now you see that . . ."
"Okay. But how do we go about . . . ?"
"That's right. You've got the first step. Now . . ."

In each of these expressions, Mr. Swade does not stop at a simple expression of praise. He goes on to provide a response that is tailored to the level of correctness of the answer given, making the praise meaningful to the student. Mr. Swade uses each response as an opportunity to move deeper into the topic. He tends to look on the bright side of every response, to see that the glass is half full rather than half empty. Responses like this blend student answers into the discussion rather than letting them become dead ends. Mr. Swade has combined probing with meaningful praise. Each of his responses leaves the student feeling good about his response and thinking more about it. This is how meaningful praise engages students in the learning process at the same time as it rewards and reinforces.

Observing Meaningful Verbal Praise

Recall that, to be effective, praise must be contingent on the performance of the specific behavior to be reinforced, clearly identified with that behavior (given immediately following the behavior), and adjusted to the characteristics of the student being praised (for example, shy and retiring, easily embarrassed, or outgoing and gregarious). These three ingredients separate ineffective praise with little or no influence on student behavior from praise that is likely to reinforce behavior and increase the probability that the desired behavior will recur. This latter type of praise is called *meaningful* praise.

The recording form in Instrument 10.3 divides praise into two categories. The first category lists the ways in which praise can be delivered to the student: orally, through body language (such as a nod of the head or a pat on the back), or written (such as

FIGURE **10.5** Four Types of Oral Praise

Gives Neutral Affirmation

Teacher uses expressions such as "Okay," "Good," and "Yep" to indicate response is accepted, but goes no further.

Expresses Surprise, Delight, or Excitement

Teacher shows some emotion, such as "Great," "That shows real talent," or "You're doing remarkably well."

Expresses Value

Teacher explains to class why the answer is correct and points out qualities used to arrive at the answer, implying superior performance.

Uses, Extends, Picks Up On

Teacher takes student response to next level, or uses it to arrive at a subsequent step in a process.

a note at the top of a paper or exercise). A second category divides praise that is delivered orally into four types (Figure 10.5).

These categories attempt to separate praise into more and less meaningful types: the first two (*Gives Neutral Affirmation* and *Expresses Surprise, Delight, or Excitement*) are generally less meaningful than the latter (*Explains Value* and *Uses, Extends, Picks Up On*). The latter two tend to be more meaningful because the praise is specific to the context in which the response was given and more tailored to the unique product of the student. Note that the teacher's responses to the first two categories could serve any correct response provided in any context by any student, which is not true for the last two categories.

Finally, notice that the first column provides an opportunity to record the beginning and ending time of the observation and, if necessary, any time the observation is stopped and started in between, which might be necessary if students turn to independent seatwork or another activity. The rate of praise per unit of class time can be recorded at these times. For example, if 4 incidents of praise were recorded after 60 minutes of observation, during which there was an opportunity for praise, the rate would be 4 praises per hour of instructional time. For comparisons across classrooms in which either more or less than an hour's time may have been devoted to observation, it is convenient to convert praise rates to a common measure using the formula

$$\frac{\text{Number of incidents of praise}}{\substack{\text{Number of minutes of observation} \\ \text{time during which opportunities for} \\ \text{praise were present}}} \times 60 = \text{praise rate/hour}$$

Praise rates can be compared across teachers and classes: They may be calculated separately for each of the five types of praise and entered in the last row of the record. To make these rates independent of one another, a type of praise should be recorded separately each time it occurs. Thus, when a teacher expresses surprise, but then goes on to explain why the response was correct, it should be recorded as two different incidents of praise. Since incidents of praise do not occur frequently, a large amount of observation time may be necessary for the rate of each type of praise to be representative of a classroom. For smaller blocks of observation time, ranging from one to several hours, a single rate combining the five individual types of praise can be used. Praise rates for academic work and conduct-related behaviors reported in six research studies reviewed by Brophy (1981) were 4.52 and 0.12 incidents of praise per hour, respectively. These data show that relatively little praise occurs in most classrooms.

Monitoring and Checking

The final behavior for engaging students in the learning process involves monitoring and checking. *Monitoring* is the process of observing, mentally recording, and, when necessary, redirecting or correcting student behavior. The teacher looks for active, alert eyes during discussion sessions; eyes down and directed at the book or assignment during seatwork; raised hands during a question-and-answer period; and general signs that indicate the learner is participating in the classwork. These signs of engagement (or their absence) can indicate when changes must be made in the pace with which the content is being delivered, the difficulty of the material, or even the activity itself.

An important aspect of monitoring that promotes engagement in the learning process is observing more than one activity at a time. This requires *withitness*, or the ability to observe all or at least many aspects of a classroom simultaneously (Kounin, 1970). Although few teachers are blessed with eyes in the backs of their heads, there are several simple ways of increasing withitness. One is changing the focus of attention as eye contact is focused on different parts of the room. For example, progress on assigned seatwork might be the focus of a teacher's observations when scanning students in the front of the class, but potential disciplinary problems might be the focus of observation when scanning the back of the class; then the sequence is reversed. Thus, the teacher switches back and forth from conduct-related observations to work-related observations with a change in eye contact. One of the greatest impediments to making this switch, however, is a tendency to focus exclusively on one student who may be having either conduct- or work-related problems. Once students become aware that the teacher is preoccupied with a single student, problems are inevitable.

An equally important aspect of monitoring is *checking* for student understanding and, when necessary, providing prompts that help convert wrong answers to right ones. Prompting is an important way of engaging learners in the learning process because it builds their confidence by encouraging them to use aspects of the answer that has already been given in working toward the correct response (Gagne, 1985).

Checking for understanding and prompting can be accomplished by asking the class to respond privately and then encouraging them to request individual help. Another approach is to call on students whether or not their hands are raised, thereby seeking out opportunities to prompt and correct wrong answers. A version of this approach is referred to as *ordered turns*, in which the teacher systematically goes through the class and expects students to respond when their turn comes. This approach has been found to be more effective than randomly calling on students in terms of producing gains in student achievement when groups are small (Anderson et al., 1979; Brophy & Evertson, 1976), but less effective than randomly selecting students to respond during full-class instruction (Anderson et al., 1982). Another approach is to have students write out answers to be checked and, if need be, corrected by a classmate. Finally, the teacher can prepare a number of questions beforehand to test for the most frequently occurring errors. Students are then asked to provide responses, which the teacher checks for accuracy and then probes when necessary. This approach has the advantage of assuming that not everyone understands or has the correct answer when no responses are heard following a call for questions. These methods for checking for understanding and probing can be summarized as

1. Ordered turns (best with small groups)
2. Calling on students randomly (best with full class)
3. Having students write out answers that are then checked by classmate
4. Asking questions (ordered or random) to check for the most frequently occurring errors

During instructional activities such as guided practice and independent seatwork, monitoring should be done within a systematic routine of checking. Rather than simply scanning the classroom, the teacher circulates among students and checks their responses in workbooks or exercises. It is important, however, that this circulating behavior is not seen by learners as punitive, but rather as a helpful response to their work. A casual glance at papers is more constructive than long interactions with individual students, whose self-esteem and engagement may be stifled by a long stay at their desk because others may see this as a sign of poor performance. Interactions with individual students should be limited to brief exchanges, lasting only about 30 seconds, and to responses that are focused on a student's particular problem. This cycle may be repeated if the teacher wants to look for other types of student errors on subsequent rounds. Monitoring and checking for progress, especially during guided and independent practice, are important tools for effectively engaging students in the learning process.

What did you notice about Mr. Swade's use of monitoring and checking behaviors? Did Mr. Swade have a systematic routine of monitoring and checking to accomplish his goals? We see that, for the most part, he did. Recall that an effective routine for monitoring and checking involves evaluating the work of as many students as possible by limiting individual student contact to brief exchanges of less than a minute. Thus, circulating throughout the classroom and giving approximately equal time to all zones of the room is important. Checking the work of individual students may be accomplished orally, in writing, or simply through body language to indicate that a particular response is correct. Some examples of each appeared in the dialogue.

For example, the teacher's response to Alex's request for help was simply to draw circles and arrows leading him to the correct response without any verbal exchange. The teacher gave Niko a verbal hint to correct a wrong answer with the words "What always goes on the bottom?" For Marcus, a simple nod of the head conveyed the message that all was correct. What do these various types of exchanges have in common? Although they employ three different channels of communication—written, oral, and visual—they are all brief and to the point. Brevity—the ability to make an evaluation quickly and then disengage to make another—is one of the most important characteristics of effective monitoring and checking. Our everyday communications tend not to be brief exchanges, and therefore it is often difficult to utilize such an approach in the classroom without being rude or incomplete. Yet the ability to avoid extended discussion with individual students, even when it is content related, is necessary during monitoring and checking.

Providing extensive assistance to individual students is not the function of monitoring and checking. Such assistance, when required, should be carried out at a later time or with specialized materials. In avoiding digressions that can lengthen individual exchanges, what is said by the teacher is as important as what is not said. The teacher's words must be chosen carefully so that a question or response is on the mark. Checks, pluses, or smiley faces written silently on papers, or simple body language, are often preferable, especially with a student who is prone to drawing the teacher into an extended discussion.

While we have given Mr. Swade some compliments on his monitoring and checking behavior, he seems to give it only a halfhearted effort. He was off to a good start, but we learn at the end of the dialogue that his monitoring and checking activity lasted for less than half of the 15 minutes allotted to the guided-practice activity. Mr. Swade then returned to his desk to grade papers. The class was left to finish the exercise without the benefit of feedback; Mr. Swade missed an opportunity to discover students who may not have been sufficiently prepared to even begin the activity. This is not uncommon. Some students will look engaged to disguise their embarrassment at not being able to begin the exercise, and teachers readily get distracted by their own uncompleted work. Since some students will disengage from practice activity at the first sign of difficulty, or when the teacher appears preoccupied or unavailable to help, the effectiveness of monitoring and checking depends on the active participation of the teacher throughout the entire practice exercise.

As students progress through the material, greater individual differences will appear. Some students who have grasped the concept race to an early finish; others who do not understand get bogged down by increasingly more difficult problems. These are reasons why teacher vigilance—monitoring and checking—should be maintained during the entire guided-practice activity: For early finishers, more work may have to be assigned; for slower students, two or even three cycles of checking may be necessary to maintain their engagement in the learning process.

Finally, Mr. Swade ended his lesson with a handout containing ten word problems. This eliciting activity differed from the preceding activities because it provided the opportunity for the teacher to evaluate the correctness of individual student responses. Yet the teacher's evaluation of these individually written responses was nonthreatening, because students were asked to respond privately at their desks. Crude, funny, or illogical responses did not become a source of embarrassment or humiliation, as they might have if individuals were called on to report their answers to the class. The success of this final eliciting activity depended on a systematic routine of (1) monitoring to encourage the students to apply themselves to the exercise, and (2) checking to ensure that students were improving the accuracy of their responses, refining them until they were increasingly correct, quick, and firm.

Observing Monitoring and Checking

As we have seen, the teacher can promote student engagement by monitoring and checking activities during assigned seatwork. At this time it is important that the teacher have frequent contact with students and that the teacher's contact is spread evenly among students throughout the classroom. Several approaches can be used to observe these teacher behaviors.

The first approach estimates the overall pattern of movement of a teacher. Although monitoring student behavior and checking student progress can be separate activities (for example, a teacher may monitor student behavior from the desk in front of the room, but circulate around the room to provide feedback and correctives), these two activities will be considered simultaneously. This is accomplished with a seven-item checklist that combines the relative number of contacts and their approximate duration as shown in the following scale.

Using one or two checkmarks, indicate which of the following is (are) most typical of this teacher's behavior during assigned seatwork.

_____ 1. No individual student contact during assigned seatwork
_____ 2. Checks the work of a few students briefly
_____ 3. Checks the work of some students briefly
_____ 4. Checks the work of most students briefly
_____ 5. Checks the work of a few students intensively
_____ 6. Checks the work of some students intensively
_____ 7. Checks the work of most students intensively

To increase the dependability of this scale, Figure 10.6 provides operational guidelines for each of its key words.

Although this scale presents broad categories of behavior, it enables us to measure monitoring by

FIGURE 10.6 Sample Guidelines for Student–Teacher Contacts

Intensity of Contact	Number of Students Contacted		
	Few	**Some**	**Most**
Brief	Checks work of 1–3 students for a minute or less each	Checks work of 4–8 students for a minute or less each	Checks work of more than 8 students for a minute or less each
Extensive	Checks work of 1–3 students for more than a minute	Checks work of 4–8 students for more than a minute	Checks work of more than 8 students for more than a minute

number of contacts and checking by duration of contact. Together, monitoring and checking form a general pattern of behavior that may be typical of a classroom. Unless special circumstances prevail, the most effective strategy is represented by the third and fourth alternatives on the preceding seven-item checklist. They allow the teacher to cover more ground with fewer classroom management problems than the fifth or sixth alternatives, which may engage the teacher in protracted conversations with individual students, perhaps causing her to miss work- or conduct-related problems occurring elsewhere in the classroom. The lengthier the contact, the more unlikely it is that the work of most students can be monitored. Frequent use of the seventh alternative would be desirable only if time permitted and classroom-management problems could be avoided. Generally, less than a minute of student contact is considered optimal, unless the class is small.

The movement of the teacher throughout the classroom can be another important sign that monitoring and checking are taking place. However, students closest to the teacher and engaged in the lesson may represent only a small portion of the classroom. Therefore, a picture or map of the teacher's circulating activity may be important for discovering implicit biases that can, over the course of time, leave some members of the class without any individual teacher contact, promoting disengagement.

The visual map of a classroom in Figure 10.7 indicates how the circulating activity of the teacher can be recorded. Connecting lines indicate the pattern of rotation. Notice how this teacher seems to favor the center of the classroom, excluding those seated along the sides and back. Also, only about one-quarter (26 percent) of the 27 students in this classroom had their progress checked by the teacher or had an opportunity to pose a question about the work. Although a single observation period may not reveal the typical monitoring and checking behaviors of a teacher, visual maps such as these can reveal

why some students may or may not be engaged in the learning process, especially if completed over more than one observation period.

Another approach to observing monitoring and checking behaviors is to combine several signs into a single format. In Instrument 10.4 the manner in which feedback is provided to the student, the time devoted to feedback, and the location of the student in the classroom are all recorded simultaneously. Figure 10.8 provides a description of each of the columns on this form. Notice that Instrument 10.4 allows you to record the mode in which feedback is provided to the learner, including the use of body language, which is often the predominant form of feedback for brief contacts. In addition, you can record three levels of duration, which correspond, respectively, to three principal reasons for initiating

FIGURE 10.7 Visual Map of a Teacher's Circulating Activity

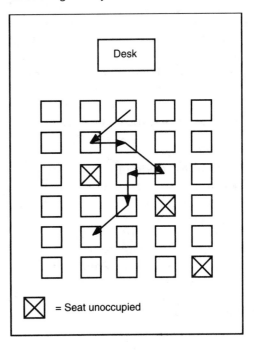

⊠ = Seat unoccupied

FIGURE 10.8 Description of Indicators for Observing, Monitoring, and Checking

Mode of Feedback		
	Oral	Teacher comments orally.
	Written	Teacher places mark on paper ("OK," check after wrong answer, smiley face, or star), writes in correct answer, or corrects one already written.
	Body Language	Teacher shakes head yes or no without speaking.

Duration		
	A Few Seconds	Teacher stops at desk only long enough to say a word or two. Student is not expected to, or given time to, respond.
	Longer Than a Few Seconds, But Less Than a Minute	Teacher engages in conversation with student but reaches closure rapidly. Student is given time to ask question or respond to teacher's comment.
	More Than A Minute	Teacher allows two, three, or more exchanges to occur. Teacher may reteach needed content, work through one or more problems with student, or give student additional problems to identify specific weaknesses. Teacher may allow noninstructional conversation to occur, which increases contact time.

Zone		
	1—Front	
	2—Left Front	
	3—Right Front	
	4—Left Rear	
	5—Right Rear	

Zone 1	Desk
Zone 2	Zone 3
Zone 4	Zone 5

student contact: to encourage, praise, or correct with no opportunity for student response; to encourage, praise, or correct with opportunity for student response; and to reteach or diagnose specific weaknesses with opportunity for student response.

Finally, the physical movement of the teacher is recorded by checking zones rather than by the process of recording movement among individual seats. Although this method is less accurate than the visual map, it can be used to detect general zone biases. Zone 1 represents the case when students are expected to come to the teacher to have their work checked. Divisions among the other zones can be determined arbitrarily by assigning an equal number of desks to each.

To conclude our discussion of engaging students in the learning process, we have summarized our reactions to Mr. Swade's lesson in Figure 10.9. How does our checklist compare with yours? We saw signs of three out of five behaviors for engaging students in the learning process in Mr. Swade's classroom. Although incomplete, Mr. Swade's monitoring and checking behaviors are also commendable. All things considered, we feel that Mr. Swade deserves high marks for this lesson.

Cultural Diversity and Student Engagement

We have seen that a teacher's task orientation and student engagement must go hand-in-hand in order to be effective. A task-oriented teacher who maximizes content coverage and gives students the greatest opportunity to learn will have little effect on learning if students are not involved, acting on, and otherwise thinking about the material being presented. Likewise, students who are actively engaged, but in ways that are irrelevant to the goals of the lesson, will fail to learn. The key to bringing these two important dimensions of effective teaching together rests with how the teacher interacts with students to invoke a willingness to respond and apply what they have been learning: to practice what has been presented with exercises, classroom activities, homework assignments, and projects. In classrooms where individual, cultural, and ethnic differences are prominent, student engagement in the learning process can be a major challenge to achieving performance outcomes.

One facet of research dealing with cultural diversity and student engagement has focused on differ-

FIGURE 10.9 Checklist for Mr. Swade's Classroom

Behavior	Observed	Not Observed	No Opportunity to Observe
1. Provides for guided practice	✓ Used two oral (choral response) and one written (individual response) exercise		
2. Provides feedback to guided practice	✓ Extends, lifts student responses and uses as transitions		
3. Uses individualized or self-directed materials and activities to promote learning, when appropriate			✓ Not enough information; check with respect to Alex on next observation
4. Uses meaningful verbal praise	✓ Affirms partially right answers		
5. Monitors seatwork by circulating and frequently checking progress		✓ Began monitoring seatwork but stopped halfway through to return to desk	

ences in fluency and oral expression among learners. For example, Kendon (1981, 1967) has studied how student fluency or quickness to respond can be influenced by nurturing and expressive qualities of the teacher. The implication of these findings is that student hesitancy in responding and becoming engaged in the learning process may, for some cultural groups, be more a function of the attitude and cultural style of the teacher than of student ability. Douglas (1975) has shown that student engagement is, in part, an expression of the interactive process between student and teacher. Specifically, her research has found that body posture, language, and eye contact form a pattern of metacommunication that is recognized by the learner and acted on according to the message being conveyed, intentionally or not. For example, a formal body posture and questions posed in an expressionless voice, without eye contact, may not invoke a commitment to respond. In other words, teachers must convey a sense of caring about the learner before engagement can take place. Engagement techniques alone (eliciting the desired behavior, providing feedback, individualizing instruction, praising, and monitoring) will not be sufficient to actively engage students in the learning process unless they are accompanied by the appropriate metacommunication expressing nurturance and caring (Noddings, 1992). Bowers and Flinders (1991) suggest some of the ways teachers can promote student engagement by conveying a sense of nurturance and caring. Their suggestions include:

❑ Use appropriate examples to clarify concepts and model performance. "Let me give you an example that will help you see the relationship."

❑ Accept student's way of understanding new concepts. "That's an interesting answer. Would you like to tell us how you arrived at it?"

❑ Reduce feelings of competitiveness. "Today, those who wish to can work with a partner on the practice exercise."

❑ Increase opportunities for social reinforcement. "If you like, you can ask someone sitting nearby how they worked the problem."

❑ Facilitate group achievement. "When you're finished with your work, you can join another group to help them solve the problem."

❑ Praise and respond to students regardless of who they are or how they perform. "Those of you who have finished the first part, keep working. I'll be helping the others."

❑ Use and expect culturally appropriate eye contact with students. "Amanda, I'm going to sit down next to you and watch you work the first problem."

❑ Recognize longer pauses and slower tempo. "Take your time. I'll wait for you to think of an answer."

❑ Respond to unique or different questions during a response. "You're asking about something else. Let me give you that answer, and then we'll go back to the first question."

❑ Balance compliments and reinforcement equally. "Let's not forget, both Angel and Damon got the right answer, but in different ways."

Although much is still unknown about cultural diversity and student engagement, one thing is clear: Students of any culture, but especially culturally, ethnically, and linguistically different learners, are more likely to engage in the learning process in an atmosphere that

1. Emphasizes the importance of unique learner responses.
2. Reduces feelings of individual competitiveness.

3. Teaches social reinforcement and peer interaction.
4. Conveys a sense of nurturance and caring.

In the remaining chapters, we will turn our attention to two equally important lenses through which to observe classrooms. These lenses—student success and higher thought process—are always observed in the context of the dimensions of student engagement. As we turn now to our next lens—student success—keep in mind the significant impact of the dimensions of student engagement studied in this chapter.

ACTIVITIES*

1. Using the checklist provided in Figure 10.2 as your guide, observe a lesson for signs of student engagement. At the end of your observation, add a brief written description to each box, highlighting at least one reason why you chose to place each of your checkmarks as you did. Using your written descriptions as a guide, write a paragraph about the reasons for the student engagement, or lack thereof, in this lesson.

2. Using the examples of five-point scales shown in Chapter 4, convert the positively stated indicators of student engagement listed in Figure 10.1 into the form of a Likert scale. Consider the vertical and/or horizontal placement of each indicator on the page, whether words will be affixed to all or only some of the response blanks, and what response alternatives will be best suited to each question. Show your scale to a classmate who has also constructed a five-point scale. Together, create a single revised version, incorporating the best features of both scales.

3. Using the seven-point, polar scale described in Chapter 4 as an example, convert the positive and negative indicators in Figure 10.1 into this scale format and observe a lesson for student engagement. At the end of your observation, complete the scale by indicating with a checkmark the degree to which this lesson achieved each dimension of student engagement. Use the code *N/O* for any items that you did not have the opportunity to observe. Reflecting on

---

*Some of the following activities may be grouped into a common activity, divided among classmates, and completed from a single observation.

your experience as a student and previous classroom observations, place an *X* on the blank that, in your opinion, corresponds to the degree of student engagement found in most classrooms. Note the difference between your ratings for this lesson and what might be typical student engagement. Cite the reasons this lesson was the same, higher, or lower on each dimension.

4. Using the form provided in Instrument 10.1 for recording eliciting activities and their proximity in time to the presentation of content, observe a classroom for an entire lesson or class period. Total the number of entries you have made in each column and in each row of the form. List any other eliciting activities that you observed during this lesson and include them in your totals. What was the preferred communication channel for presenting eliciting activities in this classroom (oral, written, or visual)? How close to the content presentation were the eliciting activities in this classroom? Identify two different eliciting activities, not observed, that would be most appropriate interspersed throughout this lesson, two that would be most appropriate as exercises at the end of the lesson, and two that would be most appropriate for homework.

5. Observe a classroom discussion or question-and-answer session. At the start of the first student question, record the question-answer-feedback sequences using Instrument 11.1 (p. 259). Complete a set of codes for at least ten question-answer-feedback sequences involving different students.

6. Using the categories of individual and self-regulating learning activities provided in Instrument 10.2 and any others that you believe are relevant, identify one example from a classroom you have observed. List your example on a 5″ × 7″ index card, with the grade and subject matter (if applicable) to which the activity pertains. Place your card with those of your classmates in a central location, so that everyone may read and copy these cards for the grades and subject matter most relevant to their teaching specialization.

7. Using the record in Instrument 10.3, observe for at least one period three different teachers teaching similar content at approximately the same level. Total the number of entries for each of the three delivery modes, the first two types of praise combined, and the third and fourth types of praise combined. Recall that these last two cat-

egories generally are considered meaningful praise. Using the formula

$$\frac{\text{Number of incidents of praise}}{\substack{\text{Number of minutes of observation} \\ \text{time during which opportunities for} \\ \text{praise were present}}} \times 60 = \text{praise rate/hour}$$

calculate the praise rate for each of the three modes of delivery and then for each of the two (combination) types of praise. In each of the three classrooms, what is the ratio of the number of incidents of the first two types of praise to the number of incidents of the last two types of praise? Did you find more instances of meaningful praise in one classroom than in the others? How would you account for the differences in terms of the teacher's personality, student ability, and lesson content? What model(s) of delivering praise was (were) preferred by the teacher in each of the classrooms?

8. Observe part of a lesson involving seatwork (for example, students completing exercises in a workbook, on a handout, or in a text), during which the teacher is monitoring and checking student progress. Draw a visual map of the classroom and indicate the placement of each occupied seat. Draw your map so that a blank space in which tallies can be placed is left to the side of each seat. During the seatwork, determine (and record) whether the student occupying each seat on the map appears engaged or disengaged by scanning each student consecutively. Enter codes, such as + for engaged and - for disengaged. Use 0 for any student whose engagement cannot be determined. Complete five consecutive rounds, placing your codes sequentially alongside each seat on the map. At the end of the fifth round, draw a series of connected lines indicating the path taken by the teacher to monitor the work of individual students during this time. Code another five rounds and complete another picture of the teacher's path. Do you see any relationship between the path taken by the teacher and your codes for engaged and disengaged students?

9. Using Instrument 10.4, which combines mode of feedback, duration of contact, and teacher movement, observe a classroom in which students are responding to an eliciting activity. Choose a student characteristic (for example, sex, ethnicity, or ability level) for which teacher bias may unintentionally occur. Place a code for this characteristic under the column labeled *Contact*, and then complete the record as indicated for each time that feedback is provided to an individual student.

Use your completed record to see if you can detect any bias about the student characteristic you have chosen. What mode of feedback is preferred by this teacher? What is the average duration for each of the three modes of feedback? Were all zones covered?

INSTRUMENT 10.1   Record for Observing Eliciting Activities

Date: _____   Lesson Content: _____

Eliciting Activity	Proximity of Eliciting Activity to Content Presentation				
	Interspersed (Throughout Content Presentation)	Immediate (At End of Content Presentation)	Interrupted (At End of Class, Separated by Other Activities)	Delayed (For Homework)	Indefinite (At Student's Discretion)
Oral Questions					
Exercises in Text or Workbook					
Problems Presented in Handout					
Activities Written on Board or Overhead					
Other					

INSTRUMENT 10.2   Categorizing the Use of Individualized and Self-Regulatory
Learning Materials and Activities

Individualized/Self-Regulating Materials

❑ Remedial/alternative learning material:

_____
_____
_____

❑ Programmed learning materials:

_____
_____
_____

❑ Game and stimulation materials:

_____
_____
_____

❑ Audiovisual media:

_____
_____
_____

❑ Computer/software:

_____
_____
_____

❑ Resource/reference/library:

_____
_____
_____

❑ Other:

_____
_____
_____

❑ Performance contracting:

_____
_____
_____

❑ Learning centers:

_____
_____
_____

❑ Peer tutoring:

_____
_____
_____

❑ Group discussion:

_____
_____
_____

❑ Teams, pairs:

_____
_____
_____

❑ Independent projects:

_____
_____
_____

❑ Other:

_____
_____
_____

INSTRUMENT **10.3**   Praise Contingent on a Specific Performance

Time	Number	Delivery Mode			Types of Praise				
		Oral	Body Language	Written	Gives Neutral Affirmation	Expresses Surprise, Delight, or Excitement	Explains Value	Uses, Extends, Picks Up On	Other
	1								
	2								
	3								
	4								
	5								
	6								
	7								
	8								
	9								
	10								
	11								
	12								
	13								
	14								
	15								
Rate									

INSTRUMENT 10.4 Format for Observing the Relationship Among Different Monitoring and Checking Behaviors

Contact[a]	Mode of Feedback			Duration			Zone				
	Oral	Written	Body Language	A Few Seconds	More Than a Few Seconds But Less Than One Minute	More Than One Minute	1	2	3	4	5
1. _____	❑	❑	❑	❑	❑	❑	❑	❑	❑	❑	❑
2. _____	❑	❑	❑	❑	❑	❑	❑	❑	❑	❑	❑
3. _____	❑	❑	❑	❑	❑	❑	❑	❑	❑	❑	❑
4. _____	❑	❑	❑	❑	❑	❑	❑	❑	❑	❑	❑
5. _____	❑	❑	❑	❑	❑	❑	❑	❑	❑	❑	❑
6. _____	❑	❑	❑	❑	❑	❑	❑	❑	❑	❑	❑
7. _____	❑	❑	❑	❑	❑	❑	❑	❑	❑	❑	❑
8. _____	❑	❑	❑	❑	❑	❑	❑	❑	❑	❑	❑
9. _____	❑	❑	❑	❑	❑	❑	❑	❑	❑	❑	❑
10. _____	❑	❑	❑	❑	❑	❑	❑	❑	❑	❑	❑

[a]These blanks can be used to record an individual's ability level (less able, LA; average, AV; more able, MA), sex (M, F), ethnicity, or other characteristic for which bias might occur.

Chapter 11

MEASURING STUDENT SUCCESS

The Elfman

I met a little Elfman once,

Down where the lilies blow.

I asked him why he was so small,

And why he didn't grow.

He slightly frowned and with his eye

He looked me through and through.

"I'm quite as big for me," said he,

"As you are big for you."

J. K. Bangs

One of the great challenges of teaching is creating an environment in which your students can succeed and yet be challenged enough to grow. Add to this the need to evaluate student growth and progress—to decide "how big" a student is—and you have what some educators view as an insurmountable task. How do effective teachers encourage student success? And how do they know when it occurs? The answers to these questions are critical for understanding effective teaching.

The Little Elf, (1968). In N. Larrick (Ed.) *Piping down the valleys wild* (p. 75). New York: Dell.

An important focus of research on student engagement has been the level of difficulty at which content is presented. One way of determining level of difficulty is to measure the rate at which students understand and correctly complete exercises based on the material taught. Three measures of success have been used to gauge level of difficulty: *high success*, in which the student understands the task and makes only occasional or careless errors; *moderate success*, in which the student has partial understanding but makes substantive errors; and *low success*, in which the student does not understand the task at all and makes many errors. Findings indicate that as the teacher becomes more task-oriented and student engagement goes up, the learner can master more difficult content with higher rates of success.

For the direct instruction model, for example where knowledge, comprehension, and application outcomes are desired, a moderate to high rate of success on practice problems, workbook assignments, and oral exercises usually corresponds with higher levels of task orientation and student engagement in the learning process, higher levels of student self-esteem, and more positive attitudes toward the subject taught (Rosenshine & Stevens, 1986; Bennett, Desforges, Cockburn, & Wilkinson, 1981; Fisher et al., 1980). The average student in a typical classroom spends about half of his time working on tasks that provide the opportunity for high success. Researchers have discovered that students who spend more than the average time in high-success activities during expository or didactic teaching have higher achievement scores, better retention, and more positive attitudes toward school (Greenwood, Delguardi, & Hall, 1984; Wyne & Stuck, 1982). These findings suggest that, during direct instruction, students should spend from 60 to 80 percent of their time on tasks that allow an opportunity for moderate to high levels of success, and that students should make only occasional careless errors the first time through the material (Rosenshine, 1983; Brophy & Evertson, 1976).

During indirect instruction, where the analysis, synthesis, and evaluation levels of behavioral complexity are emphasized, the success rate attained may be less important than the conditions under which it occurs. Here the goal is to achieve moderate success, but also to emphasize *functional failure* (Rohrkemper & Corno, 1988). Functional failure occurs when a wrong or partially correct response prompts additional cues (e.g., probes from teacher, responses of other students) that can modify the task ("Can you think of an example of your own?") or situation ("Could you write it on the board") to help the learner attain success on repeated trials. In this chapter, we will use the phrase *moderate to high rates of success* to represent both the functional failure important to attaining outcomes at higher levels of behavioral complexity and the correct, quick, and firm responses important to attaining outcomes at lower levels of behavioral complexity.

A moderate to high success rate helps produce mastery of the lesson content, but even more important is that it provides an opportunity for the student to use learned knowledge in practical ways, such as answering questions or solving problems. Tasks providing moderate to high success rates allow the pieces that are learned to fall into place, a crucial final step in the learning process. Some classrooms do not devote enough time to this stage of learning. Organizing and planning instruction that yields moderate to high success rates without being boring or repetitive—or wasting time—is a key behavior for effective teaching. In this chapter, you will learn how to observe some of the instructional activities and tasks that influence student success—and how to improve your students' chances for success.

DIMENSIONS OF STUDENT SUCCESS

Figure 11.1 summarizes behaviors that promote student engagement in the learning process at moderate to high rates of success, including:

1. Establishing unit and lesson content that reflects prior learning.
2. Providing mediated feedback to extend and enhance student learning.
3. Planning units and lessons at, or slightly above, the learners' current level of understanding.
4. Making transitions to new content in small, easy-to-grasp steps.
5. Establishing momentum that keeps students engaged in the learning process.

PRACTICE OBSERVING STUDENT SUCCESS: A DIALOGUE

The following dialogue illustrates several dimensions of student success. Review the dimensions in Figure 11.1 and then read the dialogue, using the checklist in Figure 11.2 to look for signs of student success.

In this dialogue we look into Ms. Chau's classroom, where she is teaching her students the rules of writing. The curriculum guide specifies a unit on forming and punctuating possessives, but it is vague about how to teach this topic. Ms. Chau has decided to organize her lesson into rules for using possessives. Today's lesson, which will be used as a point of

FIGURE **11.1** Indicators for Rates of Success

Moderate to High Rates of Success (Effective Teacher)	Poor Rates of Success (Ineffective Teacher)
1. Established unit and lesson content that reflects prior learning (for example, planning lesson sequences that consider task-relevant prior information)	Fails to sequence learning in advance to ensure that all task-relevant prior knowledge has been taught before moving to next lesson
2. Provides mediated feedback to extend and enhance student learning	Leaves students on their own to practice and learn immediately after presenting new content; waits until next day to show correct responses
3. Plans units and lessons at, or slightly above, learners' current level of understanding (for example, establishes bite-size lessons that can be easily digested by learners at their current level of functioning)	Packages instruction in chunks that are too large or too small (for example, teaches a lesson that is too complex too early in an instructional sequence)
4. Plans transitions to new material in easy-to-grasp steps (for example, changes instructional stimuli according to a preestablished thematic pattern so that each new lesson is seen as an extension of previous lessons)	Changes instructional topics or perspectives abruptly from one lesson to another without themes and interconnections
5. Varies the pace at which stimuli are presented and continually builds toward a climax or key event	Maintains same pace continuously, leading to a monotonous and static level of intensity and expectation

FIGURE **11.2** Checklist for Observing Success Rate

Behavior	Observed	Not Observed	No Opportunity to Observe
1. Unit and lesson organization reflects task-relevant prior learning			
2. Provides mediated feedback to extend and enhance student learning			
3. Plans levels at, or slightly above, students' current level of understanding			
4. Plans transitions to new content in small, easy-to-grasp steps			
5. Establishes momentum (for example, pacing and intensity gradually build toward major milestones)			

departure for introducing possessives, follows several previous lessons on the parts of speech.

Ms. Chau: Today we will learn how to avoid embarrassing errors such as this [points to and circles an incorrectly punctuated possessive in a newspaper headline] when forming and punctuating possessives. At the end of the period, I will give each of you several examples of errors taken from my collection of mistakes found in newspapers and magazines. You will make the proper corrections and report them to the class. Who knows what a possessive is? [Bobby waves his hand.]

Bobby: It means you own something.

Ms. Chau: Yes, a possessive is a way to indicate ownership. It comes from the word *possession*, which means "something owned" or "something possessed." Forming possessives and punctuating them correctly can be difficult, as this newspaper example shows [points to error in headline again], but I will give you two simple rules that will help you form possessives correctly. Before we can form possessives, however, we must know who or what is doing the possessing. Mary, can you recall the parts of speech from last week's lesson? [Mary hesitates and then nods.] What part of speech is most likely to own or possess something?

Mary: Well, umm . . . I think . . . I think a noun can own something.

Ms. Chau: Yes. A noun can own something. What is an example of a noun that owns something? Tommy.

Tommy: I don't know.

Ms. Chau: Debbie.

Debbie: Not sure.

Ms. Chau: Ricky.

Ricky: A student can own a pencil. The word *student* is a noun.

Ms. Chau: Good. Who can remember our definition for a noun? [Pointing to Jim.]

Jim: It's a person, place, or thing.

MS. CHAU: Good. Our first rule will be: Use the possessive form whenever an "of" phrase can be substituted for a noun. [Ms. Chau points to this rule, which has been written on the board.] Let's look at some phrases on the board to see when to apply this rule. Darnell, what does the first one say?

Darnell: The daughter of the policeman.

Ms. Chau: How else could we express the same idea of ownership?

Mary: We could say "the policeman's daughter."

Ms. Chau: And we could say "the policeman's daughter" because I can substitute a phrase starting with "of" and ending with "policeman" for the noun, *policeman*. Notice how easily I could switch the placement of "policeman" and "daughter" by using the connective word "of." Whenever this can be done,

you can form a possessive by adding an apostrophe and an *s* to the noun following "of." Now we have the phrase [writes on board] *policeman's daughter* [points to the apostrophe]. Keisha, what about our next example, *holiday of three days?*

Keisha: We could say "three days' holiday."

MS. CHAU: Come up and write that on the board just the way it should be printed in the school paper. [Keisha writes *three day's holiday*.] Would anyone want to change anything? [Susan raises her hand, and Ms. Chau nods.]

Susan: I'm not sure, but I think I would put the apostrophe after the *s* in *days*.

Ms. Chau: You're right, which leads to our second rule: If the word for which we are denoting ownership already ends in an *s*, place the apostrophe after, not before, the *s*. This is an important rule to remember because it accounts for many of the mistakes that are made in forming possessives. As I write this rule on the board, copy these two rules into your notebooks for use later. [Ms. Chau finishes writing the second rule on the board.] Now let's take a moment to convert each of the phrases on the overhead to the possessive form. Write down your answer to the first one. When I see all heads up, I will write the correct answer. [All heads are up.] Good. Now watch how I change this first one to the possessive form. Pay particular attention to where I place the apostrophe, and then check your answer with mine. [Ms. Chau converts *delay of a month* to *month's delay*.] Any problems? [Ms. Chau pauses for any response.] Okay, do the next one. [After all heads are up, Ms. Chau converts *den of lions* to *lions' den*.] Any problems? [Darnell looks distressed.] Darnell, what did you write?

Darnell: [Pronouncing each letter] L-I-O-N-apostrophe-S.

Ms. Chau: What is the noun?

Darnell: [Still sounding uncertain] Lions.

Ms. Chau: Look at what you wrote for the second rule. What does it say?

Darnell: Add the apostrophe after the *s* when the word already ends in an *s*. Oh, I get it. The noun already has the *s*, so it would be *s* apostrophe. That's the mistake you showed us in the headline, isn't it?

Ms. Chau: Now you've got it. Let's continue. [Ms. Chau proceeds with the following phrases in the same manner: *speech of the president* to *president's speech*, the *television set of Mr. Eggar* to *Mr. Eggar's television set*, and *pastimes of boys* to *boys' pastimes*.] Now open your workbooks to the exercise on page 87. Starting with the first row, let's go around the room and hear your possessives for each of the sentences listed. Spell the word indicating ownership aloud so we can tell if you've placed the apostrophe in the right place. Debbie.

Debbie: [Looking at *wings of geese*] Geese's wings . . . spelled W-I-N-G-S-apostrophe.

Ms. Chau: That's not correct. What word is doing the possessing?

Debbie: The geese, so it must be G-E-E-S-E-apostrophe-S.

Ms. Chau: Good. Next.

Alan: The author's work . . . spelled A-U-T-H-O-R-apostrophe-S.

Ms. Chau: Okay, next.

REACTIONS TO THE DIALOGUE

Which of the five dimensions of student success did you see in the dialogue? Recall that students should experience a moderate to high success rate that helps produce mastery of the lesson content and provides an opportunity for them to use learned knowledge in practical ways, such as answering questions or solving problems. Tasks providing moderate to high success rates allow the pieces that are learned to fall into place, a crucial final step in the learning process. Organizing and planning instruction that yields moderate to high success rates without being boring or repetitive—or wasting time—is a key behavior for effective teaching.

Planning Unit and Lesson Content That Reflects Prior Learning

As you can guess, obtaining a moderate to high success rate begins with unit planning: unit outcomes should be identified, and a logical sequence of lessons should be developed to achieve those outcomes. Surprisingly, teachers sometimes plan units with little or no consideration given to lesson sequence. Although certain unit outcomes may be achieved by giving learners content in any order, the cost in instructional time can be considerable. The result of this type of planning is often heard in expressions such as "I've run out of time," ". . . couldn't get to topic X," or ". . . too many interruptions to finish the unit."

Effective unit planning involves arranging lessons in a sequence that works for, not against, you. Some teachers do not realize that making each new lesson relate to a previous lesson can result in great savings in instructional time. Task-relevant prior knowledge is placed immediately preceding, or as close in time as possible to, the lesson or lessons in which it will be needed. The savings in time results from not having to reteach task-relevant prior learning—or from not having to reteach a lesson after it is discovered that the necessary task-relevant information has not been learned. A considerable amount of instructional time can be wasted by backtracking to remedy fact, skill, or con-

cept deficiencies. This waste can be eliminated by better planning. Effective unit planning results in a sequence of instruction that gradually builds to unit outcomes in a logical, systematic order. This emphasizes the importance of unit plans—without them, content may be randomly thrown at learners, some of whom may be struggling to make the transition from earlier lessons.

Lesson plans result in higher rates of success and increased achievement when

1. *Unit* outcomes are identified at higher levels of behavioral complexity than *lesson* outcomes.
2. Lesson content is planned so that outcomes of previously taught lessons are instrumental in building toward and achieving the outcomes of subsequent lessons.
3. Lesson content derives from unit outcomes in small pieces suitable for presentation in one or two instructional periods.
4. Lesson content is added to or rearranged when necessary to provide the task-relevant prior knowledge required for subsequent learning.

When lessons are planned without any thought to a higher level unit outcome, attention falls exclusively on each individual lesson without consideration to the relationships among the lessons. The result of such an assembly of isolated lesson outcomes might be confusion, anxiety, and resentment on the part of the students, regardless of how meticulously each lesson was delivered or how effective it was in accomplishing its stated, but isolated, outcome.

Let's gain some insight into this dimension by looking at how Ms. Chau's lesson fits into a sequence of instruction on the parts of speech. A graphic model of the content in today's lesson and in the previous lesson might appear as shown in Figure 11.3.

Notice from this model that knowledge of the parts of speech is task-relevant prior knowledge for today's lesson. This content had to precede today's lesson for students to be able to recognize the nouns used in forming and punctuating possessives. For Ms. Chau's lesson, the behaviors acquired from a previous lesson are required to achieve the intended outcomes for today's lesson. Also notice the progression of outcomes from the knowledge level to the application level. This series of topics begins with teaching the definition of a noun, and ends with applying this knowledge in combination with Rules 1 and 2 to form and punctuate possessives. Thus, this series of topics ends at a higher level of behavioral complexity than it began, and proceeds in a least-complex (knowledge) to most-complex (application) order.

Ms. Chau relies on an understanding of task-relevant prior knowledge to begin her lesson when she

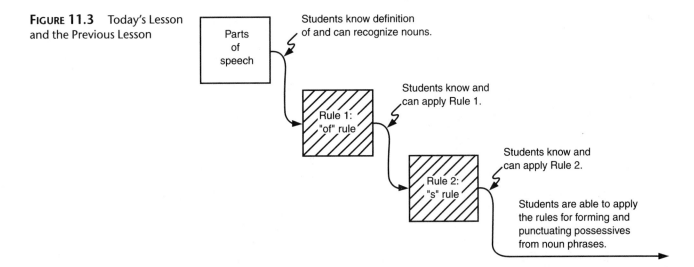

FIGURE 11.3 Today's Lesson and the Previous Lesson

asks, "Who can remember our definition for a noun?" Fortunately, Jim remembers, and this provides Ms. Chau the opportunity to present her first rule, which presupposes a knowledge of nouns. Ms. Chau's lesson may presuppose other task-relevant knowledge as well. Some of this knowledge may be familiar to students from other contexts; for example, recognition of an apostrophe and a prepositional phrase. By examining the success rate in Ms. Chau's classroom and the type of correctives used to remediate incorrect or partially correct responses, we gain an impression of how well her task-relevant prior knowledge has been taught. To determine the success rate of students in this classroom, let's examine the question-answer-feedback sequences used by Ms. Chau to evaluate and correct her students' responses.

In Figure 11.4 all the key question-response sequences in the dialogue are coded using the format suggested by Good and Brophy (1987) and described in Chapter 4 (see also Instrument 11.1). Notice that the data are recorded according to three categories of information: correctness of student answer (right, partially right, wrong response, no response), teacher response to student answer (praise, affirm, negate, criticize), and teacher feedback to student (gives answer, explains, asks other, etc.). To determine the success rate of this sequence of questions, we would divide the total number of correct (+) or correct plus partially correct (+/-) responses by the total number of student responses: (9/15)100 = 60%. Since there were no partially correct responses, our final percentage will be based solely on completely correct answers. Question 7, directed to Darnell, received no student response tally because it was nonsubstantive, asking only that Darnell read what was written on the board. It did not require that she apply any of the content of the lesson. Thus, the total number of correct stu-

dent responses to the total number of substantive questions asked by Ms. Chau was actually 9/14, not 9/15, revising the success rate upward to about 64 percent.

As noted previously, research suggests that, for direct instruction, a success rate of 60 to 80 percent the first time through the material is optimal for achievement, retention, and positive attitude toward the subject matter. This success rate helps produce mastery of the lesson content and correct, quick, and firm response patterns, while ensuring that the material is not so easy that it becomes boring and disengages students from the learning process. It also ensures that new content is covered, thus affording students an opportunity to learn. We saw that Ms. Chau's classroom met and may have slightly exceeded this mark. It is not possible to know what Ms. Chau's final success rate for this lesson will be or how heterogeneous her class is, which could require adjustments of the flow and difficulty of her presentation later in the lesson. From the trend established thus far, however, we might expect a high success rate by the end of the lesson as students are confronted with more practice opportunities and have a greater opportunity to learn from the mistakes of others. A 60 percent success rate at the beginning of a practice activity changing to an 80 percent or better success rate by the end is a good target to shoot for.

Observing Unit and Lesson Content That Reflects Prior Learning

As we have seen, lessons should be sequenced so that all task-relevant information required for a lesson has been taught in preceding lessons. The sequence of lessons within a unit can be arranged by describing the unit goal and the objectives for each

FIGURE 11.4 Coding Form and Example Data for Observing Success Rate

Number	Student	Student Response[a]				Teacher Response					Teacher Feedback						
		+	+/-	-	0	++	+	0	-	--	Gives Answer	Explains	Asks Other	Other Calls	Repeats	Clue	New Question
1	Bobby	✓					✓					✓					
2	Mary	✓					✓										
3	Tommy				✓		✓							✓				
4	Debbie				✓		✓							✓				
5	Ricky	✓				✓												
6	Jim	✓				✓												
7	Darnell						✓											✓
8	Mary	✓					✓						✓					
9	Keisha			✓				✓										
10	Susan	✓					✓						✓					
11	Darnell			✓				✓									✓	
12	Darnell	✓					✓											
13	Debbie			✓					✓								✓	
14	Debbie	✓				✓												
15	Alan	✓					✓											
	Totals	9	0	3	2	3	5	6	1	0	0	3	2	0	0	2	1

[a]See Figure 4.13 for an explanation of the symbol and codes used.

individual lesson, as shown in Figure 11.3. This graphic format can be used for any number of lessons, with the sequence shown by connecting arrows. The key to observing this dimension is noting the relationships among lessons. For each lesson objective, two questions should be asked: Has all task-relevant information needed to attain the objective been taught earlier in the sequence? and When prerequisite skills are required for a lesson, have they been taught (or are they scheduled to be taught) close in time to the lesson in which they are needed? To answer these questions and complete a graphic model of the unit, the following information will be needed from the classroom teacher who will be observed.

Unit title: _____

Goal or objective that expresses the highest level of behavior to be attained (knowledge, comprehension, application, etc.) for the unit: _____
_____

Number of lessons in the unit: _____

Topic of first lesson: _____

Objective: _____

Level of behavioral complexity (knowledge, etc.):

_____

Topic of second lesson: _____
_____

Objective: _____
_____

Level of behavioral complexity (comprehension, etc.): _____

This recording format should be continued for each lesson in the unit. The level of behavioral complexity can be determined from lesson plans, text, handouts, exercises, and so on, and then expressed as outcomes in the cognitive, affective, and psychomotor domains. Figure 11.5 provides a guide for selecting behaviors in the cognitive, affective, and psychomotor domains.

From the information already recorded, a diagram like the one in Figure 11.3 can be drawn. Connecting arrows can show the sequence of lessons planned for the unit, if relevant, and the boxes can show the objective for each lesson and for the entire unit. As the behavioral complexity increases (for example, from

FIGURE 11.5 A Guide to Selecting Behaviors in the Cognitive, Affective, and Psychomotor Domains

Cognitive	Affective	Psychomotor
1. *Knowledge*—Learner can recognize and recall facts (define terms, recall names/dates, identify words).	1. *Receive*—Learner is aware of listening to or passively attending to certain stimuli.	1. *Imitation*—Learner, when exposed to a visual model, can repeat the model.
2. *Comprehension*—Learner can interpret, translate, summarize, or paraphrase material.	2. *Respond*—Learner complies with expectations by participating or obeying.	2. *Manipulation*—Learner can follow written directions independent of a visual model to complete an action.
3. *Application*—Learner can use material in a situation that is different from that in which it was originally learned.	3. *Value*—Learner displays behavior consistent with a belief or attitude in situations with which she is not forced to comply.	3. *Precision*—Learner attains skill in performing an action independent of either a visual or verbal model, attaining accuracy and control.
4. *Analysis*—Learner can separate a complex topic into its parts, drawing comparisons and establishing relationships among the elements.	4. *Organization*—Learner is committed to a set of values and displays, provides rationale for, or communicates the values.	4. *Articulation*—Learner can coordinate a series of acts by establishing appropriate sequence and accomplishing harmony or internal consistency among different acts.
5. *Synthesis*—Learner can combine, pieces, parts, or elements and arrange them into a new, original form.	5. *Characterization*—Learner's total behavior is consistent with values (internalizes them).	5. *Naturalization*—Learner can routinely perform an action; attains spontaneity, automaticity, and smoothness.
6. *Evaluation*—Learner can make decisions, judge, or select based on a set of criteria.		

Note: Based on Bloom, Englehart, Furst, Hill, and Krathwohl, 1956 (cognitive domain); Krathwohl, Bloom, and Masia, 1964 (affective domain); and Harrow, 1972 (psychomotor domain).

knowledge outcomes in early lessons to comprehension or application outcomes in later lessons), the objectives of previous lessons should reflect the required prerequisite behavior for the subsequent lessons. If this is not the case, or if you believe the intended lesson sequence can be improved in some way, redraw the graphic model to indicate a lesson sequence in which all required task-relevant knowledge is taught prior to each lesson.

Providing Mediated Feedback to Extend and Enhance Learning

A second behavior for achieving moderate to high rates of student success is the provision of feedback that can extend and enhance an initially crude or incomplete response (Cooper, Heron, & Heward, 1987). During guided practice, when the desired behavior is elicited for the first time, correctives should be given immediately after the learner's initial response. As noted in Chapter 10, the amount of time between practice and feedback is one of the most important elements of learning. The longer feedback is delayed, the less likely it is to influence the learner's performance on subsequent attempts

to produce the behavior, because the learner must maintain a mental image of the crude first response for the feedback to be effective. Unfortunately, mental images fade quickly, especially in young learners, so the effectiveness of the feedback deteriorates rapidly with any delay. For the learner to link feedback to his image of the response, the corrective must follow immediately; for example, by calling out the right answer after each practice item has been completed during direct instruction, or by having a student write on the board how a partially correct answer was attained during indirect instruction. Also, to promote spontaneity and risk-taking behavior, which are necessary for revising and refining an initially crude response, feedback should be administered in a noncritical atmosphere.

Rosenshine (1983) has identified four categories of student response and strategies for handling these responses to extend and enhance an initially crude or incomplete response. The first category, which most teachers hope to inspire, is *correct, quick, and firm* student responses. Although such responses most frequently occur during the later stages of a direct instruction lesson, they can occur at almost any time and in the context of other types of instructional goals. A moderate to high percentage of correct, quick, and firm responses is important if students are to stay actively engaged in the learning process. Rosenshine suggests that the best teacher response to a correct, quick, and firm student response is to ask another question of the same student. This increases the potential for feedback. If time does not permit, quickly move on to another student with a similar question. The teacher should keep the lesson moving at a brisk pace, involving as many students in the practice exercise and covering as many problems as possible (Rodgers & Iwata, 1991). Attaining a moderate to high rate of correct answers will establish, a rhythm and momentum that will heighten student attention and engagement and provide for a high level of task orientation. Also, a brisk pace of right answers, especially during direct instruction, will help ensure that irrelevant student responses and classroom distractions are kept to a minimum.

The second category of student response is *correct but hesitant* responses, which frequently occur in a practice or question-and-answer session. It is important to provide positive feedback to the student who supplies a correct but hesitant response. The first feedback that should be provided in this instance is a positive, reinforcing statement, such as "Good" or "That's correct," because the correct but hesitant response is likely to be remembered more easily when it has been linked to a warm and acknowledging reply. This helps to make the student's next response to the same type of problem correct, quick, and firm.

Affirmative replies are rarely sufficient in themselves to effect significant changes in subsequent responses of the same type unless the reasons behind the hesitation are addressed. Although discovering the precise reason for a student's hesitant response is desirable, a quick restatement of the facts, rules, or steps needed to obtain the right answer often accomplishes the same end more efficiently. This restatement will aid the student giving the correct but hesitant response and reduce subsequent wrong or hesitant responses from other students who hear the restatement and incorporate it into their own responses.

The third category of student response includes *incorrect but careless* responses. Sometimes as much as 20 percent of student responses fall into this category, depending on the time of day and the students' level of fatigue and inattentiveness. When this occurs, the temptation is to scold, admonish, or even verbally punish students for responding thoughtlessly when they know the correct response. Researchers and experienced teachers agree that attempting to deal emotionally with this type of problem (for example, with statements like "I'm ashamed of you," or "That's a dumb mistake," or "I thought you were brighter than that") often results in more harm being done than good.

Verbal punishment rarely teaches a learner to avoid careless mistakes. Experience has shown that the rhythm and momentum built and maintained through a brisk and lively pace can easily be broken by off-task attention to an individual student. Emotional reaction rarely has a positive effect; the best procedure is to acknowledge that the answer is wrong and then move immediately to the next student for the correct response. The point will be made to the careless student by immediately passing the opportunity to respond and receive recognition to the next student.

The final category includes responses that are *incorrect because of a lack of knowledge*. Such errors typically occur, sometimes in large numbers, during the initial stages of a lesson or unit and throughout indirect instruction. Providing hints, using probes, or changing the question or task demand to a simpler one that engages the student in finding the correct response is more desirable than merely giving the student the correct response. The goal is not to get the correct answer from the student in any way possible, but to engage the learner in a process to find the right answer. Any time an instructional task can channel a student's thoughts in ways that result in the right answer without the teacher giving that answer, a framework has been provided for producing a correct response in all subsequent problems of a similar nature. Some common strategies for mediating feedback in this manner are

❑ Reviewing key facts or rules needed for a correct response.
❑ Explaining the steps used to reach a correct response.
❑ Asking the learner to take time to think before moving on to the next learner.
❑ Prompting with clues or hints (adjusting the situation or context).
❑ Taking a different path with a similar problem and guiding the student to the correct solution (changing the task).

The use of these strategies to make on-the-spot adjustments in content difficulty and pacing to accommodate individual learning needs is called *teacher mediation* (Duffy & Roehler, 1989). The teacher's role during mediation is to adjust the instructional dialogue to help students construct their own meanings and restructure their responses, moving them closer to the intended outcome.

Teacher mediation is accomplished by adjusting the pace and level of content (through brief reviews, questions, prompts, and wait time) to provide cognitive stimulation at the proper time to help the learner acquire the intended outcome through her own reasoning. This on-the-spot adjustment in the difficulty and pacing of lesson content should be targeted to the level of content difficulty and behavioral complexity from which the student can most benefit at that moment.

This level of content difficulty and behavioral complexity, called the learner's *zone of maximum response opportunity* (Borich, 1996; Vygotsky, 1978), is the zone of behavior that, if stimulated by the teacher, will bring a learner's response to the next level of refinement. Thus, a teacher's response directed at the zone of maximum response opportunity must be at, or near, the learner's current level of understanding, but also designed to lift the learner's response to the next level. The teacher's response directed to the zone of maximum response opportunity need not elicit the correct answer, because the learner at that precise moment may be incapable of benefiting from it. It should, however, encourage the learner to refine an initially crude response. The concept of a *zone* affords the teacher latitude within which to construct and create meanings and understandings that consider the unique learning needs of the student. Because this type of corrective feedback is delivered orally within the naturally occurring dialogue of the classroom, its effects can benefit the entire class.

During indirect instruction, the success rate after mediated feedback is less important than the instructional dialogue, which can help students create their own meanings and understandings and move them closer to the intended outcome. Typically, success rates for the entire class are considerably lower during indirect instruction than rates during direct instruction, sometimes as low as 40 to 60 percent (compared with 60 to 80 percent at the beginning of guided practice). Since time and breadth of content do not allow sampling the behavior of large numbers of students during indirect instruction, a few students who reflect the general composition of the class can be chosen to check whether the concept, pattern, or relationship has been learned by most of the class. At this time teacher mediation and the learners' zones of maximum response opportunity can play a critical role in promoting a gentle interplay between learner and teacher, pulling and pushing each participant in a student-response–teacher-reaction dialogue that helps each learner climb to the next rung of the learning ladder.

In what ways could students learn from their mistakes in Ms. Chau's classroom? Ms. Chau tends to praise or affirm correct answers, and only occasionally reacts neutrally to or negates a wrong answer. This suggests that Ms. Chau places more emphasis on motivating students to risk making a response—any response—than in passing judgment on the responses given. Presumably her goal at this stage of the lesson is to get and keep students responding by making them feel comfortable enough that their risk-taking behavior will not embarrass or humiliate them should it produce a wrong, illogical, or even funny response. Thus, Ms. Chau tends to ignore nonresponses, and sometimes even wrong responses, quickly moving to another student.

Finally, Ms. Chau tends to provide feedback to her students, either by explaining a correct response further or, in the case of a wrong response, by providing clues useful in finding the correct response. An example of explaining comes after Ms. Chau asks her first question: "Who knows what a possessive is?" Bobby replies, "It means you own something." Ms. Chau responds, "Yes, a possessive is a way of indicating ownership. It comes from the word *possession*, which means 'something owned' or 'something possessed.'" Here the teacher not only affirms the response, but uses it as an opportunity to explain more fully the meaning of Bobby's response. An example of clueing comes when Darnell looks distressed about giving a wrong response (*L-I-O-N-apostrophe-S*) to *home of lions*. The teacher responds, "What is the noun?" thereby focusing Darnell on the content of Rule 2. Still, Darnell seems not to understand, so the teacher focuses her still more with the clue, "Look at what you wrote for the second rule." These examples indicate how student responses, whether correct, partially correct, or incorrect, can be followed up with explanations and clues that further enhance the original response and provide new content. A moderate to high success rate will depend on the teacher's liberal use of feedback, which can correct and expand wrong or partially wrong student responses in ways that benefit the entire class.

Observing Mediated Feedback to Extend and Enhance Learning

The second behavior for achieving a moderate to high success rate can be recorded using the Good and Brophy (1987) student-response–teacher-reaction instrument shown in Instrument 11.1. Recall that a student's response (right, partially right, wrong, no response) is recorded, followed by the teacher's reaction to the response (praise, affirm, negate, criticize), followed by the type of feedback given by the teacher (gives answer, explains, asks other, etc.). This instrument is suitable for observing and recording student success rate pertaining to oral questions because both the teacher's reaction to a student response and the nature of the feedback given are recorded in sequence. Also, by tallying the number of correct oral responses given by students during a practice exercise, the observer can determine the percentage of correct responses. Instrument 11.1 provides example data using the Good and Brophy coding categories.

In this example, the first question-answer-feedback sequence indicates that Dave responds correctly, after which the teacher praises him and then explains why the answer was correct. In the second exchange, Mark responds to a question with a partially correct answer; the teacher affirms the answer, but then gives the complete answer followed by an explanation of why it is correct. After a sufficient number of exchanges, the success rate for all students can be determined by adding the total number of correct (or correct plus partially correct) student responses, dividing by the total completed rows), and multiplying the result by 100. The final result is an estimate of the success rate of all students expressed as a percentage—60 to 80 percent is desirable the first time through the material if the lesson is didactic or expository. If problem-solving, inquiry, or discovery learning is the goal of the lesson, a success rate of approximately 40 to 60 percent (from a steering group) may be more appropriate (40 percent representing about the minimum percentage of correct or partially correct responses needed to establish a degree of classroom momentum).

An observer can analyze why a success rate below, equal to, or above this mark was achieved by looking for patterns of teacher feedback. For example, if the teacher were to continue in the manner illustrated, a moderate to high success rate might have been achieved as a result of always praising or affirming a response when it was correct or even partially correct, and then following with an explanation to the student (with all the class listening) of why the response was correct. Patterns in other classrooms may indicate that praise, affirmative explanation, and clues tend to correspond with a high degree of teacher mediation in which correct responses are built around the students' own interpretations and meanings of content shared in the context of a classroom dialogue.

When student success is the primary focus of the observation, another instrument with an abbreviated format (Instrument 11.2) can be used to simplify the observation and recording process. Complete this record for a lesson in which guided practice will be provided in the form of oral questions to the class, recitation of workbook content,

responses to items on written exercise, and so on. Try to observe several lessons—at the beginning, middle, and end of a unit—that vary in behavioral complexity, and then compare success rates. The complexity may vary from higher success (for knowledge), to medium (for application), to lower (for analysis). These percentages can be recorded using the format in Figure 11.6.

A 60 to 80 percent success rate should be attained the first time through the material if task-relevant prior skills have been taught and the instructional content is clearly presented. A 60 percent success rate is not uncommon when only the percentage of right answers is considered, but close to an 80 percent success rate should be attained when the number of entries in both the right and partially right columns are combined, especially if the lesson is wholly or mostly didactic.

Because behavioral complexity tends to be lower for lessons at the beginning of a unit and higher for lessons toward the end, entries may occur first in the top left to bottom right diagonal of the recording format. Because not all units are placed in an order of least complexity to highest complexity, entries in other cells of the table may also occur. These entries may have the lowest success rates when lesson sequence does not take into account task-relevant prior information; for example, when behavioral complexity jumps from high for a lesson at the beginning of a unit to low for a lesson in the middle, and back to high again at the end of a unit. Be sure to note any changes in success rate over the different levels of behavioral complexity.

Other ways of calculating student success rate include averaging the number of correct student responses on a class, workbook, or homework assignment and determining the percentage of students who attain a score of, say, 80 percent correct. For example, assume ten students achieved the following scores after an assignment worth 30 points: 24, 16, 24, 25, 30, 26, 29, 24, 21, 28. Eight of the ten students, or 80 percent of this class, achieved 80 percent or more correct responses. The average score among all students is 24.7, which is slightly above the 80 percent mark ($30 \times .80 = 24$) and indicates a moderate to high rate of success when going through the material for the first time.

Another approach to determining success rate, appropriate for a heterogeneous classroom, is to record expected as well as actual scores of each student on a class, workbook, or homework assignment. For example, assume the following scores on a 30-point assignment were obtained from a heterogeneous group of ten students: 18, 28, 16, 15, 22, 29, 18, 22, 24, 26. But let's ask the teacher before

FIGURE 11.6 Comparing
Success Rate Percentages

Success Rate for Lesson	Relatively Low Complexity	Medium Complexity	Relatively High Complexity
At beginning of unit			
In middle of unit			
At end of unit			

grading the assignment to indicate what score might be expected from each student on this assignment. Each expected score is chosen to reflect a realistic degree of progress, given the student's prior learning history. Now let's assume the expected scores have been recorded for each of the ten students and placed next to their actual scores, as indicated in Figure 11.7.

Using our method for determining success rate, we find that only four students, or 40 percent of this class, are expected to equal or exceed a score of 24, or 80 percent correct. The average actual score for the class is 21.8, indicating that the performance of the class on this assignment is below the 80 percent mark. Notice, however, that eight out of the ten students met or exceeded expectations; only two did not. Thus, in terms of student expectations, this class did fairly well. When classes are heterogeneous or are marked by problem learners, absolute standards can be unrealistic indicators of success rate. In these cases, the percentage of students meeting or exceeding expectations, when formulated with a knowledge of the unique learning history of each learner, will be more indicative of the true success rate within a classroom.

Planning Units and Lessons At, or Slightly Above, Students' Current Level of Understanding

The third behavior for achieving a moderate to high success rate is matching unit and lesson plans to the learners' current level of understanding. Experience has shown that units should cover less content than might be originally desired simply because the depth and breadth of content that is comprehensible to the teacher seldom is comprehensible at the same depth and breadth to learners. Units that ramble through many historical periods, physical laws, mathematical operations, social issues, or elements of composition may prevent learners from attaining the larger concepts, organizing principles, and relationships for which the unit was intended.

Content selection mistakes at the unit level can spell trouble at the lesson level. For instance, if a unit topic is too broad, the teacher might make the component lessons broad to cover the unit content in the specified period of time. Difficulties may then occur at the lesson level when trying to establish moderate to high success rates. As lesson content becomes broader, it must necessarily become less detailed,

FIGURE 11.7 Expected Vs.
Actual Scores for Ten Students

Student	Expected	Actual	Difference
1	14	18	+4
2	26	28	+2
3	16	16	0
4	12	15	+3
5	20	22	+2
6	24	29	+5
7	18	18	0
8	24	22	−2
9	20	24	+4
10	28	26	−2
	Mean Actual Score = 21.8		

which often leaves less time for adequate periods of guided and independent practice. In the rush to cover the content, some of the content may be compromised. Also, behaviors at higher levels of complexity may be taught without adequate attention to the task-relevant prior facts, rules, and sequences that may be necessary to attain them. The temptation to walk across mountain tops may cause the teacher to miss some valleys that must be crossed as well.

Perhaps most perplexing to new teachers is deciding at which level of behavioral complexity a lesson should begin. Does a lesson always begin by teaching facts (to instill knowledge), or can a lesson begin with activities at the application, or even synthesis and decision-making, levels? All of these alternatives are possible, but each makes different assumptions about the behavioral characteristics of the students and the sequence of lessons that has gone before. Beginning a lesson or a sequence of lessons at the knowledge level (to list, recall, recite, etc.) assumes that the topic of the lesson is mostly new material. Such lessons usually occur at the beginning of a sequence of lessons that use this knowledge to build toward more complex behaviors—perhaps ending at the application, synthesis, or evaluation level. When no task-relevant prior knowledge is required, the starting point for the lesson is often at the knowledge or comprehension level. Lessons that begin at higher levels of behavioral complexity will require task-relevant prior knowledge.

The proper level of behavioral complexity with which to start the lesson depends on where the lesson falls in the sequence of lessons. Typically, a unit plan should attempt to instill a range of behaviors and to end at a higher level of behavioral complexity than it began. Some units might begin at the application level and end at a higher one, provided a previous unit has taught the task-relevant prior knowledge

and understandings required. It is also possible in some content areas to move from one behavioral level to another within a single lesson. Although this becomes increasingly difficult when lessons start at the higher levels of behavioral complexity (for example, analysis or synthesis) because of the instructional time required to achieve these more complex outcomes, it is possible and often desirable to move from knowledge to comprehension and even to application activities within a single lesson.

Finally, individual lesson content must be at the learner's current level of understanding if moderate to high success rates are to be achieved. When lengthy guided-practice or group-discussion sessions do not provide moderate to high rates of success, lesson content may be too broad and/or too complex for learners. This is a sign that the content taught may not be bite-sized, and that the material should have been divided into smaller segments. Keep in mind also that some unfinished lessons should be continued in other lessons, especially when the unfinished content represents task-relevant learning for subsequent lessons.

Do you think Ms. Chau's division of content was understandable to her students within the context of the single lesson we observed? Without knowing more about the current level of understanding of her students, the answer must be tentative. Sufficient signs exist, however, to suggest that Ms. Chau's selection of content for this lesson was understandable to most of her students. Two signs in particular point to the fact that Ms. Chau has organized her content at the students' current level of understanding: She was able to achieve a 60 to 80 percent success rate within only a brief instructional period, and her division of content within the lesson is easily recognized by her students. Figure 11.8 shows how easy it is to identify the parts of her lesson and portray their relationship.

FIGURE 11.8 Ms. Chau's Lesson

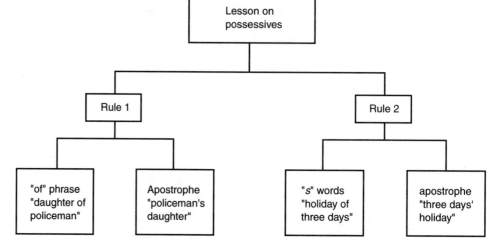

Each part is defined within the context of the lesson and labeled appropriately ("Rule 1," "Rule 2"). Definitions and examples are provided to aid the retention of each part (*daughter of policeman; holiday of three days*). Also, the presentation is organized into stages—or events—that prepare her learners to receive, understand, and practice what is presented: Her content is made more understandable by a lesson format that lets the content evolve gradually in small, distinctive steps. Figure 11.9 reviews instructional events and key phrases from the dialogue that suggest a particular model of lesson planning had been used.

Notice that we can find some reference in the dialogue to a structured approach to lesson planning. Ms. Chau not only divided her content into identifiable parts, she also divided the process by which she delivered the content into definable events known to aid learning and retention, providing a recognizable outline of a lesson plan. Ms. Chau's organization of content and its presentation in gradual steps helped students achieve a moderate to high success rate.

Observing Instruction At, or Slightly Above, the Learners' Current Level of Understanding

How a teacher achieves a moderate to high success rate can be determined from the graphic unit model (Figure 11.3) and from a tabulation of the success rates of learners (from tests, question-and-answer sessions, and practice sheets) across lessons. If the relationship between the unit goal and the objectives of individual lessons is not immediately apparent from the graphic model of the unit plan, and the average success rate for individual lessons is low, chances are that individual lessons cover more content or teach at a higher level of complexity than can be readily digested by learners. Lesson topics should fit neatly into the organizational divisions of an adopted text or curriculum guide. If a basis for lesson content cannot be found in these sources, the content may be either too broad or irrelevant to the unit goal. Both of these conditions can reduce the success rate.

Another reason for a low success rate can be the manner in which content is organized and presented within a lesson. Although there are many different ways of organizing a lesson (e.g., Hunter, 1994; Gagne, Briggs, & Wagner, 1992), most lessons (or units) should include the following instructional events:

1. Gaining the learners' attention (focusing; establishing an anticipatory learning set)
2. Informing the learner of the objective (stating the purpose and level of behavior expected)
3. Stimulating recall of prerequisite learning (reviewing task-relevant prior learning)
4. Presenting the stimulus material (input and modeling)

FIGURE 11.9 Instructional Events in Ms. Chau's Lesson

Instructional Event		Key Phrase
1.	Gaining attention	"Today we will learn how to avoid embarrassing errors such as this (circles an incorrectly punctuated possessive in a newspaper headline) . . . ."
2.	Informing learner of objective	"At the end of the period, I will give each of you several additional examples of errors taken from my collection of mistakes . . . and you will make the proper corrections and report them to the class."
3.	Stimulating recall of task-relevant prior knowledge	"Mary, can you recall the parts of speech from last week's lesson? What part of speech is most likely to own or possess something?"
4.	Presenting new content	"Our first rule will be . . . ." "You're right, which leads us to our second rule . . . ."
5.	Eliciting the desired behavior	"Let's take a moment to convert each of the phrases on the overhead to the possessive form."
6.	Providing feedback	"When I see all heads up, I will write the correct answer."
7.	Assessing the behavior	

5. Eliciting the desired behavior (providing guided practice)
6. Providing feedback and correctives (checking for understanding; closure)
7. Assessing the behavior (providing independent practice and testing)

Although not all lessons will (or should) have all of these components, each component should be discernible across a unit.

Failing to stimulate the recall of prerequisite learning (for example, by reviewing at the beginning of a lesson), elicit the desired behavior (through hands-on-activities or practice exercises), or provide feedback and correctives (by providing model answers or correcting workbooks) will result in the content of subsequent lessons becoming more difficult for most students to learn. The chart in Instrument 11.3 can be used to record how often these instructional events occur within a unit. For this record, six observations are spread across the beginning, middle, and end of a unit. Some of these observations can be completed at the same time Instrument 11.2 is used to record the percentage of correct and partially correct student responses.

For the record in Instrument 11.3, a checkmark is used to indicate the presence of any of the instructional events. The absence of checkmarks for an instructional event could indicate a bias to avoid that event frequently enough to make the unit difficult for learners to understand at their current level of understanding. The instructional events listed in Instrument 11.3 may be rephrased to follow any specific model of instructional planning, such as Hunter (1982).

Transitions Between Lesson Content

The fourth behavior for establishing moderate to high success rates involves the transitions between lesson content. Although planning lesson content in bite-size pieces helps learners make transitions between old and new content, this may not be sufficient to ensure a moderate to high success rate in question-and-answer sessions, workbook exercises, hands-on activities, tests, and practice assignments. In addition, the teacher needs to organize lesson content to establish overall themes that connect different parts of a unit. The goal is to help learners see what is being taught at the moment as part of a bigger picture. In this manner, the learner is able to build an understanding of the topic gradually and in measured steps, as opposed to receiving the big picture only at review and test times. Increasing one's understanding in a stair-step fashion is possible when there is direction and continuity among lessons; without these elements students quickly lose the underlying theme among the pieces to be learned, and learning is reduced to memorization of pieces. Unless the relationship among lessons is recognized from the start, it is unlikely to be understood by learners later. The following are common ways of relating content across (and within) lessons to create transitions in small, easy-to-grasp steps.

- *Simple to complex*—arranging unit content in a simple to complex progression so that students see each lesson as part of a hierarchy leading to more detail, greater reality, or more real-world application
- *Concrete to abstract*—arranging unit content in a concrete to abstract order (or vice versa) so that students see each succeeding lesson as a *funneling* (widening or narrowing) of facts, concepts, or principles
- *Step by step*—arranging unit content in a sequential order so that students see each succeeding lesson as a step toward a final destination or goal
- *Whole part*—arranging unit content so that a topic is introduced in its most general form and then divided into easy-to-distinguish subdivisions in succeeding lessons
- *Problem centered*—arranging unit content as a series of problems to be solved so that students see each succeeding lesson as a barrier or problem to be crossed before the next topic (lesson) can be encountered
- *Decision centered*—arranging unit content into a set of key decisions to be made so students see each succeeding lesson as a step in the decision-making process

Because some transitions across units, especially interdisciplinary units, must emphasize *lateral knowledge*, their graphic portrayal is different than disciplinary units, which emphasize *vertical knowledge* (as represented by Ms. Chau's unit plan in Figure 11.3). The graphic technique you use to express lateral knowledge must allow for content from different topic areas or disciplines to be woven in and out of lessons as the opportunity arises. Hence, a freer form, web-type visual format is required. This type of format shows how content is *nestled* within other content, how different subject areas share a common theme, how a single theme is *threaded* through different content areas, or how one field of study is *immersed* in another. Thus, all important themes and issues in an interdisciplinary plan are shown simultaneously in association with one another. The rules for creating these types of graphic outlines or webs are as follows:

- Identify the most essential theme or idea
- Place this theme or idea in the center of your web.

□ Use arrows or lines going outward from the main idea to show relationships with other, subordinate issues, topics, or content, which can become the topics of individual lessons.

□ Label the arrows and all key concepts with code words or phrases to describe the relationships you have expressed.

This approach will help you and your students visualize connections that go beyond those expressed in the textbook. The principal aim of interdisciplinary instruction is to present learners with an opportunity to discover relationships and patterns that often extend beyond a specific discipline, systematically binding different aspects of our world together. Interdisciplinary units often represent themes that can be related to several different disciplines or subject-matter areas at the same time; for example, to English or reading, science, social studies, and the expressive arts. Effective interdisciplinary units also often require learners to go beyond the instruction provided—to conduct research that requires the cooperation of other learners, the independent use of materials, and classroom dialogue in which learners are expected to reason critically, ask questions, make predictions, and, with the aid of the teacher, evaluate the appropriateness of their responses. Figure 11.10 provides an example of the use of a thematic web to express the interrelationship of ideas among lessons.

As you have seen, this dimension for achieving a moderate to high success rate involves the thematic or conceptual thread that runs across lessons and binds them into a meaningful whole at the unit level. These themes or concepts are usually presented in the form of organizers that interconnect the concepts presented in adjacent lessons. These themes or concepts are sometimes readily observable in graphic models of unit plans, which indicate relationships among content and events.

Organizers can include whole-part, simple to complex, concrete to abstract, step-by-step, problem-centered and decision-centered approaches to organizing content across and within lessons. The key to achieving this dimension is to create a theme that will provide continuity across related lessons and be apparent to students within any lesson in the sequence. In this manner, students are provided a means of keeping in touch with the big picture and, at the same time, seeing the details of the present lesson in relation to it.

How do you think Ms. Chau did with respect to this dimension? It may be difficult to tell without seeing her unit plan; however, a number of possibilities are apparent. Recall that Ms. Chau begins the lesson by showing a punctuation mistake in the headline of a newspaper. One possible approach to this sequence of lessons might be to recognize and correct grammatical errors as they appear in real contexts (for example, newspapers, and magazines).

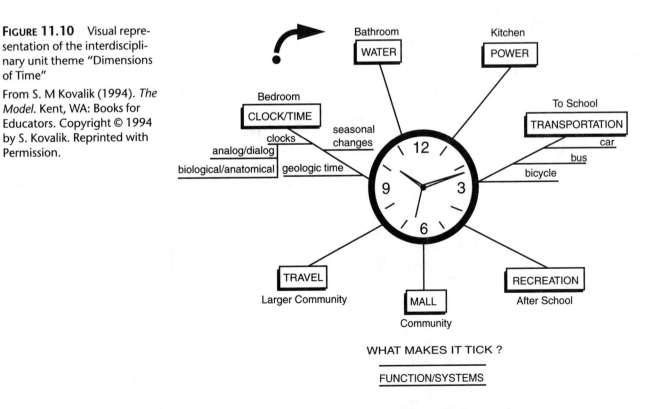

FIGURE 11.10 Visual representation of the interdisciplinary unit theme "Dimensions of Time"

From S. M Kovalik (1994). *The Model.* Kent, WA: Books for Educators. Copyright © 1994 by S. Kovalik. Reprinted with Permission.

Every lesson might begin with examples of errors that have been published in one form or another (to arouse interest) and end with exercises that ask students to find and correct the relevant errors (to apply the concepts). Another approach suggested in Ms. Chau's lesson was when and how to use Rules 1 and 2 (a decision-oriented theme). Here the goal is to recognize when various rules are applicable and to decide which rule to use in what order. Finally, Ms. Chau could use a step-by-step approach, emphasizing how rules can be used in sequence, and establishing an easy-to-remember order in which to retain and apply different types of rules. A chart could be made over the course of the unit to represent the flow of decisions that would govern the choice of one rule over another. With each of these approaches, the teacher would establish a theme at the beginning of the unit and carry it through each and every lesson, providing continuity and transitions to new content in familiar, easy-to-grasp steps.

Observing Transitions Between Lesson Content

Transitions at the beginning and end of lessons help interconnect the concepts that will be required later to achieve unit outcomes. One way of establishing an interconnection between lessons is to use advance organizers (Luiten, Ames, & Aerson, 1980; Ausubel, 1968). Recall from Chapter 7 that an advance organizer at the end of one lesson or at the beginning of the next provides learners with a conceptual preview that helps prepare the learner to store, label, and package lesson content for retention and later use. Advance organizers, presented orally or in the form of charts and diagrams, provide an overview of the day's work and the topics to which it will subsequently relate. Many advance organizers are creative inventions of the teacher that help students see the underlying thread that binds lessons together within a unit.

For this observation, you will need to use the knowledge you acquired from studying a unit plan and completing some of the previous observation records. Following the general form for recording advance organizers (Instrument 7.2, p. 144), observe two lessons in sequence, indicating whether a simple to complex, concrete to abstract (or reverse), step-by-step, whole-part, problem-centered, or decision-centered relationship can be noted across the lessons. Use your knowledge of the teacher's unit plan, if available, to help you. Note any organizers that bind these lessons together in some logical way but do not fit any of the standard designations. These creative organizers are often the most effective because they are tailor-made for a particular unit of content and for a classroom of learners who may have specialized skills, experiences, and backgrounds.

Establishing Momentum That Engages Learners in the Learning Process

The final behavior for establishing moderate to high success rates is related to several other teaching behaviors that have already been discussed. This last dimension adds a subtle but important feature to the establishment of the weekly and monthly review and testing cycles discussed in Chapter 9. This new feature involves the forward movement, expectancy, and sense of accomplishment that exist within a classroom—the *momentum*.

Momentum is established by varying the pace at which tasks are presented during the process of reaching a climax or key event. In teaching, this can be accomplished by first establishing cycles of weekly and monthly review, feedback, and testing, and then gradually increasing the pace and intensity as the time for the major event draws near. Playing the same instructional note—or keeping the same monotonous pace too long—may be as boring as listening to a drab and lifeless musical score. Consequently, rising and falling action must be established to set the instruction moving toward a discernible goal. Classroom activities that help establish a pace or tempo of rising and falling action include:

❏ Review and feedback
❏ Tests and quizzes
❏ Homework
❏ In-class workbook assignments
❏ Performance or skill evaluations
❏ Lab assignments
❏ Oral presentations
❏ Extended essays
❏ Independent projects

For example, momentum can be the result of gradually increasing the coverage and depth of weekly reviews until the time for a comprehensive monthly review arrives. The objective would be to create a review cycle that rises and falls in one-month cycles. The low point of the cycle would occur at the start of a unit, when only one week's material is reviewed. The reviews would then become increasingly comprehensive until a major monthly review restates and checks for understanding of all of the previous month's learning. Momentum is built by targeting greater and greater amounts of instruction for review, but in gradual stages so that students are not overwhelmed by unfamiliar review content and always know what will be covered. Both teacher and students continually work toward a product that is clearly seen as a meaningful intermediate step to achieve the desired behavioral outcome at the end of the unit. Most important, this creates a sense of forward movement, expectancy, and accomplishment that instills in the learner a desire to achieve at moderate to high rates of success.

What did you think of Ms. Chau's momentum—the sense of forward movement, expectation, and accomplishment in her lesson? Momentum is established by the intensity with which a lesson builds toward clearly established milestones. Recall that homework, seatwork, feedback sessions, and class quizzes are some of the vehicles with which momentum can be established within a classroom. A moderate to high success rate often depends on an organized unfolding of events such as these to give learners opportunities for accomplishment, and to keep them alert and looking forward to each new opportunity and expected activity. Momentum can be established across lessons with weekly or monthly schedules of assignments, review, testing, and feedback, and within lessons with a sequence of instructional events that gradually builds intensity and student expectation. We do not have information about Ms. Chau's weekly or monthly schedule, which would indicate the major goals toward which her students are working. We can note, however, that the brisk instructional pace established within her lesson appears to engage most of her students in the learning process. This was achieved through an orderly progression of instructional events that include a variety of presentation modes (visual, oral, and written) and classroom activities (questions and answers, examples on overheads, and recitation using problems in the workbook). All of these elements contributed to a high level of student involvement and a moderate to high success rate. Returning to Ms. Chau's classroom another time to determine the extent to which this momentum continues throughout the unit would be a good idea.

Observing Momentum

Momentum regulates the intensity with which lesson content builds toward major milestones. Homework, seatwork, prepared handouts, feedback sessions, and class quizzes leading to a major event, such as a test, term paper, research project, or oral report often create a tempo, or rhythm, of activity within a classroom. A moderate to high success rate often depends on an organized succession of events that gives learners opportunities both to practice and respond and to look forward to new and challenging activities. The rising and falling action cre-

ated by weekly or monthly schedules gives students goals to work toward and the motivation to keep working, improving their individual success rates. Without this organization and the momentum it creates, life in classrooms becomes static and dull, eventually disengaging students from the learning process and from actively practicing the concepts and skills taught.

The record in Instrument 11.4 can be used to observe major events that might create momentum and cycles of rising and falling action. Using the symbols in Figure 11.11, note the activities that occur in a classroom over a period that corresponds roughly to a grading period. Make your entries at the end of each observation so that the record represents the activities that actually occurred—not those that were planned. Up to four codes may be recorded for any given day.

A moderate to high success rate is promoted by the use of these and similar activities utilized throughout a grading period, rather than concentrated at one time (for example, tests only at the beginning and end). A variety of activities systematically placed over the entire grading period are necessary to establish a rhythm of rising and falling intensity and a sense of forward movement, expectation, and accomplishment.

We have summarized our reactions to Ms. Chau's lesson in Figure 11.12. We gave Ms. Chau high marks on this lesson because we observed at least some evidence of all of the dimensions for achieving a moderate to high success rate. If time permitted, however, we might return to Ms. Chau's classroom during a problem-solving, inquiry, or discovery lesson to see if her success can be repeated at higher levels of behavioral complexity.

Cultural Diversity and Student Success

One of the most recent advances in the study of cultural diversity has focused on the influence of teacher mediation and feedback on learner success. The work of Palincsar and Brown (1989) and Bowers and Flinders (1991) has underscored the importance of the diverse patterns teachers must use in responding to student questions and answers in a heterogeneous classroom.

There are two important dimensions of the teacher's role in controlling and modifying classroom dialogue to foster the goals of instruction. One of these dimensions is teacher mediation—on-the-spot adjustments made by the teacher to extend or refocus a student response to move the learner to the next rung of the learning ladder. The second dimension focuses on *mental modeling*, a topic addressed in the next chapter.

FIGURE 11.11 Codes for Instrument 11.4

T	Test, quiz, or departmental exam
H	Homework exercise
F	Feedback given on test or major assignment
R	Review of content (before a test or at regularly scheduled intervals)
A	In-class assignment due (workbook exercises, essay)
I	Independent study time (e.g., for catching up)
O	Oral presentation, performance, or report
L	Lab assignment/activity
R	Research project/paper due
P	Performance evaluation (assessment of how to pronounce the vowels, adjust a microscope, swing a bat, etc.)
Ot	Other

As we have seen in this chapter, teacher-mediated learning comprises on-the-spot adjustments in the level of content and pacing during a lesson in which the learner is an active participant. In teacher-mediated learning, more learners are encouraged to participate in the question-and-answer dialogue of the classroom, because the content and pacing are continually adjusted to each participant's current level of understanding. Typically, researchers have found that student success rate (frequency of correct responses) during teacher-mediated dialogues increases compared to traditional lessons in which the teacher conveys content exclusively through explaining and lecturing (Floden, 1991).

The explanation for these findings derives from the research on meaningful verbal learning (Ausubel, 1968), in which learners who were given the opportunity to construct their own interpretations and meanings from content were able to retain content longer and more easily generalize it to new contexts. The role of the teacher in these learning contexts is to take the acquired interpretations, experiences, and meanings expressed by learners to the next level of refinement through the use of follow-up questions, probes, and the responses of other learners. Thus, the teacher's response to a correct answer, a correct but hesitant answer, an incorrect or partially correct answer, or a careless answer can be chosen on the basis of the idiosyncratic needs of the learner.

These results have been applied to culturally diverse classrooms through various forms of social interaction that encourage students to construct their own meanings and interpretations, and to revise and extend them under the guidance of the teacher. Of the many techniques for promoting the concept of teacher mediation, among the most popular are *reciprocal teaching* (Palincsar & Brown, 1989) and problem-based learning (Blumfield et al., 1991). Both involve the teacher eliciting student responses at the student's current level of understanding based on personal experiences with, assumptions about, and predictions from the content to be taught. This is followed by classroom dialogue in which the teacher and learners participate in revising and refining earlier responses. The steps by which this is accomplished are

❑ *Predicting.* Discussion begins by generating predictions about the content to be learned from the text, based on
  a. its title or subheading in the text
  b. the group's prior knowledge or information pertaining to the topic
  c. experience with similar kinds of information

Following the group's predictions about what they expect to learn from the text, the group reads and/or listens to a portion of it.

❑ *Questioning.* One individual is chosen to lead a discussion of each portion of the text that is

FIGURE **11.12** Checklist for Ms. Chau's Classroom

Behavior	Observed	Not Observed	No Opportunity To Observe
1. Unit and lesson organization reflects task-relevant prior learning	✓ Lesson in sequence with parts of speech		
2. Provides mediated feedback to extend and enhance student learning	✓ Tends to praise and affirm right and partially right answers; treats wrong answers and nonresponses neutrally		
3. Plans lessons at, or slightly above, learners' level of understanding	✓ Divides lessons into small, easy-to-grasp rules		
4. Plans transitions to new content in small, easy-to-grasp steps			✓ Opportunity for several interconnecting themes, but no chance to observe related lessons to see if any are operating
5. Established momentum, for example, pacing and intensity gradually build toward major milestones			✓ Momentum evident within lesson as a result of changing activities; no evidence available about momentum across lessons

read. Afterward, the discussion leader asks questions about the information. Students respond to the questions and raise additional questions.

❑ *Summarizing.* The discussion leader summarizes the text, and other students are invited to comment or elaborate on the summary.

❑ *Clarifying.* If points in the text are unclear (e.g., concepts or vocabulary), they are discussed until clarity is achieved. In this case, more predictions may be made and portions of the text may be reread for greater clarity.

Notice how with these steps the teacher is able to support the participation of all students in the classroom dialogue. The teacher's aim is to engage as many students as possible in the learning process by providing reactions to student responses that are in their zones of maximum response opportunity. This is accomplished by (1) offering ample opportunity for students to participate in the dialogue from their perspective and (2) elaborating on student responses with prompts, wait time, and questions that guide subsequent responses. Thus, the teacher mediates the instruction by adjusting the flow and complexity of content to accommodate individual learning needs. These are important elements of instruction to look for when observing student success.

In the next and final chapter, we turn our attention to observing higher thought processes and performance outcomes. As we turn to this lens through which to observe classrooms, keep in mind the significant impact of the dimensions of student success studied in this chapter.

ACTIVITIES*

1. Using the checklist in Figure 11.2 as your guide, observe a lesson for signs of student success. At the end of your observation, add a brief written description to each box, highlighting at least one specific reason why you chose to place each of your checkmarks as you did. Using your written descriptions, write a paragraph about the reasons for the student success, or lack thereof, found in this lesson.

2. Using the examples of five-point scales in Chapter 4, convert the positively stated indicators of student success listed in Figure 11.1 into the form of a Likert scale. Consider the vertical and/or horizontal placement of each indicator on the page, whether words will be affixed to all or only some of the response blanks, and what response alternatives will be best suited to each question. Show your scale to a classmate who has also constructed a five-point scale. Together, create a single, revised version incorporating the best features of both.

3. Using the seven-point polar scale described in Chapter 4 as an example, convert the positive and negative indicators in Figure 11.1 into this scale format and observe a lesson for signs of student success. At the end of your observation, complete the scale by indicating with a checkmark the degree to which this lesson achieved each dimension of student success. Use the code *N/O* for any items that you did not have the opportunity to observe. Reflecting on your experience as a student and previous classroom observations, return to the scale and place an *X* on the blank corresponding to each scale item that, in your opinion, represents the degree of student success found in most classrooms. Note the differences between your ratings for this lesson and the typical average student success rate across most classrooms. Cite the reasons this lesson was the same, higher, or lower on each dimension.

4. Using a teacher's lesson plan, textbook, and/or curriculum guide, identify a unit goal and the lesson objectives that relate to it. From this information and following the examples in this chapter, construct a graphic model of the content taught in this unit, using either the vertical box model shown in Figure 11.3 or the lateral web model shown in Figure 11.10. Be sure to label all concepts and indicate where lesson sequence is important to achieving task-relevant prior knowledge.

5. (Instrument 11.1 may be used for Activities 5 and 6.) Using the Good and Brophy question-answer-feedback instrument presented in Chapter 4 (Figures 4.12 & 4.13), observe and code a practice or recitation session lasting 15 minutes or longer. Try to select a time when students are expected to respond orally to questions or problems in a workbook, on a specially prepared handout, on the chalkboard, or on an overhead. At the end of the session, determine student success by adding the total number of correct student responses, dividing the number by the total number of questions or problems coded, and multiplying by 100. Create a second index of student success by combining correct responses with any partially correct responses that have been coded. What is the percentage difference between these two values? If the content was presented for the first time, which index of student success might be more sensitive to the instruction that took place?

6. Turn to the Teacher Feedback section of the Good and Brophy coding form used in Activity 5. Look for a predominant pattern of teacher reaction and feedback to the student responses coded (a) correct, (b) partially correct, and (c) incorrect. Do you see any differences in the teacher's reaction and feedback to student responses in these three categories? Do these differences explain why this teacher achieved the success rates identified in Activity 5?

7. Using the Good and Brophy question-answer-feedback instrument, observe and code an inquiry, problem-solving, or discovery lesson. Try to select a lesson in which there will be student discussion and questions and answers. Use the question and answers to determine the rate of student success, and compare the rate with that obtained in Activity 5. Did you observe any teacher mediation during this lesson?

---

*Some of the following activities may be grouped into a common activity, divided among classmates, and completed from a single observation.

8. Prior to a scheduled test or graded assignment, ask the teacher to indicate expected scores that would indicate a reasonable amount of progress had been made by each student, given her ability and learning history. Using the scores achieved by each student on the test or assignment, calculate the success rate for the class by determining (a) the percentage of students who achieved 80 percent correct (if a test) or 60 percent correct (if an assignment involving new content), and (b) the percentage of students who met or exceeded expectations. How do these two values differ? Which would you accept as the most accurate index of success in this particular classroom?

9. Join a group to observe at least one lesson using the form provided in Instrument 11.3 for recording instructional events. After all members of the group have completed their observation(s), transfer all the checkmarks onto a master record. Be sure to place each checkmark in the appropriate column indicating placement in the unit (beginning, middle, or end). Analyze the master record to determine (a) which instructional events were most frequently observed, (b) which were least frequently observed, and, if apparent, (c) which instructional events were more frequently observed at the beginning of a unit than at the end.

10. Using your knowledge of scales from Chapter 4, create a five- or seven-point instrument to measure the degree to which transitions to new content within and between lessons are made in small, easy-to-grasp steps. Select from among the following dimensions to build your scales, and/or provide dimensions of your own.

> Amount of time spent introducing a new topic
>
> Use of verbal markers to place new content in perspective
>
> Amount of content contained within a single lesson
>
> Use of visual devices that show content organization
>
> Number of students off-task at beginning of new topic

When completed, make copies and exchange your instrument with other observers. As a group, pick the best scale from each observer's instrument. Using the best scale from each instrument, construct one final instrument. Observe at least one lesson with it, and report back to the group any further revisions you would make.

11. Choose a classroom with which you can have extended contact. Using Instrument 11.4, record any major activities (tests, reviews, assignments) that establish a sense of forward movement, expectancy, and accomplishment. Add any other major events you learn about in conversation with the teacher. In your opinion, does this class have a sense of forward movement, expectancy, and accomplishment? How might its momentum be improved?

INSTRUMENT 11.1   Coding Form and Example Data for Observing Success Rate

Number	Student	Student Response[a]				Teacher Response					Teacher Feedback Reaction						
		+	+/−	−	0	++	+	0	−	− −	Gives Answer	Explains	Asks Other	Other Calls	Repeats	Clue	New Question
	Dave	✓				✓						✓					
	Mark		✓				✓				✓	✓					

[a] + rights, ± partially right, −wrong, o no response, ++ praise, + affirm, o no response, − negative, − − criticize. See Figure 4.13 for an explanation of the codes used.

INSTRUMENT 11.2
Abbreviated Format for
Observing Student Success

Lesson Number _____	Right	Partially Right	Wrong	No Answer
Student Response				
1.	❏	❏	❏	❏
2.	❏	❏	❏	❏
3.	❏	❏	❏	❏
4.	❏	❏	❏	❏
5.	❏	❏	❏	❏
6.	❏	❏	❏	❏
7.	❏	❏	❏	❏
8.	❏	❏	❏	❏
9.	❏	❏	❏	❏
10.	❏	❏	❏	❏
11.	❏	❏	❏	❏
12.	❏	❏	❏	❏
13.	❏	❏	❏	❏
Totals	____	____	____	____
Percentages (totals + number of responses x 100)	____	____	____	____

INSTRUMENT 11.3   Recording the Frequency of Seven Instructional Events Within a Unit

Instructional Events	Lessons					
	Beginning of Unit		Middle of Unit		End of Unit	
	1	2	3	4	5	6
Gaining attention						
Informing learner of objective						
Stimulating recall of prerequisite learning						
Presenting the stimulus material						
Eliciting the desired behavior						
Providing feedback and correctives						
Assessing the behavior						

INSTRUMENT 11.4   Format for Observing Events That Create Momentum

	Mon.	Tues.	Wed.	Thur.	Fri.
Week 1					
Week 2					
Week 3					
Week 4					
Week 5					
Week 6					

Chapter 12

LOOKING FOR HIGHER THOUGHT PROCESSES AND PERFORMANCE OUTCOMES

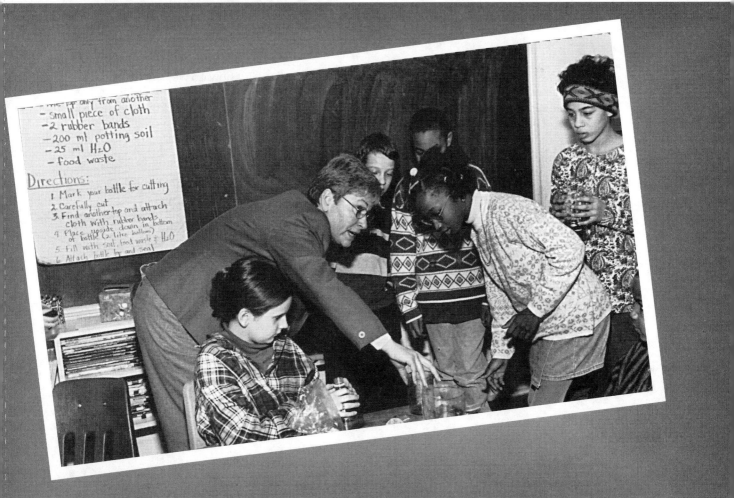

Be Like the Bird

Be like the bird, who

Halting in his flight

On limb too slight

Feels it give way beneath him,

Yet sings

Knowing he hath wings.

Victor Hugo

To give our students wings is the noble goal of education! But how do we help them find their way into the heights of higher thought processes and performance outcomes? In this chapter, we'll explore ways teachers help their students push beyond the concrete and the present to the abstract and the future . . . .

Favorite Poems Old and New, selected by Helen Ferris. Garden City, New York: Doubleday and Company, Inc., 1957, p. 280.

In this chapter we will observe teaching and learning activities that promote higher thought processes and performance outcomes, such as critical thinking, reasoning, and problem solving, that cannot be measured by paper-and-pencil tests of achievement alone. Your students, for example, may be able to recite all the rules of grammar without hesitation, but be unable to write about a simple event that they have experienced. They may understand the reasons behind world tensions but be unable to solve problems cooperatively. They may know a law of science but be unable to demonstrate how that law works in real life. They may know the cellular structure of plant life but be unable to use a microscope to see what they know. They may be enthusiastic about communicating their thoughts to close friends but be afraid to make an oral presentation to the class.

These performance outcomes require analysis, synthesis, and decision making that are believed to be stimulated more by interaction with others (peers and adults) and by an awareness of one's own learning than by books and lectures. Many of these behaviors require interaction with others to unleash the motivation required for complex thought and performance.

Teaching students to think critically, reason, and solve problems requires several unique teaching functions, including:

❑ Demonstrating mental models and strategies for learning
❑ Illustrating how these strategies are to be used to think through solutions to real-world problems
❑ Encouraging learners to become actively involved in the subject matter by going beyond the information given, restructuring it according to their own way of thinking and prior understanding.
❑ Gradually shifting the responsibility for learning to students through practice exercises, question-and-answer dialogues, and/or discussions that engage them in increasingly complex patterns of thought
❑ Monitoring, correcting, and evaluating student responses as needed

In this chapter, we will see how each of these teaching functions can be attained—and observed.

DIMENSIONS OF HIGHER THOUGHT PROCESSES AND PERFORMANCE OUTCOMES

Figure 12.1 summarizes the behaviors that promote higher thought processes and performance, including:

1. Using collaborative and group activities
2. Demonstrating mental models and strategies
3. Arranging for student projects and demonstrations
4. Engaging students in oral performance
5. Providing opportunities for students to learn from their mistakes
6. Using performance assessments

PRACTICE OBSERVING HIGHER THOUGHT PROCESSES AND PERFORMANCE OUTCOMES: A DIALOGUE

Let's look at some of the ways higher thought processes and performance outcomes can be observed in the classroom using the six behaviors presented in Figure 12.1. Use the checklist in Figure 12.2 to observe the following class.

For this dialogue, we look into Ms. Brokaw's literature class. Today's lesson begins a poetry unit. The class has just finished a unit on American literature in which they read excerpts from Jack London and Mark Twain. Some students are noticeably anxious about the change to this new and seemingly less interesting topic.

Ms. Brokaw: [A poem is written on the board; Ms. Brokaw reads it to the class.]

> *Man is but a mortal fool*
> *When it's hot, he wants it cool*
> *When it's cool, he wants it hot*
> *He's always wanting what is not.*

Today I want to illustrate some ways to understand a poem like the one I've just read. This may seem like a simple poem, but its author put a lot of care and meaning into each word. Now, let me give you an approach to study poems like these and to gain from them the meaning intended by their authors. First, let's try to identify the key words in this poem. Bobby, what do you think are some of the most important words?

Bobby: Well, I'd say the word *man* because it's the first.
Ms. Brokaw: [Still looking at Bobby.] Any others?
Bobby: Not that I can see.
Ms. Brokaw: Anissa?
Anissa: The words *hot* and *cool* have to be important, because they appear twice and they rhyme with the last words of the first and last lines.
Ms. Brokaw: Any other key words? Ricardo?
Ricardo: Well, I think *a mortal fool* is supposed to be telling us something, but I don't know what.
Ms. Brokaw: Good. So, now we've identified some words we think are especially important for under-

FIGURE 12.1 Indicators of Performace Outcomes and Higher Thought Processes

Promotes Performance Outcomes and Higher Thought Processes (Effective Teacher)	Fails to Promote Performance Outcomes and Higher Thought Processes (Ineffective Teacher)
1. Uses collaborative and group activities (cooperative learning, small groups, teamwork, panel discussion, peer tutoring)	Fails to encourage shared work and group problem solving
2. Demonstrates mental models and strategies for learning (for example how learners are to think systematically about solving a certain problem)	Fails to demonstrate how to think critically, reason, and solve problems
3. Arranges for students to apply what they've learned through student projects and demonstrations	Fails to allow students the opportunity to use what they've learned
4. Engages students in oral performance and expression (for example, encouraging the understanding of content and its organization through communication)	Fails to require students to speak out, justify their answers, and express themselves
5. Provides opportunities for independent practice that allow students to learn from their mistakes	Fails to provide supplemental material (exercises, problem sets, activity sheets) that challenge student understanding
6. Uses performance assessment of learning	Fails to assess the integration of learning in authentic contexts

FIGURE 12.1 Indicators of Performace Outcomes and Higher Thought Processes

FIGURE 12.2 Checklist for Observing Performance Outcomes and Higher Thought Processes

Behavior	Observed	Not Observed	No Opportunity to Observe
1. Uses collaborative and group activities			
2. Demonstrates mental models and strategies for learning			
3. Arranges for students to apply what they've learned through products and contributions			
4. Engages students in oral performance			
5. Provides opportunities for independent practice that allow students to learn from their mistakes			
6. Uses performance assessments			

standing this poem. Why don't we look up the meanings of any of these words we don't know or are unsure of in the dictionary. That will be our second step. Ted, look up the word *mortal* for us while we begin work on our third step. The third step is to paraphrase what you think this author is saying. Hee-Won, can you paraphrase what he is saying?

Hee-Won: I think he's saying we're always changing our minds and that's why we look so stupid sometimes.

Ms. Brokaw: We are all human, so we certainly change our minds a lot, don't we? Rhonda looks like she wants to say something. Rhonda?

Rhonda: Well, I'd say it's not because we're stupid that we change our minds, but that it's just part of who we are—we can't help wanting what we can't have.

Ms. Brokaw: So you've added a little something to Hee-Won's interpretation. What do you think, Hee-Won? Do you agree?

Hee-Won: Yeah, we're not stupid, we're just mortals.

Ms. Brokaw: Chris, do you want to add anything?

Chris: I'd say that we're not stupid at all; that to really enjoy something, we must have experienced its opposite—otherwise, we wouldn't know how good it is.

Ms. Brokaw: Now that brings us to our fourth and last step. Let's try to relate what Chris just said to our own experience. Anyone ready? Bobby?

Bobby: I agree with Chris, because I remember thinking how much I welcomed winter because of how hot it was last summer.

Ms. Brokaw: [Marcia is waving her hand.] Marcia, what do you have to say about this?

Marcia: But now that it's winter, I can't wait for the cold weather to end so I can go swimming again. [Class nods agreement.]

Ms. Brokaw: It looks as though Chris was right. We sometimes have to see both sides of something—hot/cold, good/bad, light/dark—to fully appreciate it. Now, Ted, what did you find for *mortal* in the dictionary?

Ted: It says "having caused or being about to cause death," "subject to death," and "marked by vulnerability."

Ms. Brokaw: Which of those do you think best fits the use of *mortal fool* in our poem?

Ted: Well, hmm, . . . the last one, because it kind of goes with what we have been saying about how we choose one thing and then another . . . like when we get too cold we dream of summer, and then when summer comes we think it's too hot.

Ms. Brokaw: I agree. It fits with what we all have experienced in our lives—and that means we are on the right track to the interpretation the author intended. Now, let's go one step further. Putting all of our ideas together, what is this poet saying? [Nodding to Meijean.]

Meijean: Well, I'd say life's a kind of circle. We keep going around and around, back to where we've come

from, and then trying to escape to where we've been. Maybe that's one kind of vulnerability, like it said in the dictionary.

Ms. Brokaw: That's good thinking, Meijean. Bobby, since we began with you, I'll let you have the final word.

Bobby: I think Meijean got it, because now I understand why the author thinks we're all fools: We're like a dog going in circles, chasing its tail, always wanting what we don't have. That explains the first and the last line, doesn't it? Because we are human, we are vulnerable to always "wanting what is not." Yes, so we're "mortal fools." I get it.

Ms. Brokaw: Very good. Now let's break into our assigned groups to study the next set of poems. I will give each group leader a copy of a different poem, which they will read slowly and carefully to their groups. Then each group will discuss among themselves the meaning of the poem using the four steps we just went through to understand "Man is but a mortal fool." I will write the four steps on the board while the group leaders are reading the poem to their groups. These steps will be your guide for interpreting the meaning of your poem. Assistant group leaders, please see that your group has a dictionary from the resource shelf. After about 20 minutes, I will ask each of the groups to read their poem to the class and give the group's interpretation, so each group will need to select a reader. I will be around to visit each group to help with questions or problems.

REACTIONS TO THE DIALOGUE

Which of the five dimensions of higher thought processes and performance outcomes did you see in this dialogue? Recall that these behaviors require analysis, synthesis, and decision making that are believed to be stimulated more by interaction with others (peers and adults) and by an awareness of one's own learning than by books and lectures. They involve encouraging learners to become actively involved in the subject matter by going beyond the information given, restructuring it according to their own way of thinking and prior understanding. Then the teacher gradually shifts the responsibility for learning to students through practice exercises, question-and-answer dialogues, and/or discussions that engage them in increasingly complex patterns of thought.

Using Collaborative and Group Activities

The first behavior for promoting higher thought processes involves collaborative and group activities (Johnson & Johnson, 1987; Slavin, 1987). Students must not only learn to get along in a turbulent, ever-changing society, they must also be prepared to contribute to it. Collaborative and group activities help build the skills learners will need to think critically, reason, and solve problems in an adult world, and help them acquire the social skills that can make their reasoning and problem solving effective.

In planning a cooperative learning activity, the teacher must decide

❑ The type of interactions he will have with students.
❑ The type of interactions students will have with one another.
❑ The task and materials that will be used.
❑ The roles and responsibilities that will be assigned to students.

The first goal in planning a cooperative learning activity is to promote teacher–student interaction that encourages independent thinking. Exchanges between learners and the teacher in a cooperative classroom focus on getting learners to think for themselves, independently of the text. To accomplish this goal, the teacher models, intervenes, and collaborates with learners in a question-and-answer format.

The way teacher–student interaction is developed during cooperative learning is different than in group discussion. In group discussion, the interaction is usually one on one, with verbal messages directed to individuals one at a time and adjusted to their current levels of understanding. In cooperative learning, the interaction occurs in groups of four to six members who share a common purpose and task, so the teacher's task is to fit her responses to the level of understanding common to the group. Instead of bringing individuals to a greater understanding and awareness of their own thinking, the primary goal is to help the group become more self-reflective and aware of its own performance.

"Think about that some more," "Why not check the reference book at the learning center," and "Be sure you've followed the guidelines" are expressions frequently addressed to a group of learners assigned a specific task. The teacher's role is to intervene at critical junctures and then to retreat, allowing the group to independently grapple with and go beyond information given. In this manner, the teacher monitors and collaborates with the group during brief but focused interventions, keeping them on course and following a productive line of reasoning. Teacher–student interactions are well-timed, brief intrusions into the group's thinking that stimulate new ideas.

A second goal in planning a cooperative learning activity is to promote student-to-student interac-tion that facilitates the performance of other group members. Interaction among students in cooperative learning groups should be intense and prolonged. Unlike group discussion, in which the learner is expected to take much of the responsibility for his own learning, students in cooperative learning groups gradually take responsibility for each other's learning. During cooperative learning, feedback, reinforcement, and support come from peers in the group rather than the teacher. Interactions among students constitute the majority of activity during cooperative learning, unlike the modest amount of direct student-to-student inter-action that occurs during class discussion. Groups of four to six students working together in the physical closeness promoted by a common task encourage collaboration, support, and feedback from the closest, most immediate source—one's peers. An essential ingredient of cooperative learning is the desire of each learner to facilitate the performance of his fellow group members.

A third goal in planning a cooperative learning activity is to choose a task that encourages group sharing and decision making. Cooperative learning tasks are preplanned activities; they are timed, completed in stages, and placed within the context of the work of others (for example, the tasks of other groups). The choice of task and supporting materials is important to meaningful student–student interaction. A specific well-defined task and the sharing of materials with which to complete the task (reference books, maps, calculators, videotapes, and art supplies) distinguish cooperative learning from group discussion.

Finally, the assignment of roles is important to the success of a cooperative learning activity. In addition to groups being assigned specialized tasks, individuals often are assigned specialized roles to perform within their groups. Some of the roles that can be assigned to facilitate a group's work and to promote communication and shared decision-making among its members are

1. *Summarizer*—paraphrases and plays back to the group major conclusions, to see if the group agrees and to prepare for the group's presentation before the whole class
2. *Checker*—checks controversial or debatable statements and conclusions for authenticity against text, workbook, or references, and ensures that the group will not be using unsubstantiated facts or be challenged by more accurate representations of other groups
3. *Researcher*—reads reference documents and acquires background information when more data are needed (for example, may conduct an inter-

view or seek a resource from the library); differs from a checker in that the researcher provides critical information for the group to complete its task, and the checker verifies the accuracy of the work while it is in progress or after it has been completed

4. *Runner*—acquires anything needed to complete the task: materials, equipment, reference works; requires creativity, shrewdness, and cunning to find the necessary resources, which other groups may also be diligently searching for

5. *Recorder*—commits to writing the major product of the group; may require individuals to write their own conclusions, in which case she collates, synthesizes, and renders in coherent form the work of individual group members

6. *Supporter*—chosen for his upbeat, positive outlook, praises members when their individual assignments are completed and encourages them in times of disappointment (for example, if proper references can't be found); keeps the group moving forward by encouraging less vocal group members to contribute and by recording major milestones achieved on a chart for the whole class to see

7. *Observer/Troubleshooter*—takes notes and records information about group progress that may be useful during whole-class discussion; reports to a class leader or to the teacher when problems appear insurmountable for the group or individual members

The success of a cooperative learning activity depends on communicating role responsibilities and modeling them when necessary. This is why cooperative learning bears little resemblance to loosely formed discussion groups—not only must tasks be divided among learners, but roles must be delegated to foster the orderly completion of a task.

Research on the effectiveness of various cooperative learning techniques (Slavin, 1987) has found that improved decision making, problem solving, communication, and self-esteem among students result when

1. Rewards are provided for successful performance of the group as a whole.
2. Individual accountability is maintained by selecting group tasks that require the participation of every group member for successful completion.
3. Equal opportunities for success are made available to each student by measuring individual success in terms of improvement over past performance.

What did you notice about Ms. Brokaw's use of collaborative and group learning? We noticed that

she began setting the stage for a collaborative activity by informing her students of a strategy, a plan of action, by which they could interpret the meaning of a poem. She then illustrated—one by one—each step of the strategy.

1. Identify key words important for understanding the poem
2. Look up in a dictionary the meanings of key words they are unsure of
3. Paraphrase what they think the author is saying
4. Relate what the author has said to their own experience.

Notice how Ms. Brokaw provided this strategy to her learners. First, she presented her strategy in four easy-to-follow steps. These steps were sufficiently familiar and practical to be followed by almost any student, regardless of ability or experience, and were not just divisions of the task, but actual mental steps that encouraged learners to go beyond the content presented to find their own meaning based on personal experience and individual thinking. In other words, there were no wrong answers with this strategy—only answers that could be improved to raise the learner to the next rung of the learning ladder.

Second, the strategy provided wasn't just routinely given to the learners by listing its steps on the board; the steps were illustrated in the context of a real problem. The application was for the real world and typical of other examples to which they would be asked to apply the strategy.

Third, the learners were invited to become participants in the learning, not just passive listeners waiting to be told what to do. By using a question-and-answer dialogue to provide a structure for the learners' opinions and experiences, students became an active part of the process of generating new knowledge. They were, in a sense, their own teachers, without knowing it. This was made possible through the format of an unscripted discussion, which removed any fear of producing a wrong response that might have prevented some learners from participating.

Fourth, as the lesson evolved, more and more of the most important conclusions were provided by the students—not the teacher. The highest level of interpretation, which ended the lesson, came almost entirely from the summarizing remarks of students. By the end of the lesson, the teacher's role was that of a monitor and co-discussant rather than an information provider—that role having been assumed by the students themselves as they actively applied each of the steps given earlier in the lesson.

Students working collaboratively in small groups also contributed to the higher thought processes and performance outcomes in Ms. Brokaw's classroom. Notice that the teacher's goal with this format was to promote application of the model and independent thinking. But for small-group work to be effective, it needs teacher–student interaction, student–student interaction, specification of the task and materials, and the assignment of roles. Notice that each of these elements was provided by the teacher at the end of the classroom dialogue. A particular task, which required the original interpretation of a poem using the model provided in the previous dialogue and summarized on the board, was assigned to each group. Role assignments made the execution of the task efficient and effective. There were group leaders and assistants, readers, and presenters to help provide structure and direction to the group work. A time limit was imposed that, together with group-by-group visits by the teacher, would help keep the class on task. Thus, all four elements of a collaborative activity—teacher–student interaction, student–student interaction, task specification, and materials and roles—were present in Ms. Brokaw's organization of group work, supported and reinforced by the learning strategy presented earlier in the lesson.

Observing Collaborative and Group Activities

Collaborative and group activities require teacher–student interaction, interaction among students, a specified task and materials, and the assignment of roles: The presence of these four components can determine the effectiveness of a collaborative learning activity. Instrument 12.1 provides a format to observe and record these four components. Complete this form for Ms. Brokaw's collaborative activity, indicating your judgment as to the extent to which all or some of these components were present.

Demonstrating Mental Models and Strategies for Learning

The second behavior for promoting higher thought processes and performance outcomes involves demonstrating mental models and strategies for learning. Although most teaching takes place in large- and small-group formats, a considerable portion of teaching time (as much as 40 percent in some grades and subjects) is taken up with seatwork and one-on-one dialogue, in which teacher responses must be tailored to the achievement, interest, and ability levels of individual students. This tailored interaction may occur in the context of dis-

cussion involving the whole class or during monitoring of seatwork. In either setting, the teacher's role is to assist the individual in internalizing, understanding, and applying the content being learned. These goals can be achieved most efficiently by modeling for the learner the mental processes needed to understand and apply the content to be learned. Modeling involves three steps (Duffy & Roehler, 1989):

1. Demonstrating to students the reasoning processes needed
2. Making students aware of this reasoning process
3. Helping students apply the reasoning process

These steps usually are carried out through verbal statements that help learners walk through the process of attaining a correct solution. They may begin with verbal markers like

Now I will show you how to solve this problem by talking out loud as I go through it, identifying exactly what is going on in my mind.

Think about each decision I make, where I stop to think, and what alternatives I choose—as though you are making the same decision in your own mind.

Listen to me as I think out loud, completing each of the steps you will need to answer this question.

Notice that the teacher is not giving the learner the mechanics of getting a right answer—"do step A, step B, and then step C"—but, more importantly, is providing an actual demonstration of the mental procedures that lie behind the completion of a problem.

These mental procedures help students internalize, recall, and then generalize problem solutions to different content at a later time. The teacher does not just convey information, but demonstrates the decision-making process as it occurs. By contrast, the mechanical memorization of steps rarely helps learners solve similar problems in other contexts or allows content to be recalled when the present topic has lost its immediate importance (no exam in sight, or no homework due).

Consider the following dialogue in which the teacher provides a mental model for acquiring the concept of a proportion.

Teacher: When you see a proportion, such as *4/5* (writes it on board), think of the number on top as "what is" and the number on the bottom as "what could be." Think about that box of cereal you made your breakfast from this morning. If I wrote the proportion of cereal in the box as *3/4* (writes it on board), I would say to myself, the full box is equal to the number 4—that's the "could be" part—but this morning, after I poured myself breakfast, it's only the number 3—that's the "what is" part. I can tell the box is still pretty full, since the number for "what is" is close to the number for "what could be." Juan, explain to me what it means when it says on a label that the vitamin C in one 4 ounce glass of orange juice is 1/2 the minimum daily requirement.

Juan: I'm not sure.

Teacher: Okay; what words can we use to describe the number on top?

Juan: You said, "what is."

Teacher: What does that mean?

Juan: I guess it's how much vitamin C is really in the glass.

Teacher: And now for the bottom.

Juan: You said the bottom is "what could be." Does that mean that it's all you need?

Teacher: Yes, it does—good. Now, think of another example—one of your own—in which something was less than it could have been.

Juan: Well, I finished Ms. Enro's social studies test before the end of the period.

Teacher: And how long was the period?

Juan: Umm, about 40 minutes, I guess.

Teacher: Using our words, what would you call that part of the problem?

Juan: "What could be." OK, I get it. Then, the time I actually took is what really happened? Yeah, I finished the test in about 20 minutes.

Teacher: So how would you express that proportion in numbers?

Juan: It would be 20, for "what is," over 40, for "what could be." The top is half of the bottom, so I guess one glass of orange juice gives you half the vitamin C you need in one day.

Teacher: Okay. Let's retrace the steps you just followed for another problem . . . .

Imagine that Juan relives this episode in another classroom. After the same introductory remarks, Juan is asked an identical question:

Teacher: Now, Juan, explain to me what it means when it says on a label that the vitamin C in one 4 ounce glass of orange juice is 1/2 the minimum daily requirement. [After a pause.] Look, if the number 1 is on the top and the number 2 is on the bottom, it must mean the top is less than the bottom. Right?

Juan: Right.

Teacher: So, if the top number represents what is and the bottom number what could be, "what is" is one-half of "what could be." And that can only mean the glass contains half of the minimum daily requirement of vitamin C. Got it?

Juan: Yep.

Maybe he does, and maybe he doesn't. Notice that in the first example the teacher provided mental steps for Juan to follow that moved the dialogue closer to the intended goal of the lesson. The dialogue provided a step by which Juan lifted himself onto the next rung of the learning ladder.

The second teacher simply provided the right answer. This gave Juan no opportunity to construct his own response and thereby derive a process to use for arriving at other right answers in similar circumstances. The first teacher focused on developing for the learner a process of reasoning that would give the content its own individual meaning and be consistent with the intended goal of the lesson.

Through classroom dialogues such as these, the teacher can encourage learners to construct their own meanings and interpretations; for example, to substitute their own unique constructions for "what is" and "what could be" and to share them with others through discussion and classroom dialogue. Such modeling activates a learning dialogue. By calling forth unique histories, specialized abilities, and personal experiences, mental modeling encourages higher thought processes.

Observing Mental Models and Strategies for Learning

Mental models and strategies require demonstrating the reasoning involved in obtaining a correct solution, making students conscious of the steps used, and helping them apply these steps to independently arrive at other right answers in similar circumstances. These steps often are accomplished with verbal markers, such as "Now I will show you . . . ," "Think about the steps I'm going through . . . ," or "Listen to how I think through this . . . ."

Phrases such as these are intended to alert students to the line of reasoning to use in obtaining the correct solution for themselves and enable them to construct their own meanings and interpretations that can be applied time and again to similar problems. Instrument 12.2 provides a format for recording how these three components of mental modeling are applied in the classroom. Using the dialogue in this chapter as your guide, see if you can find verbal phrases used by Ms. Brokaw during the course of the lesson that represent any or all of the steps to mental modeling.

Arranging for Student Projects and Demonstrations

The third behavior for promoting higher thought processes and performance outcomes is arranging for student projects and demonstrations. Most teachers encourage students to explore and demonstrate the concepts and principles they have been taught. Students enjoy seeing what otherwise might be considered dull schoolwork come alive by applying what they've learned. Practical applications to the real world can take the form of reports, projects, experiments, videos, drawings, scale models, and the like, which students can choose from to apply the concepts and principles they have been taught. Since projects and demonstrations are often of the student's own choosing, they pose a special opportunity to encourage higher thought processes in heterogeneously grouped classrooms.

For student projects and demonstrations to be effective in promoting higher thought processes, however, students should be given guidelines to the level of thinking and production that will be expected and should also participate in their development. These guidelines should be specific enough to ensure that the projects conform to the assignment, fit within space limitations, and are safe, and must also communicate the level of inquiry, creativity, and individuality expected. Planning these guidelines in advance and illustrating them to students are crucial steps in promoting higher thought processes. Example guidelines that can be developed from both student and teacher input are

- ❑ *Guideline 1:* Adequately represent the complexity of your topic. *Example:* "We've all heard that the brain is like a computer. Now, can you show me how the brain works like a computer?"
- ❑ *Guideline 2:* Avoid being vague or overly abstract. *Example:* "When you hear the word *horsepower*, what specific examples come to mind?"
- ❑ *Guideline 3:* Use vocabulary that is appropriate to your topic. *Example:* "How do the earth's crust, core, and tectonic plates create geologic activity?"
- ❑ *Guideline 4:* Use appropriate examples to communicate your topic. *Example:* "In what ways do you see the rapid pace of technology, such as the development of the microchip, influencing our everyday lives?"
- ❑ *Guideline 5:* Connect your topic to your own personal experience. *Example:* "Tell us some of the ways your neighborhood has taught you to appreciate that people are different."

To make guidelines clearer, sample projects or demonstrations in several categories can be exhibited to show various degrees of performance (for example, "superior," "advanced," or "meets expectations"). In this manner students get to see, and contribute to, the quality of performance and thought that is expected. Selected students can be asked to donate their completed project as an example for other classes, or a photograph or video of their work can be taken. For teachers teaching multiple classes of the same subject, staggering the time the assignment is given among classes will allow projects from one class to serve as examples for other classes.

An important addition to student projects and demonstrations is *peer review*. Peer review promotes higher levels of thinking and performance—sometimes far exceeding the results that can be obtained through teacher review. The need to show off and receive recognition is part of human nature, and having a product scrutinized by peers ensures that a captive audience of those we respect will be there to witness us at our best. Assembling a collection, gathering specimens, building scale models, and showing examples all provide opportunities to be creative and imaginative. The energy exerted by students in a peer review often results in more thorough and competent performance.

Did you notice anything about Ms. Brokaw's use of student projects and demonstrations? Unfortunately, a single observation was probably insufficient to determine the extent of her planning in this area. Think, however, about what student projects and demonstrations pertaining to the content of this lesson Ms. Brokaw might have provided to her students. For example, she could have asked her students to try writing a poem, to interpret a favorite poem, or to draw a picture that expresses their interpretation of a poem—each of these activities could stimulate higher thought processes. Use your own creativity—and higher thought processes—to propose a project or demonstration that Ms. Brokaw might use with the content of this lesson at another time.

Observing Student Projects and Demonstrations

Recall that the purpose of student projects and demonstrations is to get students to apply what they have learned. Projects and demonstrations—exhibits, experiments, scale models, videos, graphic representations, and the like—encourage students to make judgments and decisions on their own and to use their individual backgrounds, abilities, and learning histories in creative ways. Instrument 12.3 asks you to list examples of projects and demonstrations on display in the classroom that reflect the independent thought and judgment of individual students. This instrument also suggests the types of projects and demonstrations to look for, and provides an opportunity to add others that may be specific to a particular subject, grade, or classroom.

Engaging Students in Oral Performance

A fourth behavior for promoting higher thought processes and performance outcomes is engaging students in oral performance. Oral competence—the ability to express oneself through speech and recitation—is important in every subject area. Although oral performance may not be the primary objective for some subjects, few objectives in any subject will be met if the results of instruction cannot be observed and evaluated orally. Reading, social studies, science, and even math require some type of oral performance. The type of oral performance required of students can vary considerably from subject to subject, but most often it will take the form of reports to the class, reading in front of the class, stating an opinion, justifying a response, giving a speech, or performing in a skit, a play, or a demonstration. All of these require higher thought processes and forms of expression. Oral performance is one way students can share what they have learned.

Oral performances test students' knowledge and organization of a topic as well as their delivery of it. For example, recitation of an original poem involves both knowledge of the structure of poetry and the ability to deliver it orally in ways that communicate and emphasize its meaning. The ability to represent a character in a skit or play involves knowing how the character might dress and act, remembering the lines the character is to speak, and being able to convey this characterization orally to others to create a feeling of empathy. Giving a report to the class involves both having something to say and saying it in a way that promotes acceptance and understanding of a particular point of view. In other words, content and process each must be given proper emphasis.

Proper emphasis on content and process can be accomplished by observing two facets of oral performances: (1) delivery and (2) content and organization. Characteristics of delivery are

Enunciation
Pronunciation
Loudness
Word choice
Pitch
Rate
Gestures

Characteristics of content and organization are

Quality and accuracy of ideas
Logical development of ideas
Organization of ideas
Style and individuality
Wording and phrasing

More importance may be given to some categories than to others; for example, because a great deal of care and time was taken in introducing students to the library, the quality and accuracy of ideas might be considered twice as important as other dimensions of content and organization.

Oral performances in one subject may be quite different from those in another subject. Some areas of oral performance might be suitable to a class in English, writing, or reading, but not to a class in social studies. In the English class, for example, word usage might take on a greater importance than it would in the social studies class. Generally, the mechanical aspects of speaking occupy less attention in the higher grades, since these skills presumably have already been attained, and the focus of the instruction at this level is on the development of ideas, organization, style, wording, and phrasing. Thus, the oral dimensions to be observed should be flexible, varying with both subject matter and grade level.

Notice that Ms. Brokaw made several efforts to encourage oral performance among class members. First, she engaged her students orally during the lesson, preventing them from becoming passive learners. This teacher's dialogue with her students required not just student responses, but responses that encouraged students to reason out and justify their answers to the class, thereby promoting higher thought processes. Her small-group activity, by virtue of assigned roles, required a degree of oral performance from every student in the group. Group leaders would read the poem to their group, group members would discuss its meaning using the model provided, and a presenter would read the poem to the class. In this manner, oral performance was encouraged from as many members of the class as possible, in as many ways as possible. Students who didn't contribute to the class discussion could contribute to a more informal discussion within their groups.

Observing Students in Oral Performance

Oral performances include a wide range of behavior, from simply answering a teacher's question to giving a speech or performing in a classroom skit or play. In any of its varied forms, oral performance is important because of its capacity to translate content learned in one way (e.g., lecture or text) into a new and more complete form (e.g., a report to the class). For example, most oral performances require the learner to translate, summarize, or paraphrase what has been learned through books or lecture into a more integrated whole, thereby raising the learner's thought process to a higher level; for example, from knowledge of facts to the comprehension and application of these facts in an adultlike task. Since oral performance can be less time-consuming than projects and demonstrations, it can be used more often and in more varied ways.

There is little doubt that, in every classroom, students should be accustomed to expressing their knowledge as well as their ideas and opinions orally. Therefore, almost every lesson should include some attention to teacher–student and/or student–student interaction. However, besides these simple oral performances, there are other, more formal forms of oral expression that should occur over a unit or sequence of related lessons. These include assigned reports to the class, reading from one's own work, discussing an extended idea or theme, justifying a response in one's own words, critically analyzing the response of another student, and delivering formal speeches. Instrument 12.4 provides a format for observing the degree to which any or all of these examples of oral expression occur over a unit or sequence of lessons. Because some forms of oral expression are more likely than others on any given day, observations for this behavior should take place over multiple observations. Instrument 12.4 can be used to accumulate your observations.

Providing Opportunities for Students to Learn From Their Mistakes

The fifth behavior for eliciting higher thought processes and performance outcomes involves independent practice to allow students the opportunity to discover and learn from their mistakes (Marx & Walsh, 1988). This approach, called *consequential learning* (McCall, Lombardo, & Morrison, 1988), allows the learner to discover the results—or *consequences*—of his efforts to learn. It requires of the teacher the ability to anticipate student errors and to develop (or select from workbooks, texts, and resources) handouts and exercises that provide the opportunity to make these mistakes. It is by this process that the learner can expand, clarify, or revise a response. Consequential learning takes the form of exercises, handouts, problem sets, and activity sheets, tailored to the whole class or subgroups of learners, that push students toward higher levels of understanding and reveal errors that can inhibit learning.

As we saw in Chapter 11, student errors play an important role in moving learners to the next rung of the learning ladder. If an assigned problem, question, or exercise promotes an inaccurate and meaningless response, little has been achieved for the learner. But if an assigned problem, question, or exercise creates (or even intentionally promotes) a student response that is inaccurate but meaningful, the learner gains a chance to repeat the performance with better understanding. Recall that these kinds of student errors were called *functional errors*. Whether these errors are unexpected or are anticipated by the teacher, they enhance the learner's understanding of the content. Functional errors may prevent erroneous thought processes from recurring, or stimulate new thought processes to occur. Consider the following exercise designed to challenge a student's understanding of the Civil War.

> Fill in the blanks with the correct answers.
> *Abraham Lincoln* was president at the time of the Civil War.
> His government represented the *Northern* region of our country, called the *Confederacy*.

This student responded to the third blank incorrectly, but because of the relationship among the questions it was easy for the teacher to detect the nature of the error. Notice that this set of questions encouraged the learner to extend her knowledge to the point that, if understanding was incomplete or the proper relationship had not been acquired, it would become apparent in a response to a later question. But what if this teacher had raised a less thoughtful sequence of questions? Imagine the following exercise completed by this same student.

> Underline the letter representing the correct answer.
> President of the United States at the time of the Civil War:
>   (a) Douglas, (b) *Lincoln*, (c) Davis, (d) Franklin
> Regions of our country fighting were
>   (a) North vs. West (b) South vs. East
>   (c) <u>North vs. South</u> (d) East vs. West
> Name of one of the sides fighting:
>   (a) The Constitutionalists (b) *The Confederacy*
>   (c) The Pilgrims (d) The Americans

Does this student associate the Confederacy with Lincoln and the North—or not? Here it is impossible to assess the student's higher thought processes because only a regurgitation of facts was required. The teacher has no easy way to determine if there is a problem or in what area a problem might exist.

Tailoring seatwork to reflect consequential learning requires anticipating the kinds of errors that are most likely to occur and providing an opportunity for them to occur in the context of a learning experience. This means that exercises, problem sets, and activities—as well as a teacher's oral responses—need to challenge a learner's current level of understanding. They must promote a response—correct or incorrect—that is *functional* for moving the learner to the next rung of the learning ladder. This is why scripted approaches to instruction (e.g., publisher's workbooks), drills, and practice exercises are not, by themselves, sufficient to promote higher thought processes. These sources may provide practice, but may not provide sufficient opportunity for higher thought processes to occur. Frequently, these resources need to be supplemented by teacher-made or teacher-selected seatwork directed at, or slightly above, the learners' current level of understanding, so that student errors useful for providing redirection and remediation can be brought to the surface.

What consequential learning activities could Ms. Brokaw use with this lesson? A specially prepared worksheet that asks students to write an interpretation of a poem using the four steps presented in the lesson could provide an opportunity for consequential learning. This worksheet might take the form shown in Figure 12.3. Can you think of any other exercise that Ms. Brokaw might use that would clearly inform the learner of what has and has not been learned from this lesson? What might a form for recording student responses to your exercise look like?

Observing Consequential Learning

Consequential learning involves independent practice that allows students to discover their mistakes and learn from them. Independent practice that allows the learner to discover the results of his efforts to learn should challenge the learner enough that the most critical and pervasive errors are brought to the surface. Workbook problems and end-of-chapter exercises can provide opportunities for consequential learning when they are sufficiently challenging. But when published exercises provide monotonous drill either below or above students' current level of understanding, alternative materials will be needed.

Instrument 12.5 provides a format for recording independent practice opportunities that may be used in a classroom to provide students with a knowledge and understanding of their mistakes. Check for these over the course of one or more observations

Using Performance Assessments of Learning

Our final behavior for promoting higher thought processes and performance outcomes involves the assessment of learning. Classroom assessment, particularly beyond the early elementary grades, is sometimes almost exclusively based on paper-and-pencil tests that indicate, rather than directly measure, what students have learned (Gullickson, 1984). For example, we may measure an understanding of the scientific method not by having learners plan, conduct, and evaluate an experiment

FIGURE 12.3 Form for Practicing the Model Used to Interpret a Poem

Poem 1 _____

_____

_____

_____

Step 1. The key words in this poem are:

_____

_____

_____

_____

Step 2. Find the dictionary meaning of at least one key word whose meaning you are unsure of:

Word: _____   Meaning: _____

_____

Step 3: Paraphrase what you think the author is saying:

_____

_____

_____

Step 4: Describe an experience in your own life that relates to what this poet is saying.

_____

_____

_____

(a direct measure), but by asking them to list the steps of the scientific method, write about the difference between a hypothesis and a theory, or choose the correct definition of a control group from a list of choices (all indirect assessment). Or we may measure children's understanding of money not by observing them buying food, paying for it, and getting the correct change (direct assessment), but by asking them to recall how many pennies there are in a dollar, or to write down how much change they would get back from a $10 bill if they paid $6.75 for a T-shirt (indirect assessment).

There are obvious advantages to indirect assessment of achievement and learning. Directly measuring all learning that goes on in a classroom would be very time-consuming. But indirect assessment raises a problem: How do you know that the assessment is measuring what you say it is? In other words, how authentic is your assessment? Authentic assessments measure directly what teachers really care about. For example, if learners saw a teacher demonstrate how to focus a microscope, were coached to do this, and practiced doing it, then an authentic test would ask them to correctly focus a microscope—not label the parts of the microscope on a diagram.

Performance assessment of learning authentically measures higher thought processes that are often measured only as isolated bits of behavior on multiple-choice, true-false, or structured-essay tests. Resnick and Resnick (1991) assert that the performance assessment of learning can best be measured by oral reports, extended essays, projects, portfolios of student work, scientific investigations, creative scores and scripts, physical models, and similar overt signs that demonstrate that "bits" of behavior can be successfully converted into an "integrated performance" in a context different than that in which they were learned. Performance assessments typically take place over a period of hours or days in which students work at their own pace and, with the aid of guidelines provided by the teacher, select the tasks and projects with which to demonstrate their competence against a set of known criteria.

The goal of performance assessment is to reduce the importance of artificial knowledge, which may be unintentionally promoted by exclusive or heavy reliance on true-false, multiple-choice, and some types of essay tests, and to increase the importance of verbal explanations and justifications, critical thinking, and problem solving related to authentic professional and social responsibilities. A secondary goal is to diminish the weight generally accorded to traditional test-taking skills in student evaluation, especially for those for whom such skills may be weak.

Some of the most important characteristics of performance assessments are that they

- ❑ Ask learners to demonstrate understandings and intellectual skills that were modeled, coached, and practiced in class.
- ❑ Ask learners to use what they did as part of the regular classroom practice activities in a more realistic and expanded context.
- ❑ Involve the integration and simultaneous use of higher thought processes rather than the simple recall of information.
- ❑ Ask learners to do things for which the routine use of previously learned information is not sufficient.
- ❑ Set standards by informing learners what it means to perform competently in the real world.
- ❑ Reveal to students and parents the end products of schooling.
- ❑ Represent real-life challenges, rather than bookwork, which may be artificial and/or fragmented, and may have been selected because it is easy to grade.

Performance assessments, therefore, are designed to measure intellectual skills in a problem-solving, decision-making context. This problem-solving context should exhibit three important characteristics: (1) A hands-on exercise or problem to solve, which produces (2) an observable outcome or product (a typed business letter, a map, a graph, a piece of clothing, an oral presentation, or a poem) such that the teacher can (3) observe the solution process. (The teacher observes and assesses not only the product, but also the behaviors used to get there; for example, relating, composing, justifying, differentiating, and diagnosing.)

Examples of performance assessment include:

- ❑ Learners assemble a portfolio of the best examples of their writing, using poetry, essay, short story, and/or autobiographical contributions.
- ❑ Learners prepare a visual story on a crucial problem affecting their community.
- ❑ Learners select and use laboratory equipment appropriately to test a hypothesis.
- ❑ Learners program calculators to solve an equation with two unknowns.
- ❑ Learners challenge the ideas of their peers in a class discussion using three known principles of logic.
- ❑ Learners develop their own math problem and show at least two alternative ways to solve it.

Guidelines for completing and evaluating the project or performance can be developed with student input in the format of product criteria, which include key observable features of the project or performance to be judged (technical quality, accuracy, or usability) and process criteria, which include how the learner goes about completing the product or performance (use of resources, extent of group sharing, neatness, or overall effort). Sample guidelines were presented on page 272.

Observing Performance Assessments

Performance assessments are authentic assessments in which students are asked to integrate bits of knowledge that may have been learned in isolated contexts into a single, unified product. The product should allow the student a degree of flexibility regarding the form in which it is expressed and the resources consulted in producing it.

The requirements for grading performance assessments should include both product and process criteria. Product criteria include key observable features of the product or performance, such as

❑ Technical quality
❑ Accuracy
❑ Practicality or usability
❑ Organization
❑ Application of materials and resources

Process criteria include how the learner went about solving the problem or creating the product, and can include attributes such as

❑ Creativity
❑ Neatness
❑ Sharing
❑ Articulation
❑ Use of references and resources

Process criteria are often difficult to grade on an all-or-nothing basis, so they often have several degrees of effort assigned to them; for example, 3 = high effort, 2 = average effort, and 1 = low effort.

Performance assessments need not take place at the same time for the whole class. Learners can be assessed at different times, individually or in small groups. For example, learners can rotate through classroom learning centers (Shalaway, 1989) and be assessed when the teacher feels they are acquiring mastery. Or performance assessments can take place within ongoing classroom activities, rather than consuming extra time during the day.

Instrument 12.6 provides a format for observing a performance assessment. Your observation—and the performance assessment—will be more reliable if (1) the performance to be judged (process and product) is clearly specified, (2) the ratings or criteria in making the judgments are determined beforehand, and (3) two or more raters independently grade the performance.

Although Ms. Brokaw's lesson did not afford us the opportunity to observe all six dimensions directly, we can infer or imagine how they might be incorporated in future lessons. For example, efforts at writing a poem, interpreting a favorite poem, or drawing a picture that expresses some aspect of a poem could stimulate higher thought processes. Specially prepared worksheets that ask students to follow the model for a poem chosen from an approved list would provide an opportunity for both consequential learning and performance assessment. For example, an activity handout that would afford learners the opportunity to practice the model independent of their teacher and group could be provided, as was shown in Figure 12.3.

Responses from different students could be anonymously shared with the class to provide feedback as to how well the model was followed. If product and process criteria were applied to each student's response, a performance assessment could be undertaken to see how well the learners were able to integrate different pieces of information in a more realistic and expanded context. Student projects and demonstrations from past lessons (for example, on bulletin boards, shelves, and cabinets, and at learning centers) could provide evidence that higher thought processes and performance assessments were occurring.

Our reaction to Ms. Brokaw's lesson is summarized in Figure 12.4. How does it compare with your thoughts? Generally, we gave Ms. Brokaw good marks for her attempts to obtain performance outcomes and higher thought processes. This lesson provided strong indications of collaboration and group work, mental modeling, and oral performance. However, we were unable to observe student projects or demonstrations, consequential learning, and performance assessment. This will be typical of many lessons that, due to lesson objectives and time, do not allow for more than a few activities that promote higher thought processes and performance outcomes.

Cultural Diversity and Performance Outcomes

Traditionally, teachers from elementary school to college have perceived making tests and assigning grades to be two of the more bothersome aspects of teaching (Gullickson, 1984). Many have come to view these as chores that have to be done to please administrators and parents, rather than as a pattern of practice integral to the teaching process itself. In other words, some forms of testing and evaluation have become (or have been used as) ends unto themselves instead of the teaching tools they were originally intended to be. The performance assessment of

Figure 12.4 Checklist for Ms. Brokaw's Classroom

Behavior	Observed	Not Observed	No Opportunity to Observe
1. Uses collaborative and group activities	✓ Used grouping effectively		
2. Demonstrates mental models and strategies for learning	✓ Modeled correct procedure		
3. Arranges for students to apply what they've learned through products and demonstrations			✓ May relate to subsequent lessons
4. Engages students in oral performance	✓ Asked students to participate orally		
5. Provides opportunities for independent practice that challenge student understanding			✓ Plenty of opportunities, which may be followed up in subsequent lessons
6. Uses performance assessments			None required for this lesson

learning is an attempt to redress the gap between assessments that grade and assessments that teach by

❏ Reactivating previously learned skills and knowledge.
❏ Providing opportunities to practice and consolidate new information.
❏ Motivating learners to higher degrees of effort.
❏ Establishing for learners a realistic picture of their own ability.
❏ Communicating performance and progress accurately to parents, future teachers, and employers.
❏ Making allowances for differences in gender, culture, and abilities.

The relevance of performance assessment for culture- and gender-fair testing is one of its most important strengths. In heterogeneously grouped classrooms, student interest, experiences, skills, and abilities vary considerably, making some traditional test-taking formats fairer for some learners than for others. For example, paper-and-pencil tests that assume a common reading speed and vocabulary will be less appropriate for a classroom with bilingual or English Language Learners (ELL) than performance-based

projects in which learners are given some latitude in the time required to complete the activity, as well as in the focus of their efforts. Likewise, performance-based assessments provide the opportunity for learners to utilize their own unique abilities and interests to complete projects within specified guidelines that may be devised with their input. Some learners, due to their learning history, culture, or ethnicity, may excel in test-taking skills and others may not, making performance assessment a more accurate indication of learning than pencil-and-paper tests. Performance assessments have been shown to have a substantial impact on culturally and ethnically diverse learners by increasing their motivation to complete a project, influencing their choice of study patterns and learning strategies, and accessing their preferred modes of responding (Crooks, 1988). For these reasons, it is important that a range of evaluation activities be used, including performance assessment.

In this chapter we studied six dimensions of the classroom that underscore the important role of performance outcomes and higher thought processes. These dimensions were collaborative grouping, mental modeling, projects and demonstrations, oral performance, consequential learning, and performance assessment. As you begin observing these dimensions, keep in mind their significant impact on all the other effective teaching behaviors—learning climate, classroom management, lesson clarity, instructional variety, task orientation, student engagement in the learning process, and student success.

ACTIVITIES*

1. Using the checklist in Figure 12.2, observe a lesson, looking for signs of performance outcomes and higher thought processes. At the end of your observation, add a brief description to each box, highlighting at least one specific reason why you placed each of your checkmarks as you did. Using your written descriptions as a guide, write a paragraph describing some of the reasons for the level of performance outcomes and higher thought processes you observed in this classroom.

2. Convert the positively stated indicators listed in Figure 12.1 into a Likert scale. Consider the vertical and/or horizontal placement of each indicator on the page, whether words will be affixed to all or only some of the response blanks, and what verbal response alternatives will be best suited to each question. Show your scale to a classmate who also has constructed a five-point scale. Together, create a single revised version incorporating the best features of each.

3. Using the seven-point polar scale described in Chapter 4 as an example, convert the positive and negative indicators in Figure 12.1 into this scale format and observe a lesson for signs of higher thought processes and performance outcomes. At the end of your period of observation, complete the scale by indicating with a checkmark the degree to which the lesson achieved each dimension. Use the code *N/O* for any item that you didn't have the opportunity to observe, or that was inappropriate for the lesson being observed. Reflecting on your experience, return to the scale and place an *X* on the blank corresponding to each scale item that, in your opinion, represents the degree of higher thought processes and performance outcomes found in most classrooms. Note the difference between your ratings for this lesson and what might be typical across classrooms. Cite the reasons this lesson was the same, higher, or lower on each dimension.

4. Using the format provided in Instrument 12.1, observe a collaborative or group activity for (a) teacher–student interaction, (b) student–student interaction, (c) task specification and materials, and (d) role assignment. Overall, how successful do you feel this particular activity was in getting students to think critically, reason, or problem solve?

5. Using the format provided in Instrument 12.2, look for a mental strategy or model students can use to learn the content presented during a lesson. Note the steps or procedures to be followed by the students and write a brief description of them.

6. Using the format provided in Instrument 12.3 for observing student projects and demonstrations, record any physical signs in and around the classroom that indicate students have applied what they have learned. If no signs are observable, ask the teacher what opportunities students have to put into practice what they have learned.

7. With the aid of the format provided in Instrument 12.4, record the types of oral performances that occur during a lesson. Make a list of any additional types of oral responses that you believe would promote higher thought processes.

8. Using the format provided in Instrument 12.5, observe a lesson looking for opportunities for independent practice that might help students learn from their mistakes. Identify any supplemental handouts and whether they were teacher-made, assembled from different published sources, or selected from existing texts, workbooks, and other resources.

9. Using the format provided in Instrument 12.6, observe a classroom in which learners have recently completed a product or performance. In your opinion, did this product or performance provide an alternative format to accurately assess higher thought processes for culturally and ethnically diverse learners? What were its strengths? Its weaknesses?

---

*Some of the following activities may be grouped into a common activity, divided among classmates, and completed from a single observation.

INSTRUMENT 12.1 Format for Recording Degrees of Group Activity and Task Focus During Collaborative Learning

1. Teacher–student interaction

   ❑ Did not occur   ❑ Seldom occurred   ❑ Occasionally occurred   ❑ Frequently occurred

   When the teacher interacted with students during the collaborative learning activity, was it directed toward

Individuals:	Small groups:	Full class:
❑ not at all	❑ not at all	❑ not at all
❑ seldom	❑ seldom	❑ seldom
❑ occasionally	❑ occasionally	❑ occasionally
❑ frequently	❑ frequently	❑ frequently

2. Student–student interaction

   Approximately what percent of time during the activity was devoted to student–student interaction?

   ❑ Less than 25%   ❑ 26–49%   ❑ 50–75%   ❑ more than 75%

   Most of the student interaction was

   ❑ one student talking to another student.

   ❑ students talking among themselves in groups.

   ❑ students in one group talking to students in another group.

   ❑ other _____

3. Task and material specification

   Identify the task toward which this collaborative activity was directed and the supporting materials (if any) with which it was to be conducted.

   Task: _____

   _____

   _____

   _____

   Supporting materials (references, sourcebooks, handouts, etc.)

   _____

   _____

   _____

4. Role assignment

   Identify any roles assigned to individual students carrying out this collaborative activity (leader, recorder, summarizer, etc.).

   _____

   _____

   _____

INSTRUMENT 12.2   Format to Observe Mental Models and Strategies

1. *Demonstrating to students the reasoning involved.* What concept or principle was being demonstrated and how was it being demonstrated (orally, visually, or by physical demonstration)?

   _____

   _____

   _____

2. *Making students aware of the reasoning involved.* What verbal markers did the teacher use to alert students to the reasoning required? For example, "Now watch me . . . " or "Notice what I do . . . ."

   _____

   _____

   _____

3. *Helping students apply the reasoning involved.* How did the teacher involve students in actually applying the reasoning required? For example, "How would you do this problem . . . ?" or "Let's think of another example . . . ."

   _____

   _____

   _____

INSTRUMENT 12.3   Format for Observing Student Projects and Demonstrations

Identify observable signs of any of the following and describe briefly their nature.

❑ Journals, writing assignments, letters, and reports

_____

_____

❑ Physical science experiments/investigations

_____

_____

❑ Drawings and graphics

_____

_____

❑ Lifelike renderings (for example, sculpture or clay figures)

_____

_____

❑ Video/audio

_____

_____

❑ Scale models (physical replicas)

_____

_____

❑ Aquatic and plant life

_____

_____

❑ Other

_____

_____

INSTRUMENT 12.4 Format for Observing Oral Performance

	Times Observed					
	1	**2**	**3**	**4**	**5**	**6**
Oral performance	❏	❏	❏	❏	❏	❏
Students response to questions orally	❏	❏	❏	❏	❏	❏
Students read or present assignments informally	❏	❏	❏	❏	❏	❏
Students discuss idea or theme	❏	❏	❏	❏	❏	❏
Students critique or analyze responses of other students	❏	❏	❏	❏	❏	❏
Students read from text or own material	❏	❏	❏	❏	❏	❏
Students give formal speech or report	❏	❏	❏	❏	❏	❏
Other _____	❏	❏	❏	❏	❏	❏
_____						

INSTRUMENT 12.5   Format for Recording Independent Practice for Consequential Learning

			Times Observed			
Practice Opportunities	**1**	**2**	**3**	**4**	**5**	**6**
End-of-Chapter exercises						
in class	❑	❑	❑	❑	❑	❑
homework	❑	❑	❑	❑	❑	❑
Workbook Problems						
in class	❑	❑	❑	❑	❑	❑
homework	❑	❑	❑	❑	❑	❑
Supplemental Handouts						
in class	❑	❑	❑	❑	❑	❑
homework	❑	❑	❑	❑	❑	❑
Problems on Board/Transparency						
in class	❑	❑	❑	❑	❑	❑
homework	❑	❑	❑	❑	❑	❑
Other _____						
_____						
in class	❑	❑	❑	❑	❑	❑
homework	❑	❑	❑	❑	❑	❑

INSTRUMENT 12.6   Format for Observing a Performance Assessment

Identify signs of any of the following and briefly describe their nature.

❏ Product criteria (technical quality, accuracy, usability, etc.)

_____

_____

❏ Process criteria (creativity, neatness, use of resources, etc.)

_____

_____

❏ Rating scale or point system for product and/or process criteria

_____

_____

Did the product or performance require of learners any of the following:

❏ Incorporate what was learned from classroom instruction in a more realistic and expanded context?

❏ Integrate isolated bits of knowledge rather than the recall of information?

❏ Do things for which the routine use of previously learned information is not sufficient?

❏ Apply standards by which one performs competently in the real world?

❏ Represent real-life challenges, not bookwork that is easy to grade?

How to Determine Percentage of Observer Agreement for a Counting Observation System

Assume that two people have observed the same teacher for 30 minutes. During this time, one observer counts 36 instances of *asking questions*; the other counts 30 instances. The agreement between observers can be estimated from a formula suggested by Emmer and Millett (1970)

$$\text{Percentage agreement} = 100\left(1 - \frac{A-B}{A+B}\right)$$

A and B are the frequency counts of each of two observers for the behavior *asking questions*. The smaller frequency (B) is always subtracted from the larger frequency (A). Thus, the percentage of agreement between these two observers for the frequency with which the teacher asked questions during this period of observation was

$$100\left(1 - \frac{36-30}{36+30}\right) = 100\left(1 - \frac{6}{66}\right) = 91\%$$

The percentage of agreement for each behavior on the instrument is similarly determined. Behaviors for which less than 75% agreement is obtained are examined for their clarity and understanding among observers. Generally, after an initial practice session, 30 minutes of observation should provide enough data to determine a percentage of observer agreement. If a behavior fails to occur or occurs infrequently during this period, the period may have to be extended to allow for more observation.

How to Determine Percentage of Observer Agreement for an Event Observation System

Following an example from Good and Brophy (1987), Instrument B.1 illustrates two sets of codes from different observers. The codes are superimposed over one another, using the event system introduced in Figure 4.12. To determine the percentage of agreement between the two observers, we will use only those exchanges for which both observers provided codes. When one observer fails to code an exchange, for whatever reason, that exchange will not be used for determining coder agreement.

For our example, a total of five exchanges are coded. Each of these exchanges is coded according to *student response* (*right, partially right, wrong,* or *no response*). However, the second observer (whose codes appear in the top half of each box) fails to code Diane's response during the fifth exchange. Therefore, we must eliminate this exchange from our calculations. Thus, for the remaining exchanges, the percentage agreement is (4/4)100, or 100%.

We can determine the percentage of coder agreement for *teacher feedback* in the same manner. Here, perfect agreement occurs for each exchange but the last. The first coder believes that the teacher's follow-up question to Diane's partially right response is a neutral reaction. The second coder (who previously failed to code the student's response) prefers to see the teacher's response as negating Diane's answer. The second coder also sees the teacher's response as a new question; the first coder sees the follow-up question as a clue to obtaining a fully correct answer. Therefore, of the eight coding decisions pertaining to the teacher's feedback reaction, the coders agree on six: (6/8)100 = 75%. Although a larger sample of classroom behavior would be needed to estimate observer agreement, for this brief episode, agreement appears satisfactory.

INSTRUMENT **B.1**   Codes for Two Observers

Number	Student	Student Response[a]				Teacher Response					Teacher Feedback Reaction						
		+	+/-	-	0	++	+	0	-	--	Gives Answer	Explains	Asks Another	Other Calls	Repeats	Clue	New Question
1	Dave				✓			✓					✓				
2	Mark	✓				✓											
3	Susan			✓					✓								
4	Susan			✓						✓			✓				
5	Diane		✓					✓	✓							✓	✓

[a]First observer's codes are below dashed lines; second observer's codes are above.

REFERENCES

Alberto, P., & Troutman, A. (1986). *Applied behavior analysis for teachers: Influencing student performance* (2d ed.). Columbus, OH: Charles Merrill.

Alexander, P. A., Schallert, D. L., & Hare, V. C. (1991). Coming to terms: How researchers in learning and literacy talk about knowledge. *Review of Educational Research, 61,* 3, 315–343.

Anderson, G. (1973). *The assessment of learning environments: A manual for the Learning Environment Inventory and the My Class Inventory.* Halifax, Nova Scotia: Atlantic Institute of Education.

Anderson, L., Evertson, C., & Brophy, J. (1979). An experimental study of effective teaching in first-grade reading groups. *Elementary School Journal, 79,* 193–223.

Anderson, L., Evertson, C., & Brophy, J. (1982). *Principles of small group instruction in elementary reading.* East Lansing, MI: Institute for Research on Teaching.

Aronson, E. (1978). *The jigsaw classroom.* Beverly Hills, CA: Sage.

Ausubel, D. (1968). *Educational psychology: A cognitive view.* New York: Holt, Rinehart & Winston.

Ayers, W., & Schubert, W. H. (1994). Teacher lore: Learning about teaching from teachers. In J. Shanahan (ed.), *Teachers thinking, teachers knowing.* Urbana, IL: National Council of Teachers of English, 105–121.

Barell, J. (1991). *Teaching for thoughtfulness: Classroom strategies to enhance intellectual development.* New York: Longman.

Belenky, M. F., Clinchy, B. M., Goldberger, N. R., & Tarule, J. M. (1986). *Women's ways of knowing.* USA: Basic Books.

Bennet, S., Roth, E., & Dunne, R. (1987). Task processes in mixed- and single-age classes. *Education,* 3–13, 15, 43–50.

Bennett, C. (1990). *Comprehensive multicultural education: Theory and practice* (2d ed.). Boston: Allyn & Bacon.

Bennett, N., & Desforges, C. (1988). Matching classroom tasks to students' attainments. *The Elementary School Journal, 88,* 221–234.

Bennett, N., Desforges, C., Cockburn, A., & Wilkinson, B. (1981). *The quality of pupil learning experiences: Interim report.* Lancaster, England: University of Lancaster Centre for Educational Research and Development.

Berliner, D. (1979). Tempus educare. *In* P. Peterson and H. Walberg (eds.), *Research on teaching: Concepts, findings and implications.* Berkeley, CA: McCutchan, 120–135.

Berliner, D. (1984). The half-full glass: A review of research on teaching. *In* P. Hosford (ed.), *Using what we know about teaching.* Alexandria, VA: Association for Supervision and Curriculum Development, 51–77.

Bloom, B. (1994). *Bloom's Taxonomy: A forty year retrospective.* Chicago, IL.: NSSE, The University of Chicago Press.

Bloom, B., Englehart, M., Furst, E., Hill, W., & Krathwohl, D. (1984). *Taxonomy of educational goals. Handbook I: Cognitive domain.* New York: Longman.

Blumfield, P., Soloway, E., Marx, R., Krajcik, J., Guzdial, M., & Palincsar, A. (1991). Motivation project-based learning: Sustaining the doing, supporting the learning. *Educational Psychologist, 26* (2, 3) 369–398.

Borich, G. (1996). *Effective teaching methods* (3d ed.). Columbus, OH: Merrill.

Borich, G. (1995). *Becoming a teacher: An inquiring dialogue for the beginning teacher.* Washington, DC: Falmer Press.

Borich, G. (1994). *Observation skills for effective teaching* (2d ed.). New York: Macmillan.

Borich, G. (1993). *Clearly outstanding: Making each day count in your classroom.* Boston: Allyn & Bacon.

Borich, G., & Tombari, M. (1997). *Educational pyschology: A contemporary approach.* New York: Addison-Wesley Longman.

Borich, G., & Madden, S. (1977). *Evaluating classroom instruction: A sourcebook of instruments.* Reading, MA: Addison-Wesley.

Bowers, C., & Flinders, D. (1991). *Culturally responsive teaching and supervision: A handbook for staff development.* New York: Teachers College Press.

Bragstad, B., & Stumpf, S. (1982). *A guidebook for teaching study skills and motivation.* Boston: Allyn & Bacon.

Brophy, J. (1988). Educating teachers about managing classrooms and students. *Teaching and Teacher Education, 9,* 1–18.

Brophy, J. (1983). Classroom organization and management. *Elementary School Journal, 83,* 265–285.

Brophy, J. (1981). Teacher praise: A functional analysis. *Review of Educational Research, 51,* 5–32.

Brophy, J. (ed.) (1989). *Advances in research on teaching.* Greenwich, CT: JAI Press.

Brophy, J., & Evertson, C. (1976). *Learning from teaching: A developmental perspective.* Boston: Allyn & Bacon.

Brophy, J., Evertson, C., Anderson, L., Baum, M., & Crawford, J. (1976). *Student personality and teaching: Final report of the Student Attribute Study.* Educational Resources Information Center (ERIC Document Reproduction Service No. ED 121 799).

Brophy, J., & Good, T. (1974). *Teacher–student relationships: Causes and consequences.* New York: Holt, Rinehart & Winston.

Brophy, J., & Good, T. (1986). Teacher behavior and student achievement. In M. C. Wittrock (ed.), *Handbook of research on teaching* (3d ed.). New York: Macmillan, 328–375.

Brown, A. (1987). Knowing when, how to remember: A problem of metacognition. *In* R. Glaser (Ed.), *Advances in instructional psychology* (Vol. 1). Hillsdale, NJ: Erlbaum, 77–165.

Brown, B. (1968). *The experimental mind in education.* New York: Harper & Row.

Brown, G., & Edmondson, R. (1984). Asking questions. *In* E. Wragg (ed.), *Classroom teaching skills.* New York: Nichols, 97–119.

Canter, L. (1976). *Assertive discipline: A take-charge approach for today's educator.* Seal Beach, CA: Canter and Associates.

Canter, L. (1989). Assertive discipline: More than names on the board and marbles in a jar. *Phi Delta Kappan,* September 1989, 57–61.

Castaneda, A., & Gray, T. (1974). Bicognitive processes in multicultural education. *Educational Leadership, 32.*

Cazden, C. B. (1988). *Classroom discourse.* Portsmouth, NH: Heinemann.

Cazden, C. B. (1986). Classroom discourse. *In* M. C. Wittrock (ed.), *Handbook of research on teaching,* 3d ed., NY: Macmillan.

Clark, C., & Peterson, P. (1986). Teacher's thought processes. *In* M. C. Wittrock (ed.), *Handbook of research on teaching* (3d ed.) New York: Macmillan, 255–296.

Clifford, M. (1983). Thoughts on theory of constructive failure. Presidential address given at the annual meeting of the American Psychological Association, Anaheim, CA.

Cooper, J. O., Heron, T. E., & Heward, W. L. (1987). *Behavior analysis.* Columbus, OH: Charles Merrill.

Copple, C., Siegel, I., & Sanders, R. (1984). *Educating the young thinker: Classroom strategies for cognitive growth.* Hillsdale, NJ: Lawrence Erlbaum.

Corno, L., & Snow, R. (1986). Adapting teaching to individual differences among learners. *In* M. W. Wittrock (ed.), *Handbook of research on teaching* (3d ed.). New York: Macmillan, 605–629.

Costa, A. (1984). Mediating the metacognitive. *Educational Leadership, 42* (3) 57–67.

Crawford, J., Gage, N. L., Corno, L., Stayrouk, N., Mitman, A., Schunk, D., & Stallings, J. (1978). *An experiment on teacher effectiveness and parent-assisted instruction in the third grade* (three volumes). Stanford, CA: Center for Educational Research, Stanford University.

Cronbach, L., & Snow, R. (1977). *Aptitudes and instructional methods.* New York: Irving/Naiburg.

Crooks, T. J. (1988). The impact of classroom evaluation practices on students. *Review of Educational Research, 58* (4), 438–481.

Curwin, R. L., & Mendler, A. N. (1988). *Discipline with dignity.* Association for Supervision and Curriculum Development.

Cushner, K., McClelland, A., & Safford, P. (1992). *Human diversity in education: An integrative approach.* New York: McGraw-Hill.

Dahllof, U., & Lundgren, U. P. (1970). *Macro and micro approaches combined for curriculum process analysis: A Swedish educational field project.* Goteborg, Sweden: University of Goteborg, Institute of Education.

Dillon, D. (1989). Showing them that I want them to learn and that I care about who they are: A microethnography of the social organization of a secondary low-track English reading classroom. *American Educational Research Journal, 26,* 227–259.

Dillon, J. (1988). *Questioning and discussion: A multidisciplinary study.* Norwood, NJ: Ablex Publishing.

Douglas, M. (1975). *Implicit meaning.* London: Routledge and Kegan Paul.

Doyle, W. (1986). Classroom organization and management. *In* M. Wittrock (ed.), *Handbook of research on teaching* (3d ed.). New York: Macmillan, 392–431.

Doyle, W. (1983). Academic work. *Review of Educational Research, 53,* 159–200.

Duffy, G., & Roehler, L. (1989). The tension between information-giving and mediation: Perspectives on instructional explanation and teacher change. *In* J. Brophy (ed.), *Advances in Research on Teaching* (Vol. 1). Greenwich, CT: JAI Press, Inc., 1–33.

Duncan, M. (ed.) (1987). *International encyclopedia of teaching and teaching education.* New York: Pergamon.

Duncan, M., & Biddle, B. (1974). *The study of teaching.* New York: Holt, Rinehart & Winston.

Ekman, P., & Friesan, W. (1967). Head and body cues in the judgment of emotion: A reformulation. *Perceptual and Motor Skills, 24,* 711–724.

Emmer, E., Evertson, C., & Anderson, L. (1980). Effective classroom management at the beginning of the school year. *The Elementary School Journal, 80* (5), 219–231.

Emmer, E., Evertson, C., Clements, B., & Worsham, M. (1997). *Classroom management for secondary teachers* (2d ed.). Englewood Cliffs, NJ: Prentice-Hall.

Emmer, E., & Millett, G. (1970). *Improving teaching through experimentation: A laboratory approach.* Englewood Cliffs, NJ: Prentice-Hall.

Erickson, F. (1979). Talking down: Some cultural sources of miscommunication of interracial interviews. *In* Aaron Wolfgang (ed.), *Nonverbal behavior: Applications and cultural implications.* New York: Academic.

Erickson, F. (1982). Taught cognitive learning in its immediate environment: A neglected topic in the anthropology of education. *Anthropology and Education Quarterly, 13,* 49–180.

Erickson, F., & Mohatt, G. (1982). Cultural organization of participation structures in two classrooms of Indian students. *In* G. Spindler (ed.), *Doing the ethnography of schooling.* Prospect Heights, IL: Waveland.

Evertson, C., Anderson, C., Anderson, L., & Brophy, J. (1980). Relationships between classroom behaviors and student outcomes in junior high mathematics and English classes. *American Educational Research Journal, 17,* 43–60.

Evertson, C. M., Brophy, J. E., & Good, T. L. (1973). Communication of teacher expectations: First grade. *Catalog of Selected Documents in Psychology, 3,* 60–61.

Evertson, C., & Emmer, E. (1982). Effective management at the beginning of the second year in junior high classes. *Journal of Educational Psychology, 74,* 485–498.

Evertson, C., Emmer, E., Sanford, J., Clements, B., & Worsham, M. (1997). *Classroom management for elementary teachers.* Englewood Cliffs, NJ: Prentice-Hall.

Fisher, C., Berliner, D., Filby, N., Maliave, R., Cahen, L., & Dishaw, M. (1980). Teaching behaviors, academic learning time and student achievement: An overview. *In* C. Denham and A. Lieberman (eds.), *Time to learn.* Washington, D.C.: National Institute of Education.

Fisher, C., Filby, N., Maliave, R., Cahen, L., Dishaw, M., More, J., & Berliner, D. (1978). *Teaching behaviors, academic learning time and student achievement.* Final report of phase III-B, beginning teacher evaluation study (Technical Report No. V-1). San Francisco: Far West Laboratory for Educational Research and Development.

Flanders, N. (1970). *Analyzing teacher behavior.* Reading, MA: Addison-Wesley.

Floden, R. (1991). What teachers need to know about learning. *In* M. Kennedy (ed.), *Teaching academic subjects to diverse learners.* New York: Teachers College Press, 189–216.

Fraser, B. (1981). Australian research on classroom environment: State of the art. *Australian Journal of Education, 25,* 238–268.

Fraser, B., Anderson, G., & Walberg, H. (1982). *Assessment of learning environments: Manual for the Learning Environment Inventory (LEI) and My Class Inventory (MCI)* (3d ed.). Perth: Western Australian Institute of Technology.

Fraser, B., & Walberg, H. (eds.). (1991). *Educational environments: Evaluation, antecedents and consequences.* New York: Pergamon.

Fuller, F. (1969). Concerns of teachers: A developmental conceptualization. *American Educational Research Journal, 6,* 207–226.

Gagne, E. (1985). *The cognitive psychology of school learning.* Boston, MA: Little, Brown.

Gagne, R. (1977). *Conditions of learning.* Boston, MA: Little, Brown.

Gagne, R., & Briggs, L. (1979). *Principles of instructional design.* New York: Holt, Rinehart & Winston.

Gagne, R., Briggs, L., & Wagner, W. (1992). *Principles of instructional design* (4th ed.). Orlando, FL: Harcourt, Brace.

Gall, M. (1984). Synthesis of research on questioning. *Educational Leadership, 42,* 40–47.

Gall, M., Ward, B., Berliner, D., Cahen, I., Winne, P., Elashoff, J., & Stanton, G. (1978). Effects of questioning techniques and recitation on student learning. *American Educational Research Journal, 15,* 175–199.

Getzels, J., & Thelen, H. (1960). The classroom as a unique social system. *In* N. Henry (ed.), *National society for the study of education yearbook.* Chicago: University of Chicago Press, 53–81.

Ginott, H. G. (1972). *Teacher and child: A book for parents and teachers.* New York: Macmillan.

Glasser, W. (1969). *Schools without failure.* New York: Harper & Row.

Glasser, W. (1990). *Quality school: Managing students without coercion.* New York: Harper Perennial.

Glasser, W. (1986). *Control theory in the classroom.* New York: Harper & Row.

Goetz, E. T., Alexander, P. A., & Ash, M. J. (1992). *Educational psychology: A classroom perspective.* Columbus, OH: Merrill.

Good, T., & Brophy, J. (1990). *Looking in classrooms* (5th ed.). New York: Harper & Row.

Good, T., & Brophy, J. (1986). *Educational psychology: A realistic approach.* New York: Longman.

Good, T. L., & Grouws, D. (1975). Process–product relationships in fourth-grade mathematics classrooms. Final report of National Institute of Education Grant (NE-G-00-0123). University of Missouri, Columbia.

Good, T., & Grouws, D. (1979). Teaching effects: A process–product study in fourth grade mathematics classrooms. *Journal of Teacher Education, 28,* 49–54.

Greenwood, C. R., Delguardi, J. C., & Hall, R. V. (1984). Opportunity to respond and student academic achievement. *In* W. L. Heward, T. E. Heron, D. S. Hill, & J. Trap-Porter (eds.), *Focus on behavior analysis in education.* Columbus, OH: Merrill.

Gullickson (1984). Teacher perspectives of their instructional use of tests. *Journal of Educational Research, 77,* 244–248.

Hall, E. (1977). *Beyond culture.* Garden City, NY: Anchor.

Hall, G. E., & Hord, S. M. (1987). *Change in schools: Facilitating the process.* Ithaca, NY: State University of New York Press.

Harrow, A. (1972). *A taxonomy of the psychomotor domain: A guide for developing behavioral objectives.* New York: David McKay.

Hill, H. (1989). *Effective strategies for teaching minority students.* Bloomington, IN: National Educational Service.

Hilliard, A. (1976). *Alternatives to IQ testing: An approach to the identification of gifted minority children.* Final report to the California State Department of Education. Sacramento, CA: State Department of Education.

Hodgkinson, H. (1988). *All one system: Demographics of education, kindergarten through graduate school.* Washington, D.C.: The Institute for Educational Leadership.

Hosford, P. (1984). The art of applying the science of education. *In* P. Hosford (ed.), *Using what we know about teaching.* Alexandria, VA: Association for Supervision and Curriculum Development.

Hunt, D. (1979). Learning style and student needs: An introduction to conceptual level. *In Student learning styles: Diagnosing and prescribing programs.* Reston, VA: National Association of Secondary School Principals.

Hunter, M. (1994). *Enhancing teaching.* New York: Macmillan College Publishing.

Hunter, M. (1982). *Mastery teaching.* El Segundo, CA: JIP Publications.

Jackson, R. (1968). *Life in classrooms.* New York: Holt, Rinehart & Winston.

Johnson, D., & Johnson, R. (1987). *Learning together and alone* (2d ed.). Englewood Cliffs, NJ: Prentice-Hall, Inc.

Jones, F. C. (1987). *Positive classroom discipline.* New York: McGraw-Hill.

Jones, J., & Jones, L. (1990). *Comprehensive classroom management* (3d ed.). Boston: Allyn & Bacon.

Kaplan, J. (1982). *Beyond behavioral modification: A cognitive-behavioral approach to behavior management in the school.* Portland, OR: ASTEP Education Co.

Kendon, A. (1967). Some functions of age-direction in social interaction. *Acta Psychologica, 26,* 22–63.

Kendon, A. (1981). *Nonverbal communication, interaction, and gesture.* The Hague: Mouton.

Kounin, J. (1970). Discipline and group management in the classroom. New York: Holt, Rinehart & Winston.

Krathwohl, D., Bloom, B., & Masia, B. (1964). *Taxonomy of educational objectives. The classification of educational goals. Handbook II: Affective domain.* New York: David McKay.

Kulick, J. A., & Kulick, C. C. (1988). Timing of feedback and verbal learning. *Review of Educational Research,* Spring, 75–97.

Land, M. (1987). *In* M. Duncan (ed.), *The international encyclopedia of teaching and teacher education.* New York: Pergamon, 392–397.

Levin, J., & Nolan, J. F. (1991). *Principles of classroom management: A hierarchical approach.* Englewood Cliffs, NJ: Prentice-Hall, Inc.

Lortie, D. (1975) *Schoolteacher.* Chicago: University of Chicago Press.

Luiten, J., Ames, W., & Aerson, G. (1980). A meta-analysis of advance organizers on learning and retention. *American Education Research Journal, 17,* 211–218.

Lysakowski, R., & Walberg, H. (1981). Classroom reinforcement and learning: A quantitative synthesis. *Journal of Educational Research, 75,* 69–77.

Madsen, C., & Madsen, C. (1970). *Teaching discipline: A positive approach for educational development.* Raleigh: Contempory Publishing Co.

Martin, J. (1979). Effects of teacher higher-order questions on student process and product variables in a single classroom study. *Journal of Educational Research, 72,* 183–187.

Martin, R., & Keller, A. (1974). Teacher awareness of classroom dyadic interactions. A paper presented at the annual meeting of the American Educational Research Association, Chicago.

Marx, R., & Walsh, J. (1988). Learning from academic tasks. *The Elementary School Journal, 88,* 3, 207–219.

Mayer, R. (1987). *Education psychology: A cognitive approach.* Boston: Little, Brown.

McCall, M., Lombardo, M., & Morrison, A. (1988). *The lessons of experience: How successful executives develop on the job.* Lexington, MA: D.C. Heath.

McKeachie, W. J. (1990) Learning, Thinking and Thorndike. *Educational Psychologist,* Spring, 127–142.

Medley, D., Coker, H., & Soar, R. (1985). *Measurement-based evaluation of teacher performance: An empirical approach.* New York: Longman.

Meichenbaum, D. (1983). Teaching thinking: A cognitive-behavioral approach. *In Interdisciplinary voices in learning disabilities and remedial education.* Austin, TX: ProEd, 127–156.

Michaels, S., & Collins, J. (1984). Oral discourse styles: Classroom interaction and the acquisition of literacy. *In* D. Tamen (ed.), *Coherence in spoken and written discourse.* Norwood, NJ: Ablex.

Noddings, N. (1992). *The challenge to care in schools.* New York: Teachers College Press.

O'Leary, K. D., & O'Leary, S. G. (1977). *Classroom management* (2d Ed.). New York: Pergamon Press.

Palincsar, A., & Brown, A. (1989). Classroom dialogues to promote self-regulated comprehension (Vol. 1). *In* J. Brophy (ed.), *Advances in research on teaching.* Greenwich, CT: JAI Press, Inc., 35–71.

Palincsar, A., & Brown, A. (1988). Teaching and practicing thinking skills to promote comprehension in the context of group problem solving. *Remedial and Special Education, 9* (1), 53–59.

Palincsar, A., & Brown, A. (1987). Enhancing instructional time through attention to metacognition. *Journal of Learning Disabilities, 20* (2), 66–75.

Palmer, P. J. (1993). *To know as we are known: Education as a spiritual journey.* New York: HarperCollins.

Parsons, T. (1959). The school class as a social system: Some of its functions in American society. *Harvard Educational Review, 9,* 298–318.

Parsons, T., & Shills, E. (eds.). (1951). *Toward a general theory of action.* Cambridge, MA: Harvard University Press.

Pasch, M. (1991). *Teaching as decision-making: Instructional practices for the successful teacher.* White Plains, NY: Longman.

Philips, S. (1983). *The invisible culture: Communication in classroom and community on the Warm Springs Indian Reservation.* New York: Longman.

Polanyi, F. (1958). *Personal knowledge.* Chicago: University of Chicago Press.

Ramirez, M., & Castaneda, A. (1974). *Cultural democracy, bicognitive development, and education.* New York: Academic Press.

Redfield, D., & Rousseau, E. (1981). A meta-analysis of experimental research on teacher questioning behavior. *Review of Educational Research,* 51, 237–245.

Resnick, L. B., & Resnick, D. P. (1991). Assessing the thinking curriculum: New tools for educational reform. *In* B. R. Gifford and M. C. O'Connor (eds.), *Future assessments: Changing views of aptitude, achievement and instruction.* Boston: Kluwer Academic Publishers.

Richards, J., Gipe, J. P., & Duffy, C. A. (April, 1992). Beginning professionals' metaphors in an early field placement. Paper presented at the Annual Meeting of the American Educational Research Association, San Francisco, CA.

Rinne, C. (1984). Attention: *The fundamentals of classroom control.* Columbus, OH: Merrill.

Rist, R. (1970). Student social class and teaching expectations: The self-fulfilling prophecy in ghetto education. *Harvard Educational Review, 40,* 411–451.

Rodgers, T. A., & Iwata, B. A. (1991). An analysis of error-correction procedures during discrimination training. *Journal of Applied Behavior Analysis, 24* (4), 775–782.

Rogan, J., Borich, G., & Taylor, H. P. (1992). Validation of the stages of concern questionnaire. *Action in Teacher Education, 14* (2), 43–49.

Rohrkemper, M., & Corno, L. (1988). Success and failure on classroom tasks: Adaptive learning and classroom teaching. *The Elementary School Journal, 88,* 297–312.

Rosenshine, B. (1983). Teaching functions in instructional programs. *Elementary School Journal, 83,* 335–351.

Rosenshine, B., & Stevens, R. (1986). Teaching functions. *In* M. C. Wittrock (ed.), *Handbook of research on teaching* (3d ed.). New York: Macmillan, 376–391.

Rowe, M. B. (1986). Wait time: Slowing down may be a way of speeding up. *Journal of Teacher Education, 23* (January/February), 43–49.

Sadker, M., & Sadker, D. V. (1991). *Teachers, schools, and society.* New York: McGraw-Hill.

Sanford, A. J., & Garrod, S. C. (1981). *Understanding written language.* New York: John Wiley & Sons.

Savage, T. (1991). *Discipline for self-control.* Englewood Cliffs, NJ: Prentice-Hall.

Scollon, R. (1985). The machine stops: Silence in the metaphor of malfunction. *In* D. Tannen & M. Saville-Troike (eds.), *Perspectives on silence.* Norwood, NJ: Ablex.

Shalaway, L. (1989). *Learning to teach.* Cleveland, OH: Edgell Communications, Inc.

Siegel, M. (1983). Reading as signification. Unpublished doctoral dissertation, Indiana University.

Simon, A., & Boyer, E. (1970). *Mirrors for behavior: An anthology of observation instruments.* Philadelphia, PA: Research for Better Schools.

Slavin, R. (1980). Effects of student teams and peer tutoring on academic achievement and time on task. *Journal of Experimental Education, 48,* 252–257.

Slavin, R. (1981). Student team learning. E*lementary School Journal, 82,* 5–17.

Slavin, R. (1985). *Learning to cooperate, cooperating to learn.* New York: Plenum.

Slavin, R. (1987). *Cooperative learning: Student teams* (2d ed.). Washington, D.C.: NEA.

Slavin, R. (1991). *Educational psychology: Theory into practice.* Englewood Cliffs, NJ: Prentice-Hall.

Smith, H. (1984). State of the art of nonverbal behavior in teaching. *In* A. Wolfgang (ed.), *Nonverbal behavior: Perspectives, applications, intercultural insights.* New York: Hogrefe.

Smith, L., & Land, M. (1981). Low-inference verbal behaviors related to teacher clarity. *Journal of Classroom Interaction, 17,* 37–42.

Soar, R. (1968). Optimum teacher–pupil interaction for pupil growth. *Educational Leadership Research Supplement, 275–280.*

Soar, R., & Soar, R. (1983). Context effects in the learning process. *In* D. C. Smith (ed.), *Essential knowledge for beginning educators.* Washington, D.C.: American Association of Colleges of Teacher Education, 156–192.

Stallings, J. (1977). *Learning to look.* Belmont, CA: Wadsworth.

Stallings, J. A., & Stipek, D. (1995). Research on early childhood and elementary school teaching programs. *In* M. C. Witrock (ed.), *Handbook of research on teaching,* 3d ed. New York: Macmillan.

Sternberg, R. (1989). The triarchic mind: A new theory of human intelligence. New York: Penguin Books.

Swift, J., Gooding, T., & Swift, P. (1988). Questions and wait time. *In* J. T. Dillion (ed.), *Questioning and discussion: A multidisciplinary study.* Norwood, NJ: Ablex Publishing Corporation.

Tannen, D. (1986). *That's not what I meant!* New York: Morrow.

Tharp, R., & Gallimore, R. (1989). *Rousing minds to life: Teaching, learning and schooling in social context.* New York: Cambridge University Press.

Verloop, N. (1989). *Interactive cognitions of student teachers.* Arnhem, The Netherlands; National Institute for Educational Measurement.

Vgotsky, L. (1978). *In* Cole (ed.), *Mind in society: The development of higher psychological processes.* Cambridge, MA: Harvard University Press.

Walberg, H. (1966). Classroom climate questionnaires. Cambridge, MA: Harvard University.

Walberg, H. (1969). Predicting class learning: An approach to the class as a social system. *American Educational Research Journal, 6,* 529–542.

Walberg, H., & Anderson, G. (1968). Classroom climate and individual learning. *Journal of Educational Psychology, 59,* 414–419.

Wang, B., & Jones, W. (1982). Increasing metacomprehension in learning disabled and normally achieving students through self-questioning training. *Learning Disability Quarterly, 5* (2), 228–238.

Wang, M., & Lindvall, C. (1984). Individual differences and school learning environments. *Review of Research in Education, 11,* 161–225.

Wasserman, B. (1987). Teaching for thinking: Louis E. Rath revisited. *Phi Delta Kappan, 68* (6), 400–406.

Willis, S. (1972). Formation of teachers' expectations of students' academic performance. Unpublished doctoral dissertation. The University of Texas at Austin, Austin, TX.

Winne, R. (1979). Experiments relating teachers' use of high cognitive questions to student achievement. *Review of Educational Research, 49,* 13–50.

Wittrock, M. (ed.). (1986). *Handbook of research on teaching* (3d ed.). New York: Macmillan.

Wragg, E., & Wood, E. (1984). Teachers' first encounters with their classes. *In* E. Wragg (Ed.), *Classroom teaching skills.* New York: Nichols, 47–78.

Wyne, M., & Stuck, G. (1982). Time and learning: Implications for the classroom teacher. *Elementary School Journal, 83,* 67–75.

Author Index

Subject Index

Instrument Index

About the Author

Gary Borich grew up on the south side of Chicago, where he attended Mendel High School and later taught in the Chicago suburban school system of Niles. He received his Ph.D. from Indiana University, where he was director of evaluation at the Institute of Child Study, before joining the faculty of the College of Education at the University of Texas. He has been a member of the Board of Examiners of the National Council for the Accreditation of Teacher Education (NCATE) and is the author or coauthor of *Effective Teaching Methods,* Fourth Edition; *Authentic Assessment in the Classroom, Educational Testing and Measurement,* Fifth Edition; and *Educational Psychology: A Contemporary Approach,* Second Edition. Dr. Borich lives in Austin, Texas, with his wife (who is a schoolteacher) and two children. His hobbies include pottery and training and riding Arabian horses.

Contributor Debra Bayles Martin received her Ph.D. from The University of Texas at Austin and is Assistant Professor in the School of Teacher Education at San Diego State University. She is author of *Bridges: Activity Guide and Assessment Options for Effective Teaching Methods,* Fourth Edition.